Crisis Cinema in the Middle East

Crisis Cinema in the Middle East

Creativity and Constraint in Iran and the Arab World

Shohini Chaudhuri

BLOOMSBURY ACADEMIC
LONDON • NEW YORK • OXFORD • NEW DELHI • SYDNEY

BLOOMSBURY ACADEMIC
Bloomsbury Publishing Plc
50 Bedford Square, London, WC1B 3DP, UK
1385 Broadway, New York, NY 10018, USA
29 Earlsfort Terrace, Dublin 2, Ireland

BLOOMSBURY, BLOOMSBURY ACADEMIC and the Diana logo are
trademarks of Bloomsbury Publishing Plc

First published in Great Britain 2022
This paperback edition published 2024

Copyright © Shohini Chaudhuri, 2022, 2024

Shohini Chaudhuri has asserted her right under the Copyright,
Designs and Patents Act, 1988, to be identified as Author of this work.

For legal purposes the Acknowledgements on pp. ix–x constitute an
extension of this copyright page.

Cover design: Ben Anslow
Cover image: *Tehran: City of Love* © Here and There Productions 2018. All Rights Reserved.

All rights reserved. No part of this publication may be reproduced or transmitted
in any form or by any means, electronic or mechanical, including photocopying,
recording, or any information storage or retrieval system, without prior permission
in writing from the publishers.

Bloomsbury Publishing Plc does not have any control over, or responsibility for, any
third-party websites referred to or in this book. All internet addresses given in this
book were correct at the time of going to press. The author and publisher regret any
inconvenience caused if addresses have changed or sites have ceased to exist,
but can accept no responsibility for any such changes.

A catalogue record for this book is available from the British Library.

Library of Congress Cataloging-in-Publication Data
Names: Chaudhuri, Shohini, author.
Title: Crisis Cinema in the Middle East : Creativity and Constraint in Iran
and the Arab World / Shohini Chaudhuri.
Description: London, UK ; New York, NY : Bloomsbury Academic, 2022. |
Includes bibliographical references and index. |
Identifiers: LCCN 2021057273 (print) | LCCN 2021057274 (ebook) |
ISBN 9781350190511 (hardback) | ISBN 9781350190559 (paperback) |
ISBN 9781350190528 (epub) | ISBN 9781350190535 (pdf)
Subjects: LCSH: Motion pictures–Iran. | Motion pictures–Middle East.
Classification: LCC PN1993.5.I846 C48 2022 (print) | LCC PN1993.5.I846
(ebook) | DDC 791.430955–dc23/eng/20211222
LC record available at https://lccn.loc.gov/2021057273
LC ebook record available at https://lccn.loc.gov/2021057274

ISBN:	HB:	978-1-3501-9051-1
	PB:	978-1-3501-9055-9
	ePDF:	978-1-3501-9053-5
	eBook:	978-1-3501-9052-8

Typeset by Integra Software Services Pvt. Ltd.

To find out more about our authors and books visit www.bloomsbury.com
and sign up for our newsletters.

Contents

List of figures	vi
Acknowledgements	ix
A note on transliteration	xi
Introduction	1
1 Witnessing	27
2 Child protagonists	57
3 Animation	81
4 Psychogeography	101
5 Road movies	125
6 Humour	147
7 Stories within stories	171
8 Archival strategies	191
9 Sci-fi dystopia	213
Conclusion	235
Notes	238
Bibliography	282
Index	302

Figures

1.1 *For Sama*'s first-person, female witness account of the Syrian conflict is shaped by Waad al-Kateab's experience of 'being there'. *For Sama* directed by Waad al-Kateab and Edward Watts © Channel 4 2019. All Rights Reserved. — 41

1.2 Car headlights become a creative solution to power cuts when the women's football team train at night, captured by Naziha Arebi's equally inventive cinematography. *Freedom Fields* directed by Naziha Arebi © HuNa Productions 2018. All Rights Reserved. — 55

2.1 Zain exemplifies the child as a creative agent, improvizing a buggy from a stockpot and skateboard with which he tows Yonas around the city. *Capernaum* directed by Nadine Labaki © Mooz Films 2018. All Rights Reserved. — 65

2.2 Child protagonists serve as a means of creatively overcoming barriers of gender segregation. *Wadjda* directed by Haifaa al-Mansour © Razor Film Produktion 2012. All Rights Reserved. — 71

3.1 Claymation cows become a source of empathy, 'wanted' by the Israeli army. *The Wanted 18* directed by Amer Shomali and Paul Cowan, 2014 © Bellota Films, Dar Films and Intuitive Pictures. All Rights Reserved. — 95

3.2 Animation protects identities at risk in this story of an anonymous Syrian opposition activist. *Suleima* directed by Jalal Maghout © Estayqazat 2014. All Rights Reserved. — 97

4.1 Burj El Murr, a former sniper hideout in the Lebanese Civil War, looms over Beirut like the many-eyed mythological giant Panoptes, surveying current citizens and signposting a traumatic past. *Panoptic* directed by Rana Eid © Abbout Productions 2017. All Rights Reserved. — 113

4.2 Khalid's magnifying glass reflects a fragile, microcosmic image of the city, encapsulating the mood of *déjà disparu*. *In the Last Days of the City* directed by Tamer el-Said © Zero Production 2016. All Rights Reserved. — 118

Figures

5.1 Roadblocks become creative obstacles for the Speed Sisters, an all-female Palestinian motor-racing team. *Speed Sisters* directed by Amber Fares © SocDoc Studios 2015. All Rights Reserved.   129

5.2 Jafar Panahi's role as the taxi driver in *Taxi Tehran* is not just a self-reflexive gesture but results from the constraints under which he is working. *Taxi Tehran* directed by Jafar Panahi © Jafar Panahi Film Productions 2015. All Rights Reserved.   136

6.1 The episode 'Who Wants to Kill a Million?' satirizes Syrian President Bashar al-Assad with its macabre parody of the television game show *Who Wants to Be a Millionaire*. *Top Goon: Diaries of a Little Dictator* directed by Jamil al-Abyad © Masasit Mati 2011–12. All Rights Reserved.   152

6.2 Romantic comedy's boy-meets-girl format is transformed into a vehicle for exploring gender segregation and other restrictions on interacting in public space in Saudi society. *Barakah Meets Barakah* directed by Mahmoud Sabbagh © El Housh Productions 2016. All Rights Reserved.   166

7.1 Shirin's voice-over lays the nuances of her lived experience over a videogame of US soldiers invading Iran, deploying a story-within-a-story strategy. *Profession: Documentarist* directed by Shirin Barghnavard, Firouzeh Khosrovani, Farahnaz Sharifi, Mina Keshavarz, Sepideh Abtahi, Sahar Salahshoor, Nahid Rezaei © *Profession: Documentarist* collective 2014. All Rights Reserved.   182

7.2 A group of Syrian refugee women rehearse their version of *The Trojan Women* with their hands covering their mouths, pointing to constraints upon their free expression. The same constraints impacted upon the film. *Queens of Syria* directed by Yasmin Fedda © Refuge Productions 2014. All Rights Reserved.   188

8.1 A mosaic composition of YouTube clips presents stories of the multitude during the early years of the Syrian revolution and war, including a video by the first Syrian army defector, Walid Qashami. *Silvered Water, Syria Self-Portrait* directed by Ossama Mohammed and Wiam Simav Bedirxan © Les Films d'ici and Proaction Film 2014. All Rights Reserved.   203

8.2 Bassel and Noura's personal archives tell their story through their perspective to foster a more intimate understanding of forcible disappearance. *Ayouni* directed by Yasmin Fedda © Banyak Films and Hakawati 2020. All Rights Reserved. 207

9.1 A large, inflatable black monkey, found within the absurd sci-fi-like world of Sharm el-Sheik, became a playful tactic of free expression, encouraging the characters to speak about their dreams and longings as they follow him in his truck. *Dreamaway* directed by Johanna Domke and Marouan Omara © Monokel, WDR Westdeutscher Rundfunk, Fruitmarket Kultur und Medien, Fig Leaf 2018. All Rights Reserved. 224

9.2 The protagonist Hala walks past a real garbage dump in a dystopic sci-fi extrapolation of Lebanon's trash crisis. *Submarine* directed by Mounia Akl © Columbia University School of Arts 2016. All Rights Reserved. 232

A note on transliteration

For Arabic and Persian words that appear in the book, the transliteration scheme I have followed is based on the American Library Association–Library of Congress romanization system. I have not changed transliterations in personal names, film titles or bibliographic references.

Introduction

The World Free Press Index, compiled annually by Reporters Without Borders, maps the world to indicate the extent of free expression that countries permit.[1] The map's colour coding ranges from 'good' countries represented in white to 'very bad' ones in black. The Middle East is regularly swathed in black, marked as the world's worst region for freedom of expression due to prevalent conflict and censorship. Despite this, filmmakers from the region have found creative ways of telling their stories that attest to their imagination, courage and resilience. Their work points to more nuanced perspectives than either standard news images of crisis or black-and-white ideas of what is permissible or not.

This book is a study of freedom of expression, focusing on the dynamic between creativity and constraint in independent filmmaking from Iran and the Arab world. While cinematic freedom of expression is usually understood through the lens of state censorship, I investigate the numerous obstacles facing filmmakers and then, in the main body of the book, I present nine creative solutions that they apply to these constraints, drawing on my interviews with both established and newer filmmakers from the region. I explore independent filmmaking of various types, from fictional and documentary feature films designed for theatrical release to made-for-TV documentaries and short films uploaded onto the Internet. My purpose is to help readers understand the constraints of production and distribution in the region by learning from filmmakers' first-hand experiences. The book builds a theoretical framework around the constraints of filmmaking in the Middle East and creative strategies employed in response to those constraints; it offers a comparative approach – not a nation-by-nation survey – with transferable insights to other contexts, and seeks to reach a range of stakeholder audiences both within academia and beyond.

In the UN International Covenant on Civil and Political Rights (1966), freedom of expression is defined as 'Freedom to seek, receive and impart information and ideas of all kinds, either orally, in writing or in print, in the form of art, or through any other media.'[2] While the framework of human rights law enshrines this right as an abstract, universal value, for filmmakers working in contexts of crisis, freedom of expression is a lived, embodied experience. As Marwan Kraidy says, freedom is not 'a mere word' distanced from its 'actual consequences'; it is a material practice, carried out in public where bodies are literally imperilled.[3]

While this book gives credence to the idea that art flourishes in crisis, aided by the boundaries that artists are constantly pushing against, it complicates it in several respects. Claims that state censorship and other harmful constraints are helpful for creativity are problematic because they appear to condone these rights violations. They also ignore developments in art and society that led to the present moment, laying the foundations for the upsurge of creativity. In my research, I have found that creativity often flourishes at periods when restrictions are slightly loosened, or in the transition between one regime and another, like the brief 'window of freedom'[4] created by the so-called 'Arab Spring' in 2010–11 when people were emboldened to speak out after decades of discontent. As Syrian filmmaker Orwa al-Mokdad recalls about the situation in his country, 'When the revolution began people were able to express themselves more openly and more freely – at least they had the courage to do so – and it allowed the creative process to manifest itself within the population.'[5] Despite the loosening of restrictions in many parts of the region, the risks remained and indeed became greater as people were arrested, tortured and disappeared in large numbers, forcing many filmmakers into exile abroad; additionally, in Syria and Yemen, civilian areas were bombed by the government and foreign powers. The lack of full rights and the security risks are clearly negative and harmful constraints, while other types of constraints can be more productive. Therefore, this book explores how filmmakers exploit productive constraints and find ways of tackling harmful ones.

In this introduction, I clarify the book's interlocking arguments about crisis, constraints and creativity: its critical engagement with notions of the Middle East as a crisis hotspot, its emphasis on a broad array of constraints that filmmakers typically face, rather than an exclusive focus on state censorship and its understanding of creativity as shaped by material constraints. I explain the key concepts that underlie my approach and methodologies, and then provide an outline of the chapters which are focused on creative strategies that filmmakers are using to overcome constraints.

Why crisis?

More than any other region in the world, the Middle East is susceptible to being formulated as a crisis 'hotspot'. As Nat Muller writes, the 'generic image of the Middle East' is 'known to the West from "bad news"', full of stories of conflict, failed states, fundamentalism, terrorism and violence.[6] Furthermore, the term 'The Middle East', along with labels such as 'MENA' ('Middle East and North Africa') and 'Arab world' can give the impression that the region is a monolith, which belies its complexity and diversity, and is problematically associated with Orientalism: a Western mode of describing the Other.

Nonetheless, during this book's 2009–20 timeframe, the Middle East has been rocked by multiple crises, starting with the disputed 2009 presidential election in Iran that led to the Green Movement protests, a predecessor to the 'Arab Spring'. Non-violent protests in many countries across the region shared similar aspirations for sociopolitical change and helped to pioneer the use of social media to disseminate independent accounts of events. State crackdowns followed similar patterns, as rulers tenaciously clung to power, often with regional and international support, restoring authoritarian rule in many places. In 2019, a fresh wave of protests was launched, including in Lebanon, Iraq and Iran. Iraq (and the region as a whole) is still dealing with the long-term repercussions of the 2003 US-led invasion and occupation which created a security void that birthed extremist groups such as ISIS. Iran continues to undergo the highs and lows of its 2015 nuclear deal, economic sanctions and international isolation. Egypt has 'come full circle' after the 2011 overthrow of President Hosni Mubarak was followed by President Mohammed Morsi's Islamist rule and a return to military dictatorship since 2013 under General Abdel Fattah el-Sisi.[7] Libya descended into Civil War following its 2011 revolution, as did Yemen and Syria. Lebanon, where the Civil War (1975–90) casts a long shadow, has been 'sent reeling by repeated crisis' as a testing ground for neoliberal economics and host to over a million Syrian refugees (a quarter of its own population).[8] In Palestine, Israel continues to expand its occupation in East Jerusalem, the West Bank and Gaza, with restrictions on freedom of movement, goods and services that have stifled the economy and made everyday life extremely difficult. Meanwhile, the Gulf monarchies have become keenly aware that their oil resources will one day run out and therefore of the need for economic diversification that implies risks of sociopolitical change; liberal initiatives, like the reopening of cinemas and lifting of the ban on women driving in Saudi Arabia in 2018, have occurred at the same time as repressive acts such as journalist Jamal Khashoggi's murder.

Adopting the word 'crisis' to link these upheavals risks reinforcing stereotypes of the Middle East as a crisis hotspot in Western news media. Mediated as a humanitarian emergency, a crisis typically means a threat to life, property, security, physical and psychological health, marked by uncertainty and necessitating 'immediate response'.[9] Reporting of incrementally worsening conditions is minimal, as if incidents have sprung 'almost from nowhere' when they finally do break into the headlines.[10] International news media often elide political contexts of crisis and struggles for justice, treating people as victims to be helped by international aid rather than agents. However, 'crisis' can also be an accurate description of one's lived experience and diagnosis of present conditions.[11] Independent filmmakers from the region tend to undercut standard ways of thinking and behaving about crisis by making visible what is often invisible in both official state and international media depictions. Instead of the view from above, that of international players and the regime, they present the view from below, that of ordinary people's lives. In this way, they explore the fault lines of those generic images and offer something more specific.

In 2020, the coronavirus pandemic struck the world, giving us a common experience of crisis. Even citizens of so-called stable societies had to adapt to the reduction of security and freedom and daily confrontation with untimely death. The pandemic has enhanced effects of existing crises and global inequalities but, as Egyptian filmmaker Marouan Omara declares, 'Corona is now our constraint internationally.'[12] With lockdowns and social-distancing measures, COVID-19 has imposed curbs on everyday freedoms as well as unprecedented challenges to film production and distribution globally, resulting in suspended movie shoots, cinema closures and cancelled festivals, although filmmakers and exhibitors soon found creative ways of working within these restrictions. This book does not focus on the obstacles thrown up by the pandemic; that would merit another study. However, its research phase, including some filmmaker interviews, and writing up coincided with these developments which threw its themes of crisis, creativity and constraints into relief.

Why constraints?

Middle Eastern cinema is typically framed by state censorship, so much so that many filmmakers are tired of being asked about it at international film festival Q&As. As Mani Haghighi attests, 'The Western audience's exclusive focus on censorship in Iran has been a source of constant annoyance for me over the years.

I find it above all to be a passive-aggressive strategy of self-congratulation: "Ah, poor you, we are so much freer than you!"[13] The assumption that censorship is geographically and temporally distant and 'other' harks back to Cold War[14] and colonial ideologies that divided the world into the 'free' and 'unfree' according to East-West binaries. Although this view persists today, censorship studies now acknowledge censorship as a broad phenomenon emanating from disparate forces. Michel Foucault's work has been a major influence, orientating scholars towards an emphasis on censorship as a type of social discipline instead of merely an imposition from institutions.[15] Nonetheless, Foucault's abstract model of power collapses distinctions between different types of control, some of which may not be appropriate to call censorship. For this reason, 'constraints', rather than censorship, is my preferred term for generic limitations to freedom of expression. It has the advantage of highlighting the variety of obstacles facing filmmakers and shifts debates beyond state censorship, which is only one form of control and by no means filmmakers' only challenge.

In film terms, a constraint can be defined as a limitation of choices or an obstacle in the process of producing, distributing or exhibiting a movie. Exploring why artists in general might want to restrict their choices, the philosopher Jon Elster has distinguished between pre-existing constraints (such as technological, economic, institutional and societal factors) and self-imposed constraints, chosen or invented by the artist (such as decisions of style or genre).[16] Among invented constraints, freely adopted for an expected artistic benefit, Elster mentions the avant-garde Oulipo writer Georges Perec, who wrote his novel *A Void* (1969) without the letter 'e'. It is commonsensical to think that more options are better than fewer. Nonetheless, Elster suggests, some constraints have benefits. It can actually be freeing to have fewer options; it is what we do with those options that matters. Less can be more. Such restrictions challenge filmmakers to find inventive solutions.

For Elster, creativity is a two-stage process: firstly, the choice or endorsement of constraints and, secondly, choice within these constraints. Importantly, the constraints must not be too tight, leaving room for manoeuvre within them. Indeed, Elster reminds us to steer clear of overly praising constraints.[17] One of his examples is the Production Code, a form of censorship in Hollywood (1934–66) that placed numerous political, religious and cultural restrictions on what could be shown. It challenged directors to use indirect means, leading, he argues, to greater artistic sophistication that left more to viewers' imaginations. Yet, he notes, the Code was also a harmful and paralyzing constraint; many films were never made because of their incompatibility with its rules and ideologies.

Building on Elster's work, my conceptual premises in this book are: (1) every film is a product of its constraints, (2) constraints vary geographically and temporally, (3) they leave material traces on creative strategies and (4) creative evolution occurs as a result of changes in constraints. In the following section, I lay out my own typology of constraints, expanding and modifying Elster's in a way that is applicable to filmmaking conditions in Iran and the Arab world. This approach, rather than country-by-country overviews, enables us to identify similarities and differences in constraints that may otherwise not have been noticed, as well as ways in which constraints interact. Some constraints are faced by filmmakers around the world, while others arise from circumstances particular to these countries.

1. Political constraints

The state, with its security apparatus (army, police, intelligence agencies), judiciary and embassies, plays a key role determining what types of cinematic expression are allowed within a country through its legislation and forms of patronage. It can impose restrictions, and exert pressure upon filmmakers, exhibitors and critics alike – actions that signal the range of free expression in the country and the regard that the state has for it. Aside from the state, political factions have the power to make things difficult for filmmakers and civil society lobby groups can launch a campaign against a film.

In many countries, filmmakers must present a synopsis and/or script and list of cast and crew for shooting approval to state authorities, then later submit the film for a screening permit. However, as the actor and producer Khalid Abdalla says, 'shooting with permits doesn't mean that you'll be left alone.'[18] In Egypt, he observes, 'the police know that the constraints of filming create opportunities to be paid off so they come and look at your permits and start to quibble over details'.[19] Influential connections, known in Arabic as *wastat*, are important in filmmaking anywhere, but having powerful contacts to intercede on your behalf is common practice in this region. In Iran, government patronage of cinema both 'enables and limits' filmmakers' work.[20] It also promotes a culture of favouritism towards 'insiders', filmmakers trusted by the government who are not required to submit scripts for approval, and hostility towards 'outsiders', who find their work excluded.[21]

Within the region, there are certain taboo topics that 'you can't talk frontally about'.[22] Mainly, these are politics, religion and sex and, within the category of sex, queer sexuality is more policed. Additionally, criticisms of political and religious leaders are considered red lines not to be crossed. One major pressure is to portray the nation favourably. Iranian media use the phrase *siāh-namāyi* (depicting the negative aspects) to express their disapproval of filmmakers.[23] Ali Soozandeh, whose film *Tehran Taboo* (2017) was reported as anti-Iran or anti-Islamic in the Iranian press, explains, 'The picture we show to the outside [audience] must be a very clean, beautiful image, independent of what is behind it'.[24] Filmmakers sometimes get around state censorship by presenting a different version of their script from the one they intend to film. Moreover, in cinema, red lines are more open to negotiation (including through dialogue with censors) than in the press and state broadcasting: 'as long as you're not stridently explicit about your opposition to the regime as such in your film, then all kinds of avenues open up for you', says Haghighi.[25]

Neither are Middle Eastern filmmakers immune from political censorship in the West. In Britain, where colonialism has long been an unspoken past, airing that issue is not always welcomed. Several filmmakers in this book have been censored for appearing to criticize Israel (although this often arises from a misunderstanding of their work), one of the other grounds on which subject matter is judged sensitive in the West.

2. Infrastructural constraints

As Egyptian filmmaker Tamer el-Said states, 'Every film needs a machine behind it', relying on an industrial infrastructure,[26] such as film schools, production and distribution companies, cinema theatres, film festivals, galleries and television networks that produce, fund, distribute and exhibit films and provide skills training. This starts from access to films and film education, learning film language as well as filmmaking's technical craft. Iranian-Kurdish director Keywan Karimi describes growing up in Kurdistan without any cinemas; until 1995, even the VHS player was illegal. He was only able to watch serials and films on state television. 'If someone asks me, how you learn cinema in these conditions, I say that it came from one thing. I have an imagination and I do what they didn't do', by 'thinking what is a better way to tell these stories?'[27] When he went to university in Tehran, he finally had access to the cinema. Shortage of screens is a persistent problem despite the growth of regional festivals and art-house distributors. As elsewhere in the world, viewers have gravitated from theatrical screenings to (often pirated) DVD, satellite and online streaming.

Many movie theatres have closed for these reasons, but they have also been casualties of crises, destroyed during Iran's Islamic Revolution (1978–9) and the Syrian war (2011–) among other conflicts. Due to these and other difficulties, independent films are often screened abroad but not in the countries where they are set or that their filmmakers are from.

In parts of the Arab world, state support for cinema has been non-existent, inadequate or dismantled in favour of a market-led system. Despite having an established commercial film industry, Egypt had no infrastructure for independent cinema, so el-Said decided the only way to make his film *In the Last Days of the City* (2016) was to create it himself.[28] He started by founding his own production company, Zero Production, which built the infrastructure that gave birth to both Cimatheque and the video collective Mosireen. Cimatheque opened in 2015, a multipurpose space containing 'everything you want to practice in cinema', including equipment hire, workshops, a library, an archive and a screening venue that the authorities consider too small to be a theatre so it does not have to send its films to the censors.[29]

3. Economic constraints

'Cinema is fundamentally (ontologically, even) tied to capital, unlike most other art forms', Haghighi declares, pointing to money as a material constraint which, the philosopher Gilles Deleuze has said, is 'the obverse of all the images that the cinema shows and sets in place'.[30] While it would be ideal to make films that are both cheap and successful, this rarely occurs. Properly realizing ideas onscreen entails significant amounts of money and, usually, a paying audience to return the investment. Compared to mainstream, international standards, the budgets of films in this book are modest. Yet, investment in filmmaking is a risky venture – especially when combined with numerous other constraints – making fund-raising a major challenge for filmmakers.

Due to limited possibilities for distribution in their country of origin, filmmakers in the region often rely on foreign funders, co-producers, distributors, film festivals and television networks. This brings some freedom from local constraints, such as state censorship, but, at the same time, external funders and markets impose other rules and expectations. For any funding, filmmakers must meet eligibility criteria that often depend on their place of residence and nationality. Co-production arrangements may also stipulate the nationality of crew members, usually from the country providing funds. In written and unwritten selection criteria for funding applications, development labs, festivals and television sales and commissions, filmmakers' work is expected to comply with a challenging list of requirements: to be urgent or timely, implying that it has cultural value only for that moment; to be universal rather than merely 'local' (with the assumption that 'we're only talking about our own problems', which is 'condescending'[31] to many filmmakers); and to be 'authentic' to the filmmaker's country of origin, placing upon them the burden of 'explaining' their part of the world. At the same time, stories are often expected to fit pre-existing narratives of exoticism, oppressed Muslim women and Islamic terrorism. These criteria hold Middle Eastern films to standards to which Western films are not usually held, reflecting gatekeepers' preferences and fashions for subjects they want to hear about and Orientalist stereotypes inherited from other films and news media. While scholars often criticize the adoption of particular 'filmmaking formulas' in order to target festivals and be 'commercially viable' for international markets,[32] they are less sensitive to how filmmakers experience these pressures as a constraint on their free speech just as harmful as state censorship. Lebanese director Philippe Aractingi vents, 'I'm a filmmaker from the Middle East. Am I allowed to do a normal film? You know it's not allowed. Because the Europeans who read your work don't see you like that; they see you as Third World... We're put in one niche, which is drama where women are beaten.'[33] A related problem is that Middle Eastern filmmakers' dependency on European grants and markets divorces them from audiences at home.

Filmmakers feel expected to endanger themselves since films deemed risk-taking are appealing to international festivals and TV channels.[34] We can see this in the championing of Iranian director Jafar Panahi at the Cannes Film Festival. Panahi was arrested and imprisoned for several months for clandestine filmmaking during the 2009 protests. At Cannes 2010, he was honoured as an absent jury member, with an empty chair left on stage displaying his name. That year, Panahi was sentenced to a twenty-year ban from filmmaking, travelling abroad and giving interviews, as well as a six-year prison term (which he has not yet served). Despite this, he has continued to make films, including *This Is Not a Film* (2011), reportedly smuggled to Cannes in a USB stick hidden in a cake. While criticizing festivals for their 'interference', Iranian authorities have effectively condoned the films Panahi has made since his ban; in some respects, it suits them, since it ostensibly demonstrates that he is a 'free' citizen in his country,[35] just as his censorship makes his work of interest to international festivals.

Several films in this book are made with support from Arab cultural organizations such as the Doha Film Institute, Arab Fund for Arts and Culture and

Bidayyat, which claim to be looking for something different in the projects they fund. For example, the Lebanon-based Bidayyat was founded during the Syrian revolution specifically to 'protect' emerging Syrian documentary filmmakers from rules imposed by film and TV markets and let them develop their ideas 'more freely... with small budgets and alternative artistic practices'.[36] Because Western and Arab NGO grants tend to be small, they rely on filmmakers finding additional sources to finance projects. Filmmakers piece together funding from multiple sources or shoulder substantial costs themselves. For his film *300 Miles* (2016), al-Mokdad won funding from Bidayyat and the British Council but, in the four years it took to make, the film cost $50,000 and he had to personally finance half of it.[37]

To avoid political and economic constraints, some filmmakers adopt an artisanal mode, performing most production roles themselves, and often display their work in galleries as well as cinemas.[38] One such figure is Iranian filmmaker Mania Akbari, now living in exile in the UK: 'I make my films with very little money and this low-budget cinema is not tied to the film industry's rules and concerns over revenue as it has its own special audience.'[39] Even so, 'I face countless financial obstacles that slow down the project, delay it and sometimes permanently abort its progress.' Due to budget constraints, many filmmakers resort to donated labour although this is not a sustainable strategy, especially during economic crisis. As Iranian filmmaker Shirin Barghnavard states, 'Living in Tehran is super-expensive now. Today, it is very difficult to work in the film industry with a low wage. You have to pay your rent and bills, which are expensive compared to income.'[40] The need to earn a living is another constraint underlying filmmaking, which is affected by the wider economic situation, as in Iran, where sanctions and inflation have made life several times costlier.

4. Technological constraints

Since the late 1990s, the rise of cheaper and portable digital video cameras and editing software, combined with the Internet, has facilitated independent filmmaking everywhere. In countries such as Iran and Syria where filmmakers were hitherto reliant on state support for hiring equipment, it has enabled filmmakers to bypass these infrastructural constraints.[41] It has also fostered underground filmmaking throughout the region. By 'underground films', I mean films shot illegally, without official permits and distributed secretly in the home country, at festivals abroad or on the Internet. Produced on the run, with a limited budget and small crew, underground filmmaking entails numerous personal, professional and legal risks, so many films lack credits to protect participants' identities. Their subject matter is often taboo or sensitive, dealing with subjects thought 'inappropriate by the state and its restrictions on expression and free speech'.[42]

These technological changes have empowered more people (including women and other marginalized groups) to tell their stories, and to tell them more directly; they have also enabled identities and experiences not often filmed before to find representation in cinema. In particular, the Internet has provided an alternative virtual public sphere where films can be made accessible to audiences within the country and abroad in ways that bypass state censors and other gatekeepers. However, putting works online for free does not allow filmmakers to recoup their costs. Moreover, authorities can block websites, filter content and switch the Internet on and off, resulting in blackouts, as has often occurred during mass protests across the region. Far from a free, uncensored domain, the Internet increases possibilities for tracking dissidence by our electronic footprints. Additionally, as Chapter 8 explores, online posts can be removed by the platforms themselves, who retain ownership of the material and whose 'terms of service ... count for more than freedom of speech'.[43]

As video becomes the dominant means of production and streaming the prevalent mode of spectatorship, older definitions of film as generated on celluloid and designed for theatrical exhibition become increasingly untenable – cinema itself is said to be in 'crisis' as a result of these new media offering alternative models to both 'the capital-heavy motion picture industry that employs dozens of specialists in the production of a single work' and 'commercialized distribution networks' that determined public accessibility of films in theatres or on television.[44] Yet, as we will see in the chapters, film is a mixed medium, always incorporating newer media; hence, my definition of 'film' remains open, applying to different forms of moving images.

5. Societal and religious constraints

Filmmakers must comply with social and religious customs of Arab-Muslim society if they want to distribute their films within the region. What directors might ask actors (especially women) to do and wear is often constrained by Islamic codes of honour and modesty (*hejāb*). Iran's Islamic Republic has strict regulations governing onscreen depiction of female characters, who must always be veiled, even in scenes at home with their families when this would not be realistic. As we will see in subsequent chapters, filmmakers creatively work around these constraints to explore characters' private lives and intimacy.

Partly due to religious rules about public space and gender segregation, filmmakers can encounter interference from citizens on set.[45] While directing outdoor scenes for *Wadjda* (2012) in Saudi Arabia, Haifa al-Mansour communicated via walkie-talkie from a van so as not to be seen publicly interacting with male crew members. Despite these struggles, a greater proportion of female directors exists in the region's independent filmmaking sector – up to 50 per cent in Palestine and Lebanon – than in the West, where the figure stands at around 12 per cent in Europe and 5 per cent in the United States.[46] Palestinian filmmaker Annemarie Jacir surmises that this may be due to the absence of the entrenched prejudices against women present in more established film industries.[47] For her debut feature *Salt of This Sea* (2018), her French producers expressed concern whether her Arab crew members would respect her as a young, female director; yet, during the production, it was the French crew members that gave her trouble. These examples demonstrate the problems of assuming that Arab-Muslim societies are the sole source of women's oppression, as Lila Abu-Lughod has highlighted in another context.[48] As Egyptian filmmaker Mohamed Siam puts it, Westerners tend to have 'a very medieval idea about Islam'.[49] These negative views also underlie social prejudices against filmmakers from the region when they emigrate to the West. Palestinian filmmaker Basil Khalil believes unconscious bias against foreign names has counted against his career progression in the British film industry, making it harder to jump through hurdles.[50]

Filmmakers from the region frequently report that self-censorship plays an inhibitive role during the creative process before any state censorship. Self-censorship, however, is not always a matter of making conscious choices to exclude politically contentious elements. Social and religious norms can also be internalized in ways that make it difficult to combat or even be aware of them. As a form of voluntary and involuntary self-control, self-censorship might be regarded as an internalized social and/or political constraint. We can see this in, practices of public dissimulation prevalent in authoritarian states, as Lisa Wedeen has analysed in Syria under Hafiz al-Assad: 'citizens acted "as if" they revered the leader', manifesting compliance to the regime in their outward behaviour, while differing from it in their actual beliefs and values.[51] Dissimulation fosters separate private and public worlds, recalling the precautionary practice of hiding one's religious belief to avoid persecution, known as *taqiya*, in Shi'a Islam.

Filmmakers who grew up in these cultures of dissimulation are accustomed to speaking indirectly: saying one thing and meaning another. Iranian filmmaker Sadaf Foroughi believes this occurs so instinctively in her creative process that she does not even think of it as self-censorship.[52] Yet, self-censorship is not confined to the Middle East. As Saudi producer and comedian Hisham Fageeh states, 'If I said what I wanted to say I'd be in trouble all the time. I've lived in the States and you self-censor there sometimes; there's always a sense of self-censorship.'[53]

6. Security risks and ethics

Security risks are a major challenge to filmmaking in the region, many of them exceeding 'inevitable risks' that generally occur when a film is made.[54] Filmmakers sometimes venture into extreme situations, such as the conflict in Syria where they face kidnapping and killings by the regime and assorted militias. For security reasons, anonymity or pseudonyms are often essential while inside the country while those who have left have greater freedom to sign their work in their own name.[55] Under these conditions, it is not always possible to film in person. US-based Syrian filmmaker Sam Kadi directed his documentary *Little Gandhi* (2016) over Skype from Turkey, relying on activists on the ground in war-torn Syria to operate camera and sound equipment, and to smuggle footage across the border.[56]

Although both filmmakers and their subjects are vulnerable, risk is unevenly distributed, often disadvantaging whoever remains in the danger zones and faces long-term consequences. Filmmakers sometimes highlight these discrepancies. In *Those Who Remain* (2016), Lebanese filmmaker Eliane Raheb's documentary about the Akkar region on the Lebanese border, feared to be the doorway for a potential ISIS invasion from Syria, the protagonist Haykal points out to her, 'you are doing your interview and you will leave.... We will remain here!' Documentary filmmaking sharply demonstrates these ethical dimensions because it deals with real people whom filmmakers are obliged not to put in harm's way. Yet ethical responsibility applies more broadly to how filmmakers treat actors and crew, in either documentary or fiction, including 'at risk' or vulnerable groups such as child actors, many of whom play versions of themselves as we will see in Chapter 2. When dealing with people at risk, filmmakers sometimes exercise self-censorship for ethical reasons, even if it means losing an opportunity to tell a good story. Risks attached to a film extend to its afterlife in distribution, as it can become more dangerous through national and international visibility. As explored in Chapter 8, Yasmin Fedda took these responsibilities very seriously for her documentary *Queens of Syria* (2014), measuring risks to her participants over time.

7. Travel restrictions

When attending festivals abroad, cast and crew often encounter obstacles to travel such as bureaucratic processes for visa applications and even visa refusals, depending on what passports they have. Barghnavard made her documentary *Invisible* (2019) partly to express these frustrations about limitations imposed by your passport which defines your nationality and how others see and treat you. Additionally, many filmmakers experience restricted mobility within their own country, as in occupied Palestine, or country of residence, which hampers their ability to make films and accompany them on their journey through distribution. As a Syrian refugee in Lebanon, al-Mokdad was confined to a specific geographical area in Beirut and could not travel with his films; his brother Eyas al-Mokdad, a Belgian national, attended festival screenings and Q&As on his behalf. In some cases, filmmakers classified as 'dissidents' in their home country are banned from international travel, as has happened to Jafar Panahi in Iran; their passports can also be confiscated upon their return after travelling abroad. Travel restrictions, and filmmakers' creative solutions to them, are explored in Chapter 5 on Road Movies.

8. Temporal constraints

Deadlines are examples of temporal constraints that some people find concentrate their creative powers.[57] For independent filmmakers, dependent on prestigious festivals for premiering their films and thereby gaining recognition that leads to distribution opportunities, the festival network is a source of time pressures, imposing schedules for completion.[58] Aside from these routine factors, further deadlines are enforced by the state of crisis in which filmmakers live and work. Karimi obtained a seventeen-day shooting permit for his film *Drum* (2016) while he was awaiting trial for posting a trailer of his previous film on YouTube. Knowing that he had to shoot whatever he could in case he was unable to continue shaped his decision to shoot each scene without cuts.[59] Filmed in black and white with long takes in decaying buildings in the older, historic part of Tehran, *Drum* recalls Hungarian auteur Bela Tarr's style, as critics noted, yet it is as much a product of temporal constraints as artistic influences.⁶⁰ Furthermore, because film production (including lengthy editing processes) often takes significant time, films that began under one set of circumstances may be released under a completely different one, such as another political regime with different limitations upon free expression. Several filmmakers in this book have run into these temporal obstacles.

9. Environmental constraints

In *A Room of One's Own* (1929), Virginia Woolf wrote that 'a woman must have money and a room of her own if she is to write fiction.'⁶¹ A physical environment can affect creativity, particularly in unstable places where it is difficult to concentrate and basic services are not reliable for reasons of conflict, sanctions, official corruption and incompetence, interfering with even simple tasks such as charging cameras and uploading films, let alone more complex aspects of production. According to Rania Stephan, 'All filmmakers face external factors that hamper their work but in Lebanon you have more', such as slow Internet or not having electricity or a quiet space. There are 'a lot of little annoyances that take your energy' so 'you have to be really focused and resilient'.⁶² As film scholarship is increasingly recognizing, filmmaking practices have an environmental impact.⁶³ But environmental factors also impact filmmaking practices. 'I live in Cairo, one of the most polluted cities in the world' with 'all the variation of constraints you could imagine', Omara told me. 'In other places, maybe making a great film is a big achievement; in Egypt, making *a* film is a big achievement.'⁶⁴

Aside from political constraints that force some filmmakers into exile abroad or internally within their country, environmental limitations prompt many to emigrate for more stable working conditions. However, when they emigrate they risk separation from their sources of inspiration in the people and places with which they share a history, language and culture. When their environment changes, it can be a dislocating experience, throwing up new challenges such as redefining themselves and gaining fluency in another language.

10. Linguistic constraints

Not only is language the medium of dialogue, voice-over and titles, it is essential to all aspects of filmmaking, from writing funding applications through to pitching, scriptwriting, directing and communicating with audiences. In the Arab world, many dialects are spoken, an 'obstacle hampering the inter-Arab exchange of movies' since people from different parts can find it difficult to understand each other.[65] While the Modern Standard Arabic used by newscasters, politicians and poets is familiar to most educated Arabic speakers, it is not the language of everyday expression. Most of the films in this book are in Arabic or Farsi, in a variety of dialects. The region has a history of languages being imposed as a result of colonial conquest, which marginalizes other spoken languages and dialects. Depending on funding stipulations and market considerations, filmmakers can find choice of language foisted upon them. Through the hegemony of English and French, language continues to operate as a neo-colonial tool as some gatekeepers deem subtitled movies a barrier to commercial appeal.

11. Formal constraints

Elster uses the term 'formal constraints' to refer to an artist's anticipation of audience expectations and how this formally shapes a work; he classifies them, along with 'material, technical or financial restrictions', as 'hard' constraints, as opposed to 'soft' constraints such as conventions.[66] 'Hard' constraints come from external sources; all constraints discussed so far come under this category. However, that is not to say that they are fixed and unchanging. Maybe, one day, filmmakers will no longer encounter Orientalist stereotyping, as audiences, funders, festivals and broadcasters change their habits of thought and practices.

Formal constraints include classical Hollywood narrative which favours clear, coherent storytelling in three (or five) acts with believable characters: a globally dominant form. Most films in this book abide by these constraints, although they also challenge or deploy them towards other ends in experimental practices, as shown in Chapters 5, 6, 7 and 8. Film length is another constraint. Running times have historically been determined by commercial reasons, such as exhibitors' or broadcasters' programming schedules, resulting in the standard ninety-minute theatrical feature or forty-eight-and-a-half-minute television documentary (the latter allowing for advertisement breaks). In television documentary particularly, 'you're literally counting every second', entailing ruthless compromises for anything that doesn't fit clear storytelling.[67] Because they rarely have theatrical releases, short films are less attractive than features to investors, who want to ensure returns on their investment. Lebanese filmmaker Mounia Akl found a creative way of overcoming this constraint by convincing funders that her graduation short *Submarine* (2016) (discussed in Chapter 9) was an investment for her future feature, *Costa Brava Lebanon* (2021).[68] For Lara Zeidan, director of *Three Centimetres* (2018) (in Chapter 5), graduation shorts and film schools, whether in Lebanon or abroad, offer spaces of free expression: 'In Lebanon there are a lot of LGBT films that come out of film school because there is this safety there where you can use film as a way of self-expression instead of thinking of the audience and how it's going to be received'.[69] Furthermore, as we will see in Chapter 7, because short films are held less tightly to screening permit requirements, even more established directors are using them to circumvent rules by creating features from strings of shorts.

12. Self-imposed constraints

Self-imposed constraints are chosen by artists and consist of two types: pre-existing conventions and invented constraints.[70] Like metre and rhyme in poetry, conventions can stimulate play and innovation. Genre falls into this category if it is chosen by the filmmaker as their expressive medium rather than imposed by their production company or exhibition platform. The science-fiction genre is a chosen constraint in Larissa Sansour's work in Chapter 9. Sansour's premise is that life in Palestine is stranger than reality and merits not a realist or documentary approach but a science-fiction treatment. Therefore, any topic that she wants to address about the crisis, such as the politicized use of archaeology, she often drops into a science-fiction framework. Genre innovation is almost inevitable in crisis contexts that force filmmakers to twist genres beyond their usual parameters. In Chapter 5, for example, we will see how the road movie is transformed.

Invented constraints occur when artists devise the rules and limitations by which they will abide. For Elster, an artist has greater freedom when they choose their own constraints and make choices within them; consequently, constructing constraints is an assertion of freedom. The Dogme '95 movement epitomizes this type of constraint in filmmaking. Led by Danish directors Lars von Trier and Thomas Vinterberg, Dogme '95 launched a manifesto with ten filmmaking rules known as the 'Vow of Chastity', forbidding artificial props and sets, 'temporal and geographical alienation', 'superficial' action involving guns or murders and genre movies, among other restrictions.[71] Dogme rules turn external pressures into internal ones which, it might be argued, suit Danish filmmakers working in relative safety and/or struggling for subject matter; Middle Eastern filmmakers in crisis conditions have enough constraints in their external environment, with no shortage of stories, and therefore no need for further restrictions. Yet, this is complicated by the fact that Danish directors (like many other filmmakers elsewhere) also make use of hard, external constraints, such as economic limitations, as 'opportunities for creativity'.[72] Conversely, Middle Eastern filmmakers, too, make use of chosen constraints to hone their creative approach. The Iranian director Abbas Kiarostami was adept at working with external constraints and imposing further ones on himself, inspiring the creative strategies considered in Chapters 2 and 5. Some of the filmmakers I interviewed have appropriated Dogme and Oulipean techniques. 'I do put constraints in my films, but throw them out as well', Aractingi says.[73] This is entirely in keeping with Dogme spirit. The rules are like a scaffold to stimulate creativity and can be ditched when they have served their purpose. Additionally, some filmmakers, especially those with an experimental bent, have invented their own constraints. Lebanese filmmaker Rana Eid declares, 'If we don't have a challenge in this film, let's create one!'[74] In her documentary *Panoptic* (2017) (in Chapter 4), which explores the Lebanese Civil War's unresolved legacies, she determined only to use reflected sound on location in order to convey the atmosphere of detention centres and former torture chambers through their sound qualities.

Why creativity?

The word 'create', in English, is about making, originally referring to divine power; only after the acceptance of creation as human activity were the terms 'creative' and 'creativity' coined in the eighteenth and twentieth centuries, respectively.[75] These developments were anticipated in the Muslim and Arab world by Sufi philosophers who, by the ninth century, had intuited that human beings have a 'creative element'.[76] In Sufism, creativity happens in an intermediate world between our empirical reality and the universe of angels known as the 'imaginal realm' where ideas and dreams assume tangible forms.[77] For filmmakers that I interviewed, creativity holds many associations, from imagination and spiritual yearning to problem-solving, labour, suffering, resistance, healing and necessity. 'Creativity is often a response to the "un-making" of the world, when the pavement is crumbling under your feet and you no longer recognise the people around you', Iraqi filmmaker Maysoon Pachachi told me.[78] Whereas crisis and conflict are a radical unmaking of the world, creativity is imagined as their antithesis, capable of putting the parts together again.

Creativity is a favoured word among artists and has popular currency. As Kraidy observes, it was widely used by journalists, activists and academics in their coverage of regional protests, pairing it with words like 'revolution', 'dissent', 'protest' and 'resistance' to describe a range of activism and art.[79] Yet, with the exception of Gilles Deleuze (whose ideas seep into this book), creativity has generally been neglected in film theory, perhaps due to the way it seems to elevate the artist over other forces and ignore the material base of production, conjuring up mystical and Romantic notions of 'inspiration' and 'self-expression'.[80] However, even in mystical and Romantic thought, 'inspiration' is not necessarily something that just happens; frequently, the impetus for creativity is believed to come from elsewhere: the artist moved by larger forces, such as a Muse who dictates their thoughts. For Sufis, 'spontaneous creativity is impossible'; it needs pre-existing conditions, namely self-perfection and mystical ecstasy. Sufism, therefore, lays claim to being the first philosophy to consider questions of 'stimulating creativity'.[81]

This book proposes a model of creativity as shaped by constraints. The twelve-part typology above shows how creativity is always constrained. Constraints also complicate ideas of authorship – not only Romantic notions of artists as solitary geniuses but also the abstract philosophizing that often goes under the name of auteur theory that 'has less to do with the way movies are made than with the way they are elucidated and evaluated'.[82] In this book, I adopt Mette Hjort's notion of 'practitioner's agency': a more grounded approach that emphasizes how filmmakers' choices are shaped by constraints but also how their choices transform those constraints into creative opportunities.[83] I cover several categories of filmmakers, each constrained in different ways that affect their creative approaches: filmmakers based in the region, exiles who have permanently left their country, voluntarily or involuntarily, émigré and second-generation filmmakers of dual nationality who travel to the region to make films and filmmakers from the West, who collaborate with filmmakers from the Middle East. Those predominantly based abroad trade positions of relative safety for riskier ones when they work in the region. However, constraints are usually greater for filmmakers based in the country. In my analysis, I try to take account of these different 'life worlds' and 'safety-nets'.[84]

Allegory has formed the dominant framework for interpreting Middle Eastern cinema, a mode of interpretation that goes hand in hand with the emphasis on state censorship, its impetus being to study how filmmakers 'defy' censors through this particular creative strategy. In its most basic form, allegory is a mode of expression that says one thing while meaning another, creating a literal layer and an allegorical one. It is often deemed a means of political resistance against authoritarian regimes, since it disguises core meanings through symbolism and metaphor, capable of 'smuggling' in contentious ideas. The Cold War paradigm of the dissident artist is a key influence; as Angus Fletcher states, 'In times of political oppression we may get "Aesop language" to avoid the censorship of dissident thought.'[85] Historically, allegory has suited filmmakers working in state-sponsored cinema, as Rasha Salti shows in films developed under the auspices of Syria's National Film Organization, founded by the Ba'ath Party. One of the paradoxes of Syrian cinema, Salti observes, is that it managed to create a space for subversion and critique under one-party state sponsorship that suppresses dissent and imposes official dogma. Filmmakers were aware of red lines, so they came to 'operate through guises, stratagems, allegory and metaphor' to avoid detection and slip under the censors' radar.[86] For example, Ossama Mohammed's *Stars in Broad Daylight* (1988) subverts the regime's own symbols and alludes to state oppression through a character resembling President Hafez al-Assad.

Negar Mottahedeh interprets the cinema of Iran's Islamic Republic as 'displaced allegories' of 'the national situation and constraints on the industry'.[87] However, as I argue in this book, films simply *are* products of their constraints; there is no need to interpret this allegorically. Along with allegorical readings, there is a tendency to interpret filmmakers' choices as techniques that draw attention to limits of representation, emphasizing 'that which cannot be shown' and asking viewers to seek out hidden meanings beyond what appears onscreen.[88] In contrast to these approaches, which stress state censorship at the expense of other constraints, I focus on filmmakers' creative use of a variety of limitations, their ability to get around or work within them. As Saudi filmmaker Ahd Kamel says, it's about 'harnessing the constraints to do what you can't do.'[89]

Another problem with allegorical interpretation is the inclination to see each film as a coded message seeking to overthrow a government, which reduces filmmakers' creativity to political messaging.[90] Films from non-Western countries are also often taken as national allegories in the manner proposed by Fredric Jameson: every third-world text is an allegory of '*the embattled situation*' facing that society, so an individual's story is always that of the public, even when not presented as such, because of 'a different ratio of the personal to the political' from 'western habits of reading'.[91] Jameson's argument has been criticized for its generalization of 'third-world' cultural production. However, it finds a certain confirmation in the tensions between personal stories and collective struggles and the battles between filmmakers and their Western(ized) collaborators, as we will see with *5 Broken Cameras* (2011) and *For Sama* (2019) in Chapter 1.

Moreover, practices of dissimulation have fostered a habit of saying things indirectly in Middle Eastern societies, as much due to cultural customs as living under dictatorships. This tendency, which prefers allegory and other cloaked expressive forms, will not disappear overnight. In her work on Iranian cinema, Michelle Langford has persuasively argued that allegory is not merely a response to state censorship; instead, it is sustained by enduring poetic traditions.[92] She regards allegory as expressing images' potential to open up to other dimensions of meaning – to shift from the immediate, concrete and particular to the broader, abstract and universal. In this book, I am not arguing that allegory has been entirely replaced; indeed, all films remain open to allegorical interpretation. However, we are witnessing a shift away from the allegories that characterized the region's cinema in the past towards more direct and multiple creative strategies.

In moving beyond allegory, this book is anticipated by the work of Viola Shafik and Laura Marks. Shafik has discussed various creative strategies for articulating dissent in Tunisian, Egyptian, Syrian and Palestinian films before the Arab uprisings through the performativity of actors' bodies and address to the spectator's body.[93] Using Deleuze's writing on the fold and classical Islamic philosophy, Marks has proposed an aesthetics of unfolding/enfolding, referring to how both funding and censorship selectively make experience perceptible.[94] Since experience is difficult to depict directly, she identifies creative strategies that dwell on filters of information such as surveillance and self-censorship, or unfurl hidden aspects of experience.[95]

Today, the range of creative strategies emanating from independent Iranian and Arab filmmaking is much wider than previous scholarship in this area has acknowledged. Elster suggests that the number of possible creative strategies is unlimited because of how artistic evolution occurs: 'Whereas constraints arise by necessity or choice, conventions [or creative strategies] *evolve*'.[96] As the constraints change, so do creative strategies for getting around them, as shown by the uprisings that, at least temporarily, broke the 'wall of fear' that kept populations in states of dissimulation. While government crackdowns ushered in a more repressive climate in many places, landing filmmakers in trouble and forcing great numbers to leave their countries, many of them became emboldened to tell their stories more directly, no longer considering allegorical expression and poetic indirectness as obligatory although, as we will see, their directness depends on the degree of risk and range of free expression in contexts in which they work.

The films produced in this period arise from a state of crisis, registering the pressures under which they were made: they are crisis-images related to, yet distinct from, previous eras. For my notion of the crisis-image, I draw on Deleuze who characterizes the breakdown of action in the movement-image and transition to the time-image as a crisis within cinema that resulted from the crisis of the Second World War.[97] Emerging in the war's aftermath, the time-image captures the landscape's physical and mental scars through motifs such as circuitous journeys and child protagonists who see rather than act. In Chapter 2, I engage more fully with Deleuze's arguments, and also critique his view of child protagonists as passive seers. If the time-image was a new way of thinking about crisis for post-war European cinema, the creative strategies elaborated in this book are filmmakers' techniques for understanding their contemporary circumstances and coping with their constraints. The term 'strategy', however, may sound too deliberate for the creative process. In this respect, filmmakers' choices may be better understood as 'tactics' or ruses. Michel de Certeau distinguishes between 'strategy', a term that he reserves for institutional power, and 'tactics', that describes how ordinary people watch for opportunities in their path as they walk about the city, using the space differently from the ways intended by urban planners. His idea of tactical play – inspired by an anthology whose title translates as *The Book of Tricks: The Political Strategy of the Arabs* – is helpful to understanding the creative strategies in this book.[98]

The rise of documentary, previously often regarded as 'a subordinate cinematic form',[99] but now gaining greater visibility and market appeal, plays an important role in the shift towards more direct creative strategies. Documentaries contain direct relationships with lived realities, since they record real people and places. As Khalid Abdalla remarks about filmmaking from the region, 'The palette of documentary on the whole is often more interesting and wider than a lot of the fiction films because the circumstances are pretty extraordinary. What you can capture is often more cinematic than what you might be able to recreate.'[100] In crisis conditions, reality presents filmmakers with 'found' stories that rival fiction's inventive powers. On the other hand, when shooting documentary is considered too politically charged, fiction serves as a shield. Moreover, as we will see in the chapters, blending documentary and fiction can open new spaces that challenge restrictions.

The concept of indexicality captures well what I mean by directness in creative strategies. Charles Sanders Peirce defined the index as part of his classification of signs: unlike icons that resemble their objects, and symbols that gain meanings through usage, indices are 'physically connected' to what they represent, taking the form of a trace (such as a footprint or photograph) or a pointing signifier (like a weathervane or deictic pronouns such as 'this').[101]

Film itself is an indexical medium as it captures space and time. In film theory, indexicality has tended to be associated with realism, as in the work of André Bazin or Siegfried Kracauer, who remarked on film's ability to 'record and reveal physical reality'.[102] However, indexicality is available to a variety of styles, as well as different media.[103] Indexicality elucidates the political dimensions of the creative strategies I discuss, as many of them stem from their filmmakers' direct engagement with political events. Made in the midst of upheavals, their films bear an indexical relationship to crisis: not merely representations of crises, they are products of crises. Creative strategies bear traces of the circumstances under which films were made so that each film is 'a record of its working constraints'.[104] These constraints may be foregrounded to varying degrees, but contextualizing them is essential to understanding the creative strategies adopted. In such conditions, the very act of making films is a political gesture. This is distinct from the ways in which political cinema has been defined in the past, as politically and formally radical like dissident allegory or collectivist films from the 1960s and 1970s known as 'Third Cinema'. Constraint forms a large part of a work's meaning, which is located not merely in its story of resistance or its political 'message'.

Methodology of filmmaker interviews

This book is partly based on forty-two semi-structured depth interviews with directors and producers that I carried out between 2015 and 2021. On average, each of the interviews, which were mostly face-to-face or via video link or telephone, lasted about two hours. As the book originated from a series of events in which I participated and curated, the interviews came out of those events and, as I began researching the book, I selected other filmmakers on the basis of their regional production contexts. I have also drawn on published interviews, including with some filmmakers whom I did not interview.

Film scholarship tends to study finished films; the journey towards their creation, the difficulties that filmmakers must overcome and their inventive tactics for doing so rarely receive attention as alternative sites of meaning. In contrast to the view from 'in front' of the film, my interviews with filmmakers provided me with the view from 'behind', consisting of their first-hand accounts of constraints in crisis contexts.[105] For many filmmakers, the finished film is not the end point but the start of conversations with audiences, considered as 'part of the making process'.[106] My interviews focused on the circumstances in which they were working, their creative processes, how external and self-imposed constraints shaped their films' development and their journey through distribution. Where filmmakers or their collaborators might be exposed to harm, interview contributions have been anonymized and sensitive details have been removed.

Much has been made recently about raising the voices of those outside the global north in academic debate. In this book, I use practitioner perspectives as voices of authority and treat them as theorists in their own right in their reflections on their practice. Some filmmakers referred to theorists themselves, citing Western thinkers such as Deleuze and Lacan as well as Sufi philosophy. In their films made in crisis conditions, we can recognize elements of critical theory which they lived 'in a very embodied way'.[107] Conversely, talking to them led me to reflect on how critical theory takes shape in situated contexts; as mentioned in Chapter 4, much twentieth-century French critical thought was formed in Algeria with the help of native 'informants' whose intellectual contribution was barely acknowledged. The major ideas and interviews in this book are constructed through situated encounters between myself and the filmmakers, co-produced with them as interlocutors rather than informants.

Organization of the book

This book's goal is not a comprehensive study of filmmaking in the region but, rather, a theoretical framework for analysing cinematic freedom of expression that may be useful beyond this corpus of films and filmmakers. Despite the Middle East's interconnectedness as a cultural sphere, there is a tendency to treat these cinemas hermetically in national cinema or area studies; there are even few comparative studies of Arab and Iranian cinemas. This book's comparative approach illuminates transnational similarities and differences within the region and beyond. As we will see, Iranian cinema is an exemplary model of inspiration and practice for many Arab filmmakers.

Each of my nine chapters focuses on a creative strategy that filmmakers have adopted in response to constraints. The nine creative strategies studied here are not exhaustive but rather indicative of the many possibilities. These strategies do not exist in isolation, but often intersect with each other and a given film could potentially use several. Each chapter shows how the creative strategies have emerged out of earlier world cinema practices, gesturing to the cinematic histories of these crisis-images, and explores case-study films in close analysis through attention to their material production circumstances. The case-study films have been chosen to illustrate the possibilities of the creative strategy with which the chapter deals, with the purpose of fleshing out my theoretical framework. The choices are inevitably shaped by my own physical and cinematic journeys through the region and what I had access to. Many other examples could be offered, both from those countries that I have discussed and others, so I hope that my analysis will provoke debates about other films in the region and elsewhere in relation to their constraints and creative strategies.

Chapter 1 introduces my argument that films bear an indexical relationship to their constraints and crisis conditions through the creative strategy of witnessing. My first two case studies, *5 Broken Cameras* (2011) and *For Sama* (2019), are constructed from conflict footage filmed in situ in Palestine and Syria, respectively, by filmmakers identifying as citizen journalists and retrospectively shaped into cinematic narratives through collaboration with foreign co-directors; I explore the constraints and possibilities of these relationships in what Tamur Ashuri and Amit Pinchevski call the field of media witnessing. In the second set of case studies, *Whose Country* (2016), and *Freedom Fields* (2018), set in Egypt and Libya, respectively, I show how these documentaries witness unexpected turbulent changes in both their content and style.

In Chapter 2, I explore the use of child protagonists to overcome societal, political and infrastructural constraints, identifying a shift from their earlier allegorical deployment to a more direct, experiential one that emphasizes their responses to crises that they witness (*War Canister* (2013), *Capernaum* (2018), *300 Miles* (2016)). I argue that children's license to say the unsayable and do what cannot be done becomes even more direct and politicized in a shift towards teen protagonists (*Wadjda* (2012), *Ava* (2017) and *Amal* (2017)).

Animation creates its own world by hand or computer; Chapter 3 investigates how it offers a creative solution to constraints such as missing footage, restricted access and the need for anonymity as well as censorship, in the case studies *The Green Wave* (2010), *Tehran Taboo* (2017), *The Wanted 18* (2014) and *Suleima* (2014). Chapter 4 focuses on psychogeography, a tactic that explores psychological and historical layers beneath official narratives of places by travelling around them and recording their ambiance. It discusses psychogeography as a way of 'witnessing' cities undergoing crisis that is more direct than allegory although less direct than the reportage-style witnessing in Chapter 1, as exemplified by *Writing on the City* (2012), *Tehran: City of Love* (2018), *Panoptic* (2017), *In the Last Days of the City* (2016) and *A Day and a Button* (2015). Continuing the theme of travel, Chapter 5 turns to tactical insights that filmmakers have drawn from the road movie genre, used to overcome various obstacles to freedom of speech and movement in *Speed Sisters* (2015), *Taxi Tehran* (2015), *Three Centimetres* (2018), *From A to B* (2014) and *Mondial 2010* (2013).

While witnessing is a thread that runs through the book, Chapters 6–9 place greater emphasis on storytelling constraints and strategies. Chapter 6 describes humour as a tactic deployed in different comic modes matched to filmmakers' purposes and extent of free expression in their working contexts: from direct satire that mocks the powerful and punctures spectacles of power (*Top Goon: Diaries of a Little Dictator* (2011–12)) to surrealist humour that exposes situational absurdity (*It Must Be Heaven* (2019), *Ave Maria* (2015) and *Pig* (2018)) and indirect modes of deadpan humour and romantic comedy (*Tehran: City of Love* (2018) and *Barakah Meets Barakah* (2016)). Chapter 7 turns to stories within stories as a versatile storytelling tactic in crisis conditions, capable of being shuffled in any order, sharing multiple perspectives and dodging censorship (*Profession: Documentarist* (2014), *Queens of Syria* (2014), *Tales* (2014)). Archival strategies create films from existing footage; Chapter 8 explores storytelling from electronic archives as a means of accessing alternative microhistories of contested events and bypassing production constraints, as shown in *The Three Disappearances of Soad Hosni* (2011), *Silvered Water, Syria Self-Portrait* (2014) and *Ayouni* (2020). Finally, Chapter 9 examines sci-fi dystopia: when reality becomes stranger than fiction, filmmakers can make creative use of 'found' dystopias for commentary upon present-day crises, as we will see in *Atomic Heart Mother* (2015), *Dreamaway* (2018), *Nation Estate* (2013) and *Submarine* (2016).

1

Witnessing

In the documentary *Syria's Disappeared* (2017), Mansour Omari, a Syrian detention centre survivor, relates how he smuggled out a garment sewn from his fellow prisoners' rags bearing their names that they had inscribed in their own blood and rust from their cells. The regime kept records of its tens of thousands of detainees but denied their families knowledge of arrests. By carrying this evidence into the outside world and living to tell the story himself, Omari is a powerful witness of activists' enforced disappearance in post-uprising Syria. *Syria's Disappeared* juxtaposes such survivor testimony with the story of an international war crimes investigation into abandoned intelligence documents found during the war that are matched with thousands of photographs documenting tortured corpses taken by a regime defector codenamed Caesar. With this insider evidence, the film bears witness to regime crimes and appeals to the international community for release of remaining detainees and justice for them and their families.

Both documentary filmmaking and journalism frequently engage in witnessing practices. As Barbie Zelizer claims, the phrase 'they were there' bears 'special resonance for journalists', indicating 'a physical presence that enables reporters to accomplish newswork.'[1] In the web 2.0 era, moreover, anyone possessing a portable camera or mobile phone can document crisis and instantaneously share images online. The term 'citizen journalist' conjures up an ordinary person 'unexpectedly caught up' in moments of crisis and compelled to bear witness, contributing insider, 'bottom up' perspectives in contrast to the top/down, outsider views of professional news corporations.[2] Witnessing has been taken up with particular urgency in the Middle East, where state media are not trusted to cover events truthfully. In Palestine, filming and uploading citizen videos with eyewitness testimony of atrocities by Israeli soldiers and settlers has become an established practice for combating Israeli media hegemony. Since the 2009 Iranian protests, videos documenting demonstrations and state repression have proliferated, including footage of the death of Neda Agha-Soltan, a young woman shot by security forces in Iran in 2009, of the 2011 Maspero Massacre in Egypt, uploaded to YouTube by the video collective Mosireen and of a woman, Malak Alawiye, kicking a ministerial bodyguard brandishing an assault rifle during the 2019 Lebanese protests. These captured moments had transformative effects on narratives of those events.

Witnessing is one of the most prevalent creative strategies emerging from filmmakers in the region and the closest to journalism, especially citizen journalism, although some scholars have disputed the validity of this label for diverse output produced by assorted parties in these conflicts.[3] While there are important differences between short videos that witness on the spot, reacting to events as they happen, and feature-length films made over a longer duration that retrospectively shape the rushes into a story, this chapter emphasizes links between them, as footage from the former inspires and forms the raw material of the latter and several filmmakers have been involved in both stages. My first set of case studies is works by two filmmakers who can be considered 'citizen journalists': the Palestinian director Emad Burnat, who worked as a volunteer for Reuters news agency as he documented protests against the Israeli Separation Wall being built in Bil'in, his West Bank village, footage that he subsequently turned into the film *5 Broken Cameras* (2011) with his Israeli co-director Guy Davidi, and the Syrian filmmaker Waad al-Kateab, who sent her footage of the siege in the Syrian city of Aleppo to the UK's Channel 4 and later co-directed the documentary *For Sama* (2019) with British filmmaker Edward Watts. Al-Kateab has publicly embraced the identity of citizen journalist, describing herself as such in her biography on her 'Action for Sama' website and in award acceptance speeches.[4] The chapter's second set of case studies are documentaries that witness countries in transition: *Whose Country?* (2016) and *Freedom Fields* (2018), filmed by the Egyptian director Mohamed Siam and British-Libyan director Naziha Arebi in post-uprising Egypt and Libya, respectively. Siam and Arebi see themselves as filmmakers rather than journalists, while Sara Afshar, the British-Iranian director of *Syria's Disappeared*, positions her work as investigative journalism, evoking the professional rigour and neutrality associated with that field. As we will see, tensions between filmmaking, activism and (citizen) journalism are intrinsic to cinematic witnessing, registered in each of these films and their production conditions.

My approach to witnessing differs from the idea of 'representational limits' in Holocaust studies influential in scholarly literature on other conflicts since the Second World War, which posits that certain overwhelming experiences are beyond the realms of representation and make bearing witness an impossibility.[5] This Western, modernist framework is not suited to all types of witnessing and cannot account for the specific challenges and conditions of filming in crisis zones. In my conceptualization, witnessing is a *direct* strategy intended to capture the onslaught of conflict and other crises. Traditionally, a witness is a first-hand observer who recounts what they have experienced with their own eyes. However, in the enlarged understanding of who or what can be a witness generated by new technologies, a camera or other device can fulfil the role, capable of bearing witness even without human presence.[6] As a photographic medium, film automatically registers traces of events it captures; in the digital era, this indexical relationship with the object photographed, far from being lost, is retained in the camera's digital file. Moreover, films do not just bear traces of what they *represent*; their production circumstances leave material residues on them. Just as the garment that Mansour Omari smuggled out of the Syrian detention centre contains remnants not only of those people and events, but also the limited technology available to record them, so *films act as witnesses to their constraints*, which they register in their content and style.

The constraints of witnessing in protests and conflict zones can be likened to another form of street-based witnessing: political graffiti. Both graffiti and cinematic witnessing are forms of underground culture, produced without official permission, circumventing state censorship and monopoly of official media. Like graffiti art, witnessing deploys basic equipment (a small digital camera or mobile phone) because of economic exigencies and security risks. Working in public spaces under dangerous conditions, graffiti artists and videomakers also operate under time constraints, necessitating speed and secrecy to avoid lethal violence. During Iran's 2009 protests, filming furtively from windows and balconies of homes and offices was a way of testing the waters before being emboldened to capture events from the ground.[7] On the streets, protesters raised their hands to film with their phones, or videoed clandestinely from devices hidden in their shirt pockets, as Syrian activist Bassel Safadi demonstrates in the documentary *Ayouni* (2020). These constraints leave their imprint on witnessing styles, resulting in characteristics such as blurriness, unstable framing and variable sound.

Being there and risking their lives was part of the mission on which many of these filmmakers embarked. Their witnessing approaches martyrdom, a radical act of self-sacrifice; notably, in Arabic and Persian, the word 'martyr' (*shahīd*) derives from 'witness' (*shāhid*).[8] Across the region, 'martyr' commonly refers to anyone 'who puts his or her body on the line of defence against brutal repression'.[9]

The uprisings broke protesters' barriers of fear from decades of authoritarian rule and censorship, although risks and penalties intensified. Being caught while documenting protests and regime atrocities could result in imprisonment, confiscation of one's cameras and hard drives and even death. Under such extreme repression, anonymity is often necessary. As Joshka Wessels remarks, writing of Syria, while earlier creative resistance was 'an indirect and coded protest against the authoritarian regime', witnessing was a *direct* protest: rather than coding their work, video-makers 'coded themselves' with pseudonyms, as using real names would imperil them.[10] However, filmmakers manage risks not only to themselves but also to those they film, as we will see in the case studies.

The style of witnessing videos has been compared to the filmmaking movements *cinéma vérité*, Third Cinema (with its aesthetics of imperfection) and Dogme '95. The documentary movement *cinéma vérité*, distinguished from observational 'fly-on-the-wall' Direct Cinema by filmmakers' interactions with their subjects, arose in the wake of 1960s leftist political struggles and the advent of handheld 16 mm cameras that facilitated a similar immediacy in low-budget, street-level shooting that small digital cameras are renowned for today. As Kari Andén-Papadopoulos writes, the 'vérité aesthetic' of citizen videos 'heightens the effect of "realness" and "closeness" already so powerfully signified by the sense of viewing events from the involved perspective of those who lived or experienced a crisis as it was actually happening'.[11] Sixteen-millimetre technology was also adopted for capturing revolutionary struggles against colonialism in 1960s and 1970s Third Cinema. In his manifesto 'For an Imperfect Cinema' (1969), Cuban filmmaker Julio García Espinosa called for a politically committed cinema that no longer abides by mainstream cinema's rules of technical perfection nor standards of taste and artistic quality needed for endorsement by elite culture.[12] Drawing parallels with Third Cinema, Hamid Naficy claims that Green Movement videos' 'aesthetics of imperfection' heightened their witnessing power, while Chad Elias and Zaher Omareen have adopted the term 'Imperfect Cinema' for amateur videos from the Syrian Revolution which, they say, express 'a new audiovisual language … tied to the technological and aesthetic properties of the mobile phone'.[13] Meanwhile, in his performance/lecture *The Pixelated Revolution*, Lebanese artist Rabih Mroué has linked Syrian videos to Dogme '95 whose rules, as we saw in this book's Introduction, stipulate various technical restrictions as a provocation to filmmakers to renew their art.

Several critics have objected to such comparisons, arguing that witnessing videos are determined merely by 'necessity' and 'limitations', ruling out 'voluntary and premeditated stylistic choices' that usually accompany a film's making: 'The luxury of cinema is not allowed to those who record in the fatal conditions of a war', they claim.[14] The objections raise questions of the videos such as 'Is this cinema or not?' and 'Are the producers filmmakers or not?' There are terminological shifts: for example, Naficy describes practitioners as 'filmers' or 'videographers' rather than 'filmmakers', while retaining the word 'cinema' for the overall phenomenon.[15] On the other hand, Mohammed Ali Atassi asserts a stronger view that such videos 'belong to a world far different from that of cinema... Their producers usually do not term their productions "films", and they do not identify as filmmakers.'[16]

So is this cinema or not? The exclusions we make when we deem something isn't cinema relate to the ideological standards that García Espinosa critiqued in his manifesto and what William Brown has more recently called 'non-cinema'; Brown argues that the latter's marginality serves capitalist imperatives, although 'there is much that is cinematic in non-cinema as there are non-cinematic aspects in cinema'.[17] Instead of opting for one or the other, I want to emphasize the tensions between cinema and non-cinema, filmmakers and non-filmmakers. As García Espinosa remarked back in 1969, 'we are filmmakers because we have been part of a minority which has had the time and the circumstances needed to develop, within itself, an artistic culture; and because the material resources of film technology are limited and therefore available to some, not to all.'[18] Even then, he speculated that the evolution of film technology might lead to it no longer being 'the privilege of a small few'. As economic and technological constraints have changed, so have possibilities of cinematic creativity for everyone, no longer restricted to specialists. The body of witnessing videos is produced by diverse actors, who are not *merely* recording events but sharing their dreams of a better future during demonstrations and their ordeals during times of bodily injury, funerals, gunfire and air attacks: a form of creative agency. While many of them have not been educated in filmmaking, some were already professional filmmakers. Others are self-trained, and some of these, such as Syrian director Orwa al-Mokdad, identify as filmmakers and see themselves as making conscious artistic decisions.[19] Moreover, partnerships form between these groups; for example, *Little Gandhi* (2016) was directed by émigré Syrian director Sam Kadi over Skype supported by video activists on the ground during the Syrian conflict.[20] Further, as we will see in *5 Broken Cameras* and *For Sama*, filmmakers from the region and foreign co-producers and co-directors collaborate, although not without tensions and controversy about how their witnessing footage is shaped into a cinematic narrative for wider audiences.

As Georgina Van Welie, co-writer of *Whose Country?*, states, 'In work like this, it is not always about choices; it's about opportunities – you go in and you get footage that you can and you can't get more than that, as opposed to choosing settings freely'.[21] Yet even when the filmmaking context is dictated by conflict and changing political circumstances, it still presents choices, as Naziha Arebi, director of *Freedom Fields*, recalls, 'When you're up against those constraints, you have to make quick decisions from a smaller range of options.'[22] Like graffiti, which few would argue is not creative despite its often hasty execution, witnessing has *both* artistic and constricting possibilities; these are not mutually exclusive. Comparisons with Dogme 95 *are* pertinent, because they remind us that the work of image-makers of all kinds is shaped by constraints, some chosen and some externally imposed. In the words of British-Palestinian director Yasmin Fedda who led the 2015 workshops for Syria's Mobile Phone Film Festival, these witnessing videos testify to a 'will to create' despite these constraints.[23] Further, as we will see in the case studies, when witnessing footage is incorporated into professionally produced films, with its markers of uncertainty, haste and lack of technical polish indicating circumstances under which it was shot, this itself is a stylistic choice and can present creative opportunities.

Despite proliferating more than ever before thanks to new technologies, acts of witnessing are mediated in their journey from crisis zones to audiences. Tamur Ashuri and Amit Pinchevski's concept of witnessing as a 'field' of unevenly distributed resources and power struggles between different agents, each with their own goals and agendas, helps to illuminate 'the possibilities and constraints' in this media landscape although, as my case studies show, practitioner interviews add nuance to this theoretical framework.[24] Eyewitnesses strive to gain access to mediators – here, TV networks and other news outlets, NGOs and film festivals – in order to mobilize international solidarity and action, and mediators seek compelling images from eyewitnesses. In these asymmetric relations, mediators wield more power, yet mediators and eyewitnesses are mutually dependent. Eyewitnesses are uniquely advantaged by having 'been there', although entering the field and getting heard is a struggle. For their part, mediators rely on eyewitnesses to relay events on the ground.[25]

Mediators act as gatekeepers, who select, commission, edit, upload, broadcast and archive testimonies, and train and equip citizen witnesses. It is mostly they who shape a narrative from 'otherwise chaotic event[s]', providing a platform for it to be witnessed by others.[26] Witness videos uploaded by broadcasters and other media organizations appear far higher in search results than those uploaded by witnesses themselves.[27] Such is the power of the platform. Television networks also incorporate footage into standard news reporting format or can issue directives about filming and choice of subject matter when commissioning. News and current affairs programmes, in particular, are driven by what is new. For Sara Afshar, this made it harder to pitch her documentary *Syria's Disappeared*, since it was about an ongoing issue, even though it presented new evidence. It also coincided with a time when fascination with ISIS was dominating mainstream media and young Britons were travelling to Syria as ISIS recruits. Afshar's documentary lacked this British 'angle' that national broadcasters were looking for. Nonetheless, almost all the broadcasters she approached understood the wider significance of her story and were willing, in the end, to commission it.[28]

The crisis of witnessing

In al-Mokdad's documentary *300 Miles* (2016), an activist, Adnan, bemoans worldwide apathy to Syrians' plight: 'If only someone in Japan cared!' Yet, he confesses that he has never cared about distant wars and crises. Syrian activists have found that their witnessing videos have not become 'the agents of change' that they believed they would at the revolution's start.[29] Their feelings are shared by other filmmakers and activists in the region, aware of the energy and risk it takes 'to capture a story that might not make a difference anyway'.[30] Paradoxically, while the visibility of suffering via circulation of documentaries, NGO and news images has gone up, actual conditions have worsened around the region. For Gil Hochberg, this casts doubts on witnessing's political efficacy; the problem is no longer that the world doesn't see – the crisis of witnessing associated with the Holocaust – but that 'the world spends too much time seeing, and that this seeing serves no political intervention'.[31]

However, lack of political intervention cannot be solely blamed on the inefficacy of witnessing. Framing by mediators often makes it difficult for audiences to grasp what is happening in conflict zones. Lilie Chouliaraki's study of UK newspapers' reporting of the August 2013 chemical weapons attack in the Damascus suburb of Ghouta, Syria, shows that only half of them placed the story on their front pages. Their coverage, moreover, did not 'personalize those dead: we know nothing about them, their lives and histories. As a consequence, we may be appalled by these mass killings, but we are not invited to relate to the victims as human beings'.[32] The people who died just became statistics. Outrage 'compellingly registered' in video footage by Syrian activists serving as the story's source was half-heartedly taken up, pointing to a 'selective humanization' at the core of Western journalistic practices: some deaths are viewed with indifference, if not satisfaction, some are fully mourned and commemorated, and others are mentioned but ultimately forgotten.[33]

Moreover, in the social media era, images tend to become detached from their context; they 'circulate rather than communicate'.[34] Although suspicion of images predates the digital, dating back to earlier debates about photographic authenticity, doubts about their veracity have spiralled, marking the rise of what Adi Kuntsman and Rebecca Stein call 'digital suspicion', expressed in allegations of doctoring and Photoshop manipulation.[35] Kuntsman and Stein are interested not in whether images are actually true or fake, but rather in 'the political framework' in which digital suspicion is mobilized, as states exploit doubt regarding digital images in order to neutralize oppositional voices. For example, in Israeli social media, hoax pictures of dead and injured Palestinians circulating on the Internet have been taken as evidence that all such images are fakes – part of a longer history of Zionist suspicion of Palestinian narratives that holds Palestinian eyewitnesses to be 'unreliable' in order to deny their claims of indigeneity, land rights and Israeli aggression. Similarly, the Syrian government and its supporters have used video hoaxes purporting to come from Syria as proof that all such footage is fake, thus supporting the state's official perspective that there is no revolution, just a 'media conspiracy', and that it is fighting terrorism: the choice is Assad or Islamic extremists. Established before the rise of ISIS, this narrative has been amplified through international media by foreign journalists embedded with the regime. As Chouliaraki's analysis shows, a range of Western media tends to doubt the credibility of Syrian activists' footage, responding lukewarmly to its moral demands. Even though the Ghouta chemical attack videos were verified by British journalist Eliot Higgins (who later founded the investigative journalism website Bellingcat), that technical proof was not sufficient to authenticate them for everyone.[36] Paradoxically, questions of whom we trust are subjective and are not settled by verification (although that work is important and necessary). As we will see in *For Sama*, establishing trust is crucial to successful witnessing.

The relative lack of international response to the Syrian crisis can be better explained by a lack of political will to hold the regime accountable, vetoes by Assad's powerful ally Russia on the UN Security Council and fiascos of preceding wars in Afghanistan, Iraq and Libya. According to Marc Lynch, Libya was 'a decisive turning point' in the region showing, first, that protests *could* lead to external action and, second, that intervention could descend into civil war; it also 'led Russia to block further such United Nations resolutions'.[37]

Despite scepticism surrounding witnessing, images from the uprisings *have* spurred action and intervention, as protests across the region inspired each other. As Libyan filmmaker Mohammed Maklouf declares, 'if we didn't see these images, which changed people's minds around the world, nothing would have happened'.[38] Witnessing *does* work. For Leshu Torchin, claims about the crisis of witnessing are short-sighted 'in the face of longstanding history of the use of film in the formation of public opinion and witnessing publics'.[39] Mere exposure of suffering is not sufficient; there is, she emphasizes, a need for practical strategies – shaping images into powerful stories to make testimony compelling and targeting it strategically to mobilize specific audiences in desired ways. Aside from the usual festival, theatrical and community screenings, TV broadcast and Internet streaming, this may involve private screenings for policy and decision-makers. Moreover, witnessing is most effective when it is part of a wider campaign: 'material practices that accompany watching' are crucial to a film's efficacy, not merely the act of watching itself.[40]

Due to a pessimism about witnessing, several scholars have posited a shift away from first-hand witnessing of crisis towards more self-reflexive, hybrid and experimental engagements later on.[41] The argument often implies that witnessing is somehow superseded by more sophisticated modes of expression. However, changing circumstances often demand a return to a position of witnessing, as I learnt from Khalid Abdalla, who performed in and co-produced *In the Last Days of the City* (2016), a hybrid of fiction and documentary produced just before the Egyptian Revolution when direct witnessing was not possible except under immediate threat of imprisonment, so the filmmakers had to adopt a different way of 'making things visible'.[42] After the revolution started, he and others switched to witnessing as part of the Mosireen collective, stepping from 'a moment of fiction' to 'a moment of documentary, where the camera's role was to do its best to capture first of all the moment that was being lived':

> Actors who were in our film were imprisoned. And you had to film testimonies to make sure that they could be released. From very simple things like that to working to dismantle narratives upon which authority is claimed. For example, the military taking the moral high ground to dispel accusations of torture, saying they could never do such a thing. But then you go and interview someone who has been tortured and it's clear that they're lying. Likewise, the streets became a place where things you could only dream of filming are suddenly being said, right there, or have become possible to capture as images. All you need to do is go out, film it, then put it out into the world to mean everything that you want to say.[43]

Witnessing arises from an urgent sense of political and ethical responsibility; it captures what reality is offering then and there, when conditions permit. According to Abdalla, although fiction and documentary are always capable of combining in hybrid forms, witnessing as a direct form of expression takes precedence at those opportune moments, contrasting with fiction, which is suited to when reality is not expressing what you want to say and you need to (re)create it.

Citizen journalist filmmaking: *5 Broken Cameras* and *For Sama*

For me it is not a film, it's my story.

Emad Burnat[44]

Witnessing as an urgent calling pervades *5 Broken Cameras* (2011), Emad Burnat's first-person eyewitness account of protests against the Israeli separation barrier (also known as 'the Wall') in the Palestinian West Bank village of Bil'in. Here the Wall was routed to separate Bil'in from an Israeli settlement, cutting off the villagers from half of their agricultural land. 'Whenever anything happens in the village, my instinct is to film it', Burnat, an olive farmer by trade, explains in the movie. Using his personal cameras to record the footage, his testimony of the protest movement and confrontations with the Israeli military takes us into the conflict's frontline. Burnat had a press permit as he had worked as a volunteer for Reuters for two years, sending them footage of the protests. He learnt filmmaking that way, but otherwise had no formal training. As Bil'in protests attracted attention from Israeli and international activists, some came to participate and make films, and Burnat lent them parts of his footage. Eventually, he decided to transform the 700 hours of footage he had shot over a five-year period into his own documentary: 'The media only give you one part of the truth. I wanted to tell my own story and work more freely.'[45] He sought to use the camera as a 'witness and for change', to open the world's eyes to the injustice of Palestinian land being stolen to build Israeli settlements and the Israeli army's use of teargas and live ammunition against non-violent protesters.

The film opens with pixelated images, by which we realize we are seeing through the aperture of a damaged camera, hit by Israeli bullets. During the demonstrations, Burnat's cameras are broken, one after another. The third camera saves his life when a soldier shoots at him and the bullet gets lodged inside. His other cameras are struck by teargas canisters or smashed by soldiers or settlers. Divided into segments, each corresponding to footage captured by successive broken cameras, the film closes with intertitles that inform us of their fate. While filming with the sixth, Burnat was hit by a stun grenade, but the camera was unharmed and carried on filming. At first, he believed that the camera could be 'a strong witness' for use in court and serve as a shield against violations: 'When I film, I feel like the camera protects me. But it's an illusion', he says in his voice-over, as neither the camera nor presence of international and Israeli activists creates immunity from soldiers' violence. The camera itself is a fragile, material object. As a witness, it not only captures events, but also bears the material wear and tear of the battle. When Burnat's friend Adeeb is shot in the leg, it focuses on his wounds, in testimony to his bodily suffering. The tragic death of Bassem Abu Rahma (nicknamed El Fil, 'the elephant'), a well-known protester and Burnat's friend, is also caught on camera: the Bil'in protests' first 'martyr'.

Within the film we can see some of the challenges Burnat faced. He is shot at, arrested and at risk of being killed. Under house arrest, he keeps the camera running. At other times, he is forbidden from filming, as Israeli soldiers declare that the area is under 'military closure' and shut down the camera or confiscate it, all forms of pre-emptive censorship. Burnat reported to me that he had been beaten up several times by both soldiers and settlers who tried to stop him filming and seized his camera; nonetheless, he endured these dangers in order to witness: 'You risk your life. I accept that.'[46] In addition, there were political pressures from the Palestinian Authority, which would not sponsor him; as Burnat says in voice-over within the film, 'If you don't fit the resistance image, you're on your own'. He filmed for five years without any funding, while supporting his family under harsh economic circumstances. 'How do you get new cameras when you have no money?' he asked me.[47]

While the news tends to focus exclusively on violent events, *5 Broken Cameras* also gives us a sense of what everyday family life is like under these pressures. Burnat bought his first camera to film his youngest son Gibreel, born just as protests began in 2005. Gibreel's early years coincide with the five years of protest documented in the film; footage of him growing up marks the passage of time and culminates in his fifth birthday. As he gets older, he joins the protests, sees people he knows getting arrested and shot at, and starts asking questions about soldiers, learning about life's injustices. Despite the bleak reality, the film avoids reducing its characters to the singular identity of victims by emphasizing their agency and creative resistance. In order to claim Palestinian land, settlers lay down trailers, a strategy that the protesters adopt and turn against their oppressors, graffitiing the words 'Welcome to Bil'in' on their own trailers. For

Burnat, it was important to show this creativity as it was one of the reasons why Bil'in became an inspiring symbol of non-violent resistance. The film itself is part of a wider campaign created by Bil'in's Committee of Popular Resistance against the Wall and Settlements, which organizes weekly protests and embraces non-violent, creative ways to further its cause.

It was Burnat's co-director Guy Davidi who suggested structuring the footage through the broken cameras.[48] Davidi was an Israeli video activist who had participated in the protests. Burnat approached him because he needed a producer (following a meeting with the Israeli-owned production company Greenhouse) and he thought Davidi could help to screen the film in Israel and change the mentality there. Davidi therefore came on board after Burnat's five-year shoot. They completed the first edit together at Burnat's house. The script, including the voice-over, was written after the edit. Davidi claims he wrote it, then Burnat reviewed it.[49] However, Burnat stresses its collaborative nature, arguing that Davidi could not have written the script on his own because it expresses inner feelings, 'telling our story from the inside' in a way that would be impossible for outsiders. He accepts that Davidi did offer ideas to make the film 'more powerful' by recommending that Burnat should be at its centre: 'He told me it is my story, my experience, so he gave me the idea to show more footage of myself, like my accident'.[50] In this episode, Burnat crashes a tractor into the separation barrier. Paradoxically, this saves his life because it entitles him to be treated at an Israeli hospital; if he had been taken to an 'average Palestinian hospital', he probably would not have survived. Initially, Burnat was resistant: 'I didn't want to focus on this side of the story. It's not easy to show myself bleeding at the hospital'.[51] He was concerned that fellow Palestinians, for whom this is a collective struggle, might wonder why he had made it a story about himself.

Yael Friedman has argued that, despite Davidi's pro-Palestinian politics and his belief that he empowered Burnat's voice, the duo's collaboration reflects colonial power dynamics: a collective, Third World struggle has been shaped into a Westernized personal story, the fault lines of which appear in the disjunction between the film's activist images and its audio track with its contemplative voice-over and message of healing and reconciliation.[52] My conversations with Burnat corroborate his difficult relationship with Davidi, although he insists that his family was always going to be the through-line, especially Gibreel growing up. In the film's production and distribution, Burnat also faced linguistic challenges related to colonial dynamics. When he and Davidi worked together, they communicated in Hebrew, a language Burnat learnt while employed as a landscape gardener in Israel. Later, when they began doing Q&As internationally,

Burnat felt disadvantaged because Davidi's English was better and therefore, initially, he had less control of how the film was presented. When I met him, several years on, Burnat was still tirelessly touring the film, now on his own (and with excellent command of English).

Although funders were initially reluctant to finance a film about Palestine until convinced of the story's strength by a trailer, neither they nor Greenhouse pressured the filmmakers to change the storyline – Burnat was adamant that he would never accept such an imposition. With no Palestinian film funds that he could feasibly draw upon, he decided to take Israeli funding (along with European funding) in order to facilitate screenings for Israeli audiences, one of the most important witnessing publics for this film. One major drawback of this, however, was the film's subsequent classification as Israeli, preventing it from being screened in Arab countries.

In Israel, *5 Broken Cameras* was shown on television and in cinemas. While its reception in Israel was mixed, the film was very successful internationally. In 2013, it was Oscar-nominated for Best Documentary Feature and the directors jointly won numerous other awards, including the 2013 International Emmy. It was even screened at the European Parliament. Burnat recognizes that the creative choices that he and Davidi took have strengthened the film's power to move international audiences. According to him, the film has changed some people's minds, but not the reality on the ground: 'The situation is getting worse every day.'[53] The villagers still face Israeli occupation, together with expansion of settlements and confiscation of their land. As regional crises have proliferated, Burnat believes that international attention has shifted from Palestine to other countries; now the challenge is to keep it in the spotlight. For him, the villagers' protests in Bil'in were the inspiration for the 'Arab Spring' which came several years after their non-violent struggle started: 'I think this way of resistance affected them in these Arab countries. It was effective and they started their own revolutions.'[54]

In 2019, *For Sama* was released into a media landscape which, by that time, had already been 'saturated' with images from Syria; the conflict had dropped in the news agenda and the global public was reportedly tired of hearing about it. The film's creative choices were shaped with this crisis of witnessing in mind. It begins with its protagonist and co-director Waad al-Kateab talking affectionately to her baby daughter Sama in their bedroom. Suddenly an aerial attack is imminent, and she hands Sama to someone else as she grabs her camera, and they all make their way to a basement shelter underneath the hospital they have made their home, as al-Kateab's husband, Hamza, is a doctor. The film establishes trust in al-Kateab as a witness through her voice-over, which narrates her personal account in the present tense, tethered to her thoughts and feelings of 'being there', while her handheld camera's blurry, unsteady style registers the fear, danger and uncertainty of the impending attack. These techniques confer a sense of immediacy that invites us into besieged Eastern Aleppo in 'a shared witnessing perspective'.[55]

Contrasting with dominant male viewpoints on conflict, *For Sama*'s female, first-person account stands out, especially as a mother's perspective. It is structured as a letter from a mother to her daughter, an epistolary format that the Arabic title *ilà Sama* ('To Sama') captures more than the English title does. Epistolary devices are not new to crisis cinema; indeed, they are often used to bring together protagonists separated in space and time.[56] *For Sama* draws its particular power from a mother's act of telling her child the story of her fight for freedom and justice for her country's future generations. This 'very personal and yet, at the same time, universal story' is 'key' to the film's success, as Donatella Della Ratta notes.[57] Such a structure was possible because al-Kateab had already chosen to record more light-hearted personal moments, alongside the bloodshed and destruction, to save them for her daughter and give her a more rounded picture of life during these times. Her camera remains switched on, even in private moments such as when she discovers from her home pregnancy-testing kit that she is pregnant with Sama. The non-linear storytelling gives us flashbacks to the Revolution's early days and up to 2015, when the opposition were still hopeful of winning, before returning us to the siege in 2016. These tonal shifts transport us from moments of joy and levity to moments of mortal danger and gravity and back. The flashbacks reveal the beauty of those early experiences despite the pain and hardship. Filmed in home interiors, the private moments lend audiences insights into the effects of conflict on ordinary lives and contrast with protest footage, which is largely of public places.

Al-Kateab's perspective as a mother is reflected in her choices of what to film and the stories she tells. In one scene, a pregnant woman is rushed into the hospital in a critical condition. Her baby is apparently stillborn but is repeatedly turned upside down and patted until its deathly pale body chokes into life. Al-Kateab captures the miracle birth and against-odds survival of both mother and child. When she films her friend Afraa's young son, he starts to weep as he voices his desire to stay in Aleppo when many of his friends have left. Al-Kateab's hand slips into the frame and gently touches the boy to console him, a gesture expressing the film's care and sincerity towards these testimonies. The crying mothers and children are not simply victims; they are people whose stories and presence demand acknowledgement and sympathetic hearing.

When protests broke out, al-Kateab was in her graduation year at Aleppo University and she began filming them on her phone, deciding to put aside her studies in order to focus on the revolution. As she told me, 'This wasn't an individual decision, something that I decided to do for myself' – thousands of people were flocking to the streets to do the same thing, realizing this was a 'unique and important' period that could alter Syria and the entire region following decades of silencing and denial of rights by the regime. 'We were all hearing our voices for the first time and taking the camera was a very simple response to what I was seeing in front of my eyes.'[58] She tried to capture events as they unfurled, uploading her footage to YouTube and sending it to Arab television channels. Her cousin, a protest coordinator, warned that she should not chant along with protestors if she wanted her footage to be used, since a reporter simply observes and also security forces could identify her directly. Yet she found she could not separate herself as a filmmaker or journalist. In her view, this shaped *For Sama*'s approach, as it 'was also relying on the experience of that situation, not just being an observer.'[59]

In 2016, al-Kateab began working as a freelance reporter for Channel 4's series *Inside Aleppo*. By that time, Russian forces were involved in the bombing. Channel 4 was seeking locals who could capture news stories for them, a common method of outsourcing when areas are inaccessible to their own correspondents.

Figure 1.1 *For Sama*'s first-person, female witness account of the Syrian conflict is shaped by Waad al-Kateab's experience of 'being there'. *For Sama* directed by Waad al-Kateab and Edward Watts © Channel 4 2019. All Rights Reserved.

Hearing about Channel 4's search from a friend, al-Kateab emailed them with her details and links to her previous work. They were immediately interested and asked her to do more filming for them, which she did. On her part, she could tell the relationship was different from her previous experiences with news channels which usually 'talk to you once, take the story, that's it'.[60] Instead, a week later, she received an email from Channel 4 news editor Ben de Pear congratulating her on her report which had gained one million views. 'One million people seeing this in just week!' Al-Kateab is still staggered by this.[61] Some scenes in *For Sama* first appeared in *Inside Aleppo*, such as the miracle birth and a hazardous journey back to Aleppo from Turkey where al-Kateab and her husband were visiting his parents, travelling the last stage by foot and singing a lullaby to Sama to calm her during those tense moments. In *Inside Aleppo* the channel's own voice-over commentary is laid over the footage, as often happens when international media incorporate citizen videos, a suppression of their own soundtrack that reduces their 'affective power'.[62] However, removing al-Kateab's voice was necessary at that time to protect her identity as she was still in Syria.

Al-Kateab describes her collaboration with Channel 4 as one of mutual benefit: there was no other reporter there who could deliver that material for them and she was able to amplify her story on their platform. She already had her camera kit and all they supplied her with was one lens before the siege occurred. They did not tell her what to film but would ask her to follow a particular person or to know more about certain matters, and they gave feedback, helping her to understand how to structure a story. In contrast to her experiences with other channels, they urged her not to take risks in order to film and made efforts to get her out of Aleppo by petitioning the UK Parliament and Red Crescent. Yet despite their exhortations, danger was everywhere in those circumstances. Even the basement shelter was not entirely safe due to the regime's use of ground-to-ground rockets to deliver chemical attacks.

During the war, Syria became divided into areas controlled by the regime, the Free Syrian Army (FSA) and other opposition groups, Kurdish forces and (from 2013) ISIS.[63] These corresponded to different zones of freedom of expression. In Eastern Aleppo, which was partly controlled by the FSA, al-Kateab maintains that it was much better than under Assad's dictatorship: 'Even for the camera, no one can stop you in the street if he has a gun and asks you what you are doing. Even if that happens, and it happened a few times', people would challenge the gunmen's authority to do this, 'whereas if you were in the regime area filming something not permitted, you'd be arrested and no one would know where you are.'[64] Her view correlates with a poll of Syrian video activists which found that 'areas where film-makers are most free to film inside Syria are FSA-controlled areas', where filming is permitted everywhere apart from military positions, although that freedom is diminished by risks of kidnapping when extremist groups are nearby.[65]

Al-Kateab feels that the war's challenges were heightened for her as a filmmaker and as a woman, especially as a mother. Filming in the hospital, she was always encountering the dead and injured from the bombings: 'Every time you see the scenario in front of your eyes, you realize this could be my daughter, this could be me'.[66] Even when she turned the camera off, she had no escape from the situation, unlike filmmakers who come, film and leave. Moreover, as a filmmaker, she could not simply forget these scenes: 'everything you have seen with your eyes is recorded and saved and you have it on your laptop and your hard drive' and editing the footage made her relive the trauma.[67] Whenever she closed her eyes, she knew that was not the end of it; she revisited it every day. It was challenging to work in a conservative community where she had to convince people that what she was doing was important and 'I have the right to do this, like any male filmmaker.'[68] Despite the fact that women had a strong presence both as protestors and video activists in the uprisings in Syria and elsewhere in the region, some of al-Kateab's male colleagues in Aleppo preferred her to edit their material, although she insisted on capturing and editing her own: 'They said, "We can go outside, risk ourselves and bring you whatever you want – you just edit".[69] These prejudices against women associate them with indoor work: editing is an indoor activity, whereas filming entails going outside. When al-Kateab left Aleppo she discovered that these inequalities extended beyond Syria. In 2017, she collected her Royal Television Society (RTS) award for Camera Operator of the Year in the UK, the first time that any woman had won the prize: 'I was shocked – oh my God, I thought it was just our community. You realize this is not a struggle limited to one geography; it's a life struggle for everyone.'[70]

What added to the difficulties was that Syrian society was not camera-friendly. Previously, the camera was an entity controlled by the regime that would instruct people what to say and cause trouble if they said anything 'wrong'. In building her relationship with the community, al-Kateab had to generate understanding that 'this is something for our use, not for our harm.'[71] A product of many years of dictatorship, this suspicion of cameras is pervasive: other Syrian activists have reported that it exists in both regime-controlled and liberated areas.[72] Al-Kateab explains that the regime targets filmmakers and journalists 'because they didn't want this story to be saved. But also, if under any circumstances, I was arrested with this archive, everyone who appeared in any clip would be dead. And that's a very big responsibility' for which no assurances can be given to anyone.[73] Nevertheless, if she did not film what they have been through, the story would never be saved 'not just for today or tomorrow but for the next generation'. In one scene in *For Sama*, a mother arrives at the hospital to find her young son is already dead. 'Wake up, wake up, I've brought milk for you!' she cries. She notices al-Kateab. 'Are you filming?' she asks, then defies expectation by insisting, 'Carry on!' Al-Kateab respected the wishes of those who did not want to be filmed, either by turning her camera off or labelling the footage accordingly. There were many stories that she had to omit due to these ethical constraints. During one fateful night when she and her family were away, the hospital was bombed, witnessed in the film through the hospital's security cameras. In contrast to restless, choppy handheld footage, a security camera's gaze implies a neutral position, legitimating the act of witnessing in a different way during the filmmaker's absence. The film switches between different security cameras on the premises as they capture the unfolding chaos and destruction. This material, too, al-Kateab had the presence of mind to store in her archive, which consists of over 500 hours of footage. As she only possessed one hard drive, it was difficult to keep all the footage secure. On the other hand, making backups would have increased risks of the archive falling into the wrong hands. When she and her family were evacuated from Aleppo, she thought of burying it in the ground and finding a way of retrieving it later. In the end, she gambled on taking it with her, despite the perils if she was captured.[74]

When al-Kateab left Aleppo, she initially felt that her sacrifices had been for nothing. Her videos for *Inside Aleppo* had received half a billion views altogether. So many individuals and countries had known what was happening, yet they did nothing. What motivated al-Kateab to turn her footage into a larger story was realizing the power in her archive. While *Inside Aleppo* focused on the siege, she felt it was important for audiences to know the whole journey from the Syrian Revolution, when it all started, in order to grasp why she and Hamza took the decisions they did, including their return to Aleppo with their daughter (for which she had received some criticism when *Inside Aleppo* was released).[75] The genesis of *For Sama* began when she came to the UK for the RTS award ceremony and revealed her archive's existence to Channel 4. Previously, they had not known what else she had been filming, since she had only sent them news footage of besieged Aleppo. She and the news-team jointly agreed the idea of producing a longer piece, initially fifteen or thirty minutes long. However, when al-Kateab showed them her material, it became clear that it would need to be of feature length. At that point, other organizations became involved, including

ITN and the US channel Frontline PBS, and al-Kateab was introduced to her co-director Watts with whom she then worked for two years. As her voice-over states in the film, 'Millions of people see my reports. But no one does anything to stop the regime.' *Inside Aleppo* made her realize that the situation could not be changed in the naïve way that she had hoped – that more was needed to keep attention on the story and to apply pressure on politicians. Both she and Watts were frequently told 'there have been enough films about Syria', warning them not to expect much from *For Sama*. As Watts recollects, 'It was a travesty to hear that because it's so important for Waad and all of us to witness this story.'[76] The film's 'whole creative approach', he says, was designed 'to counter that apathy'.

Some commentators have criticized Watts's involvement as a white, male, British co-director. Della Ratta interprets his role as 'a guardian, rather than that of a peer or co-author', belonging to a type of 'neo-orientalism exploiting Syrian image-makers who have access to the "field" yet, in the eyes of western media industries, are probably not powerful enough to produce a storytelling that would be considered compelling and marketable to global audiences.'[77] It is true that one reason why Channel 4 invited Watts was to 'translate' al-Kateab's story into 'a form that a Western audience could understand'.[78] Another was his commitment to Syria and his conviction that Western media reporting of the Syrian crisis had been obfuscated by Russian and Syrian regime 'war on terrorism' propaganda. He believed that the public should know that at its core the conflict was about 'people like you and me' fighting for democratic values 'and we did nothing'.[79] As we saw with the collaboration between Burnat and Davidi in *5 Broken Cameras*, shared values do not prevent (neo-)colonial dynamics but although this kind of viewpoint has some truth, it lacks nuance as it does not consider the agency of all parties involved, the terms on which mediation in the field of witnessing occurs *for them* and the constraints and possibilities.

Al-Kateab and Watts began working together remotely while she was in Turkey following her evacuation, and then in person when she claimed asylum in the UK.[80] Their relationship was adversarial at times. 'Part of the great fight between Ed and me', al-Kateab says, was turning the film into her personal story, which had not been her intention.[81] Like Burnat in *5 Broken Cameras*, al-Kateab wanted it to represent collective struggle, while Watts argued that this was best expressed through her own story, which acts as a conduit to collective experience. As part of the research process, Watts built up a picture of al-Kateab's life by going through the footage and interviewing her to understand the key emotional points for her as well as factual details. One of the earliest ideas was to include these interviews to camera in a chronological telling of the story. That changed when the 'For Sama' idea arrived, after the co-directors had already been working together for a year – Watts describes it as 'a kind of epiphany' as they were immersed in al-Kateab's footage, the story of Syria and problem of how to tell her story.[82] As we have seen, her style of filming was already personal and became even more so when she became pregnant, imparting a sense of dialogue with her unborn child.[83] Their decision to structure the film as a letter to Sama melded with the way her life was dedicated both to Sama and the future of Syria and its children. Watts believed it 'would help an audience to understand the day-to-day dilemmas that Waad was facing: do you run to protect your baby or do you stay and fight for their future but risk losing everything? That extreme tension was important to convey to the audience and the letter format could transmit it.'[84] In his words, this approach 'freed' them from the country and chronology of events, becoming 'much more about the human dilemma'; it enabled them to structure the film as an engaging narrative in five acts, with flashbacks: '1. Falling in love, 2. Being pregnant, 3. The moment of ultimate choice in the siege, 4. The catastrophe, 5. The aftermath.'[85]

The voice-over idea came later, and they worked on it last. Initially, Watts sketched it out, drawing on his interviews that contained al-Kateab's distinctive language and conceptualization of her own thoughts and actions. His script flagged what the audience needed to know at particular points and how scene transitions could take place. Then, al-Kateab made it hers, offering alternative suggestions. Sometimes they had to work harder to find a meeting-point between what each of them wanted. When they had finished what they thought was the final cut, Watts sent it to an acquaintance whose views he valued as a documentary editor, receiving the feedback that the voice-over's emotional truth and intensity could be pushed further. Despite already working on the film for two years, an incredibly draining process, al-Kateab agreed to redo the voice-over, working on it by herself first 'to dig out the truth of her feelings', then both directors distilled those emotions into the narration.[86] As Ashuri and Pinchevski note, enunciation of emotional states is crucial to eyewitnesses' performative claims about what they saw when they were there, bringing together witness and audience in an 'experiential closeness'.[87] Honing the voice-over made the expression of al-Kateab's feelings more specific, original and intensely personal and enhanced her testimony's credibility.

While the handheld camera weds us to al-Kateab's perspective much of the time, the five acts are punctuated by drone footage revealing the city's large-scale destruction. These drone shots have attracted attention because of a perceived contradiction between their grand cinematic quality and the raw immediacy of warzone witnessing which, some critics believe, excludes creative choices – a false dichotomy, as I argued earlier. According to Della Ratta, 'This drone view adds the spectacular to the film and makes it look like a proper mainstream documentary made for the consumption of Netflix and other similarly global palates.'[88] Al-Kateab obtained her drone shots from a friend in Aleppo.[89] There, activists were using drone technology to document the scale of devastation wrought by Russian-aided Syrian regime bombing of the city, and uploading their footage to YouTube.[90] With the ability to see events from above and from a wider angle than possible for a person on the ground, drones 'send eyes where our bodies can't easily go unencumbered'[91] and have extraordinary witnessing potential. *For Sama*'s drone footage was filmed on location while al-Kateab was in Aleppo (she and her child even appear in one shot). The drone shots have a structuring role, marking transitions between chapters and revealing a macro perspective, in contrast to the micro perspective of al-Kateab's footage, 'conveying in a subliminal way that these personal moments are happening across the city.'[92] Watts also saw them as offering audiences 'a breathing space', confirming one of Della Ratta's reservations.[93] However, *both* directors were concerned about overwhelming the audience, especially with graphic footage.

Some of their discussions revolved around the witnessing value of graphic footage versus engaging the audience with the story. Even with the final version, they were convinced, having repeatedly heard about 'Syria fatigue', that audiences would find it unbearable; they never expected its worldwide release and acclaim. Al-Kateab recalls sitting in the audience at the South by Southwest Film Festival première in Austin, Texas, waiting to see how many people would walk out. Instead, people came to her, moved, asking what they could do: 'Every time I heard this question from someone in the audience I was just, like, I did it, I gained what I wanted.'[94] It gave her a feeling opposite to her despondency about effecting change when she left Aleppo. From the Prix d'oeil at the Cannes Film Festival to a BAFTA and Oscar nomination for Best Documentary, *For Sama*'s profile has been raised by multiple awards, attracting more viewers who perhaps otherwise would not watch a documentary on Syria.

For Della Ratta, *For Sama*'s emphasis on motherhood erases the political context of the Syrian revolution, ensuring that we see al-Kateab as an individual, but not the wider struggle. Her critique highlights how highly charged this territory is, when few Syrian films galvanize such attention and many witnesses struggle to get heard. It evokes the general pressures on Middle Eastern cinema to fit within Western models, which limits what filmmakers are allowed to say and how they say it. However, *For Sama* was Oscar-nominated in the same year as another Syrian film, *The Cave* (2019), which witnesses in a different way, despite sharing a hospital setting.⁹⁵ Moreover, it has moved many people around the world and made them want to act. This is why, al-Kateab explains, she set up the campaign Action for Sama, consisting of small actions that audiences can take.⁹⁶ Linked to this impact campaign, the film is not just a harrowing vision that people can promptly forget when they have finished watching, since it encourages them to do something practical – from sharing what they have witnessed on social media to donating to humanitarian workers, asking their MP to watch the film, uploading their own creative response and organizing community screenings. As Torchin says of material practices that accompany witnessing more generally, this strategy 'enables an audience to channel their emotions into action rather than allow them to dissipate or get transformed into frustrated outrage'.⁹⁷ Changing people has value in itself, but people can also put pressure on governments. The filmmakers have specific goals for pressuring decision-makers, having screened the film at the United Nations, and prompted a UN enquiry regarding the bombing of hospitals. Their use of the film as an impact tool insists that the fight goes on even if Assad regains controls of Syria.⁹⁸ When the film screened at Cannes, al-Kateab, Watts and Hamza al-Kateab held the sign 'STOP BOMBING HOSPITALS'. At Q&As for the film's 2019 theatrical release, the trio emphasized 'what you see in the film is still happening now' in rebel-held Idlib, where the Syrian regime aided by the Russian military has continued targeting hospitals. When I interviewed her, al-Kateab was working on a legal case against the regime for its attacks on hospitals, albeit without expecting any results, having been disappointed, like many people in Syria, so many times in the past. Ultimately, the film is a tool in this ongoing struggle: 'to keep the story being told day by day'.⁹⁹

Witnessing countries in transition: *Whose Country?* and *Freedom Fields*

In the next two case studies, the filmmakers were forced to adapt creatively to changing political circumstances, an experience shared by many productions across the region during this turbulent period. Both are documentaries shot on location, in which the stories took an unexpected turn and the footage changed meaning and status. *Whose Country?* (2016) witnesses Egypt as it transitioned from revolution to counter-revolution. Its director Mohamed Siam participated in the Egyptian revolution while he made two documentaries *Whose Country?*

and *Amal* (2017) simultaneously. In *Whose Country?* his interest was less in 'my side', the activists, and more in 'the other side', plain-clothed police.[100] The murder of Khaled Said, a young man beaten to death by police in June 2010, had been a rallying point for the revolution. More fundamentally, the police demanded Siam's attention because they belong to the security apparatus that forms Egypt's 'deep state'. Alongside the intelligence community and state 'thugs', a vast, far-reaching police force works 'to guard the regime, monitor the opposition and stifle dissent', generating a continually fearful atmosphere.[101] *Whose Country?* consists of first-person accounts, both by Siam, whose late father was a criminal investigator, and a policeman nicknamed 'Abu Habiba'. What makes the film unprecedented is that in Egypt it is not usually feasible to film police. Asking them questions is illegal and can lead to arrest; even accredited journalists must seek permission for interviews, thereafter being redirected to a media spokesperson adept at presenting the official line.[102] As Siam explains, 'Egypt has always been a hard place to film and express yourself.'[103] But after the revolution, Abu Habiba was emboldened to speak out as he would not have done previously.

With its testimony from a policeman, speaking to camera about details of police brutality and corruption, *Whose Country?* is more direct than any previous depictions of the subject in Egyptian cinema, in which its sensitivity was mitigated by the shield of fiction and use of actors.[104] It was challenging to obtain these interviews even during the more open political climate immediately after the revolution. As we see in the film, Siam met Abu Habiba at a protest outside a Cairo police station where low-ranking officers were demonstrating against their fifty-dollar-a-month salary for which they endured extensive shifts and long daily commutes from the Nile Delta, due to the state's policy of not employing those with loyalties to areas they are policing. Siam met secretly with Abu Habiba for six months, building his trust, before he was willing to be filmed. By this time, President Mubarak was on trial and Abu Habiba felt free to talk. Although hardly paid enough to live on, we learn that he accepted his job because of its security and because he and his colleagues could supplement their wages through bribe income. By spending time with Abu Habiba in his family and work settings, we get to know him, his affectionate relationship with his small daughter jarring with our knowledge of his probable complicity in police abuses he recounts.

Shot between 2011 and 2013, *Whose Country?* was made within a small window of opportunity. During that time, the country, which had belonged to the military, briefly passed to the people, levelling some differences and offering the chance to talk to 'the enemy'. Even within that window there were at least three different regimes in place, each with a different calibration of freedom of expression. In the film's narration of this history, the revolution was 'hijacked' by the Muslim Brotherhood, whose leader Mohammed Morsi was elected president in 2012 and within a year became the 'new oppressor', leading to protests for his resignation and his removal by the army in 2013. In ironic contrast to confrontations between police and protesters during the revolution, people welcomed the police back. By the end, when military dictatorship returned, Egypt had revolved 'through 360 degrees, back to square one'.[105]

Changing circumstances made the production highly time-sensitive. Siam's relationship with Abu Habiba was inevitably affected, as he remarks in voice-over, 'I sensed that the window that had opened between us was about to slam shut'. Both men despaired about what was happening to their country. As hopes for change receded, so did the opportunity to ask questions. Their interviews began to peter out during the Muslim Brotherhood period. Abu Habiba's motives for participating in the documentary also shifted. Previously, he took a moral stance in speaking out against injustices, claiming that was why he left the police force before rejoining it after the revolution. In the final interview, undertaken during the new military regime, he asserts that he was mistreated by another officer before he quit and was rehired before the revolution, as if attempting to overwrite the previous record.

The risks to both men are palpable, highlighted in Siam's voice-over and in a scene where Abu Habiba, with his daughter on his lap, gestures to Siam who is filming them and bids her to repeat, 'If my father is harmed because of you, I'll cut you with a knife'. Later Siam disclosed to me, 'The more as I was doing the film, and the country was changing and the revolution was declining, I understood that what I had in hand could be critical'.[106] After the military takeover, a crackdown began on activists, human rights organizations, filmmakers and journalists, disappearing people from their homes and imprisoning them for long sentences without trial. Such counter-revolutionary measures led many in the region, like Siam himself, to leave their country for a life of exile because of their activities since the uprisings. In the film, the words 'Whose Country?', uttered first by the policeman and later echoed by Siam in his concluding voice-over, encapsulate corresponding feelings of despair and disconnection from one's country.

Siam wanted to protect Abu Habiba as he still lives in Egypt. 'I felt maybe less could be more', he says, explaining his stylistic decisions such as avoiding location titles and shots that might enable viewers to track his protagonist.[107] In the public trailer, Abu Habiba's face is blurred. Another policeman whom Siam interviewed does not feature (as he had requested, if the revolution failed). The entire film bears subtle traces of its changing circumstances. An opening title declares that 'Due to the political climate in Egypt at the time of completing this documentary, many of the local film production crew requested to remain anonymous'. Contrary to their enthusiasm at the start, some producers and Arab funders withdrew, as it was no longer possible to release the film in Egypt nor, due to similar transitions from revolution to counter-revolution, in many other parts of the region.

Therefore, *Whose Country?* had to be made more appealing to international audiences and distanced from Arab regimes. During the last six months of post-production, British screenwriter Georgina Van Welie was hired as a co-writer at the request of the film's Kuwaiti producer, Talal al-Muhanna. Her role was to craft a narrative structure and an English-language voice-over. It was al-Muhanna's decision to involve Siam's personal story, underlining the relationship between the filmmaker and his subject, although Siam himself wanted to focus on his interactions with Abu Habiba. The voice-over, which al-Muhanna had outlined through interviewing Siam about his childhood, included psychoanalytic elements that Van Welie thought were 'too Western', not true to the material of a documentary about Egypt made by Egyptians: 'We used some of that but reined it back', she says.[108] Seeing her role as a mediator between the filmmaker's and producer's conceptions of the story, her input was attuned to Siam's 'less is more' approach. Together, the team had to 'maximize the significance' of the interview footage with Abu Habiba.[109] As a non-Arab voice in the creative process (although she has lived in Kuwait and has Arab family connections) Van Welie also advised on what needed to be clarified for an outside audience and where titles were needed for historical markers, writing them herself. Upon release, Siam's team kept the publicity low-key, avoiding press interviews, social media advertising and promoting news of awards. All these precautions 'hurt the film's distribution because they didn't push it' but were felt to be necessary for avoiding 'unwanted attention from certain authorities towards the participants of the film'.[110]

When Naziha Arebi began *Freedom Fields* (2018), she thought she was making a documentary about the Libyan national women's football team playing their first international match. After the country's 2011 revolution, she had gone to live in Libya where cinema production had been scarce under former ruler Muammar al-Gaddafi and few film theatres functioned. Previously an artist and theatre-maker, she taught herself to use a camera and co-founded the collective HuNa Productions to develop Libyan cinema as a tool for social change. *Freedom Fields* was made over seven years in total, with five years of filming, during which circumstances changed dramatically. Political instability following Gaddafi's overthrow led to a protracted civil war, as armed revolutionaries formed rival militias, financially and militarily supported by foreign powers, and Islamist groups entrenched themselves in the security voids of the divided territory ruled by three factional governments. 'As Libya changed, the film changed, and became darker', Arebi recalls.[111] It could no longer be, she says, a 'tidy film about a women's football team'.[112] Under deteriorating security, the women were banned from travelling and football disappeared from their lives. As with *Whose Country?*, uncertainty about the film's direction worried funders who had been keen on the film during its early development; they questioned whether it could be finished and, indeed, whether there was any point, since there was no longer any football. At a vulnerable point in the middle of production, funding began to run out. Nonetheless, Arebi persisted, discovering 'alternative routes and ways to fill in the gaps'.[113] Since she did not know if football was ever going to return to the women's lives, she decided to film its absence and found a new focus in the team's creative resilience: although their dreams promised by the revolution were crushed, they sought other ways to experience their freedoms, despite massive hurdles.

So *Freedom Fields* witnesses the country in transition through the team's professional and personal struggles in post-Revolution Libya. Its year-by-year structure makes it a record of changing circumstances. The war is captured in the background, as smoke plumes rise into the sky and gunfire is heard in the distance, while, in the foreground, ordinary life goes on. Since there had been few previous films about or from Libya, the documentary carried a heavy burden of expectation that it should be more explanatory and comprehensive. An earlier cut contained title cards but was discarded as 'too didactic'.[114] With the help of her executive producer Huda Abuzeid and co-producer Flore Cosquer, Arebi managed to keep those pressures at bay and 'let the film be what it's truly about', which she felt was both 'a blessing and a curse', as it made the production more financially difficult.[115] As the characters living through the crisis did not have the privilege of a wider perspective on events, this approach felt more truthful to their experiences. Much of the conflict takes place off-screen, yet its presence vibrates within the frame. Arebi explains, 'When you live in a conflict zone, that's often what happens – you hear things and you feel the paranoia but you don't really know what's going on. You scroll through Facebook but you don't really know what's happening down the road.'[116] As one character says in the film, 'Even if it's bullets, tell me it's fireworks'.

Three personalities from the women's team come to the fore: the exuberant goalkeeper Halima, Fadwa, whose outspokenness inspires a 'we are all Fadwa' moment and Nama, resilient despite the tough life she leads as a refugee from the forcibly-evacuated town of Tawergha. The film is filled with sensory details of their intimate lives that, as well as reflecting Libya's wider situation, are shot through with minor pleasures that sustain these women in difficult times. The team faces numerous limitations: they receive threats from Islamic extremists who object to women playing football; the Libyan Football Federation, itself led by a corrupt management, cancels their participation in an international tournament because of security concerns; amid rising conservatism, they are suddenly not permitted to travel without a male guardian and the war and state failure bring power cuts and border closures. In their determination, and with strategic help from others, they invent ways around the obstacles and become what Arebi calls 'accidental activists'. Initially, they train in daylight, supported by armed guards, one of whom we see burning a hate letter from a religious extremist. After a long hiatus following cancellation of their international tournament, the women decide to compete as a private team, training secretly at night. When floodlights are extinguished by a power cut, locals drive their cars onto the pitch, enabling the women to train, illuminated by their headlights. Finally, the team get to fulfil their dreams and participate in an international tournament but realize they are not prepared and are unable to excel on the pitch. Undaunted, they set up their own grassroots NGO, HERA, using football as a tool for social development and trauma relief for girls in schools and refugee camps.

Arebi's struggle in making the documentary shadows the women's struggle and leaves imprints in its audiovisual textures. The conflict impaired freedom of movement and travel, resulting in closure of Libya's airport which was limiting both for the women trying to participate in an international tournament and for Arebi's film crew, who were not able to fly there. Therefore, for much of the shoot, she had to perform all the technical jobs herself, including first camera and sound, while Libyan cinematographer Sufian Arara assisted on second camera. Without a male guardian, it was difficult for Arebi to travel on the road, just as it was for the women. When Halima is travelling alone across the border and the police order her to turn around, we witness the scene in darkness with muffled sound. Arebi, who was filming, placed the camera under the car seat, which is why the sound is low, in order that the police would not know she was filming. Although we only see one unaccompanied woman in the car, Arebi was also there, finding herself (and her camera) caught in the same position.

In a country where filmmaking, like football, is seen as 'a man's job', Arebi faced further difficulties as a female filmmaker.[117] The existence of multiple governments in Libya necessitated seeking filming permits from assorted authorities. Under no circumstances could she explain that the film she was making was about a women's football team, so she had to find alibis. Yet being female was sometimes an advantage, since she could follow her protagonists into female-only spaces barred to male crew members, and achieve the film's distinctive intimacy. As a woman, it was also occasionally 'easier to negotiate with armed groups or people trying to stop filming because they didn't see me as such a threat.'[118]

When the civil war started in 2014, it became more dangerous to film in public places. Having started with a small camera, Arebi had moved to a larger camera and now she returned to the small camera, shooting only from enclosed spaces or discreetly from the hip: 'That was really important that I don't put them [the women] in danger and myself in danger. Being somewhere with a camera, you're not "fly on the wall", you're frickin' obvious! With that comes responsibility.'[119] The small camera drew less attention, while filming from inside cars became a safer solution during the war. As the situation became more chaotic, so did the camera style, imparting 'the chaos and energy... that was there in real life', which was left in the edit because it captured the feeling of those moments.[120] The rush of movement attained by shooting from inside cars, too, became part of the film's kinetic style; it was also the viewpoint upon the landscape that Arebi shared with her protagonists. Throughout the filmmaking process, power cuts were a recurrent problem 'because we couldn't charge cameras, we'd be in the dark half the time, or something major was happening and we'd cut out', so she decided to let them suffuse her style and they, too, 'became a motif in the film'.[121] Power cuts stimulated her creativity as well as that of her characters: during the team's nocturnal training, their figures are silhouetted by car headlights, with striking chiaroscuro effects.

Despite similarities between her struggles as a filmmaker and the team's struggles, Arebi was aware of the privileges of her dual Libyan-British nationality, even admitting that if she was 'fully Libyan' it would have been harder to make this film, since the field of independent filmmaking is so 'Western-centric' and its processes, such as funding applications, are often conducted in English.[122] The fact that she was half-Libyan affected her relationship with the women who, she says, initially 'felt sorry' for her because of her previous lack of access to Libyan culture; they desired to make her 'more Libyan'.[123] She felt this made the dynamics 'more equal', levelling out her power as a filmmaker bearing the camera and ability to edit. Moreover, when the women founded their own NGO, her privileges became useful to them; they acted as mediators for each other.

Figure 1.2 Car headlights become a creative solution to power cuts when the women's football team train at night, captured by Naziha Arebi's equally inventive cinematography. *Freedom Fields* directed by Naziha Arebi © HuNa Productions 2018. All Rights Reserved.

Like Siam, Arebi had to negotiate the risks of her film's release, although in this instance more because of social, gender-based constraints. Out of responsibility to her characters living in a politically unstable, conservative society in Libya, she exerted self-censorship in the editing. During the shoot, she built trusting relationships that gave her unprecedented access to the women's lives and she was able to film anything, yet this was based on tacit understanding that her edit would not endanger them. The country's lawlessness and instability made public reactions uncertain and, since the women were already being threatened for playing football during the production, it was quite possible that the film could lead to physical attacks. Therefore, it demanded 'tweaking' to pass some conservative social norms; from Arebi's perspective, this self-censorship was acceptable to allow the film to be screened for Libyan, not just international, audiences, provided that changes were minor and did not alter its core, namely women playing football.[124] A further factor in these safety precautions is that Arebi herself wanted to continue filmmaking in Libya, just as the women desired to carry on their work there. She and her producer made the difficult choice of not striking financial deals with some broadcasters who had differing expectations in order to retain full control of the edit: 'It's not just a film. It's their lives. It's my life', she stresses.[125] Security considerations forced her to balance the need to promote the film and the NGO with safeguarding her protagonists. The trailer utilizes shots where their faces are turned away or silhouetted and they do not appear in social media promotion. The women have been present, however, at screenings in Libya where the film has been self-distributed due to lack of public functioning cinemas, one advantage of which is greater control over who attends. Some of the women have also travelled with the film internationally and, as a witness to their struggles, it has lent greater visibility to, and facilitated support for, their NGO.

Conclusion

Witnessing is a direct creative strategy, not only in terms of what it represents but also in its exemplary indexical relationship with production constraints. Use of the strategy is matched to the urgency of circumstances and desire to show the world what is happening in order to bring about change. In the asymmetric media landscape in which acts of witnessing take place, collaboration with mediators plays a crucial role in how stories are shaped into a form to be witnessed by others. My case studies display different types of witnessing and reveal nuances in the power dynamics through the agencies of key people involved. In *5 Broken Cameras* and *For Sama*, witnessing footage produced by citizen journalists was powerfully restructured with the help of mediators which propelled the films through festival, activist and mainstream networks, presenting both opportunities and another set of constraints. In contrast, *Whose Country?* and *Freedom Fields* demonstrate another type of witnessing, that of filmmakers capturing countries in transition and registering changing political circumstances in their content and style. Instead of high impact upon witnessing publics, the latter take a more cautious approach precisely because of film's witnessing power and worsening security in their respective countries.

2

Child protagonists

In *For Sama* (2019), as we saw in Chapter 1, the camera is always close at hand to capture Sama's early months. We see baby clothes, toys, a milk bottle; we hear lullabies and nursery rhymes. These universal markers of childhood encourage us to empathize with a story of life in besieged Eastern Aleppo. This is one example of a strategy increasingly common in the region's filmmaking as well as in international news media. As a privileged vehicle for emotional identification, the child powerfully conveys local and national crises to international audiences. News agencies and NGOs frequently present children as innocent and blameless victims to highlight injustices in a manner that seems 'apolitical' or, at least, above politics.[1] The cultural construction of children as pure, innocent and neutral, as well as spontaneous and natural, is shared by modern Middle Eastern societies. Elias Jamal suggests that 'Idealized children – innocent, sweet, cute, and adorable – are reflections of adult concerns about their own state, bearing little resemblance to real children who vacillate between innocence and awareness, morality and immorality, cruelty and kindness, foolishness and wisdom'.[2] Adults tend to cling to idealized views of childhood despite the fact that most children do not lead 'sheltered and innocent lives'.[3] As Omar al-Ghazzi observes, 'The myth of childhood innocence empties the child figure of its political agency to fulfil the symbolic demands placed on it'.[4] Among these is adults' desire for children to embody 'hope', a 'future orientation' that detracts from their 'actual experiences' in the past and present.[5]

The belief that the child is 'other' to the adult lends the figure to allegorical usage in cinema. As Stephanie Hemelryk Donald, Emma Wilson and Sarah Wright claim, the child is 'a powerful symbol for nations coming to terms with shifting political or social changes' and 'can act as a pivot between national, local concerns and wider, transnational identifications'.[6] Filmmakers in the Middle East have made distinctive use of children, producing (to borrow Hamid Naficy's typology) 'Films *for* children, films *about* children, films in which children are *substitutes* for adults or a *pretext* for dealing with adult issues, and films *with* children acting in them'.[7] In the period covered by this book, there has been a shift from allegorical uses to a greater focus on children's actual experiences, including in documentaries as well as fiction films using documentary methods. While children's roles remain rooted in cultural ideals of childhood and cinematic traditions, such as melodrama and neorealism, this chapter shows how the strategy is becoming more direct and politicized, as it shifts from allegorical modes towards experiential images of child and teenage being that indexically register the crises they are undergoing, as exemplified in *War Canister* (2013), *Capernaum* (2018), *300 Miles* (2016), *Wadjda* (2012), *Ava* (2017) and *Amal* (2017). While the child often functions as an ostensibly apolitical figure, it helps filmmakers tackle sensitive subjects by deflecting political implications. In the transition to teen protagonists, we find a riskier variant of the strategy, since teenagers are regarded as more contentious than younger children, although less so than adults. As we will see, the gender of the child or teenager is also significant to the political and cultural sensitivity of the portrayal, indicating links with the depiction of women, another important topic in the region.

Neorealist forerunners

While other traditions of child performers exist, Italian neorealism is the world cinema practice that has impacted most on filmmaking in the region.[8] The movement innovated by using documentary methods such as real locations and non-professional actors, among them children, for its fictional stories of everyday crisis during and immediately after the Second World War. Among the best known of Italian neorealist films with child protagonists are Roberto Rossellini's *Germany Year Zero* (1948), in which twelve-year-old Edmund wanders through war-devastated Berlin, and Vittorio De Sica's *Bicycle Thieves* (1948), where another young boy, Bruno, accompanies his unemployed father in a desperate search through Rome's streets for a stolen bicycle upon which their livelihood depends.

For Gilles Deleuze, the child in Italian neorealism plays a key role in the crisis of the action-image. In his account, Italian neorealism's use of post-war settings, such as demolished cities and wastelands, gave rise to a new type of protagonist, who sees rather than acts, producing pure optical and sound situations.[9] This paved the way for a new kind of image – the time-image – which directly embodies time. According to Deleuze, the child becomes prominent in neorealism because its 'motor helplessness' renders it 'all the more capable of seeing and hearing'.[10] His notion of the child as a witness reflects a wider sense of disempowerment in crisis situations. Nevertheless, his attribution of passivity and lack of agency reinforces cultural assumptions about children, contrasting with how resourceful and active they often are in cinema, let alone in the real world. In many films featured in this chapter, the child functions as both a witness and resourceful agent.

Deleuze's argument is essentially about a relationship between cinematic strategy and crisis. But although the time-image emerges from a situation of crisis, that of the Second World War, this transition is mainly registered on the formal level of the image for Deleuze rather than the constraints of filmmaking. As well as exploring post-war economic crisis, Italian neorealism's creative strategies also arose *from* this crisis. This led its directors away from commercial studio conventions, such as the star system and constructed sets, and towards real locations and non-professional actors, including children. By demonstrating possibilities for filmmaking without large-scale infrastructure, they set a model for creativity within constraints for resource-strapped filmmakers everywhere. For Satyajit Ray, the founder of Indian art cinema, watching *Bicycle Thieves* was a 'life changing experience'.[11] It was partly through Ray's *Apu Trilogy* (1955–9), which features several child actors, that Italian neorealism inspired Iranian cinema, but there were also direct influences. The Iranian director Jafar Panahi, who used child protagonists in his early films *The White Balloon* (1995) and *The Mirror* (1997), saw *Bicycle Thieves* when he was a student and stated that it 'affected me more than any other film'.[12]

Aside from Italian neorealism's influence, there are many factors behind the prevalence of children in Iranian cinema. The trend began before the 1978–9 revolution and reached its heyday in the 1980s and 1990s. One important driver has been the Institute for the Intellectual Development of Children and Young Adults (also known as Kanun), a state organization producing educational films for children that supported the early work of Abbas Kiarostami and Bahram Beyzai, among others. But filmmakers also realized that children are a means of overcoming the constraints of gender segregation.

Widely practised in Muslim societies, gender segregation prevents 'interaction between men and women not related to each other by either marriage or blood'.[13] It 'divides all social space into male and female spaces' – the public realm of men, that of religion and power, and the private realm of women, that of domesticity and sexuality – through practices of seclusion and the veil (referring to various head, face or body coverings) known as *hejāb*, a code of modesty. Lowering one's eyes to avoid eye contact is another technique fostered for occasions when the sexes do meet. While these traditional norms are increasingly violated without social censure or legal penalties throughout the Arab and Muslim world, they are more strictly enforced in Iran's Islamic Republic and institutionalized in its censorship processes.

Under the Islamic Republic, it became obligatory for women to wear the veil in public and their adherence to modesty codes is policed. Islamicization was extended to cinema, which the state aimed to reform. Because cinema is considered a public realm, women must observe *hejāb* onscreen at all times even when they are portrayed indoors with family members or in historical settings – situations where it would not actually be applicable. In the absence of detailed guidelines on depicting male-female relationships, filmmakers became familiar with censorship criteria through 'trial and error'[14] and developed their own conventions for creatively working around them such as transforming the desiring gaze between the sexes to an 'averted' gaze.[15] In the early years, filmmakers often avoided adult female protagonists; later they turned to films with children. This use of children expressed an underlying belief in their innocence and that their interactions are 'sexless' and platonic.[16] Children served to 'purify' the cinematic image, sometimes functioning as intermediaries between adult men and women.

As Hamid Reza Sadr states, 'children were freer than adults; they could go anywhere and do more or less anything'.[17] In terms that resonate with Deleuze's account of the action-image's break-up, Sadr describes how children liberated the narrative of 1980s and 90s Iranian films, which developed episodic narratives with minor actions, such as roaming around city streets or rural environs. These films presented the world through a child's perspective as it undertook an everyday quest with minimal assistance from adults who were typically interfering or unhelpful. In *The White Balloon*, for example, a little girl, Razieh, wants to buy a goldfish for Nowruz (Persian New Year) but loses her money in a street grate. She enlists the help of her brother and another child, an Afghan balloon seller, who retrieves it for her with his stick and some chewing gum. Leading us through a frequently inhospitable and confusing urban maze, or trekking between villages in often treacherous conditions, children in Iranian cinema from this period display the ability to cross boundaries and navigate between different spaces. In so doing, they brought to light aspects of Iran's sociopolitical realities, such as after-effects of the Iran-Iraq war (*Bashu, the Little Stranger* (1989)), the plight of the country's Afghan minorities (*The White Balloon*) and Kurds' hardships on the Iran-Iraq border (*A Time for Drunken Horses* (2000), *Turtles Can Fly* (2004)).

Films using children are less likely to offend audiences (including censors) because they convert political judgments into 'the realm of personal experience and feeling', Sadr surmises.[18] From questions of 'why do people feel this way?' they turn to explore 'how does it feel to have such feelings?'[19] According to Michelle Langford, however, some Iranian films harness children to model ideologically 'correct' values and behaviours. The audience learns didactic lessons not by being *told* them, but by 'seeing, hearing and feeling' through the child's perspective.[20] The strategy of child protagonists often makes them vehicles of allegorical meanings beyond their control. Nonetheless, it goes beyond allegory when it attends to the specificity of their embodied experiences and idiosyncratic viewpoints. Cinematic focalization techniques, such as point-of-view shots and shots from a child's height, create an alignment between the audience and the child's visual perspective. However, just as often, as Karen Lury suggests, speaking of the boy in Tarkovsky's *Mirror* (1975), it is the child's gaze *into* and *away* from the camera that 'unfolds his unsaid but imagined personal experience' into the 'material evidence' of images.[21] The child's agency and subjectivity are emphasized when films narrate how experiences *felt*: 'warm or burning, fascinating or frightening, mundane or magical, sometimes all at the same time'.[22] As a multisensory medium, film expresses itself most powerfully in ways other than direct speech and finds an ally in the young child whose communication is primarily non-verbal. Even so, several films in this chapter feature highly vocal older children, who articulate bold statements that evade the censure they would meet if spoken by adults, permitting them to say the unsayable.

As amateur actors, children give mesmerizing performances that appear to be genuine. Sadr writes, 'Unlike film stars, children were also real people...Because children have an existence in the world independent of their film appearances, we can believe that they are more real than the other characters'.[23] Rather than belief in the 'authenticity' of the child's performance, Langford takes this to refer to a reality-effect that supports the child's allegorical and ideological function. Whilst I agree with this, I read Sadr's statement in a different way, taking it to mean that, since amateur (child) actors inhabit the real world, they bring its determinants into the film. This is not to say that movies provide unmediated access to children but, to use Margherita Sprio's wording, it points to the 'existence of other realities beyond the diegetic world of the film' where 'real life' and performance collide.[24]

In neorealist filmmaking, non-professional actors often have deprived backgrounds similar to the characters they portray and return to them afterwards. The practice blurs boundaries between their real and onscreen lives in ways that raise ethical concerns, especially for children. Furthermore, the lack of health and safety regulations on film sets in many countries allows filmmakers to use children as much as they want, without concern for long working hours or effects on their welfare, as one Iranian director admitted in the course of my research. On the one hand, the use of child protagonists is a creative means of producing cinematic art under constrained conditions. On the other, it can be a form of exploitation.[25] Moreover, neorealist filmmakers often use minimal crew and equipment to blend into real environments. This facilitates capture of unknowing performances from non-professional actors, often to great effect. Yet it also generates problems of consent, as Amina Maher who played the ten-year-old boy in Kiarostami's *Ten* (2002) claims, 'My real life was filmed without me being aware of it and was sold out to the world as a fiction film!'[26]

The child as a witness to crisis

The episodic narratives of child protagonists wandering through city streets that are characteristic of neorealism – in both its Italian and Iranian variants – have inspired other filmmakers in the Middle East. Sometimes there is direct borrowing. At other times, filmmakers gravitate to child protagonists because they are working within constraints similar to those in post-war Italy or Iran's Islamic Republic. The use of child protagonists was conducive to conditions in post-war Iraq, where the UK production company Human Film established the Iraqi Independent Film Centre (IIFC) with Iraqi filmmaker Mohamed al-Daradji to support the rebirth of Iraqi cinema after the US-led invasion and occupation. The IIFC encourages filmmakers to tell real-life stories, especially about children and their daily struggles. In one IIFC-produced film, a fictional short called *War Canister* (2012) directed by Yahya Al-Allaq, a ten-year-old deaf boy, Hamoudi, steals an oil canister to help his struggling family in Baghdad. The film dramatizes the everyday experience of post-war fuel shortages through his point of view and that of a friendly bus conductor, also a child. When the canister leaks and the driver orders Hamoudi to leave the bus, the conductor finds a solution by sealing the puncture with his chewing gum, evoking *The White Balloon*. During the film, the canister is lost, found and shared with a little girl whose family is also short of fuel. Instead of regarding the child's theft of the canister as a crime, we are invited to consider it as an outcome of desperate need. Because they live through the fuel crisis themselves, the children act both as witnesses to how it affects their lives and as active agents within that environment, managing to survive by helping each other.

As well as being produced in crisis conditions, *War Canister* was made under several self-imposed constraints. It arose during a workshop led by al-Daradji, who specified the following rules: 'all scenes had to be shot using a static camera, no music was allowed in the montage, and the film actors had to be non-professional'.[27] These rules helped al-Allaq to be creative within limited resources, as post-war Iraqi filmmaking suffered from chronic lack of investment and training of film personnel. His non-professional child actors came from a Baghdad orphanage. Ashraf Hisham, who plays the bus conductor, added his own creative input by composing the song that he sings on the bus. As al-Allaq recalls, Ashraf asked him, 'Is this film going to be in the cinema? Is everyone going to watch it?' The child wanted al-Allaq to include the song as an appeal to his mother: 'She left us here in the orphanage. I wish for her to hear my song wherever she is. Maybe then nostalgia will pull her back to me'.[28]

In neorealist style, Nadine Labaki's Oscar-nominated fiction feature *Capernaum* (2018), from Lebanon, employs real street children.[29] It follows a twelve-year-old, Zain, who lives in overcrowded lodgings with his family, working several jobs to support them. According to Labaki, 'This is a real story of real people who you see every day on the streets but you don't really look at them'.[30] *Capernaum* focuses on unregistered people – street children, migrant workers, refugees – who lack rights, because they either cannot afford to pay for identity documents or are in the country illegally. Labaki regards the child protagonist as a 'magnifying glass' that gives visibility to these problems.[31] Aside from the *kafala* (sponsorship) system that determines migrant labour conditions in Lebanon, a motivating factor for the film is the Syrian refugee crisis. At the time of its production, Lebanon had the world's largest number of Syrian refugees per capita and most street kids in Beirut were Syrian refugees. *Capernaum*'s protagonist is played by one, Zain al-Rafeea, whose family lived in the same conditions as his character's family in the film. Cedra Izam, who portrays his eleven-year-old sister Sahar, was also a Syrian refugee street girl in real life. By emphasizing the universal injustices of their situation as children, and by making them Lebanese rather than Syrian, the story sidesteps tense relations between Syrian refugees and Lebanese hosts.[32]

Labaki preserved the integrity of her child actors' spontaneous performances in situ by long takes and not calling 'Action!' at the start so that her performers were not made conscious of a difference between real life and filming. This was aided by the use of real locations with available lighting (without lighting cables that impede actors' freedom of movement) and a small crew, consisting of two cameramen and a boom operator, accompanying the director during shooting. While the real Zain's personality is not identical to his character's, Labaki channels aspects of who he is and his experiences into his role. Although sentimental melodrama pervades *Capernaum*, as it does some of its neorealist forerunners, she depicts her protagonist in a more complex fashion by rendering his harsh life through haptic film language as well as shots from a child's height as he wanders through Beirut's chaotic streets. When Rahil, an Ethiopian migrant worker whom he befriends disappears, Zain is left with her baby boy Yonas, without any parental protection. Their hunger is conveyed haptically as Zain feeds Yonas a diet of ice and sugar, a technique he learnt from his own mother. We can imagine that Zain's precocity is due to his upbringing which has taught him to behave like a little grown-up. Frequently, the film focuses on his face, with its expressions of defiance and pain. At times violent and foul-mouthed, Zain challenges ideas of childhood innocence and survives on his wits. After money, water and food run out, he roams the city, attempting to sell tinware and bottled opiates, towing Yonas along in a buggy improvised from a skateboard and stockpot – an image of his own creativity under crisis.

Zain's story reveals an unjust bureaucratic system in which people without ID cards are not entitled to any support, among them children whose parents cannot afford to register them. However, Labaki chose not to attack the authorities, which would certainly be provocative in Lebanon, especially given that she secured access to a military-run detention centre for her film.[33] Instead, her film feels the anger that Zain feels. This is directed at his sister's husband, whom he injures with a knife after she is denied medical treatment and dies of pregnancy complications, and his parents, whom he sues in court for bringing him into this life.[34] In their efforts to improve their non-professional cast's real lives, Labaki and her husband and producer Khaled Mouzanar arranged for UNHCR representatives to meet al-Rafeea and his family, resulting in their resettlement in Norway. Within the film, Zain's triumph is more modest: through the court case, he gets his story heard and, finally, an ID card, although he remains jailed for the stabbing. Even as a victim of poverty and of the system that fails him and his sibling, the film shows him asserting his agency.

In the Syrian War, children became prominent witnesses of crisis, even producing and circulating their own images with the aid of digital technology. For example, during the 2016 siege and bombardment of Eastern Aleppo, seven-year-old Bana al-Abed reported her experiences from a Twitter account managed by her mother. As al-Ghazzi notes, Syrian opposition activists have attempted

Figure 2.1 Zain exemplifies the child as a creative agent, improvizing a buggy from a stockpot and skateboard with which he tows Yonas around the city. *Capernaum* directed by Nadine Labaki © Mooz Films 2018. All Rights Reserved.

to harness the child's emotional power for international witnessing publics, appealing to ideas of children as 'truth seers and truth tellers supposedly able to speak and give meaning beyond muddled geopolitics'.[35] In Orwa al-Mokdad's documentary *300 Miles*, however, we find a child from the Syrian opposition in a more complex role. Al-Mokdad began filming on his phone as an opposition activist during the Syrian uprising, then produced two short films before *300 Miles*, his first feature. *300 Miles* is structured as a cinematic letter between him and his seven-year-old niece Nour, forming an important predecessor to *For Sama*. The title refers to the distance that separates them – al-Mokdad is in Aleppo in northern Syria, while Nour is in their hometown, Deraa, in southern Syria. The letter format bridges this distance which would normally take a few hours to travel by car yet became impossible to traverse safely during the war as the country was divided by front lines and different armies and militia. Nour is a powerful character. She is creating her own film: a video diary presenting the war from her perspective, as she learns about life, the world and the conflict.

When he began making *300 Miles*, al-Mokdad discussed with his brother Feras, with whom Nour lived along with other family members, the ethics of involving her in the film.[36] They decided to let her participate since she, like many other Syrian children, had been living on a daily basis with the war, which had already shattered her childhood. So that it would not be traumatically 'stuck' inside her, they wanted her to talk freely about it. Therefore, they gave Nour a camera, with al-Mokdad directing her from afar. His own interest in including Nour was driven by 'the representation of innocence'.[37] He himself was filming from the frontline in Aleppo, presenting the war from an adult perspective, 'full of blood, fear and anguish'. For him, Nour functions as a 'counterbalance'. He conferred with Feras about putting her in particular places, where she had the creative freedom to film whatever she wanted. These places are where al-Mokdad used to play during his childhood. Nour acts as his 'eye' in those places to which he no longer has access, 'keeping those memories alive'.[38] Addressing her uncle, she shows him the trees he used to climb, the remains of a swing that he built and the olive and lemon trees he used to pluck. In part, the child figures as a means of recapturing the innocence that al-Mokdad and other Syrian opposition members have lost in the war. In his voice-over, he addresses Nour: 'I erase the war planes, colour the destruction, and erase the checkpoints… and look for the murdered martyrs and scattered friends around the world. I erase the maps and the distance and redraw the world through your eyes'. Having been detained himself by Syrian army intelligence during the war, al-Mokdad reflects that this 'extreme violence… practically destroys a human being'.[39] Although personally he survived it, he feels he is not the same person anymore.

Sequences on the frontline in Aleppo dwell upon quiet moments rather than combat action, in keeping with the film's introspective feel, as al-Mokdad states: 'This contradiction between the noise of the war and the silence in the film is a representation of the actual inner struggle of the war. The war isn't only happening outside; it's happening inside, a struggle for the people going through it.'[40] Accompanying a Free Syrian Army (FSA) commander, Abu Yarub, al-Mokdad poses awkward questions about how the opposition has lost its bearings and probes an activist named Adnan about the ethical consequences of starting the revolution. Al-Mokdad critically interrogates the movement he is part of, pushing his interviewees to their limits.

Although the war has invaded her imagination, Nour explores it from a lighter perspective, offering relief from the film's foreboding intimation that the opposition is losing its fight against the Syrian regime. Al-Mokdad says he was astounded by the shots that she took, because they were 'so innocent'.[41] But, like him, Nour asks difficult questions, revealing herself as innocent *and* aware. In one scene, she asks Feras what 'cleansing' means. She has overheard her father (a FSA commander) saying on the phone that his friend has been 'cleansed'. The unfamiliar word marks the limits of her comprehension, but she demands to make sense of it. When Nour is unconvinced by Feras's initial answer, he finally explains that cleansing means 'assassination'. His decision to answer her plainly, rather than manipulating reality to make it softer for her, shows the difficulty of isolating children from the conflict.

Nour's creative input is strikingly bold. In her video diary, she relates the destruction that has befallen Syria, 'for one reason only – Bashar!' Her words have a startling directness, a contrast to Western news reporting on aerial bombardments in Syria that often avoids attributing responsibility to al-Assad's government, in the interests of 'impartiality'. Nour's camera zooms in on the bombing in the neighbouring town Busra where residents have lacked electricity for twenty-five days. Her creative agency is channelled into witnessing the war's violence and everyday effects on civilians. However, Nour, like her uncle, is no mere mouthpiece for the opposition. Through the film we glimpse her perspective on the world, which is different from the jaded activists. 'I wish we could just stay alive', she declares. 'Why?' asks Feras. 'Because!' she exclaims, 'It is just more beautiful to be alive. It might get more beautiful… If he [Bashar] dies we'd rebuild [Syria] hand-in-hand with the whole world.' The film ends with Abu Yarub walking into the mist. Nour's eye is superimposed on the landscape, then the scene shifts to her and her brother watching the sunrise. For al-Mokdad, these final shots, filmed by Nour herself, reflect a contrast between her and the adult protagonists who 'went into the darkness and didn't have a future'.[42] While this evokes the familiar symbol of child as the future, ending the film without layering any interpretation on these images allows Nour to have the last word as a maker of her own meanings.

Coming of age: another type of crisis-image

Susan Moeller relates how news reporting constructs a 'hierarchy of innocence' that places infants at the top, 'then, in descending order, children up to the age of 12, pregnant women, teenage girls, elderly women, all other women, teenage boys, and all other men.'[43] She suggests it is harder to describe teenagers as 'innocent', as their lifestyles nowadays are influenced by 'violent video games' and mobile phones.[44] However, this age group's loss of innocence has a wider significance for the films in this part of the chapter. Teenage years are a formative period in which individuals come to discover and understand social structures, and become politicized. They are a time of testing social and ideological boundaries, finding one's sexuality and identity and discovering whether one fits in or stands out. For filmmakers in the region, this makes it riskier to focus on teen protagonists, especially teenage girls who are becoming women.

Coming-of-age films have roots in the *Bildungsroman* genre of novels of formation, which trace a protagonist's development from youth to adulthood.

In cinema, they typically explore conflicts with parents and themes of 'problem youth', in home, school or college settings. The process of growing up offers another kind of crisis-image akin to Deleuze's time-image. Firstly, adolescent characters are 'inherently in a state of crisis' in the sense of existing in a ritually significant threshold moment.[45] Secondly, as a medium that captures time, cinema is uniquely placed to convey these transitional states, as the protagonists' bodies are performed or filmed changing and evolving onscreen. For a teenage girl, becoming a woman engenders crisis when she encounters the demands and expectations laid down by family, school, law and religion. As Lyn Mikel Brown writes, adolescence 'disposes girls to see the cultural framework, and girls' and women's subordinate place in it, for the first time. That their reaction to this awakening would be shock, sadness, anger and a sense of betrayal is not surprising'.[46] Coming-of-age films reveal how young women have to stand up to systems of social and political power, using tools at their disposal to defy or navigate them. In her work on girlhood in contemporary culture, Sarah Projansky builds on the idea that girls have a 'different' voice, one of the tools they possess both in film and life, but which is at risk of being lost when they are socialized into women. Moreover, in being held up to ideals of girlhood, girls can easily slide from 'fabulous' to 'scandalous'.[47]

The obsession with virginity is a specific limitation that girls encounter in Muslim societies, serving to regulate their bodies, although that obsession is not exclusive to the Middle East or even to Islam. As the Iranian filmmaker Mania Akbari told me, 'staying a virgin in Islamic societies has been associated with the identity of a healthy woman and with healthy body. This was especially true when I was a teenager.'[48] The Persian term *pāk* ('pure') evokes 'both physical healthiness and spiritual purity, two converging concepts regarding virginity. For many men it is crucial to be the first owners of that body.'[49] In Arab and Muslim society, belief persists that the hymen is the 'most important part of the girl's body'.[50] Failure to preserve it for her wedding night risks various punishments, from shame and divorce to death. Family honour is inextricable from a girl's honour, and located in her premarital virginity and chastity after marriage. Honour for a boy does not carry this meaning and while a boy can regain honour when lost, a girl cannot.[51] Teenage years are significant because it is usually then – or, more specifically, during puberty – that girls learn that their behaviour is important to family honour. It is at this time that modesty codes and gender segregation are implemented, although this varies according to class and geography.

In Iranian cinema, the turn to teenage girlhood began during Mohammad Khatami's presidency (1997–2005), when there was a loosening of censorship restrictions and a shift away from child protagonists to a more direct tackling of 'more adult' and 'risqué' themes,⁵² such as delinquency, drug addiction and prostitution – although that more liberal climate was reversed when Ahmadinejad came to power in 2005. The Khatami period also witnessed the rise of underground digital filmmaking, including Akbari's film *20 Fingers* (2004), which partly explores the topic of virginity.⁵³ In this cycle of films, we find a new focus on teenagers and adult women – sometimes, as in Panahi's *The Circle*, an attempt to imagine the challenges when the girls in the earlier children's films grow up. The relative freedom of Khatami's presidency also fostered new subcultures: Iranian youth, discouraged from verbal forms of free expression, turned to 'nonverbal, embodied protest, embedded in what they wore or did not wear on their hair, their bodies, and their feet' and displays of 'intimacy in public places particularly toward members of the opposite sex'.⁵⁴ This, in turn, had effects on their onscreen representation. Just as public behaviour and looking relations became bolder and more direct, so too did the camera's gaze and that of film characters.⁵⁵

A film made in the early Khatami era, Rasoul Sadrameli's *The Girl in the Sneakers* (1999), can be seen as an intermediary between the earlier films with child protagonists and later films with teen protagonists. In its opening shot, the film distinguishes its central character, fifteen-year-old Tadai, by her white sneakers and her manner of walking on the kerb rather than footpath, both signs of her non-conformism. Her stroll in a park with her boyfriend Aideen is interrupted when police arrest them for breaching gender segregation rules. Concerned for their respectability, Tadai's parents file a lawsuit against Aideen and send her for forensic examination of her virginity. The day after, Tadai runs away from home, wandering the streets, selling her jewellery to obtain money and repeatedly trying to call Aideen so they can escape together. Adults to whom she turns for advice prove unhelpful or try to take advantage of her. After many escapades (including almost being raped) she is finally reunited with Aideen in the park. Disillusioned and heartbroken when he declares he no longer wishes to marry her, she disappears into the night. The film's resolution, where the runaway is presumed to return home, might be seen as a corrective to her rebellion. However, we never see Tadai return to her parents – her future, signalled only through her disappearance into darkness, is left ambiguous.

As *The Girl in the Sneakers* indicates, the teenage girl protagonist disrupts the established narrative traits of children's films that helped filmmakers overcome rules of gender segregation and censorship – here, interacting with boys results in arrest, and wandering the streets leads to her being taken for a prostitute and makes her vulnerable to rape. At the same time, the restrictions imposed on women present further creative opportunities for filmmakers. They engender tensions between girls and the institutions of the family, school, religion and the law that are, from a scriptwriter's perspective, dramatically 'interesting'. This higher level of oppression helps to explain why teenage girls possess a greater appeal to filmmakers than boys. Naficy suggests that both *The Girl in the Sneakers* and *The Circle* were internationally acclaimed 'because they confirmed the erroneous grand narrative abroad of women in Islamic Iran as passive victims of a ruthless patriarchal system'.[56] As discussed in this book's introduction, stereotypes of oppressed Muslim women form part of the Orientalist expectations of international film festivals and script developers. Filmmakers from the Middle East (especially female filmmakers) are themselves aware of these dangers and often resist them by focusing on the everyday (rather than the sensational), emphasizing girls' agency rather than victimhood and not portraying men one-dimensionally as oppressors. The following three films, two of them directed by women, are centred on eponymous teenage girl protagonists and render crisis through their perspectives as they negotiate threshold moments and deviate from prescribed behaviour.

Teen protagonists: *Wadjda*, *Ava* and *Amal*

With its everyday story of a ten-year-old girl who wants to ride a bicycle, Saudi director Haifaa al-Mansour's debut fiction feature *Wadjda* (2012) is directly inspired by Iranian cinema. Following these conventions, the child protagonists Wadjda and Abdullah roam relatively freely outside compared to adult couples. They are even able to walk on the streets and play together, although this stretches the limits of plausibility for many Saudi spectators. Al-Mansour's use of child protagonists was a creative strategy for overcoming the constraints of gender segregation which she herself faced during the film's production. At the time the film was made, cinemas had been banned in Saudi Arabia for three decades due to the influence of clerics representing Wahhabi Islam (the conservative form of Sunni Islam that dominates in Saudi Arabia). Despite obtaining an official filming permit, al-Mansour encountered problems with cultural disapproval of cinema, especially in conservative areas where locals tried to halt the production. For this reason, she chose to respect rules of gender segregation by not working alongside her male crew outdoors and directing scenes remotely, using a walkie-talkie and a monitor in a van. As *Wadjda* was the first feature film shot entirely within Saudi Arabia, lack of infrastructure was another constraint, necessitating use of a mainly foreign crew (as well as foreign funding) and a cast largely drawn from Saudi television and open calls for non-professionals, including children.

Since she is a child, Wadjda's transgressive behaviour is more likely to be condoned than an adult's, and it frequently provokes humour for the audience. Age-wise, however, she can be classified as a 'tween', a girl between childhood and teenage years.[57] The first sign of Wadjda's tween (or aspiring teen) identity is in the opening which differentiates her from other schoolgirls by the black Converse trainers she wears underneath her school uniform. She listens to Western pop music as a means of rebellion and wears blue nail polish to express her individuality. In addition, she plays a violent video game with her dad, a moment that shows the emotional bond between them that Wadjda later finds is less significant to him than his desire for a son, and she witnesses him leave her mother for a second wife for this reason. On the cusp between childhood and adolescence, she learns the lesser value that society gives women.

According to traditional customs of gender segregation in Saudi Arabia, women were not supposed to be seen in public, other than covered in full-length black veils (*abayahs*), a practice that is changing in parts of the country. As Ahd Kamel, who plays Wadjda's headmistress Ms Hussa (and is a filmmaker herself) told me, in this closed society it is already taboo 'to open the door and see beyond the women who are dressed in black and the men who are dressed

Figure 2.2 Child protagonists serve as a means of creatively overcoming barriers of gender segregation. *Wadjda* directed by Haifaa al-Mansour © Razor Film Produktion 2012. All Rights Reserved.

in white in public'.⁵⁸ In its intimate, interior scenes between Wadjda and her mother, the film opens the door to this inner world.⁵⁹ The camera is constricted in these spaces just as mother and daughter are confined to the kitchen and bedrooms when Wadjda's father entertains male guests in the living room. The women 'make way' to avoid trespassing into male spaces. When they leave trays of food at the living room door, the camera stops there, just as they do. When Kamel was growing up, she was taught she had to be modest and cover up in order to be a 'good lady'.⁶⁰ In Islam, these practices do not stem from a belief in women's inferiority or passivity but rather from the conjecture that 'women are powerful and dangerous beings'.⁶¹ As Fatima Mernissi points out, the word *fitna* ('beautiful woman') also means 'chaos, disorder'.⁶² In *Wadjda*, Hussa declares, 'A woman's voice is her nakedness' – a saying that implies that women's voices, as well as their appearance, are a sexual provocation to men and therefore women should be both mute and covered. She admonishes Wadjda for her lack of an *abayah* and for playing hopscotch in the courtyard where workmen can see her. In order to go to school, girls (in the film) walk through the streets and courtyard, spaces of disorder because they are gender-mixed. Even inside the all-girls' school, other dangers lurk; Hussa publicly shames a pair of girls for their lesbian desire.

Bicycle-riding is traditionally forbidden for girls in Saudi society, linked to anxieties about hymen loss through accidents and sporting activities. The film gently parodies these fears when Wadjda is learning to ride a bicycle on the rooftop. Upon hearing her mother approach, she falls off the bike and grazes her knee, crying out, 'I'm bleeding!' Her mother instinctively covers her eyes in shame, thinking that Wadjda has lost her virginity. Despite the limitations she faces, Wadjda has boundless ingenuity and spirit. She enters a Quran recitation competition to gain the cash prize to buy her bicycle. Her mercenary motivation has further transgressive aspects since memorizing the Quran is supposed to be part of a child's religious socialization. When she wins, she is congratulated by Hussa for her exemplary devotion and perseverance. Wadjda rapidly transforms from 'fabulous' to 'scandalous' by audaciously declaring that she will use her prize money to buy a bicycle, one without training wheels 'since I already know how to ride one'.

A subplot about Wadjda's mother's reliance on a chauffeur for travelling to work refers to Saudi Arabia's ban on women drivers, in force at the time of the film's making. In an interview, al-Mansour has suggested that the film's concerns are not specifically a girl's right to ride bicycles or women's right to drive cars, but more generally about 'denial of basic human rights to women and girls in the name of Islam and Saudi tradition'.[63] Given that Saudi Arabia is a 'religiously conservative place', she is aware that she has to work within those boundaries, pushing them 'bit by bit'.[64] *Wadjda* explores these issues sensitively because it focuses them through the medium of a girl and a bicycle. Bicycling in a public space has powerful connotations of freedom, change and self-determination in a society with obstacles to mobility.[65] Wadjda realizes her goal – her mother rewards her persistence by buying her a bike when Hussa withdraws the prize money – and races Abdullah into an open horizon, unlike the closed spaces shown before. Dealing with everyday restrictions rather than ultra-dramatic events, the film has helped to prepare the ground for social changes. The driving ban, which women had campaigned against since the 1990s, was finally lifted in 2018, as were the bans on cinemas and women riding bicycles. With changes afoot, al-Mansour returned to Saudi Arabia to make her fourth feature *The Perfect Candidate* (2019), about a woman who stands for local elections. For this film, she had no need to direct from a van.

Inspired by its Canadian-Iranian director Sadaf Foroughi's own adolescence in Iran, the fiction film *Ava*, her debut feature, explores growing up under a strict, traditional society. Its sixteen-year-old protagonist, Ava, is a model student and talented violinist, who starts to rebel against the constraints imposed by her parents, school and wider society. The use of the coming-of-age genre, which rests on the universality of teen experience, acts as a shield against criticisms about its political nature. When I discussed this with Foroughi, she remarked, 'It wasn't deliberate but it's totally true', adding that 'children can say things that if we heard an adult say, we'd go, "oh God!" With an adolescent woman, maybe it's a little difficult in Iran, more difficult than a child of course, but it's easier than an adult because whenever anyone asks you a question you can say, "It's not about now – it's about my adolescence"'.[66] Her words evoke the Shi'a tradition of *taqiya* which, as mentioned in this book's Introduction, is the precautionary practice of dissimulating or denying one's religious belief to avoid persecution. Yet, dealing with female adolescence itself posed problems for Foroughi at script approval stage, which took one year. Iran's Ministry of Culture and Islamic Guidance told her that 'they did not want a woman shooting a film about women'.[67] So she altered her script: she changed her protagonist's gender, made the narrative structure more straightforward and removed the subtext. With these changes, she obtained shooting permission, but she shot her original script, acting as her own producer, which gave her complete creative control over its realization.

Apart from Ava's parents and headmistress, most roles are played by non-professionals, including the protagonist. Like al-Mansour, Foroughi respected laws and customs in her country of origin while making her film and believes they aided her creativity.[68] When women are veiled, she explains, they express themselves more with their hands. Some shots are composed to give greater expressivity to characters' hands, while the rest of their body is out of frame. *Ava*'s experimental cinematography, mise en scène and sound express its teen protagonist's alienation and the generation gap between her and her parents. While the film uses some real locations, Ava's family home is a constructed set, built specifically to emphasize characters living in the same space but in separate worlds. The set design was inspired by the Danish painter Vilhelm Hammershøi, whose paintings depict an interior world inhabited by solitary figures. Taking us into the private middle-class realm of Ava's family, the film becomes like a chamber drama with this artificial set filled with purposefully placed objects, such as an antiquated rotary phone that serves themes of eavesdropping as Ava tiptoes around overhearing her parents talking about her and attempts private calls without being overheard herself. As in a chamber play, where the audience can hear actors whisper, sound ranges from the almost inaudible, conveying Ava's auditory perspective. Scenes and characters go in and out of focus to highlight her increasing isolation from others.

When her mother, Bahar, discovers that Ava has secretly met Nima, a boy in her music lessons, she takes Ava for examination by a gynaecologist to reassure herself of her virginity. Of course, this would not happen if Ava were a boy. Bahar starts to disapprove of Ava's music lessons, which she now believes are not just academically useless but also improper, leading to mixing with boys. At home, she puts Ava under surveillance and tighter restrictions, even threatening to break her violin. As in other coming-of-age narratives, Ava's parents represent both parental authority and 'a larger cultural authority' that she is fighting against.[69] They are also hypocritical, another genre trait, as Ava discovers when she stumbles on their secret: they were forced to marry when Bahar got pregnant, breaching the same rules against premarital sex that Ava is suspected of breaking. At her equally controlling all-girls high school, the headmistress Ms Dekhoda warns pupils over a loudspeaker that they are under constant observation and admonishes them with a tale about a schoolgirl in another district who disposed of her abortion in the school washroom, which Ava's classmates suspect is concocted to lecture them on virginity. Obsessed with the school's reputation, Dekhoda wears white gloves, as if protecting herself from contamination. Modesty is enforced by the regulation black veils worn by pupils over dark, loose tunics although, like her cinematic predecessors Tadai and Wadjda, Ava refuses to fully comply by sporting trainers: hers obtrude in bright red.

Through school and home life, Ava encounters the many limitations laid on women in a religiously conservative patriarchal society and she fights back with a steely determination. With a child's naivety combined with an adult command of language, her voice is her tool, as she answers back to her parents' and headmistress's bullying. Significantly, Ava means 'voice' in Persian. Playing the violin is her means of creative expression which is why Bahar's threat is so painful to her. As a reviewer noticed, 'a teenage girl who presumes to challenge her parents and teachers is made to feel like a dissident in a police state'.[70] Initially, Ava simply attempts to express herself, not rebel against those institutions. However, her actions become a rebellion against them as they try to silence her and she refuses to submit to their demands.[71] In mounting frustration, Ava cuts her hand during class, an act where violence erupts suddenly as the film cuts from her toying with scissors to blood flicking onto the wall. With associations of virginity loss, the blood adds to red colours that build gradually through the film, expressing Ava's rebellion and sexuality.

Ava's attempt to assert her personhood is a huge challenge in this environment where external determinants overwhelm internal motives. With the full weight of society's rules and laws behind them, her family and school hit back at her, upholding their cherished notions of honour, and their blows are harder than hers. In the last scene, just after she has been expelled, Ava crosses the street and gazes quizzically into the camera. This open ending belongs to what Foroughi calls the film's 'interactive form', allowing the audience 'the space to complete the film along with me, as the one who created it'.[72] Viewers are left wondering how much of the story is about repression under the Islamic Republic and how much of it is about being a teenager. As I mention in this book's Introduction, I am not arguing that allegorical modes have been entirely replaced. What I am emphasizing, rather, is a *shift* towards greater directness. The openness of Ava's ending exemplifies this by leaving both possibilities – allegorical and literal readings – hanging in the balance.

Amal (2017) is a feature documentary that follows a teenage girl, Amal Gamel, from adolescence to adulthood over a six-year period against the backdrop of the 2011 Egyptian Revolution and its aftermath. Her coming of age mirrors the country's transition during this turbulent period, interweaving the personal and the political. The director Mohamed Siam, who made *Amal* simultaneously with his first feature-length documentary, *Whose Country?* (discussed in Chapter 1), met her on a protest while looking for a male protagonist. Amal transformed his perspective and trajectory. Initially, he filmed her during the revolution when she was just fourteen years old, thinking just to portray her at that point in time.

However, as the revolution unexpectedly turned into counter-revolution, he decided to continue following her, marking anniversaries over a six-year period until she was twenty, and the film became an intimate coming-of-age story. Each year that passes after the Egyptian revolution, together with her age at the time, is marked by a title superimposed on a running track. Amal herself appears poised to run at the start position, wearing a tracksuit and Superman T-shirt. The passage of time is also registered by physical indicators, such as hairstyle, *hejāb* and changing figure, as Amal grows up before our eyes, her body literally becoming-woman onscreen.

This lends *Amal* a dramatic structure akin to fiction – in fact, Siam's background was in fiction cinema, working as a casting director, before he made these two documentaries – inviting comparisons with Richard Linklater's fictional coming-of-age movie *Boyhood* (2014), which charts a boy's development from childhood to late teens.[73] With a cast aging in real time during its twelve-year shoot (including a non-professional child actor in the lead role), *Boyhood* was heralded as the first single-part movie to film its characters over such an extended period.[74] However, several documentaries from the Middle East were also filmed over a prolonged time due to tumultuous circumstances after the uprisings, as we saw in Chapter 1. These are the conditions that gave rise to *Amal*'s structure, rather than any direct influences from *Boyhood*. Because *Amal* was about a girl growing up, seemingly not as controversial as *Whose Country?*, Siam considered applying for official filmmaking permits but everyone he spoke to about it discouraged him, intimating that the coming-of-age format offered no shield for a documentary on the revolutionary generation in the present climate.[75] Therefore, like *Whose Country*, *Amal* was made underground and could not be shown widely in the Arab world.

The uncertainties that accompany any film produced over a long duration were exacerbated by changing political circumstances in Egypt. Initially enthusiastic about the project, Amal became more cautious as time wore on, warning Siam that they could no longer do everything they wanted. Furthermore, as the producer Myriam Sassine explains, 'It was complex for Amal to maintain this special relationship with Siam', as she was 'constantly evolving', growing up from a girl into a woman, her moods and priorities shifting as the film progressed.[76] These constraints affected Siam's access to her and the amount of footage he captured – twenty-five hours altogether, which is slim given the period that the film covers. However, because the film is made so artfully, nobody would be able to guess it.

Home-movie footage of Amal as a little girl, excavated from her family archives, is integrated into the narrative, showcasing her exuberant personality.

Constantly the centre of attention, she bellows 'Happy Birthday' lyrics at her mother's birthday celebration and blows out the candles herself. Amal has a star quality that demonstrates the performative nature of child and teen actors: she is playing a character onscreen, as well as being herself. The home-movie footage adds emotional dimensions to the documentary, fleshing out Amal's relationship with her father, whose death a few years before the revolution plunged her into loneliness. In the home movies, he is always by her side or filming her. With characteristic flamboyance, Amal attempts to take the camera herself, declaring 'I want to film!' Her father gently reprimands her, explaining that he is recording her early years for posterity. As Moeller notes, parents avidly film their children's early years, such as 'first smile, first bite, first step' but often lose interest when they become teenagers, except for 'scheduled events such as holidays, graduations, and family reunions'.[77] *Amal* recontextualizes childhood home movies within the more neglected teenage years. With their grainy, faded qualities, the home movies help to express the film's themes of change and loss. Despite the chronological structure suggested by the racetrack device, Siam uses the home movie footage to cut across the linear storyline. In the voice-over, written in collaboration with her, Amal is introspective and downbeat, quite different from her high-spirited public persona. Together with the home movie footage layered into the narrative, this expresses her perceptions of time, not merely her sequential progression from childhood to womanhood.

In an early scene, we encounter the fifteen-year-old Amal at a street demonstration, insulting riot police. Although her small body makes her look vulnerable, she is fearless, expressing her anger at her first love's death at the Port Said stadium riots that year. With her short hair and hoodie, she looks and acts like a boy, believing that finding her place on the streets beside male revolutionaries depends on this performance. When her friends plan to attend a sit-in commemorating the riot victims, they warn her, 'Sit-ins are not for girls… Someone will harass you'. Footage of the 2011 Tahrir Square protests, when Amal was beaten and dragged along the ground by policemen, is shown slowed down with the sound cut, as if she were recalling it in a dream. Despite performing as a man, Amal is repeatedly held to cultural demands and expectations for women which identify the female body with honour. In this, her experience is representative of many women who participated in the Egyptian revolution when the army subjected women to 'virginity tests' and accused them of sexual impropriety. Their bravery in coming out to demand their rights in public was interpreted as 'looseness' and lack of respect for authority.[78] Three years after the Revolution, Amal is pictured with her boyfriend. Her erstwhile short, curly hair is now long and straight, and she is wearing make-up. Her boyfriend tries to police what she wears, complaining that she does not wear her veil consistently. Although Amal's feminine appearance seems to fulfil gender expectations, she remains defiant, asserting, in voice-over, 'People look at me like a woman, but treat me like a child'.

Central to this coming-of-age story is Amal's politicization, forged by her experience of the revolution and her ideological split from her family, who belong to the establishment: her father was a policeman, her mother is a military prosecutor and her uncle is the governor of Cairo. Seen as a 'necessary step' of adolescence, 'physical and ideological separation from parents' is a coming-of-age genre trope.[79] These ties to genre and adolescent experience make Amal's politicization particular and universal at the same time, dramatized in heated exchanges with her mother about the then upcoming 2012 presidential election. Neither of the two candidates, Chafik (who belonged to the deposed, corrupt Mubarak regime) and Mohammed Morsi (leader of the Muslim Brotherhood), speaks for the revolutionary generation. For Amal, herself too young to vote, the choice is between 'two evils', and she is certain that Chafik is the bigger evil. Her mother, however, favours him. Amal accuses her of continuing to support Mubarak, despite the brutal crackdown he ordered, with teargas, torture and killings, which she herself witnessed first-hand, while her mother watched state propaganda. But even her mother saw Amal's bruised body after policemen abused her on Tahrir Square. 'If you vote for a military candidate, I'm going to disown you', Amal reproaches her, abruptly ending the conversation by removing her mic and walking out, slamming the door behind her – an extraordinary moment, not only for its frankness but also because Amal decides that she does not want to 'perform' anymore, reminding us that the film is dependent on her. The scene recalls the moment halfway through Panahi's *The Mirror* where the child protagonist Mina looks directly into the camera, rips off her arm cast and declares that she will not act anymore. But whereas in that film, the child's assertive agency is contrived by the director as a self-reflexive gesture that reveals the technical apparatus and crew behind the film, in *Amal*, the protagonist's *actual* agency threatens the production.

Later, Amal is pondering her life options at a cafe, where she is studying with a friend. She looks visibly different, studious and modestly dressed with a veil. 'Nobody gets what they want in Egypt', she says, resignedly. Despite her name which, as her friend says, means 'hope' in Arabic, she expresses disillusionment as she realizes her limited choices upon coming of age in post-revolutionary Egypt. Many of her friends from Tahrir Square have been killed, are in jail or have left the country. Those who remain are mired in the country's social, political and economic crisis. Amal contemplates joining the police, thinking she might change the system from inside. In the final shot, Amal is aged twenty and feeling her pregnant belly on the racetrack. The electronic dance rhythms of Mash'rou Leila's song 'Ashabi' give the film an uplifting ending which is belied by Amal's voice-over and the lyrics, speaking of loneliness and a desperate attempt to fit in. For Siam, Amal's personal story is representative of the revolutionary generation 'who have to find their place, whether they are going to be part of the system or defying the system or leaving the country'.[80] Now coming of age, this generation that underwent a utopian experience has to relinquish its dreams and somehow find a way of surviving with limited choices.

Conclusion

As a creative strategy inherited from neorealist practice, child protagonists offer filmmakers from the region a means of working within traditions of gender segregation and infrastructural constraints caused by crisis. Precisely because children are held to be uncontentious, they create safe grounds for speaking about difficult topics, acting as witnesses to the crises that permeate their daily lives. While filmmakers remain invested in children as symbols of the future and proxies for adult agendas, this chapter has charted a shift away from this allegorical usage towards a more direct and politicized approach that emphasizes children's experiential perspectives: not only does this highlight their creative agency and idiosyncratic worldviews but also their interactions with their crisis environment. Along with this, there has been another shift towards teen protagonists whose coming of age generates another kind of crisis image as they evolve into adults and test the limits of their societies in their bid for self-expression and search for identity. The use of teen protagonists throws into relief the licence afforded to child protagonists and shows how the strategy becomes riskier and more politicized in proportion to the child's age, particularly for teenage girls who are becoming women.

3

Animation

Marjane Satrapi's animated feature *Persepolis* (2007) narrates turbulent events in Iran from the perspective of its child and teen protagonist, Marji. When Marji's uncle Anoosh tells her about his dissident past, the story comes to life through simple but striking black-and-white backgrounds and characters that move like puppets, almost as if the child who is hearing the story drew these images herself. After Anoosh's arrest and execution, Marji appears to float in a black void, conveying her sense of loss and isolation, surrounded by two miniature swans that he sculpted for her from his prison bread. During the Iran-Iraq War (1980–8), a missile falls in her neighbourhood and Marji sees a disembodied hand in the rubble; the film focuses on her horrified expression, then fades to black. Through colour palette, movement, shape, texture and character design, the animation does not just document the brutalities but evokes a subjective world and feelings of what it is like to live through such events. By shifting attention from physical violence to Marji's dream-like imaginings and the horror present in her look, its abstract style poses an alternative both to graphic explicitness and news images of crisis.

Like the memoir upon which it is based, *Persepolis* was a critical and commercial success, although it was temporarily banned in Lebanon and provoked controversy in Iran and Tunisia.[1] Along with the Israeli film *Waltz with Bashir* (2008), it led a wave of animation films from and about the Middle East, many of them produced outside the region by émigré directors. Through its case studies of *The Green Wave* (2010), *Tehran Taboo* (2017), *The Wanted 18* (2014) and *Suleima* (2014), this chapter explores animation as a creative solution for overcoming some of the constraints that beset live-action production during crises in the region, such as difficulty of access to locations, absence of live-action material, need for anonymity and censorship. In animation, the filmmaker creates a world by hand or computer, something that can, theoretically, be achieved anywhere and does not require filming on location. This lends it the ability to bring to life places, events and experiences 'that might otherwise prove logistically difficult or impossible to depict onscreen using other production methods'.[2]

As we will see, in addition to overcoming constraints, animation offers many opportunities, one of which is that abstract, generic animated characters can often elicit wider audience empathy than live-action counterparts.[3] This underlies Satrapi's preference for animation in the movie adaptation of *Persepolis*. Live-action, she says, 'would have turned [it] into a story of people living in a distant land who don't look like us… The novels have been a worldwide success because the drawings are abstract, black-and-white'.[4] Animation creates an aesthetic distance from reality, lending it a degree of abstraction that invites audiences to complete the images with their imaginations. In this respect, it bears an affinity with the prohibition on figurative images in some branches of Islam where only God holds the creative power of image-making. Laura Marks suggests that Islamic art has been stimulated by this constraint since avoidance of figurative representation liberates artists from the need for realism and allows new, aniconic creative forms to develop.[5] This is exemplified by Arabic calligraphy with its lively shape-shifting letters that bounce around like animated characters.[6] Calligraphy is among several proto-animated forms from the Middle East that have led writers to locate the origins of animation there.[7] However, this is not how animation evolved in the region; instead, it took shape through encounters with animated movies from abroad.

Animation studies scholars often assert that animation is a strategy of free expression, in one form or other. According to Paul Wells, anything is possible in animation since it is free from our world's physical laws. Animated characters can stay suspended in mid-air or fly, defying gravity. With these properties, the medium has the potential to 'resist the conventions of the material world and the "realist" representation that characterises live-action cinema'.[8] Line, shape and colour, too, have shape-shifting properties. In his writings on Disney, Soviet filmmaker Sergei Eisenstein enthused about animation's ability to adopt any shape and reject 'allotted form'.[9] He distinguished this protean quality in Disney's early animations from technical developments and commercial imperatives driving it towards more realistic representations. For Nea Ehrlich, the 'constructed nature of animation' brings 'limitless' representational options, assuring 'artistic freedom' and the creator's 'omnipotence'.[10] From this, there is only one step to arguing, as Wells does, that because animation does not have to refer to 'the real world', it can operate outside its moral and ideological boundaries.

Yet although animation seems free from constraints, in practice it comes with its own limitations, which make it difficult to sustain the ideology of the free artist running through some of these claims. As Iranian-born filmmaker Ali Soozandeh told me, 'it depends on the story you want to tell. If you want to tell a story about everyday life, you cannot really be abstract in animation because the story would be unbelievable. But if you have a fantasy story or a story for children, you have fewer limitations.'[11] Not all forms of animation can embrace its freedoms, since factors of genre and intended audience often make filmmakers lean towards the photorealistic characteristics of live-action cinema rather than the abstraction of avant-garde animation or cartoons.[12] The widespread view that animation is for children means that, despite international breakthroughs such as *Persepolis* and *Waltz with Bashir*, adult animation is still perceived as niche by funders and distributors. Soozandeh explains, 'As live action, you have hundreds of examples, but for animation for adults you have only five, ten, twelve examples and that's not enough for people who want to invest in a film.'[13] For his film *Tehran Taboo* (2017), Soozandeh's team had to create a trailer to convince funders that the adult themes and story would work in animation; eventually it was co-financed by German and French television stations ZDF and Arte.

Other limitations are time and money, as well as technological capabilities and the production company's priorities. Traditionally, animation is a time-consuming, expensive process, requiring vast amounts of human labour, as was the case for *Persepolis* which Satrapi opted to make as 2D handmade animation. A team of twenty artists traced character movements at a light box, using top drawings as a guide – a painstaking process that was costlier than the average French live-action film at the time.[14] Digital technologies have increased affordability, since many arduous jobs, such as colouring and drawing 'in between' movements, are achievable on computers, although showing fluid movement is still time-consuming.

Animation is generally thought to be non-indexical because it does not record objects and people before the camera in the same manner as live action. However, as Marks suggests, 'Animation indexes the hand that made it, the labor and time that went into it.'[15] The diverse materials and techniques that animators adopt leave indexical marks on the art itself, extending to computer-based animation, which indexes the software and hardware that produced it. Animation is indexical in this broader sense, pointing to its production processes. For example, the reversion to traditional hand-drawn animation in *Persepolis* renders it distinctive in an era when 3D CGI animation has become industry standard, driven by an obsession to make films more photorealistic. As Satrapi explains, 'the hand can make something the machine can never do'.[16] Because of the indexical quality of animation, I argue that, just like other films in this book, the animated films in this chapter are documents of their working constraints.

There is a long history of animation providing solutions to filmmaking constraints during crises. An early example is *The Sinking of the Lusitania* (1918) by the US animator Windsor McCay, which portrays the sinking of a British passenger ship by a German submarine in 1915. Since there was no footage of the actual disaster, McCay aimed 'to draw a historical record', as the opening titles state. In a live-action prologue, we see him gathering testimony from a first-hand witness, the journalist August F. Beach, and working on the drawings with a team of artists. Despite purporting to be factual, the account is embellished with imagined details, such as startled fish fleeing from a torpedo. *The Sinking of the Lusitania* is a significant precursor of the films in this chapter because it uses animation to 'witness' crisis in the absence of live-action material. For Annabelle Honess Roe, it inaugurates the tradition of animated documentary in which animation serves as an alternative to the standard documentary practice of dramatic re-enactment – 'a way of creatively treating actuality', she says, invoking John Grierson's influential definition of documentary.[17]

In former communist Eastern Europe, animation helped filmmakers to overcome state censorship. The conditions in which they operated were similar to those faced by filmmakers in the Middle East: 'direct questioning of the government or society were forbidden, and vagueness of narratives or complete abstraction were looked upon as highly suspect. The most favoured films were uplifting or educational, with clearly delineated plots.'[18] As in the Middle East, filmmakers knew which topics they should avoid, such as direct criticism of politicians and the state, and found ways of working around these constraints. According to Wells, animation was able to flourish in Eastern Europe partly because of its association with 'harmless' children's entertainment. On the one hand, this marginalized animators' work. On the other, it carved out an 'apparently unguarded space to create films with surface pleasures and hidden depths'.[19] Symbols and metaphors aided in evoking these other meanings. For example, the Czech puppet animation *The Hand* (1965) by Jiri Trnka is a 'seemingly innocent fable' about a sculptor tormented by a hand, a symbol for the state that alludes to restrictions on artistic expression.[20] Many Eastern European animators chose to work with wooden puppets, their 'rigid' faces, 'incapable of stretching to show a smile or speak'.[21] Yet, as we see in Trnka's film, the sculptor is remarkably expressive, by dint of subtle manipulations of movement, lighting, setting, camera angle and framing. For Trnka, the puppet's inflexibility was a productive constraint, since it 'forces the artist to find a narrative solution more creative than merely showing a smile or frown'.[22] Although much Western literature on Eastern European animators focuses on state censorship, other types of constraints, including self-imposed ones, were just as important to their creative endeavours.

In Iran, animation has been supported by training centres and festivals since the 1960s. For example, the Centre for the Intellectual Development of Children and Young Adults (Kanun) brought animation into its remit of children's films and, in 1966, launched its International Festival of Films for Children and Young Adults which gave prominence to Eastern European animation, inspiring Iranian filmmakers with this alternative tradition.[23] Kanun also sent filmmakers to European countries, especially in Eastern Europe, in order to learn animation skills. One of Iran's preeminent animators, Nourredin Zarrinkelk, himself sent students to train at Trnka's workshop in Czechoslovakia. Along with festivals, Iranian television offered opportunities for encountering world animation. When the Islamic Republic was formed, the introduction of Islamic rules and regulations reduced the diversity of broadcast animation; however, Eastern European and Japanese animation remained on air.[24]

Before the Revolution, Iranian animation mainly consisted of experimental shorts – for example, Zarrinkelk's satire *Mad, Mad, Mad World* (1975) in which a globe reveals countries shape-shifting into birds and beasts that squawk, consume and squabble with each other. Filmmakers such as Zarrinkelk and Ali Akbar Sadeghi attempted to create a distinctively Iranian style of animation influenced by Persian miniature paintings, folktales and black-and-white lithographs in illustrated books, leaving their mark on newer generations of animators such as Satrapi whose magic realist monochrome style in *Persepolis* recalls these works. During the Islamic Republic, state support for animation has continued, enabling Iran to remain one of the few countries in the Middle East with an animation tradition and infrastructure. However, the state uses animation to promulgate its Islamic and cultural values. For example, SABA Cultural and Artistic Incorporation, created in 1994, is the government's major investor in animation and exerts a huge influence on policies for television animation. Studios and filmmakers blame its bureaucratic approval process and political and ideological criteria for the shortcomings of animation in Iran.[25] Despite this, diverse animations for the purposes of entertainment, satire and education are made there. However, while Iranian live-action films are widely known abroad, regularly appearing at international film festivals, Iranian animation is less globally visible.

By contrast, in the Arab world, there has historically not been much support for animation. Apart from constraints of budget, infrastructure (including training schools and dedicated festivals) and state control and censorship of traditional media, the widely held assumption that animation is only for children may have been a factor.[26] The Jordanian animator Tariq al-Rimawi reports that, for many years in the Arab world, imported animation films and television programmes were aimed at children; Eastern European animation, which could have offered an alternative model, did not tend to be screened. Ironically, given the relative lack of home-grown production, many animated films in the West and Japan have been inspired by Arabic (and Persian) stories and aesthetics, especially from *The Thousand and One Nights*.[27] However, as al-Rimawi points out, Western animations of these sources are filled with Orientalist stereotypes – for example, Walt Disney's *Aladdin* (1992). While animation's generic representations can facilitate cross-cultural identification, they can, just as easily, be racist. In the absence of direct encounter with other people and places, the animator's creative control over the animated world can reinforce existing worldviews and the invisibility of the marginalized.[28] This has urged some Middle Eastern filmmakers to create animated characters that are more recognizable to them or battle this stereotyping. For instance, in *Persepolis*, Satrapi partially deracializes her characters and individualizes their facial and bodily features to counter the stereotyping of Middle Eastern characters that constructs them as inferior and 'other'.

In 2008, the Syrian filmmaker Akram Agha made the animated short *The General's Boot*, expressing dissent through synecdoche: army boots evoke the authoritarian state and its repressive apparatus, while worn shoes stand for ordinary people. Immediately after the Tunisian and Egyptian uprisings and just before the Syrian one, Agha uploaded the film to YouTube.[29] As we saw in Chapter 1, 'the Arab Spring' temporarily expanded the boundaries of free expression by showing the power of social media and diminishing the grip of censorship. It also stimulated interest in animation in the region, as filmmakers and activists were emboldened to produce and distribute overtly political work online, including earlier banned animated films. As al-Rimawi recounts, it resulted in 'an explosion in the exposure of Arab animation artists and their work to the world, in comparison to the very limited opportunities and freedoms of the past'.[30] In addition, more affordable digital technologies have assisted animation's rebirth in the Middle East, accompanied by new training opportunities through university courses offering animation and hubs for nurturing local talent.[31]

New technologies have moreover enabled the use of animation in an ever-widening range of contexts. From cinema and television, through advertising and music videos to video games, visual effects, data visualization, virtual reality and gifs, animation is now present in a broad 'animation spectrum'.[32] One outlet has been human rights reporting. Amnesty International, Human Rights Watch and journalists for the Al Jazeera channel AJ+ have used animation, often combined with anonymized survivor testimony, to raise awareness of crimes such as mass killings in Syria's detention centre Saydnaya, torture in Ethiopian prisons and genocidal rape of Rohingya women in Myanmar.[33] It is also increasingly incorporated into human rights documentaries to tell empathetic stories about individuals whose rights are at risk or have been violated. Documenting violence raises ethical problems, such as how to represent subjects with dignity, that constrain what can be shown by responsible filmmakers. Since animation is not limited by what can be or has been filmed, and is capable of visually rendering what lies beyond the observable world, it lends itself to alternative ways of witnessing crisis. As we saw in *Persepolis*, this can shift the emphasis to subjective perspectives, such as witnesses' emotional reactions and memories, rather than graphic violence. It thus helps to solve both ethical and logistical problems generated by crisis, such as missing, censored or inappropriate footage, restricted access and the need for participant anonymity. The following case studies provide specific examples of how animation acts as a creative solution to these constraints.

Storytelling in the absence of much live-action footage: *The Green Wave*

The feature documentary *The Green Wave* (2010), directed by Ali Samadi Ahadi, an Iranian based in Germany, tells the story of the Green Movement, a popular movement to elect the reformist Mir-Hossein Mousavi in Iran's 2009 presidential election. It transformed into a protest movement when the election result returned Mahmoud Ahmadinejad as president, leading to widespread speculation of fraud. The state responded to protests with torture, rape and killings. Providing a record that was off-limits to conventional news media, since foreign reporters were expelled, *The Green Wave* informs an international audience about these human rights breaches, to ensure that they are not forgotten. It uses animation to depict what would otherwise be undepictable through the storylines of two fictional animated characters, Azedeh and Kaveh, whose words and experiences, spoken by émigré Iranian actors, are taken from blogs written at the time. The storylines link different types of factual material: YouTube footage of protests and state brutality filmed on mobile phones by citizen witnesses, date-stamped transcripts of blog entries and Twitter posts and interviews filmed later in Europe with human rights campaigners and exiled Green Movement supporters.

Soozandeh was *The Green Wave*'s art director, an émigré himself, having left Iran at the age of twenty-five to study filmmaking in Germany, where he began creating animation for documentary films. He explained to me, 'The problem was we had no images for telling the story. We had a lot of YouTube clips made by Iranians inside Iran with cellphones, but we wanted to tell the fictive story of two characters.'[34] Since live-action re-enactment was beyond the documentary's limited budget, the production team opted for animated illustrations, which could visualize the textual content of blogs and tweets while still protecting the identities of their writers in Iran who would face certain punishment if they openly testified.

The animation was based on drawings by illustrator Alireza Darvish in the style of comic book panels using a predominantly green colour scheme, reflecting the Green Movement's iconography. Working within the documentary's budget constraints, the team chose a limited form of animation in which the characters are still, with movement suggested through mobile camera and backgrounds, offering another challenge: how to tell a story with still characters. Generally, 2D animation moves between two extremes, full and limited animation, even within a given film. Exemplified by Disney films and, to a lesser degree, by *Persepolis*, full animation necessitates more images per second to generate fluid animated movements. Limited animation, on the other hand, uses fewer drawings per second with less character movement. To save time and money, it recycles sequences and deploys camera movement to generate impressions of motion, while voice-over narration avoids the complex drawings needed for synchronizing movement to dialogue.[35] Like *Waltz with Bashir*, which uses computer-based cut-out animation, *The Green Wave* belongs to the pole of limited animation. Furthermore, it contains hybrid images that are both still and moving, produced by combining drawings with live-action mobile phone footage. In one scene, Kaveh recalls the day of his arrest, when he was travelling on a motorbike with his friend who was filming on his mobile. As he describes how they were attacked and beaten by plain-clothed security forces, footage of such an event is replayed on the wall behind the animated character, as if projecting his memories onto a screen. Despite lack of character movements, the animated images evoke a plausible dramatic story-world, drawing in viewers to engage with documentary content.

In order to establish documentary credibility for the film's claims about a peaceful reform movement suppressed by state brutality, animated sequences are incorporated strategically. Attempts are made to lessen the animation's fictional character by, for example, displaying the dates of the blog entry that form the basis for each scene's imagery. Verbal and visual testimony reinforces the animated sequences, and vice versa. At the same time, animation vividly dramatizes events, switching from the past tense narration by interviewees in the audio track to a present tense visualization in the animation that enacts their words and experiences with a powerful immediacy. The journalist Mitra Khalatbari describes how the city 'turned into a military zone' after Supreme Leader Ayatollah Khameni endorsed Ahmadinejad in his 19 June Friday night sermon, licensing the Basji militia to violently punish protesters. Police and militia members were everywhere, charging on motorcycles towards a large group of protestors and dispersing them into side-streets. The film visualizes Khalatbari's anecdote of a boy emerging onto the street. Seemingly oblivious of events, he enters the supermarket, buys a tub of yoghurt and walks out again. A police squadron approaches on motorcycles and beats him up, leaving him lying on the street, bleeding over the spilled yoghurt. The scene is dynamically presented through a variety of angles, including the reactions of two female witnesses – Mousavi supporters dressed in green – paralysed in shock, standing in for Khalatbari.

It is the animation that enables viewers to experience the motorcycle gang's attack, even though it was not filmed, or the overcrowded prisons, where cameras are not allowed. Through animated illustrations of Kaveh's story, the film evokes the inhumane conditions inside Kharizak Prison, where he is detained in a cell with 200 other wounded protesters. Azadeh, meanwhile, is shown being arrested and taken to Evin Prison, where she is interrogated for being on Mousavi's election campaign team. Alternating with interviews, which give credence to the visuals, the animation builds subtle details about these places. For example, in the courtyard, Azadeh finds names of former prisoners etched on the wall – a detail that makes this place, unknown to those outside, more imaginable.

'Thinking without censorship': *Tehran Taboo*

Even more than *The Green Wave*, Soozandeh's fictional feature *Tehran Taboo* is concerned with using animation to overcome censorship. It opens with snow falling in the beam of car headlights. When the car halts by the kerb, a sex worker and her young boy step inside. Animated in sultry browns and reds, the prostitute offers the driver a blowjob while her son sits in the backseat, gazing through the window. Moments later, the driver crashes the car in a fit of outrage when he sees his daughter holding hands with a man on the street. *Tehran Taboo*'s three storylines show characters encountering sexual restrictions and the double standards that accompany them, resulting in one type of behaviour in public and another in private. It arose from Soozandeh's own questioning of the restrictions under which he had grown up; restrictions that are not specific to Iran but characterize Middle Eastern societies and their diasporic communities more generally, such as the concept of female honour, which is linked to family honour (as discussed in Chapter 2).

Animation has a long history of dealing with taboo subject matter, harking back to sixteenth-century flip books consisting of erotic drawings that show sexual acts when flicked, a proto-cinematic form of pornography that 'recognises the possibility in "animation" of expressing feelings and thoughts about taboo subjects without inhibition'.[36] Through its title and opening scene, *Tehran Taboo* advertises itself as taboo-breaking. As an animated film made in the diaspora, it circumvents both the need for location shooting in Iran and state approval. It depicts many controversial subjects – sex acts, prostitution, nudity, alcohol, drug-taking, underground clubs, crowds gathering to take photographs at public executions, political corruption, divorce, abortion, premarital virginity loss, sex-trafficking and suicide – many of which have been tackled in Iranian cinema since the Khatami era, as mentioned in Chapter 2. As Soozandeh acknowledges, 'none of these issues are taboo in Iran – everybody knows "it" and everybody does "it". The taboo is, in our culture, talking about the problems in public.'[37]

What distinguishes *Tehran Taboo* from cinema made within Iran is that it can address these topics directly, 'without thinking of censorship', while filmmakers active inside Iran must find creative ways around the restrictions, traditionally by speaking indirectly.[38] But, Soozandeh adds, 'talking directly is not the usual way in our culture. I see the faces of Iranian audiences in the cinema when they see the film. They are shocked. They cannot really believe that we show a blowjob in a film about Iranian society.'[39] During the film's première at Cannes, there was a brief backlash from Iranian newspapers claiming that it was 'anti-Iranian' or 'anti-Islamic'.[40] But altogether there were more negative reactions from Iranians *outside* Iran than from Iran itself.[41] Despite often living with greater freedoms, diasporic communities can cling onto cultural customs and values more faithfully than those within the country itself. So it is not surprising that, accustomed to indirectness as an accepted cultural and cinematic norm, many diasporic Iranians found the film's direct manner unsettling and 'vulgar'.

The animation technique used in *Tehran Taboo*, rotoscoping, aids its directness. Soozandeh describes it as a process lying 'between live action and animation'.[42] Rotoscoping is recognized for its ability to create 'animated images that move with a high degree of realism', since it captures the actual movements of real bodies.[43] This made it suitable for *Tehran Taboo* which aims to create a plausible story world for an adult audience. However, rotoscoping can make the actors recognizable; therefore, the animation cannot protect identities in the way that it does in *Suleima*, as analysed later in this chapter. Soozandeh told me that he discussed this issue with his actors, who had no problems with it. As Iranians living and working in Europe, appearing in the film did not pose a significant risk. Moreover, some actors were particularly keen to take part to highlight the theme of double standards. For example, Zahra Amir Ebrahimi, who plays Sara, used to be a famous actress in Iran, starring in the TV series *Nargess* (2006–7). After a video of her having extramarital sex circulated on the Internet, she could no longer work in the country and was forced to leave. In *Tehran Taboo*, her character's story is that of a discontented housewife who finds her life destroyed by a prank sex phone call, which bears parallels with what happened to her.

With rotoscoping, viewers can perceive the ghostly traces of live-action figures beneath the animation, an 'uncanny sense of reality haunting the animated image'.[44] In *Tehran Taboo*, it endows characters with life-like appearances, capturing the subtleties of actors' expressions, from their realistically animated eyes to their idiosyncratic gestures, and artfully renders them in striking colours: predominantly green, brown and red. Soozandeh says he sought to make the film colourful: 'When I think back to my childhood in Iran, the images I remember are very colourful images... When I watch films from Iran, they are not really colourful and that's why I wanted to go further with colour, because I miss the colour in Iranian films.'[45] Despite this, the film has a dark mood, since it dwells on characters worn down by everyday pressures. The animation expresses the predicaments sitting heavily upon their features with shadows created by mixing complementary colours.

The film depicts an imaginary Tehran that evokes its distinctive look and atmosphere yet is not intended to be cartographically accurate. Its districts were recreated in CGI animation using photographs of stores, buildings and streets; the backgrounds and animated characters were later composited together. Pulsating with colour and movement, this animated Tehran is a surreal space, mutable and disintegrating like in a nightmare. Red and green are predominant in scenes involving the prostitute Pari, contrasting colours which create jarring effects and accentuate her scarlet headscarf. A nightclub bathes the musician Babak and other dancers in swathes of pink and purple. Other city scenes are more subdued, with buildings forming a beige background against which dark shadows are cast.

Rotoscoping came with its own challenges, especially of giving actors and crew orientation when filming on a soundstage with green screen and minimal props. In order to establish a connection to the scene, the entire environment and its sounds have to be imagined. Rotoscoping software enables separation of layers of the image – characters, backgrounds, colours, lights – so that animators can work on and 'fix' in place particular parts. But because there were different teams working separately on different layers, it was difficult for them to imagine the result and remain motivated during the long post-production process, which took thirteen months for the animation alone. Furthermore, while rotoscoping has the advantage of bringing 'a bit of reality to the animation', it imposes constraints upon the scope of the world that is created: filmmakers cannot turn it into something very abstract, as they generally have to abide by physical laws.[46]

Yet, despite its realism and directness, *Tehran Taboo* retains a degree of abstraction by virtue of its use of animation. As Soozandeh accepts, 'this abstraction creates a distance to the story we see. It helps us, as the audience, to create a room in our head for self-imagination.'[47] Viewers fill in the gaps of what isn't being shown. This counterbalances the film's sex and violence, which might be more confrontational if shown in live action. Moreover, there is one scene in *Tehran Taboo* in which the colours become unreal, which Soozandeh identifies as the limit of the film's abstraction. In this scene, Sara walks across a bridge. Around her, figures are animated in blood red as we hear voices in her head echoing on the soundtrack: snippets from the prank sex phone call that Pari made from Sara's phone and Sara's conversation with her mother-in-law, who warns that the culprit will be found. The abstract colours express the danger that Sara finds herself in, knowing that the phone call will be traced to her. As Stanley Cavell, otherwise known as a detractor of the medium, perceptively notes about animation, 'The difference between [the animated world] and the world we inhabit is not that the world of animation is governed by [different laws]... its laws are often quite similar. The difference is that [in animation] we are uncertain when or to what extent our laws and limits do and do not apply'.[48] This uncertainty becomes especially poignant in Sara's story. When she finds herself accused, she attaches herself to a kite on the rooftop, determined to show she is an angel, complete with wings, and leaps off, tragically lacking gravity-defying cartoon abilities.

Replacing the missing Palestinian archive: *The Wanted 18*

The feature animated documentary *The Wanted 18* (2014) tells a story of civil disobedience in the occupied West Bank during the First Intifada (1987–93). Deciding to boycott Israeli goods, Palestinian residents in the town of Beit Sahour bought eighteen cows from a kibbutz in order to set up a cooperative farm and produce their own milk. The subversiveness of this backyard farming lay in demonstrating to the occupying power its lack of control. The Israeli army subsequently declared the cows a security threat, turning them into fugitives from the law. *The Wanted 18*'s co-director Amer Shomali, who has a background as a cartoonist, first read about the events in a comic he came across during his childhood in a Palestinian refugee camp in Syria, as he tells us in voice-over in the film's opening. Shomali relocated to Palestine in 1997. By then, the First Intifada was long over, but the comic remained an inspiration for *The Wanted 18*, for which he was partnered with a Canadian co-director, Paul Cowan. The film took five years to make, its lengthy schedule owing not only to the geographical distance between key collaborators but also its complex, mixed-media composition, consisting of Claymation, comic book-style pen-and-ink drawings, still photographs, archival footage, interviews with witnesses and dramatic re-enactments with their children playing their younger selves.

The context is that of a missing Palestinian archive. Palestinian films are an important archive of Palestinian experience, yet historically these archives have been full of gaps and subject to erasure. Filmmaking units established by the Palestine Liberation Organization (PLO) in the 1960s and 1970s operated statelessly. In 1982, when Israel invaded Beirut (then the PLO's base), the PLO archive was lost. Palestinians have also lacked control over 'the ideological frames' through which their images are circulated.[49] On the one hand, they have been associated with terrorism through the hypervisibility of Palestinian violence on the news and, on the other, with victimhood, under the humanitarian gaze of organizations such as the United Nations Relief and Works Agency for Palestine Refugees in the Near East (UNRWA) which built its own archive. As Shomali found when his team looked for archival footage from the First Intifada, most of it 'came from news agencies and they either filmed the Palestinians as victims or as terrorists'.[50] No camera, it seems, had recorded Palestinians engaging in non-violent resistance, such as teaching children at home when Israeli forces closed schools or milking cows to produce their own food. 'So basically we took the animation as a tool to recreate an alternative archival footage as if we had the chance to represent ourselves in that time', Shomali explains.[51]

The Wanted 18 is part of a growing trend for using animation as a substitute for a lost Palestinian archive: a method of accessing an otherwise inaccessible past.[52] The lack of filmed material makes the motivation for using animation similar to *The Green Wave*. However, *The Wanted 18* puts a humorous spin on these issues, as animated cow sequences are used as documentary evidence. These Claymation sequences are filmed in black and white, with backgrounds that minimalistically evoke the settings, and are made to blend in with other footage, playfully suggesting their equivalence as documentary sources. While the re-enactments show scenes from the Palestinians' perspective, the Claymation portrays the cows' takes on the same events. Moreover, the cartoon style occasionally punctures the more conventional documentary formats, as when pen-and-ink drawings spill into the same frame as the interviews through split-screen compositions.

While humour as a strategy in itself is the topic of Chapter 6, here it can be seen as a function within animation, for animated films frequently provoke laughter.[53] Although not all animated films are funny (nor are they intended to be), the use of animation can add humour which, in the case of *The Wanted 18*, reinforces the absurdity of circumstances related in the story. The cows are distinctively animated, with their own voices and personalities, the principal characters being Rivka, Ruth, Lola and Goldie. In interview, Shomali has mentioned that there are three language-versions of the film to date: 'The English version, where the cows and I are speaking in English, another where we speak in Arabic... and a French version.'[54] Animated animals who talk often derive their humour from their partial resemblance to human traits or, conversely, traits that defy physical laws such as stretching, squashing, bouncing and walking off a cliff unharmed. From this we can extrapolate that animations are perceived as funny to the extent that they transgress physical laws; when they confirm more realistic expectations, they tend towards the tragic, as we saw in *Tehran Taboo*. Human traits build audiences' rapport with the cows. Shomali suggests, half-jokingly, that the cows

Figure 3.1 Claymation cows become a source of empathy, 'wanted' by the Israeli army. *The Wanted 18* directed by Amer Shomali and Paul Cowan, 2014 © Bellota Films, Dar Films and Intuitive Pictures. All Rights Reserved.

are the main site of identification because 'it's easier for [the] Western audience to sympathize with the cow rather than a Palestinian'.[55] Moreover, he says, 'people get bored after 60 years with all the films and reports about Palestine.' The animated cows, therefore, revitalize what has come to be seen as 'tired' subject matter; the bitter irony of this strategy is not lost on some of the film's audiences and certainly not its makers.

At first, the cows object to being bought by the Palestinians, and try to escape. On their side, Beit Sahour residents have no experience of cow-rearing, since this does not belong to their traditional culture or existing skillset. In one scene, shot from a cow's point of view, a clay Palestinian is pictured hopelessly trying to milk a cow. In another, clay-animated scene, the military governor wakes up in a sweat from a nightmare in which cows are parading with Palestinian flags. From being in opposition, the cows and Palestinians become unlikely allies in their joint experience of being targeted as security threats. When the military governor comes to take photographs of each cow with its identification number, the cows pose for suspect profile photos against height chart backgrounds. A huge military search campaign is launched after they disappear. Now they are 'wanted cows' which is a 'joke', as one interviewee remarks, while another recalls soldiers carrying photos of cows. The film animates this scenario with a cow on a 'WANTED' poster in the street and cows hiding behind bushes and in people's houses as soldiers hunt for them. The clay puppets' hardness and weight are recruited to convey the absurdity of hiding these large animals from the Israeli army as well as to empathize with their weariness, as they are reluctantly shunted from place to place, part of *The Wanted 18*'s ironic tactic of centring animated cows as sources of empathy instead of Palestinians.

Protecting anonymity: *Suleima*

Filmmakers have a responsibility to protect their interviewees' anonymity when the topic is sensitive or when the participant's security is at risk. A common convention in live-action documentary is silhouetting the interviewee; animation serves as a 'more creative' alternative for achieving the same anonymity.[56] Using an avatar, animation 'veils' the subject's identity, keeping their face and body hidden as well as preserving their safety and dignity. Anonymity may also encourage participation if interviewees are reluctant to come forth. The promise that the animation will not resemble them gives them an opportunity to talk more freely. This is the premise behind the Syrian feminist collective Estayqazat's project of animating Syrian women's testimonies, which are sexually and politically frank in ways that would have been impossible if the women had appeared on camera, due to both security concerns and social customs around female honour. Appropriately, the collective's name means 'She has awoken'. The short films in Estayqazat's *Trilogy of Voice* (2014), distributed on their YouTube channel, are about Syrian women gaining freedom of expression and it is through animation that they exercise this right.[57]

Since the Syrian War began, animation production has been halted in Syria and many animation artists have gone into exile.[58] For the animated short documentary *Suleima* (2014), which forms part of Estayqazat's trilogy and portrays a Syrian opposition activist, the organization commissioned the animator Jalal Maghout, who left Syria for Germany in 2013. Maghout worked from a voice-recorded testimony of the anonymous woman upon whom the character of Suleima is based. What drew him to her was that she was not a well-known opposition activist, but rather 'an ordinary woman who can reflect the situation of thousands of people who are working and helping others anonymously'.[59] As miriam cooke relates, 'Women from all walks of life and from many different regions inside Syria played a crucial, if poorly covered, role' during the Syrian uprising, coordinating and taking part in demonstrations.[60] A Syrian-Palestinian woman working in a hospital in Ghouta (in the outskirts of

Figure 3.2 Animation protects identities at risk in this story of an anonymous Syrian opposition activist. *Suleima* directed by Jalal Maghout © Estayqazat 2014. All Rights Reserved.

Damascus), the witness whose story is told in *Suleima* attempted to rescue fellow protesters when they were arrested by the security forces and was twice detained herself in the process. She is an unsung heroine for these times, bravely defying both the regime and her family, who consider her active role in the opposition to be inappropriate because she is a woman.

As Maghout explains, although he only had 'a voice recording of her telling the story ... [i]t was enough to build an image of an ordinary, nondescript woman, who trusts her abilities and values'.[61] The animation reconstructs the witness in a way that does not resemble her, substituting her physical appearance with an animated personality inspired by her words and manner of speaking.[62] Her character and world are visually realized through the animator's creativity, using mainly 2D paper animation with some cut-out and 3D computer animation, while her voice-over and dialogue are spoken by an actress. All these elements serve to conceal the witness's identity for ethical reasons. As Maghout attested near the time of the film's making, 'any kind of reference to her real character will put her in a real dangerous situation since she is still active till now in the humanitarian field in Syria.'[63]

Honess Roe has asked whether replacing physical bodies with an aestheticized animated counterpart depoliticizes and disempowers people who are already marginalized.[64] But in *Suleima*, the fact that we have no sense of the real

Suleima's actual appearance does not rob the film of its political meaning. Instead, the constraints imposed on the animator by the necessary anonymity of the character empowered him (as well as the character) to create a stand-in through animation, which testifies to her existence and her courageous acts of resistance. The animation begins with sounds of clapping at a street demonstration, where protestors hold placards saying, 'Stop the killing. We want to build a homeland for all Syrians'. As security forces drag away Suleima under arrest, she reflects in voice-over about what brought her to this point: 'If I could go back in time I would do more than I have already done'. This line, which is repeated near the end, affirms her determination, hope for change and defiance of state repression.[65] The black-and-white animation (with occasional colour for artificial lights) that designates the present shifts to a sepia flashback looking back to her life before the revolution, including her childhood under the rule of Hafez al-Assad. Suleima recalls when, as a little girl, she realized the meaning of *Mukhabarat* (secret police). Even at home, one must whisper because state surveillance is everywhere – an idea visualized through her child's perspective as giant security cameras rear up behind a wall as she strolls down a street. As in *Persepolis*, the animation's evocation of childhood renders the images accessible to a wider audience, while the graffiti emblazoned on the wall, 'We shall strive to restore our usurped rights and shall fight against imperialism, backwardness etc', articulates revolutionary ideals. Among the events that Suleima recollects is the regime's aerial bombing of Hama following an uprising there in 1982, in which between 10,000 and 40,000 people are estimated to have been killed, part of what formed her resolve to join the revolution as an activist. The film uses animation to embody subjective memories of this massacre, which has been suppressed in the official record. It underlines that this history of pre-revolution Syria is important to understanding the present.

For Maghout, a fascinating aspect of animated documentary is that 'you can be less loyal to the documentary material you have. You are free to add and create from your artistic view.'[66] In animated documentary, we are invited to accept the animated images as a means of transporting us into the witness's thoughts, although they are interpreted through the animator's third-person perspective.[67] Maghout regards *Suleima* as a form of self-expression but one that emerges from 'common feeling' between him and his subject. This can be seen in scenes reflecting shared experiences of growing up under dictatorship in Syria, but also in his empathetic depiction of a female activist estranged from her family and treated unequally in the resistance. In animation, empathy is partly expressed through synaesthesia, where sense impressions belonging to one sense are experienced through other senses. When Suleima is beaten up, the blows are conveyed through the strokes of the drawing as well as thuds on the soundtrack. As a child, shouting her hatred of Hafez al-Assad, her voice's loudness is comically visualized by making a security guard's hair and clothes waft in the wind.

The advantages of animation for this subject matter are summed up by Maghout himself: 'For me, animation is an effective medium to depict an unattainable situation. For example, our memories, fantasies and dreams, the people whom we cannot meet in person and the places we cannot visit and, of course, in this case, to protect the persons who are involved in the film.'[68] Set during the early years of the revolution when Syria was largely off-limits for film crews, and moving back and forth in time, *Suleima* enables us to 'visit' the country, and its past. Like *The Green Wave*, it provides access to the regime's detention centres by illustrating witness testimony of torture and detention. As in *Persepolis*, the focus is not the brutality itself, but the way the character feels about it. Sitting in her cell, Suleima would hear the beatings of fellow prisoners, which was worse, she says, than being beaten herself. Her testimony tells of a prison doctor, who would stitch up prisoners' wounds without anaesthetic and force them to walk immediately. Every twelve hours, Suleima was permitted to go to the toilet and each time she would pass prisoners, hanging in the same position. We see her clasp her hands around the hands of one prisoner, although she is unsure if he can feel it. The animated imagery, together with voice-over and sound-effects, emphatically and empathetically imparts this intimate experience to viewers.

Conclusion

This chapter has explored animation as a creative strategy for overcoming some of the constraints of live-action filmmaking in the region. It has shown how animation serves as an alternative to live-action re-enactment when images and access to locations are unavailable (*The Green Wave*), circumvents censorship (*Tehran Taboo*), acts as a substitute for missing archives (*The Wanted 18*) and offers a means of protecting the identity of individuals at risk (*Suleima*). Moreover, its use is not confined to these functions, since the medium has expressive possibilities that enable it to evoke the subjective worlds of memory and emotion, elicit audience empathy, provoke laughter and imagine the unimaginable. Creating empathy is particularly important for these filmmakers who are dealing with groups of people who are often denigrated in mainstream media; animation offers a way of overcoming this through its generic, abstract characters. Yet, while animation gives filmmakers considerable creative and interpretive freedom, in practice it is accompanied by many of its own constraints (including time, money, type of story and intended audience) which are registered in the form that the animation takes. It can be employed with startling directness, yet it is, at its core, an abstract medium that takes an aniconic approach to crisis-images.

4

Psychogeography

Fuad Abdulaziz's documentary *Sana'a: A Symphony* (2020) brings together a poet, radio presenter, singer, photographer and videographer to capture different aspects of Yemen's capital. When Saudi-led airstrikes began in March 2015, Abdulaziz could no longer return to the city to complete the film as he had intended. So his contributors sent him footage of their wartime experiences. In the radio presenter's video diary, the nightly aerial attacks are a symphony of fear and despair, but during daylight she climbs to her rooftop and gazes at the city she loves, as if relieved it is still there. One of Abdulaziz's influences was the work of social theorist Michel de Certeau, who contrasted two ways of looking at the city: one is a totalizing perspective that reflects the panoptic design of urban planning; the other is from the space inhabited by residents, usually at street level.[1] It is the inhabitants' perspective that we find in *Sana'a: A Symphony* and the films featured in this chapter, which map the psychological and historical layers of their respective cities, and the shifting social relationships that accompany urban transformations. Often the city functions as a character in its own right, a witness to its inhabitants' lives and historical events. The movies archive their cities as they were when they were filmed. They offer complex, nuanced perspectives not usually found in either official state media or international reporting, which often take the view from above.

It is no coincidence that this strategy, which I am calling psychogeography, has emerged in contemporary Middle Eastern cinema at a time of turbulent change and destruction in the region. It is part of the general movement towards more direct forms of expression than allegory that I am tracing in this book but, although it is a form of witnessing in itself, it is not as direct as the documentary-type reportage that witnesses events as they unfold, covered in Chapter 1. This chapter centres on documentaries and fiction films about four cities in the region: Tehran (*Writing on the City* (2012) and *Tehran: City of Love* (2018)), Beirut (*Panoptic* (2017)), Cairo (*In the Last Days of the City* (2016)) and

Damascus (*A Day and a Button* (2015)). These films display an acute sense of place that comes from a love for these cities as well as a critical take on them. Psychogeography helps me frame how they express sensitive aspects of urban realities when other strategies are unavailable due to constraints such as lack of infrastructure and state censorship. Like any other strategy, it is not immune from censorship itself. In fact, four films discussed in this chapter have been censored or made underground in their respective countries.

Psychogeography is associated with the writings of Guy Debord, a leading figure of the avant-garde group Situationist International, which was an influence on de Certeau. According to Debord, the term psychogeography has Middle Eastern origins, coined by 'an illiterate Kabyle', around 1953. The Kabyle, who belong to the Amazigh people formerly known by the colonial term 'Berber', live in northern Algeria. Debord's interlocuter remains nameless, pointing to the colonial context under which much French theory from this period emerges. Debord goes on to define psychogeography as 'a study of the precise laws and specific effects of the geographical environment… on the emotions and behaviour of individuals'.[2] As a practice, psychogeography is rooted in both a Marxist critique of capitalist alienation and a surrealist urge to delve beneath everyday surfaces. Challenging official and other totalizing perspectives on the city, such as urban redevelopment schemes, road networks and tourist images, it explores different routes, taking us horizontally into marginal areas and vertically into the past.

One psychogeographic tactic is *dérive* or drift, as it is sometimes translated into English: an unplanned journey in which a person abandons their everyday routine and allows themselves to be 'drawn by the attractions of the terrain and the encounters they find there'.[3] The purpose of the *dérive* is to create an alternative mapping of the city with its distinctive zones and ambiences. Walking is integral to it, since it is on foot that one may more easily deviate from existing routes and discover places off the official maps, as we will see in *A Day and a Button*. In metropolises that are inhospitable to pedestrians, promoting 'swift circulation' via highways, walking is a subversive activity in itself, its street-level exploration capable of challenging official city planning.[4] The *dérive* affords a different way of moving around the city, apprehending it not merely through one's eyes but engaging all bodily senses through the corporeal experience of walking. The film theorist Giuilana Bruno advocates the idea of 'embodied psychogeography', drawing parallels between the Situationists' psychogeographic mapping and filmic 'site-seeing' in which the camera wanders around a city with a haptic gaze.[5] As Thomas Deane Tucker suggests in his study of walking in cinema, the camera acts as a pedestrian, creating 'a *peripatetic point of view*' that he links to the concept of the *flâneur* (the urban stroller in the work of Charles Baudelaire and Walter Benjamin) as well as psychogeography.[6] For the film viewer, this offers a virtual tour of the city, though not to the usual tourist destinations.

Precursors of this strategy are found in city symphony films such as *Manhattan* (1921), *Berlin, Symphony of a City* (1927) and *Man with a Movie Camera* (1929) that responded to the changing urban environment – the dynamism of its architecture, machinery and crowds – in order to capture its visual poetry and visceral sensations. Often structured as a day in a city's life, these documentaries map lived urban space, tracing patterns of interactions between built environments and their inhabitants. While their use of location shooting places them in the real world as witnesses to actual events, city symphonies flamboyantly reimagine city topography through montage and other forms of image manipulation which poetically inflect the witnessed reality, an approach taken by *In the Last Days of the City*. True to their name, city symphonies are attuned to urban rhythms, which they hear acutely as if listening to music. Despite being made as silent films, the 1920s films are packed with 'sound', using movements within the frame and editing rhythms to convey the cadences of the city. Sound is a particularly important feature of *Panoptic*, which is also closely allied to the city symphony tradition, as is *Sana'a: A Symphony*.

In cinematic styles that mix documentary and fiction, location shooting brings street life into the narrative. As film theorist Siegfried Kracauer noted about this technique in Italian neorealism, incidents from the background street may enter the scene and enrich the narrative with their 'found' stories.[7] By filming the diverse and unpredictable 'flow of life' in real locations, contemporary movies from the region can capture elements that were not part of the approved treatment or script. Another psychogeographic topos inherited from Italian neorealism is the urban ruin, as location shooting bears witness to wartime destruction. This plays a key role in Gilles Deleuze's theorization of the crisis of the movement-image in post-war Europe, giving rise to what he calls 'any-space-whatevers' – indeterminate settings such as wastelands and derelict and disused sites – that transformed the landscape and heralded the cinematic time-image, which represents time directly.[8] While derelict sites belong to specific histories and are far from indeterminate for locals, Deleuze's idea of the ruin as a witness is highly pertinent to films in this chapter which often gravitate to destroyed walls and derelict buildings that leave traces of past conflicts on the urban fabric.

Budgetary and infrastructural constraints in the immediate post-1945 era stimulated the use of location shooting in Italian neorealism. For similar reasons, independent films in Iran and the Arab world often rely on real locations that are rich in the kind of textural and historical detail that is difficult to recreate on set. However, this has not been uniform practice throughout the region. As Viola Shafik points out, 'Egyptian realism remained a child of the studios, with all that this meant for faithfulness to detail and creating an appropriate atmosphere'.[9] To achieve this with a degree of artistry requires a large budget and infrastructure, including highly trained specialists in art direction, costume design and casting as well as extras. As the British-Egyptian actor Khalid Abdalla, whose career spans Hollywood and Arab films, explains, such resources have

> a huge effect on what you can and can't do, in terms of the palette of what you're able to express. I think the most successful kind of censorship is infrastructural, not the figure at the top who says cut this out, don't do this or do that... How many films can I think of from our region that stun me in terms of their art direction and what that allows the camera to do? Very few. Generally, what they're relying on is their locations, real locations which they might happen upon which have those interesting walls, those things that allow space to communicate.[10]

As we will see in the following films, location shooting is a practical solution to this constraint, laying the foundation for creative psychogeographic strategies that reveal the city's material conditions and allow silent histories to speak. Each of these films exemplifies a different psychogeographic method, which my interviews with the filmmakers and the theories of Debord and other critical thinkers of urban space have helped me to elucidate.

Tehran

The city in Iranian cinema is often a palimpsest of social and political crises. This tendency can be traced to the reform period of Mohammad Khatami's presidency, which created a more open climate in which filmmakers could comment on social, economic and political issues more or less directly through Tehran's urban landscape, as Rakhshan Banietemad does in her fiction film *Under the Skin of the City* (2001). As Blake Atwood says of Banietemad's films in general, 'Tehran functions as an affective surface that captures and mirrors the emotional responses and impulses of its inhabitants'.[11] More direct and radical, Keywan Karimi's documentary *Writing on the City* (2015) explores Tehran's historical and psychological layers through graffiti on its walls, which bear witness to events from the 1978–9 Revolution to the 2009 Green Movement. An Iranian-Kurdish filmmaker, Karimi studied sociology at Tehran University. It was there that he became interested in the sociologist Henri Lefebvre, whose work influenced the Situationists and de Certeau, and psychogeography as a tactic.[12] *Writing on the City* is inspired by an anthology of Lefebvre's essays on urban space, *Writings on Cities*.[13] For Lefebvre, the space in which we live is a social space, produced by social relations. In municipal buildings and thoroughfares, space is in the service of the state or governing authority, reflecting official ideologies. In *Writing on the City*, the invisible hand of the state is apparent everywhere within the city, asserting its power through the organization of urban space.

Karimi claims *Writing on the City* is a film that changed his life, since it led to his arrest and imprisonment.[14] He began it in 2012, when one of his university professors, who wrote a book named *Graffiti in Iran*, invited him to make an accompanying film. However, once Karimi started researching the topic, discovering graffiti from the time of Revolution and even the 1953 coup d'état, he realized that he could not just focus on present-day graffiti. Searching through the dusty archives in Iran's National Library revealed to him 'how the Revolution removed the power of the other groups' in urban space.[15] He completed a first edit of *Writing on the City*, which was not as uncompromising as the final version would be, before an international festival tour for his short film *The Adventure of a Married Couple* (2013). Upon his return to Iran, he was arrested and his computer hard drive was seized during a raid on his home because he had posted a trailer for *Writing on the City* on YouTube. The hard drive was returned, erased, resulting in the loss of his first edit. In 2015, Karimi was given a six-year prison sentence, which was later reduced to one year. He was finally released in 2017 after serving five months in Evin Prison, Iran's jail for political prisoners.

These experiences altered Karimi's approach to his film, which he re-edited while under trial: 'Especially after the arrest, what I wanted to do is tell everything direct.'[16] First, he removed an interview that featured in the first edit and replaced it with voice-over. Although this voice-over is poetic and philosophical, qualities associated with earlier Iranian films, it tells us directly what happened in those times and spaces. The arrest, moreover, led Karimi to consolidate his idea of the city as a character in the film: 'we have a city like a human body that has a skin, and the skin is like the scars of an operation – it gives you a history of what happened on this body'.[17] In other words, the film reads the history of Tehran through the writing and images on its walls, a relatively direct political and creative strategy. It focuses on two types of graffiti: official graffiti, consisting of state-commissioned murals, and unofficial graffiti produced in resistance to state discourses, reminding us of policies that have devastated the city and its people. Created by city dwellers in secret, often at night, unofficial graffiti are images and texts that communicate in public spaces, circumventing censorship and denial of voice in official media. The film juxtaposes these official and unofficial perspectives on the city; it reads the walls in order to delve under the skin of those official discourses and, as the voice-over puts it, 'discover the dwellers' dreams'.

Writing on the City is composed of 60 per cent archive materials and 40 per cent Karimi's own footage. Karimi remarks, 'There is always a *flâneur* figure in my films, either he is a lawyer (in *Drum*) or he is the wandering ghost of the city (in *Writing on the City*). Besides, it is my own relationship to the city.'[18] In *Writing on the City*, the wandering camera is like the ghost of the city. It escorts us into its past and evokes suppressed histories that offer alternatives to official historiography. During the Revolution, people got their news from graffiti on the city's walls, since they did not trust the Shah's official media. With his editing, Karimi emulates camera pans from right to left, reading revolutionary slogans in Farsi written under the cover of darkness that would be whitewashed by government agents in the morning. After the Revolution, the new Islamic regime ordered the graffiti to be cleared, a systematic attempt to remove other voices in the public sphere: Marxist slogans faded away, replaced by religious sayings, attesting to Karimi's view that a Marxist revolution was transformed into an Islamic one. During the Iran-Iraq war (1980–8), the walls no longer narrated Revolutionary ideals but rather support for the war, with murals honouring martyrs. Later, in the Khatami era (1997–2005), martyr portraits receded behind advertising billboards, reflecting the Islamic Republic's turn to neoliberalism as a new way to survive in the globalizing era. The film reveals the layering of these images, the old hidden behind the new, and descends into the underground metro where, the voice-over tells us, 'another life is going on beneath the surface'. Here, war murals are forgotten in murky corners. Under Ahmadinejad's presidency (2005–13), on the other hand, there was an attempt to revive revolutionary and war ideology. New, colourful and imposing murals display revolutionary leaders, their portraits no longer stern but mild and smiling. Murals of flora, fauna and rural life also appear among new property developments, creating a fake green environment in a polluted city.

Alternating between a female and male narrator, the voice-over creates counterpoint, part of the dialectic that the film establishes between historical events.[19] In a reversal of traditional gender roles, the female narrator recounts the time of the Revolution and the Green Movement in the first and final third of the film, whereas the rise of neoliberalism in the post-war era, a comparatively dull period of Iranian history according to Karimi, is voiced by a man in the middle third.[20] During the Green Movement, people returned to the streets and walls were used for protest slogans again. The authorities unsuccessfully asked Karimi to cut this sequence, but the film's radical character exceeds this by far. Graffiti is a short-lived artefact, routinely erased by municipal authorities. By capturing graffiti through archival footage and scenes shot by Karimi himself, *Writing on the City* grants greater longevity to these ephemera. It preserves traces of a repressed past and dredges buried layers to the surface as the city's political unconscious. Night-time, time-lapse footage shows graffiti artists at work, operating clandestinely because of risks of getting caught by police. The film also enters public toilets which, the voice-over tells us, 'for decades functioned as de facto political whiteboards' outside the otherwise ubiquitous gaze of CCTV cameras. To date, *Writing on the City* has not been officially shown within Iran, although it has screened on BBC Persian (which can be seen, via satellite TV, within the country) and it has propelled its director to international fame, eliciting a tribute from Situationist International member Raoul Vaneigem when Karimi was sentenced.[21]

Although not a documentary but a fictional drama, Ali Jaberansari's *Tehran: City of Love* utilizes an implicitly psychogeographic strategy because of its concern with character and environment. It consists of three intersecting stories, those of an ex-body builder, a beauty clinic receptionist and a funeral singer, each searching for intimacy in a city where love cannot be expressed freely. The film cuts back and forth from one story to another, following the characters as they circulate through the city, engaged in their daily activities. Sensitivity to the specificities of the city's locations enables it to explore its characters' *habitus* (a disposition produced by a particular kind of environment) and to deal with homosexuality, religion and dating, all of which are potentially controversial issues in Iran.[22]

Places in the film – a modern and a traditional gym (*zūrkhāneh*), a beauty clinic and a cosmopolitan-style café – are not the typical ones of internationally exported Iranian cinema.[23] They are communal spaces of work and leisure, reflecting spatial practices of consumerist society; the habitual axes to which characters are drawn in their itineraries around the city. Furthermore, a mosque is shown in the context of funerals rather than just prayer. Since the film appears to present 'a comfortable, modern picture of Iran', Jaberansari has related that he has been accused of working on the regime's behalf.[24] However, his and his co-writer Maryam Najafi's unusual choice of locations lends a different perspective on the city. Because the locations are both modern *and* traditional, the film moves across the divides created by the reconstruction project that transformed Tehran's historical core and led an emerging middle class to relocate to new residential areas, while poorer communities remained in the old city.

Moreover, in contrast to many other city films, which offer orientating overviews or shots that interrelate the different spaces, there are few exterior shots in *Tehran: City of Love* – and certainly no touristic vistas of the Milad Tower and Alborz mountains. Characters are seen arriving at places or leaving them, or driving through the highway network but, other than that, they are always inside. Jaberansari explains that it was a self-imposed constraint not to show much of the city and instead focus on interiors.[25] At the development stage, the script consultant questioned the lack of exterior shots; no changes were made, but the conversation allowed Jaberansari to defend his choices and sharpen his vision of the relationship between his characters and their environment.

As an émigré filmmaker who keeps close links to Iran, similarly to Sadaf Foroughi (whose film *Ava* is discussed in Chapter 2), Jaberansari feels he has a privileged insider-outsider position whenever he returns, affording him a certain distance to observe and artistically reflect on aspects of Iranian culture in his films. According to his own psychogeographic insight, many pressures tend to be internalized in Iran, an environment where citizens largely lead a double life, displaying oneself in public and another in private.[26] The impact on storytelling is that Iranian dramas tend to be situational with the impetus deriving from external forces, such as bad husbands, fathers-in-law or the regime itself, rather than characters themselves, as in the films of Tahmineh Milani or Asghar Farhadi. Because these forces are so internalized, characters rarely exhibit outright emotions and barely know themselves. For Jaberansari, this lack of self-knowledge also means that Iranian Cinema tends not to explore characters deeply; instead, many are depicted as 'types'.[27] In *Tehran: City of Love*, he turns this constraint to his advantage for expressing themes of same-sex love and intimacy. His characters are informed by external forces – namely, the environment that they inhabit, which materially affects their behaviour, resonating with Lefebvre's statement: 'Every space is already in place before the appearance in it of actors... This pre-existence of space conditions the subject's presence, action and discourse'.[28] This lends the space psychological dimensions that materialize in the characters' stories so that, in its mapping of the city, the film performs a psychosocial analysis of urban space.

With regard to the story of ex-body builder Hessam, Jaberansari explains,

> We knew the kind of story we wanted to tell and we specifically chose it in an environment which was the space of the gym... The gym was for me a very interesting environment because of the way gym culture has been adopted in Tehran especially. The gyms have turned into social clubs, because there is no nightclub or pub to hang out. But then they are segregated by sex, so [there are] men only and women only gyms.[29]

In gender-segregated societies, homosociality forms the norm, encouraging strong same-sex bonds, even as homosexuality remains illegal. Moreover, Jaberansari remarks, men-only gyms are spaces in which male bodies are displayed and 'there's this obsession with the male physique.'[30] As the gyms in *Tehran: City of Love* are real locations, he did not need to embellish what can be found there, he jokes. The rapport between Hessam, who works as a personal trainer in a modern gym, and his younger client, Arshia, who seeks his coaching for a championship, is established in this homosocial space. Pulsating techno from the gym's sound system forms a background to their 'courtship' as Hessam trains his protégé, stretches his limbs and measures his vital statistics. Arshia flexes his muscles as they both look at themselves in the mirror, a shot that draws attention to their mutual gaze and similarities of their muscled, tattooed bodies, evoking same-sex desire. Jaberansari underlines that Hessam was not written as a homosexual; rather, the character is unaware of his own same-sex desire.[31] His desire for Arshia, barely perceptible to himself, emanates from this environment. Furthermore, their intimacy is readable in terms of conventions of *dūstī* ('friendship'), '[a] male homosocial love, sometimes with homoerotic undertones, [which] played a crucial role in many *filmfārsī* plots.'[32]

It was very important for the filmmakers to juxtapose this modern gym with the traditional *zūrkhāneh* gym, which features as the place where the funeral singer Vahid trains. In this domed building, men stand in a circle and exercise with pairs of wooden clubs, whirling them rapidly to a drumbeat and clanging bell. The film focuses on old, black-and-white photographs on the walls depicting bare-chested men posing with their hands tucked inside each other's shorts – again, these were found on location. The *zūrkhāneh* embodies Persian traditions of chivalry and sportsmanship within a homosocial community. Like the modern gym, its iconography and practices evoke different reactions depending on the cultural perspective from which they are viewed, as Jaberansari explains: 'from a Western point-of-view it would be very homoerotic but it might not be for someone inside the culture. So all of this created enough space to tell this story'.[33] The juxtaposition between modern and traditional gyms grounds the relationship between Hessam and Arshia in a cultural context. At the same time, the filmmakers sought to be, as Jaberansari puts it, 'a bit more playful, not just to go for the [interpretation that] they're just buddies. But that's the line we could say to anyone who wanted to question it – what are you talking about? It's two buddies. That space between these readings was the grey area where we could manoeuvre.'[34]

In contrast with *Writing on the City*, *Tehran: City of Love* was approved for both production and screening permits. Jaberansari explains it was always his intention to 'stay within the boundaries – not to do an underground film.'[35] Since Hessam and Arshia's relationship was in the script, he was naturally apprehensive when it was submitted for approval, although the censors did not pick up the homoerotic aspects. Of course, the script omits details such as the length of characters' gazes and other bodily gestures that can suggest same-sex desire. Despite that, the finished film was approved for exhibition after being submitted in a slightly re-edited version. The authorities requested some changes – mainly, removal of some male nudity – but not ones that affected the storylines, testifying that, in this case, psychogeographic tactics were successful at dodging censorship.

Beirut

As Lina Khatib suggests, several films about the Lebanese Civil War (1975–90) use psychogeographic methods: 'The Civil War left its mark on the physical appearance of the city, and on the cinematic imagination of Beirut', scars that were 'both physical and social as both the buildings and people shared the suffering'.[36] In keeping with the 1991 Ta'if Accord, which declared amnesties for perpetrators, the city's redevelopment by the company Solidere sought to erase traces of the war, clearing the downtown areas. Several Lebanese filmmakers whose formative experiences are defined by the war have sought to excavate its hidden legacy from beneath the official version of the city imposed by reconstruction projects. Their work taps into feelings that the Civil War is ongoing. The July 2006 war with Israel revived memories of that earlier war and sectarian tensions resurfaced. Life has not returned to normal – violence still seems to lurk, capable of breaking out at any moment in full-blown conflict between sectarian parties. The artist-filmmaker duo Joana Hadjithomas and Khalil Joreige have commented that the culture of amnesty has affected freedom of expression, forcing filmmakers to censor themselves in fear of reprisals.[37] As Rana Eid, director of the documentary *Panoptic*, explains, 'In Lebanon there isn't a classic dictator, where you know that you're against this person.'[38] The ruling power is based on a sectarian system inherited from the Ta'if Accord, which allowed perpetrators to assume political positions. This has led to a mafiaesque structure of government whose corrupt and dysfunctional nature was apparent to citizens for decades and has been further exposed in the 2020 Beirut Port explosion and ongoing economic catastrophe.

During the Civil War, Beirut was divided between east and west. Most films on the topic focus on this division whereas, in *Panoptic*, Beirut is divided between overground and underground. This inversion of the city brings to the surface the Civil War's ghostly presence. Eid's idea for her film arose when she discovered an immigration detention centre underneath Tahwita Bridge.[39] It prompted her to think of events during the war, when militias carried out kidnappings, torture and killings underground and civilians took refuge in subterranean shelters. As Eid relates in her voice-over, the generation that survived the war 'emerged from the shelters but not from underground', evoking a past that haunts the present. In *Panoptic*, we explore the city from symbolic sites used as underground detention centres, from the present-day immigration detention facility to past torture chambers in Burj El Murr, a former sniper hideout, and Hotel Beau Rivage, former headquarters of Syrian intelligence in Lebanon: the city's official story is retold through another story of the underground.

With her background in sound design – she has worked on numerous films previously as a sound designer and continues working in that field – Eid also lends another perspective on Beirut by attention to its sounds in *Panoptic*, her directorial debut: 'If you want to really understand a city, you have to listen to what it's saying.'[40] The film opens with a sound montage that immerses us in Beirut's soundscape for two-and-a-half minutes. It commences with an ominous throb, an inexorable pulse upon which other rhythms – construction noises, the call to prayer and car horns – are superimposed. In voice-over, Eid speaks about taking 'refuge in sound' in underground shelters during her childhood when the war's violence was concealed from sight yet heard continually. The film then shifts to present-day Beirut where sounds barely die down at night. Roads teem with cars with gleaming headlights, overlit by electronic billboards, accompanied by ambient traffic sounds and a percussive beat as if vehicles are humming on the tarmac. In the absence of visuals other than a black screen, this opening invites spectators to 'open their ears'[41] to the city and listen to its rhythms.

As well as the production of space, Lefebvre was interested in the city as a lived space with its own rhythms performed by everyday work and leisure activities: 'The interaction of diverse, repetitive and different rhythms animates... the street and the neighbourhood'.[42] Usually these sounds are mixed up, difficult to distinguish from each other, yet Lefebvre describes how 'the attentive ear' can separate them out, identify their sources and perceive how they interact as a multiplicity. Eid, like Lefebvre, is a rhythmanalyst. The sounds in *Panoptic* are all recorded on location, integrated into the film without added sound effects but layered to create a distinctive sound architecture. Unlike the conventional precedence of visuals over sound, sound acts as our primary guide to meaning. Most of the sound in the film is out of sync, reflecting a city out of sync. Non-synchronized sound produces unsettling effects. In *Panoptic*, visual and sound mismatches render the hidden past and present 'visible' by linking the overground with what remains invisible underground. From the surfaces of Beirut, the Middle East's nightclub capital, the film descends into the detention centre beneath Tahwita Bridge, where undocumented domestic and manual workers (of whom Ethiopians form the largest group) are imprisoned. Here soldiers patrol, moving in slow motion, appearing and disappearing like ghosts. When Ethiopian marathon runners later pass overhead, we hear sounds from underground, underlining the irony that while some Ethiopians are celebrated as champions, their compatriots are forgotten below. As Eid explains, 'The challenge was to destroy the perspective – when you see the bridge, the sound is from under the bridge. So the idea that we're always underground is communicated through sound'.[43] In order to work 'out of sync', she captured visuals and sounds separately, although sound formed her primary orientation. During the shoot, she initially arrived at each place to hear its acoustics, closing her eyes and listening through her headphones.

The primacy given to sounds contrasts with the objectifying visual logic of the panopticon, a model observational tower from which the film takes its name. For Michel Foucault, the panopticon forms the paradigm for state surveillance and it exemplifies vision as a dominating power.[44] In *Panoptic*, Burj El Murr and Hotel Beau Rivage are shot from low angles, emphasizing their commanding vision as they tower over the cityscape; they remind citizens that they can turn into observation targets at any moment. As Lefebvre writes, 'Verticality and great height have ever been the special expression of potentially violent power'.[45] These buildings functioned as means of terrorizing the population during the Civil War and still evoke fear today. Formerly Beirut's tallest building, Burj El Murr is a grey tower block with numerous square windows. Now pocked with

Figure 4.1 Burj El Murr, a former sniper hideout in the Lebanese Civil War, looms over Beirut like the many-eyed mythological giant Panoptes, surveying current citizens and signposting a traumatic past. *Panoptic* directed by Rana Eid © Abbout Productions 2017. All Rights Reserved.

bullet holes, it is a forlorn witness to the war when its upper floors were used by snipers and its lower floors for torture and imprisonment by militias. In her voice-over, Eid describes it as 'a giant that never closes its eyes', 'surveilling us', comparing it to the mythological giant Panoptes with his hundred eyes of which he would close fifty when asleep and keep a lookout with the remainder.

The buildings that Eid films are under military jurisdiction, revealing for her a 'military system beneath everything that's governing the country'.[46] *Panoptic* touches on surveillance and atrocities carried out by the Lebanese army and militias, and additionally by the Syrian government during the Syrian occupation of Lebanon (1976–2005), which are very delicate subjects. Eid is herself the daughter of an army general, who had died a few years previously. She initially made a rough cut featuring interviews with military personnel. However, these were discarded with creative input from her editor, Rania Stephan, who discerned that the film was ultimately about Eid's relationship with her deceased father, her city and her otosclerosis.[47] The task was then to find a corresponding form for these ideas. The voice-over became a requiem to Eid's father and a trip into the city guided by her personal memories: 'It was like I was walking with the city', she reflects.[48] On the voice-over, Eid also meditates on her otosclerosis, a hardening of ear tissue that threatened her with deafness and paralysis. Although it was successfully operated upon, her illness modified her listening; indeed, she believes 'The ear problem helped me how to hear. When you have a difficulty you can work with it, not against it'.[49] In the film, her personal history of disease is related to the political as she identifies her body with the city in a line that rings like a refrain: 'The city is calcified.' As the generation who were children during the war and 'discovered' it afterwards, 'we're physically and psychologically not ok,' she explained to me. 'The sicknesses that we have are extremely similar to the sicknesses of the city.'[50]

Like the psyche, the city has layers: past burdens are pushed underneath. In one scene, we enter Burj El Murr's interior and descend a shaft to its lower floors, which are heaped with rubbish. Water visibly seeps up from underground. 'It's like it's unclean, rotten', Eid remarked in 2018, somewhat prophetically, given the later Beirut Port explosion. 'The foundations of the city are going to collapse… Beirut has been destroyed several times. So, it can destroy itself. Bad energy goes somewhere. It's going to come back to us.'[51] Eid uses reflected sound – sound that reflects off other objects – in order to convey the atmosphere of these former torture chambers through their acoustics. She remarks, 'In those spaces, there is not much reverb because they are empty and rotten. So how sound moves in the space has changed completely. You cannot understand the dimension of the space. It's a labyrinth. In Burj El Murr there's no reverb at all because the walls are wet. It's strange, soundwise.'[52] In Beau Rivage, we hear a clanging door, dripping water and a dog inexplicably barking – reflected sounds that are like ghosts of that place. Plunging underwater off the city coast, the film discovers an armoured personnel carrier (APC) dumped on the seabed and travels across its rusty surface. Archive footage from the war is sonically and graphically matched to the underwater scene, as if the vehicle is steering through a war-devastated landscape, coming to life with these ghostly superimposed images.[53] The abandoned APC is both an actual and symbolic relic of the war that has been repressed underground. Crystallization of her ideas into this final form helped Eid to address sensitive topics, since it made the film more contemplative and less accusatory: 'During the editing process, Rania told me not to accuse – remember the core of your film, it's about mapping the city and understanding those layers. They [the perpetrators] will be accused automatically at the end of the film.'[54] Eid says the process taught her 'to be in action mode and not reaction mode. It helps the creative process not to be angry while doing things. Do it with love, not with hate. I was doing it because I love Beirut and I love the sounds of Beirut.'

Among the locations, the crew found Beau Rivage psychologically heaviest to film, since it evoked unresolved traumas under Syrian occupation. To Eid's knowledge, it was the first time that the hotel had been filmed. The Syrian occupation, a taboo subject at the time, remains difficult to comprehend. As Eid explains, when she was growing up, Israel was a more straightforward enemy, presenting a clear set of disputes and mutual hatred (her own home was bombed by Israel during the war, as shown in *Panoptic*). By contrast, relationships with Syrians were more fraternal, rendering them an ambiguous 'enemy'. At Beau Rivage, Eid's voice-over tells us, 'upper floors were used as a hotel, the lower ones to imprison and torture people'. Elsewhere the crew could rely on army presence for help, if needed. However, here they were completely alone, apart from a receptionist. Disorientating sounds added to the ghostly, oppressive atmosphere: 'we kept hearing a ticking clock and couldn't locate it'.[55] Strewn in the laundry were army uniforms and other clothes, intimating the Syrians' hurried departure in 2005. In the film we can see that the hotel is 'open' but it is eerily empty. Tables are laid out in the restaurant yet no guests materialize. In the sickly yellow lighting, old-fashioned fittings reveal the deserted rooms as a time capsule of their violent past. Traces of bloody hands can even be seen on the walls. Filmed in double-exposure, the image itself becomes ghost-like.

Despite Eid being an army general's daughter, which gave her a certain leverage, obtaining shooting permits for these military-controlled locations was a lengthy, difficult process: one-and-a-half years for the immigration detention centre, six months for Burj El Murr and almost two years for Beau Rivage. Despite gaining shooting permits from the army, *Panoptic* was denied a screening permit by General Security, which acts as the censorship authority in Lebanon, just before the film's scheduled première in Lebanon at the Beirut Days Festival. General Security asked Eid to remove scenes in the detention centre, because officers can be seen and it is illegal to film them. She refused. As a result, *Panoptic* cannot be exhibited in Lebanon (although, ironically, it is now available to watch within the country on Netflix). The authorities deny this is an act of censorship, presenting it instead as her decision not to re-edit the film. Eid was not surprised that the film was 'banned' because it deals with the military system, and it was released into a climate when it had become much harder to criticize the army and government.

Cairo

The idea that the city functions as an archive of the past and site of memory is implicit in films about Beirut and the Lebanese Civil War. However, while *Panoptic* explores symbolic sites that serve as monuments to a repressed, violent history, in Tamer el-Said's *In the Last Days of the City* the entire urban space is 'a sedimentation of the past'[56] that evokes memories. As Geraldine Pratt and Rose Marie San Juan argue in their study of cinema and urban space, documentary and fiction movies shot on location create an archive of the city by their inadvertent or deliberate recording of a specific time and space, sometimes becoming the only document of places swept away by processes of urban change. Films themselves produce memories, which 'can destabilise the present by giving uncanny inklings of all possible worlds that have existed and can be made to exist in the same space'.[57] The notion of film as an archive, capturing aspects of the city on the cusp of change or disappearance, and activating virtual possibilities in the past, imbues the psychogeographic strategy of *In the Last Days of the City* (henceforth referred to as *In the Last Days*).

In the Last Days was first conceived in 2006, at the time of the July War in Lebanon and the height of sectarian violence in Iraq following the US-led invasion, when Cairo appeared to be comparatively calm and stable. However, for its residents, living under economic pressures in the last years of Mubarak's presidency, there was a sense of the country and wider region being on the brink of explosion. A planned nine-month shoot began in 2008 but, due to financial and production issues, filming did not finish until about six weeks before the 2011 Egyptian Revolution. Completion of the editing took a further five years, as el-Said and his lead actor and producer Khalid Abdalla battled with financing their project and negotiating editors. In parallel with this, they launched Cimatheque, an alternative film centre, and the video collective Mosireen, both by-products of the film (discussed in the Introduction and Chapter 1), as well as participating in other films – and indeed in the Revolution itself. Like many other films in this book, *In the Last Days* was produced in one political environment, and released in another. However, as Abdalla puts it, it has a 'strong antenna' to changes that gripped Egypt and the region, having been, he says, 'made with foresight' and 'edited in hindsight'.[58]

This sensitive tuning to reality is helped by the film's hybrid form: although it is a fiction film, 'it was filmed more like a documentary film... or somewhere between the two'.[59] Abdalla explains, 'Cairo is a city that you rarely see on film in the way that we shot it. It's a very loud city and you'd have to have a big budget to recreate it fictionally, close off streets and fill them with extras.'[60] Since the filmmakers did not have the capacity to do this, they shot on location in the midst of the bustling city. This itself was beset by problems: 'very often we'd be shooting a scene and the best take would have someone looking into the camera'. At moments, fiction and documentary collide, raising questions of 'Is this really real? Were the events staged?' By registering elements 'that otherwise remain hidden, normalized, treated as if they don't exist', this approach, in

Abdalla's view, permits more to be seen than the documentary-type witnessing footage that became prevalent during the Revolution.[61] A witnessing approach was impossible anyway. *In the Last Days* was made under 'circumstances where the route to participate doesn't exist, unless you're immediately going to go to prison'; therefore, it necessitated a different way of filming, of 'making things visible that otherwise you can't witness'.[62] Greater investment of time and money was needed for editing, colour-grading and so on, in comparison to the urgency with which Mosireen's short videos were produced to witness crackdowns on street protests denied and twisted by state media narratives.

The hybridity of fiction and documentary in *In the Last Days* is reflected in its story, in which the protagonist Khalid is a filmmaker making a documentary, roaming the streets of Cairo armed with a camera in search of shots that will make sense of his reality. Along with this film-within-a-film, the narrative concerns his friendships, his endless search for a new flat and his break-up with his girlfriend Laila, a translator, who is about to leave Egypt forever. Friends from Beirut (Bassem) and Baghdad (Hassan and Tarek, the latter now living in Berlin) arrange to send him footage of their respective cities, creating constellations between these different metropolises in relation to stories of loss and departure. The films that Khalid and his friends are making and the film that we see converge, as we fluidly pass back and forth between them. El-Said's own flat was used as the location for Khalid's home, framed by a large window overlooking the city's rooftops. Suspended on a string is a magnifying glass in which the window view is reflected upside down – a fragile microcosm of the city which Laila, during her last visit, gently balances on her palm. The magnifying glass forms what Deleuze calls a crystal image, reflecting the film's *mise-en-abyme* structure.[63]

In the story, the aimlessness of Khalid's documentary exasperates his editor who exclaims, 'Beirut, Baghdad, your parents, Laila, Hanan, Maryam. What's the link? We just go round in circles!' *In the Last Days*, likewise, goes against the grain of goal-driven narrative, with an ineffectual hero who simply looks on instead of acting. Instead of the action-image, the film handles its subject 'contemplatively in terms of how you see'.[64] It might frustrate us narratively but deserves our attention because so much is happening in the image. 'The city gave us its gifts', Abdalla says, highlighting the film's ability to catch Cairo's actual sights and sounds as characters walk or drive around. As the protagonist resides in el-Said's flat, he meets the same characters that the director met in the street daily: an old woman selling carnations, a vagabond eating bread, watchful soldiers and street-children roaming through busy traffic. Often a scene starts

Figure 4.2 Khalid's magnifying glass reflects a fragile, microcosmic image of the city, encapsulating the mood of *déjà disparu*. *In the Last Days of the City* directed by Tamer el-Said © Zero Production 2016. All Rights Reserved.

with something else as the focus, then Khalid enters it. The film imbibes the atmosphere of the city's café culture and the faded grandeur of its downtown sandstone architecture. It arrests reflections in vehicle windshields, turning them into palettes mixed with the city's colours.

At the heart of *In the Last Days* is a sense of *déjà disparu* ('already disappeared') – that what made the city unique is slipping away, together with the desire to cling to elements that one loves in it.[65] The film develops this mood in different forms, from the personal (vanished times evoked by Khalid's photos with Laila and his friends) to the changing social and political fabric of the city. Pious stickers in apartment blocks intimate a rising tide of Islamism, while mannequins' apparel in a shop window is modestly changed to *abayehs*. *Déjà disparu* is also communicated through sound design. Sometimes the characters' dialogue is heard over their contemplative faces before they have spoken, a technique that lends the moment a quality of memory just as it is being lived.

Foreboding of tumultuous change was already implicit in the story, but with the Revolution 'suddenly everything that we had shot acquired a different meaning'.[66] Most of the editing took place after the shoot, during 'the heyday' of the Revolution and 'as the revolution turned to counterrevolution' and it was finished 'when the counterrevolution became the new order'.[67] There were about 300 hours of footage. Contrary to how a fiction film is normally made, since the costs would be prohibitive, *In the Last Days* was 'written' during the edit. 'Throughout that period, the footage kept reflecting different intensities', Abdalla comments. The editing became 'a filtration process. Rather than trying to express ourselves, it was more a matter of finding what the footage was trying to express.'⁶⁸ The film works like an 'unconscious optics', a notion elaborated by Walter Benjamin, registering details that have become more significant with time.⁶⁹

For example, in one scene, the four friends gather on a rooftop overlooking Tahrir Square, not yet the revolutionary symbol it became after 2011; the choice of location was fortuitous. When the friends drive around downtown Cairo in an open truck, with Khalid angling his camera and microphone upwards, we pass buildings filmed from this canted perspective, among them the art deco Radio Cinema with its distinctive vertical tower, later adopted as a TV studio by comedian Bassem Youssef before his satirical show *El Bernameg* (2011–14) was shut down and he was forced into exile. In another scene, Khalid joins street celebrations after Egypt wins an African Cup football match four – nil: fans approach his camera making a four symbol with their hands, a signal that later came to imply support of the Muslim Brotherhood following the 2013 Rabea Massacre in which army and security forces killed hundreds of pro-Morsi protestors (*rabea* means 'fourth' in Arabic). The Egyptian authorities subsequently criminalized the gesture.⁷⁰ Additionally, the film captures the 2010 demonstrations, when protestors called for the downfall of military rule prior to the Revolution, an action that now takes us by surprise because it has been erased from official history and collective memory. Throughout the film, we hear radio news broadcasts from the time. One of them refers to a military campaign in Yemen, which also strikes a prescient note, pointing forward to the Yemen Civil War (2014–).

In terms of its appeal to the international market, *In the Last Days* is untimely. When it was being made, the spotlight was on Iraq and there was a lack of interest in Egypt; then, after the Revolution, Egypt became a sought-after topic but the film's production was so protracted that, by the time it was released, interest in Egypt had faded and moved elsewhere, to Syria, for example. In another sense, however, the film is very timely. In the light of subsequent events, tensions captured by its footage have become internationally readable, whereas previously they were readable mainly at a local level. In Abdalla's view, this owes to the foresight and hindsight with which the film was made: the feelings it intimates that 'this can't go on forever' and that the region is on the brink of explosion were confirmed when it exploded spectacularly on the world stage in 2011, turning what 'we could already see' into 'something that everyone can see, relative to their own closeness or farness to things.'⁷¹

While *In the Last Days* is relatively direct, pointing to specific realities in its mapping of the city, it remains quite elliptical. Many elements that it 'captures naively', as Abdalla says, 'require a lot of intellectual engagement to unpack. And, in turn, that unpacking reveals why it's so culturally dangerous, why it's potent in dealing with uncomfortable territories.'[72] There is speculation that the film did not receive a screening permit in Egypt because it showed the 2010 protest that anticipated the 2011 Revolution. While the filmmakers were always aware that there might be problems screening it in Egypt, the most significant fact explaining its controversy is that it was produced and released in different political climates. The film began under Mubarak, when it gained official shooting permits and, apart from infrastructural constraints that dogged the filmmakers throughout, was 'made freely' in terms of the strategy that it adopts.[73] It was completed during the counterrevolutionary military regime led by Sisi, when El Said was told he did not have the right papers and instructed to remove a couple of references to the military (to which he agreed for the Egyptian release). The film was invited to screen at the Cairo International Film Festival, yet it was withdrawn at the last minute and the same happened at Sharm el-Sheikh Film Festival. Gradually, it became apparent that the film had been banned, albeit (like *Panoptic*) without an official stamp.

Damascus

In the documentary short *A Day and a Button* (2015), the director Azza Hamwi walks the streets of Damascus in 2014, filming with a camera hidden in her bag. Her hidden camera technique reflects the constraints under which independent Syrian filmmakers operated during the Syrian uprising and subsequent war. As we saw with *For Sama* in Chapter 1, filmmakers had greater freedom of expression in rebel-held Free Syrian Army areas in comparison to areas ruled by either Assad's regime or ISIS, where much filming was carried out in secrecy, at peril of their lives. Hamwi herself uses a pseudonym to protect her anonymity. With her, we traverse the regime-controlled area of Damascus in the film's first half, then an opposition-held area in the second, crossing different zones of freedom of expression. Made in a playful-critical spirit similar to that of the Situationists, the film intuitively adapts the practice of *dérive* for its risky circumstances. It not only shows us the divided city of Damascus from the street-level perspective of one of its inhabitants, but also how a seemingly mundane recording of an urban walk can be an act of resistance.

City walks in European cinema, shot on streets such as those of Paris and Rome, are often read in terms of the *flâneur*, who is traditionally male and upper-class. As Bruno remarks on this gendering, 'A male loiterer is a *flâneur*; a female is a "streetwalker." Denied the space, and pleasure, of *flâneurie*, woman's territorial horizon is phantasmatically as well as literally restricted'.[74] Constraints imposed by gender and class are perhaps even greater when the act of walking is considered in Middle Eastern cities, given traditions of gender segregation (discussed in Chapter 2). As a woman venturing into war-torn and militarized public space, lacking the leisure of loitering, because of her gender as well as security risks, Hamwi is decidedly not a *flâneur*; she is, rather, a *dériveur*. Unlike a conventional stroll, her filmic walk through the city is alert to psychogeographical effects, making visible what is invisible in state discourses.

The film begins by showing Hamwi's act of hiding the camera in preparation for filming in public space. She inserts the camera into her shoulder bag and sews a lace bow over it to conceal it. This takes place in a homely domestic interior; however, it is overshadowed by hints of threat: the sinister image of her cat pawing an insect caught in a net curtain while, visible and audible through the window, a regime helicopter hovers overhead – 'a flying demonstration' that, Hamwi remarks in voice-over, is actually 'a flash mob protest that ends with the security forces firing stray bullets'.

Outside, Hamwi walks with the camera filming at thigh-level, pointing at her shoes and bouncing against her body, accompanied by her clothes' rustling sounds. The concealed camera not only creates a peripatetic point-of-view but also an embodied, first-person perspective on the city. Debord describes the *dérive* as 'a technique of rapid passage through varied ambiences'.[75] As she walks, Hamwi's camera registers fleeting aural and visual impressions of the city. Through the lace, we glimpse sunlight on railings, an old, mildewed wall and a corrugated iron garage door with the official Syrian flag painted on it: red, white and black with two green stars. 'This place has not changed', Hamwi reflects, implicitly contrasting the regime-controlled area with the rebel-held one. Each area is distinguished by its colours, both the symbolic ones of the flag and everyday colours that reflect conditions in that place.

In the regime-controlled area, Bashar al-Assad's voice and image predominate. We hear his words, repeated as a refrain throughout the first half: 'Today we meet at a cross-point in the history of our country!' In the Arab world before the 2010–11 uprisings, public space was governed by the cult of the leader.[76] When Hamwi enters a square decorated with al-Assad's portraits, his voice resounds again, affirming his continued control of public space. Even roadblocks and vendors' carts are painted in the official flag's colours, and graffiti validates the leader: *manhibak ya Bashar* ('we love you Bashar'). The film catches strains of a popular military song ('I wish I were a soldier at the checkpoint beneath her house. I'd stay up all day and night, just to take her ID card'), prompting Hamwi's voice-over to move from the identity of place to the national identity card, the carrying of which is compulsory in Syria, although 'you'll be arrested with or without it'. Her movement through the city reveals its structures of power, in which freedoms are incessantly under attack as citizens are under constant surveillance and the watchful gaze of their pictured leader. She wanders into a narrow, cobbled street in the old city with cafes serving *manoushe* (flatbread with savoury fillings). Suddenly, a man stops her and points, saying 'Forbidden, young lady'. The moment recalls Debord's statement: 'cities have psychogeographical contours, with constant currents, fixed points and vortexes that strongly discourage entry or exit from certain zones'.[77] An arbitrary no-entry point demonstrates that this part of the city is more closed than open, gesturing to government and military sites to which civilians are usually denied access except when they are arrested and disappeared.

The screen goes black and, when the picture returns, we are riding in the front passenger seat of a car with a bullet-smashed windshield. Hamwi has taken a different route, moving into the 'liberated', rebel-held zone, only ten minutes from the regime-controlled area. Amidst sounds of explosions, we enter into bright daylight. No longer is the camera hidden; here, one can film openly. The liberated zone is like 'a different planet' although it is part of the same city, Hamwi observes in her voice-over. The surrounding urban space is dishevelled. We pass a collapsed building where a twisted curtain rail and curtain can be glimpsed in its ruins: this was once someone's house, perhaps their living room. Hamwi meditates on the division of land that sometimes arbitrarily throws people under different zones of control: 'Maybe they chose it, maybe they didn't'. Smiling children, wearing bright casual clothes, travel to school on a cart and queue for sparse food. Their colourfulness contrasts with the grey, dilapidated buildings whose facades droop to the ground, a witness to the people's stand against the regime for which they were constantly bombed and besieged while being deserted by the outside world. At a demonstration, people clap and chant an anti-Assad song. They are holding flags, both a black flag indicating a group with an Islamic affiliation and the Syrian opposition flag with its red stars. Several demonstrators are openly filming, marking this as a place where Assad no longer rules. Yet, the sound of an aeroplane overhead reminds us of his control of airspace.

Journeying back by car, we return to the regime-controlled area's warm earthen colours. The camera is hidden once again, lending a restricted view on the landscape as it hurtles past. Assad's billboards line the streets and buildings are intact; this area does not get bombed. Through the voice-over, Hamwi articulates her struggle with her identity, located in the city but torn apart by the two different Syrias existing in it: 'I can't figure out my identity anymore'. As darkness falls, the screen fades to black and helicopter sounds are heard again, she longs to return to her bed and her cat. Merlin Coverley states, 'The *dériveur*... conduct[s] a psychogeographical investigation and is expected to return home having noted the ways in which the areas traversed resonate with particular moods and ambiences'.[78] In a similar fashion, Hamwi makes psychogeographic observations on place and identity. Urban walking with a hidden camera, she records random sights and sounds, along with the different ambiances of the regime-controlled and liberated areas. In the spirit of the *dérive*, her film maps Damascus in a new, playful fashion, exploring the psychological rift of the two Syrias behind its official facade.

Conclusion

Psychogeography is a creative strategy that allows filmmakers to explore under the skin of official representations of the city, unearthing its hidden psychological and historical layers. It tells the story of the city from the space of the inhabitant, often a pedestrian walking on foot: an intimate, perspective 'from below' that contrasts with the view 'from above' characteristic of state and international media. Through location shooting, capturing walls, ruins and impacts of the urban environment upon residents, psychogeography overcomes some of the infrastructural and storytelling constraints that hamper filmmakers as well as offering opportunities for clandestine filmmaking. In the next chapter, we turn to the creative possibilities afforded by the road movie, featuring movement across diverse landscapes in a moving vehicle that is simultaneously a private and public space.

5

Road movies

While the films in the last chapter featured travel, what distinguishes the road movie is the importance of the road and moving vehicles to the story and characters. The genre is usually identified with Hollywood films such as *Easy Rider* (1969) and *Thelma & Louise* (1991) which recount journeys of rebellion and self-discovery, often with the thrilling, forward impulse of action entertainment. The open road tapering to a vanishing point on the horizon bears the promise of freedom and mobility. When reworked in other contexts, the road movie often dramatizes contrasts between the genre's mythologies and the starker realities of the territories in which the films are set. Kay Dickinson has observed how the fantasy of the open road is subverted in Palestinian 'roadblock' movies of the Second Intifada era (2000–c.2005) which confront curfews, checkpoints and segregated roads.[1] Laura Marks finds that the resulting obstructed movement is not confined to road movies from Palestine but belongs to a wider Arab genre that occurs in other places where 'roads are blocked off for specifically political reasons'.[2]

However, the delayed or interrupted journey is not unique to the Arab world. As this chapter shows, it is part of the genre's broader connection to crisis, and it is not the only feature of road movies from the Middle East. While filmmakers from the region have adapted road movie motifs to expose restrictions on freedom and movement, the genre has also presented them with creative ways of overcoming these obstacles. The road movie, as we shall see, is not just about vehicular traffic; it is also about the tactics that enable films to be produced and to circulate both within and outside geopolitical borders. With my case-study films, I sketch out three tactical insights drawn from the genre. Firstly, blocked passage stimulates creativity, as illustrated in Amber Fares's *Speed Sisters* (2015). Secondly, the vehicle is a simultaneously private and public space, lending itself to creative uses pioneered by Iranian directors Abbas Kiarostami and Mania Akbari and further innovatively utilized in Jafar Panahi's *Taxi Tehran* (2015) and Lara Zeidan's *Three Centimetres* (2018). Finally, the road movie's foreground and background dynamics of characters and landscapes marry popular appeal with political consciousness, as deployed in different ways by Ali Mostafa's *From A to B* (2014) and Roy Dib's *Mondial 2010* (2013).

The road movie often arises from, and explores, crisis. Prototypical road films such as *The Grapes of Wrath* (1940) established important motifs of the genre during the Great Depression, when the Dust Bowl crisis forced Americans to migrate westwards in pursuit of work. In the voyage form that Gilles Deleuze identifies as characteristic of the time-image that he claims arose in Italian neorealism, protagonists take unpredictable journeys through real post-war landscapes; the initial quest is frequently interrupted and delayed by periods of stasis.[3] Like psychogeography, discussed in the last chapter, road movies permit real or staged background events to enter into, and sometimes disrupt, the story. In *Voyage to Italy* (1953), for example, a religious procession literally arrests a couple's road trip through Naples. Through windscreen shots, now a genre staple, the car acts like a camera, capturing the surrounding landscape and people – paradoxically, by means of an enclosed, private capsule. As Nadia Yaqub notes, the road plays a central role in Palestinian literature and cinema, dating back to the 1948 Nakba that saw over 700,000 Palestinians expelled from their homeland and generated a refugee crisis leaving millions of Palestinians 'on the road'.[4] In *The Duped* (1972), an early Middle Eastern road movie, three undocumented Palestinian refugees take a fateful journey across the Iraqi desert in search of work, dependent on a Palestinian driver, who has legal status, to smuggle them inside a water tank across the border to Kuwait. The film exemplifies what Rebecca Stein calls '*discrepant mobility*', a term that she uses for the effects of the 1948 expulsions and limits upon free movement in occupied Palestine, but that has relevance to the broader Middle East and beyond.[5]

In this chapter, discrepant mobility is registered not only in the stories that road movies from the region tell, but also the circumstances under which they were made. Since it often involves being on the road, filmmaking rests precariously on the ever-shifting ground of travel permits and other obstacles to free movement. Palestinian filmmaker Annemarie Jacir, discussing her experiences of working in her homeland, remarks that, added to the usual constraints of independent filmmaking, there are the 'Kafkaesque restrictions of military occupation – which are not just the obvious ones of checkpoints and permits – but come up in the most mundane and basic ways: picking up a crew member from the airport, speaking Arabic on set and having the police called on you, and renting equipment.'[6] Palestinians with West Bank identity cards are barred from Israel unless they obtain special permits, reinforcing just how different Palestinian experience is from that of Israeli and foreign passport holders, who can move between Israel and the West Bank seamlessly.⁷ Conflicts impair freedom of movement for filmmaking more generally. As we saw with *Freedom Fields* and *Sana'a: A Symphony* in Chapters 1 and 4, closures of international airports and other restrictions on mobility during the civil wars in Libya and Yemen jeopardized the completion of these films and altered their creative approach.

Free movement is equally crucial for film distribution. When Jacir curated a Palestinian film festival in New York in 2003, it was a major feat to obtain the videotapes for the screenings, due to checkpoints around Palestinian towns and curfews in the West Bank and Gaza.⁸ Since then, technological advances such as digital formats and fast broadband, where this is available, have made it easier to submit films to festivals. Or, failing that, as the Iranian director Jafar Panahi says, 'All you need to do is find a traveler, somebody who is going abroad, and give them your movie in a USB flash drive'.⁹ Even before the digital age, Iranian filmmakers relied on travellers to smuggle films in their suitcases to international festivals; Panahi recalls storing his films in packages bearing labels of films by other directors in order to deter suspicion.¹⁰ Transporting films in suitcases remains a fallback during periods of prolonged Internet blackout in Iran, as happened in the run-up to the 2019 Sydney Persian Film Festival.

People, like films, have traditionally relied on roads and other routes to travel to festivals and screenings. Jacir flew from Palestine for the London première of *Wajib* (which is Arabic for 'duty'), tweeting that it was her *wājib* to attend.¹¹ She regards such attendance as part of her role as director: 'We make films to share with people – and this is a way to share them, to connect to your audience, to meet them and speak with them'.¹² Nonetheless, many Middle Eastern filmmakers, along with their cast and crew, are prevented from attending international screenings by visa denials. The difficulty of obtaining visas reinforces a system of differential access to mobility depending on what passport(s) one has. For example, when *Freedom Fields* (a documentary about a Libyan women's football team) premiered at the Toronto International Film Festival, Fadwa was the only cast member whose visa application was approved. Later, the director Naziha Arebi was able to bring nine of the women to Amsterdam for the IDFA festival, where they livened up the proceedings by ululating during the screening. Due to President Trump's so-called 'Muslim' ban, Arebi, herself a holder of both Libyan and British passports, was barred from attending the Blackstar Film Festival, confirming her belief that, when travelling to the United States, being half Libyan cancels the benefits of her British passport.[13]

Further restrictions hinder filmmakers from travelling within the region. As artist-filmmaker Larissa Sansour explains, against the background of hostilities between Lebanon and Israel, 'It's very hard for Palestinians to go to Lebanon, which is just next door. I entered there on my Russian passport because my mother is Russian.'[14] Palestinians travelling to Lebanon on a Palestinian passport are rarely granted visas. Similarly, the Lebanese cannot enter Israel to go to Palestine. In the most extreme cases, travel bans are imposed on filmmakers. Jafar Panahi's sentencing by the Iranian state prohibits him from travelling abroad as well as from filmmaking. This excludes him from attending international festivals, although he can travel freely throughout Iran. For Panahi and other filmmakers whose work is featured in this chapter, the road movie has served as a creative solution to these restrictions through tactical insights such as the following.

Tactical insight #1: Blocked passage is a stimulus to creativity

As Marks writes, 'blocked movement intensifies creative energy'.[15] Obstacles can force people to be creative, in order to find a way around them; for many, this is a form of survival amidst absurd and harsh constraints. This is true of both the filmmakers and their characters in these road movies, who are shown as creative agents, not victims in states of dependency, even as the films highlight injustices of restricted movement. For example, in Amber Fares's film, Marah, Noor, Mona and Betty, along with their captain Maysoon, are 'the Speed Sisters', an all-female Palestinian motor-racing team. They compete against men and against each other for the title of fastest woman. Initially backed by the Palestinian Motorsport Federation as independent racers, they were formed into a team with funding from East Jerusalem's British Consulate.[16] Living in Palestine at the time, Canadian-Lebanese director Fares was first hired to film promotional videos for them, then realized the potential for a feature documentary when she saw 'a classic racing dynamic' in Marah and Betty's rivalry.[17] Betty hails from a wealthy family of racers. Striking a pose next to her car, she declares, 'Betty Saadeh – I'm a brand'. In contrast, Marah lives in a refugee camp in Jenin; her mother is a driving instructor and her father, Khaled, is a dental technician, whose family was expelled from Haifa in 1948. *Speed Sisters* follows the team through two racing seasons; its first half is dedicated to the first season, which

Figure 5.1 Roadblocks become creative obstacles for the Speed Sisters, an all-female Palestinian motor-racing team. *Speed Sisters* directed by Amber Fares © SocDoc Studios 2015. All Rights Reserved.

Betty wins, while the other half ends with Marah's victory in the second season, despite the Federation's inconsistent and arbitrary rules favouring Betty over her.

Speed Sisters makes knowing references to the racing movie, a subgenre of the road movie characterized by racing car choreography, as well as racing rivalries such as that between Brazilian Formula One champion Ayrton Senna and his fellow driver Alain Frost in the documentary *Senna* (2010). The film's sound design consists of motors and skidding tyres, as well as a medley of Arab heavy metal, rap and pop songs. With their mobile protagonists, race and road movies contain thrilling possibilities, not least of which is the thrill of high speed that the Speed Sisters revel in. These women are determined to embrace the highways, despite obstacles in their path. When Noor appears on an Aljazeera TV show, the irony of speed rallies taking place in Palestine is not lost on the presenters, because every few minutes you encounter a checkpoint. 'Exactly', she replies. 'We don't have open spaces where we can put cones and train freely'. Road and race movie fantasies of automotive speed and empowerment are juxtaposed with the shrinking of Palestinian space, a reality that the team confronts regularly when they are training. Near Ofer Israeli detention centre, they found a small empty lot where they train in the vicinity of a watchtower, soldiers and barbed wire. One day on their way to their training ground, soldiers signal for them to stop their car. Betty steps out and approaches the soldiers –

as a daring driver, she is accustomed to taking risks and assumes that a pretty, blonde woman like her will not be harmed. Suddenly, she is shot in the back though, luckily, not severely hurt. The film captures the moment. Fares recalls, 'We were just about to leave and then I yelled at Lucy [the cinematographer] to turn on the camera', which she did, then Betty was hit within seconds.[18] The scene's gravity is leavened with humour when Betty later recovers and Maysoon and Noor make light-hearted fun of her. Noor points out that, if you're Palestinian, Israeli soldiers are indiscriminate: they don't care if you're blond, dark, ugly or pretty. Despite the injustices of living under occupation, neither the film nor the characters dramatically dwell on such moments; they move on with characteristic Palestinian resilience.

Early on, Marah repurposes her family's black Volkswagen, making it lighter and faster by removing its glass, wipers and outer steel – an act that reflects her economic precarity. The family previously lived under twenty-four-hour military curfew, when they were only allowed to leave their home for two hours a day to buy food and water. Khaled, who knows that curfews can be imposed at any time, toils long hours in his workshop, manufacturing dental prosthetics to support Marah financially and buy her a new car. With their Jerusalem IDs, Maysoon and Noor can travel to the sea at Jaffa whenever they want, unlike Marah, Betty and Mona whose West Bank IDs require them to obtain permits. For most West Bank Palestinians, visiting the sea is a form of freedom of movement beyond their ken, as shown when Marah gets a permit (with the film crew's help, Fares explained to me). But, first, she must walk through the turnstiles at Qalandia checkpoint, while Noor simply drives through with her Israeli numberplate.[19] Arriving at the sea, Marah dives in, fully clothed. 'They took the most beautiful place we had', she exclaims. 'Imagine if we could come here every day!' – a politically charged statement that articulates a national longing for freedom of movement, open spaces and connection with the land and sea. It gathers emotional force from earlier scenes that established her limitations, which are temporarily transcended on the road trip.

Cinematically, Fares wanted to counterbalance the liberation of racing with the obstacles of living under occupation: 'The car is an appendage for race car drivers... It's their own private space, which gives them freedom, even with roadblocks. They have some degree of control where to go'.[20] This freedom is contrasted with what can be seen outside the cars as they drive through checkpoints surrounded by Israel's road signage and Separation Wall. The races happen in repurposed venues in different cities, taking us on a journey through Palestine, starting with a wholesale vegetable market in Jenin, then Bethlehem's presidential airstrip and the Jericho security forces academy. The racecourse itself is filled with obstacles. Fares approached it as 'a microcosm of the occupation' – with its roadblocks, rules changing at a whim and an autocratic disdain for questioning, 'it is very similar to what the occupation is to them [the Palestinians].'[21] In the film each race is introduced with a map of Palestine, indicating the location of the city, and a diagram of the track with its obstacles. Gopros (action cameras) mounted on windscreens inside the cars enable us to experience the track from the characters' perspectives, as they wend in and out of roadblocks.

Inevitably, the filming of *Speed Sisters* was affected by mobility restrictions. The Israeli army stopped the film crew on several occasions and, once, they were pulled over by the Palestinian police. Fares was also told to stop filming at military checkpoints which, she emphasizes, is a red line:

> Once you live there, you understand the boundaries and how far you can push and how far you can't. Until you become comfortable in that environment. As a foreigner you have to learn that stuff. I was able to make *Speed Sisters* because I'd been living there for years before I had even picked up a camera to film the girls, so I had an understanding of what the game is and who all the players are and how far I can push things. At a checkpoint, if a soldier comes up to me and tells me to stop, I'm going to stop, I'm not going to push it. But you try to get away with what you can.[22]

Despite this, Fares believes that 'It is easier to film in the West Bank than it is in a lot of places that I've filmed [including the US]. Gaza's a little bit trickier.'[23] For her, this is because 'In Palestine, people are much more used to having cameras around, whether it's NGO films or the news. For a long time, it was such a hotbed of the news cycle that people are more open to it.'[24] This cemented her view that 'each place has its own constraints that you have to deal with in making a movie and Palestine has its set that aren't any better or any worse' than anywhere else.

Nevertheless, as Fares acknowledges, her Canadian passport lends her greater freedom of movement than the majority of Palestinians: 'I don't have the same constraints and, in terms of the mechanics of the occupation, none of that applies to me.'[25] Furthermore, being a foreigner, unable to speak the languages well enough to understand underlying tensions, she admits that she may have been unaware of some of the constraints upon her: 'In Palestine, I have been saved so many times by a shop owner who said "come in", when there's a clash, "don't go down that street, there's something going on".[26] At the same time, although she is not Palestinian, as an Arab Muslim woman living in Palestine, Fares enjoyed an insider/outsider status that gave her unprecedented access to the community, helping her to build relationships with the women and their families. She believes her gender was another factor that 'allowed me to move in those spaces', pointing out that, unlike men who often receive rough treatment from Israeli soldiers, as a woman, 'there's an underestimation of what you're doing', which means 'you can get away with more'.[27] However, as Betty's experience shows, gender exceptionalism does not always work.

The Speed Sisters appealed to Fares precisely because of her insider/outsider identity: 'I'm not even sure if a Palestinian would look at those women and see an opportunity of making a film about them because they may see them as too fringe or not really telling the Palestinian story. Ultimately, my goal was to show women in a context where people from my hometown in Canada could identify with them.'[28] Breaking international audiences' stereotypes of Arab women was uppermost in her mind. This influenced how Fares handled pressure to show pushback from the community while the film was in development: 'Anytime we pitched it in the West, people were like, where's the tension? Obviously, these women just can't be racing like this. There must be some guy or a father who didn't like them racing.'[29] In contrast to Western assumptions of oppressed Arab/Muslim women, *Speed Sisters* shows men being overwhelmingly supportive of the women's ambitions, particularly in the story of Marah and her father but also in conversations with male racers. Instead of trying to manufacture or amplify the disapproval, which did exist, Fares decided to convey it more subtly, in the manner that the women experienced it. In one scene, Maysoon reads out comments from the Internet after Noor's Aljazeera interview, among them complaints that sports and fashion are not the way to liberate Palestine and that the women should focus on reading the Quran instead. Fares explains, 'You want to show a place in a critical light, but I also don't want to take liberties of criticizing it with a viewpoint that's just North American'.[30] She believes that this approach, together with the fact that *Speed Sisters* was made and edited in Palestine (with a Palestinian editor and co-producer) benefitted its reception there as well as abroad. In Palestine, audiences could see it as a reflection of their lives, including the support networks that exist. Internationally, the genre enabled the film to appeal on different levels and attract audiences beyond the usual activist crowd.

Tactical insight #2: The vehicle is a simultaneously public and private space

'Inside the car is another world' runs *Speed Sisters*'s tagline. The vehicle belongs outdoors yet it is enclosed and sealed off from the street, making it a space that is both public and private. The film historian A. L. Rees writes, 'the car is a social machine; only racing cars are for soloists, the rest carry passengers'.[31] Although we might note that, in *Speed Sisters*, racing is also a team sport, the road and the vehicle are certainly sociable settings in many road movies, affording opportunities for conversation and chance encounters. In classical Hollywood, it gave rise to the genre motif of 'the people', as in *It Happened One Night* (1934) where the protagonist finds herself in an enforced intimacy with fellow travellers from different social classes. During the Production Code era (1934–68), Hollywood filmmakers were alive to the car's creative possibilities: not only did the set-up of '[t]wo people in the front seat... make for easy classical framing and keep the dialogue going', it allowed sexual tensions to be intimated at a time when sex was not permitted onscreen.[32]

The car as a vehicle for freedom of expression has been utilized in different creative ways in films from the region. An influential practitioner of this strategy, the Iranian director Kiarostami has frequently organized his films around the car and road trips.[33] For him, the car's appeal is twofold. Firstly, as he suggests in his documentary *10 on Ten* (2004), the act of sitting side-by-side, rather than face-to-face, encourages people to talk more freely, since they can make eye contact only when they want to. Secondly, the car's mobility compensates for the relatively static camera and supplies a varying backdrop. In the feature film *Ten* (2002), Kiarostami uses the car to bypass Iranian film censorship codes that stipulate wearing of *hejāb* at all times, even at home when women would not normally veil themselves, which prevents realistic portrayal of intimate conversations in domestic interiors. *Ten* is shot almost entirely inside a car, filmed with two digital cameras affixed to the dashboard. Its narrative consists of ten dialogues between a female driver, Mania, and her passengers who, apart from her son, are all female – non-professional actors playing versions of themselves. According to Mania Akbari (who stars in the film along with her own car and family members) the actors were not aware that they were being filmed, which raises profound ethical questions, as mentioned in Chapter 2. In his interview with Geoff Andrew, Kiarostami claimed he sometimes directed from the backseat or followed in another car, monitoring the performances on a screen.[34] With these self-imposed constraints – including the single set (the car), limited camera angles and a remote director, and the absence of a film crew – he showed the creative possibilities for making films this way. The car's public/private space provides the stage for intimate conversations that touch upon sensitive topics, such as women's rights in Iran. In one scene, Mania's passenger, a young woman whose fiancé has left her, removes her veil, revealing her shorn hair – an act that appears to be a personal gesture of freedom (since shaving her hair removes the need for the veil to cover it up) as well as a sign of mourning.

After *Ten*, Akbari turned to making her own, low-budget digital films. Intense conversations held in moving vehicles are a recurring feature of her Iranian movies. They maintain a dialogue with *Ten*, although the latter was made during a traumatic period in her and her child's life, as mentioned in Chapter 2. For example, *20 Fingers* (2004) consists of six episodes, each portraying a conversation between a man and a woman (played by Akbari and Bijan Daneshmand) travelling through Tehran or neighbouring areas by car, motorcycle, telecabin, train or boat. The film leaves it open as to whether the man and woman represent the same pair or different couples. They speak about sexual relations with unprecedented frankness for Iranian cinema at the time. In the different episodes, the woman boldly articulates her desires, broaching topics such as abortion, adultery and homosexuality. Each episode is improvised around Akbari's script and filmed in one long take, a self-imposed constraint that enhances the intensity of these dialogues that are all about women's alienation from and desire to have control over their bodies. The body and sex formed 'a great part of the battles I had to fight as a woman raised in an Islamic society', where a woman's body is expected to be pure and virginal, Akbari explains. 'For many men, it is crucial to be the first owners of that body… Later it became the subject of my films, this instinctive understanding of women's situation, that things can't continue the way they are defined.'[35] The opening scene of *20 Fingers* implies an act of rape in the darkness of a car's backseat when a man attempts to ascertain if his girlfriend is a virgin after she relates a childhood anecdote of playing 'doctor' with a male cousin. Akbari's Iranian films were made underground and none of them have been officially screened in Iran 'but a lot of people watched them on the black market.'[36] Having left Iran in 2012 during a wave of government crackdowns on filmmakers, she still makes films and installation art about female desire and the body in exile in the UK. However, she now faces different types of constraints and moving vehicles with their private/public spaces are no longer prominent in her work.

In Jafar Panahi's *Taxi Tehran*, his third feature since his 2010 sentence, a succession of passengers take a ride in a taxi, among them a DVD smuggler named Omid, a woman with her injured husband, Panahi's argumentative young niece Hana, two women carrying their goldfish to a shrine and the defence lawyer Nasrin Sotoudeh. The taxi driver is none other than Panahi himself, disguised in a grey beret. Like *Ten*, *Taxi* takes place inside a car, largely filmed by a dashboard-mounted camera. Its use of the car as a private/public space is shaped by its clandestine conditions of production and mobility restrictions imposed on the director. All Panahi's post-filmmaking ban films have necessitated sealed locations. This is because, as he says himself, 'Anybody who wants to use public locations in Iran for making a movie has to have permission from the government... Otherwise he or she will be arrested by the police and their equipment confiscated'.[37] Panahi's first two films after the ban, *This Is Not a Film* (2011) and *Closed Curtain* (2013), were made in indoor, private spaces: his Tehran apartment and his beach house near the Caspian Sea, respectively. This production constraint gives *Closed Curtain* its title, as well as its story about a filmmaker trying to hide his dog (following an Iranian law banning such pets in the home) by keeping the curtains closed. Fundamentally, the black drapes across the window are there to conceal the shoot 'so that nobody from outside could see us'.[38] Mahsa Salamati argues that all of Panahi's post-ban films involve the 'creation of "other spaces"', or what she calls, using Foucault's term, 'heterotopias': 'Once we enter these spaces we are bound to stay, as the camera never leaves'.[39] On a more literal level, however, the camera never leaves these confined spaces for safety reasons.

In order not to attract attention and minimize risks to his collaborators, Panahi employs a limited cast and crew in his post-ban films. Despite these precautions, Mojtaba Mirtahmasb, co-director of *This Is Not a Film*, had his passport confiscated and later the same happened to Kambuzia Partovi and Maryam Moqadam, co-director and actress of *Closed Curtain*, when they were due to leave the country to attend the Berlinale premiere – repercussions that curtailed their own freedom of movement. 'That's why I really have to reconsider what I'm doing and come up with a small-scale project that I can shoot and sound-record myself without involving other people', Panahi explains. 'By necessity my movies are becoming more and more minimalistic'.[40] It is also in this light that we can understand Panahi's own appearances in these films: 'if there is a part I can play, I just do it myself'.[41] Not only, or primarily, instances of authorial self-reflexivity, which is how they are usually interpreted, these cameo or 'star' appearances are a product of constraints under which he is working.

While these restrictions would be limiting to most filmmakers, they are particularly so for Panahi who regards himself as a socially committed director, reflecting his surroundings in his movies. Before the ban, he filmed in bustling, urban, exterior spaces. At the time of *Closed Curtain*, he commented, 'When you go inside, you feel so limited. In our case, we couldn't even look out the window because of security'.[42] By contrast, his next two films, *Taxi Tehran* and *3 Faces* (2018), are both road movies – the former set in Tehran, the latter in the remote countryside. By means of the car, a sealed, private space within the public realm, and small digital cameras, they permit him to shoot outside and reconnect with the social side of his filmmaking. In *Taxi Tehran*, the shared taxi is a social machine. It enables Panahi to capture the city and its inhabitants via the road movie motif of 'the people', as passengers share brief encounters within the vehicle. Their conversations touch on debates on human rights and cinema as well as offering occasions for much merriment and humour. Unlike *Ten*, the dashboard camera points inwards *and* outwards, turning the windscreen into a mobile viewpoint on the city. It is supplemented by other cameras within the narrative reality to follow the action from different angles. For example, when the injured man and his wife scramble onto the backseat, Panahi lends Omid his mobile phone to record the man's last will. Panahi not only stars; he is a cinematographer, too, manually turning the dashboard camera to film events outside the car. While he is certainly in charge of the location, 'the one who decides what part of the reality outside is to be captured',[43] *Taxi Tehran* is not just a self-reflexive self-portrait but makes creative use of the vehicle as a social ensemble.

Figure 5.2 Jafar Panahi's role as the taxi driver in *Taxi Tehran* is not just a self-reflexive gesture but results from the constraints under which he is working. *Taxi Tehran* directed by Jafar Panahi © Jafar Panahi Film Productions 2015. All Rights Reserved.

Sotoudeh, whose cameo is significant, shared with Panahi the Sakharov Prize for Freedom of Thought in 2012. Known for defending political prisoners, Sotoudeh has herself been repeatedly imprisoned for her work and, like Panahi, has been banned from leaving Iran and practising her profession. During the conversation she quips, 'Although you are released from prison, the outside world is only a bigger prison', since the authorities are always watching. Before leaving the cab, she adds that Panahi had better remove her words from his film otherwise he will be accused of *siāh-namāyi* ('showing the negative aspects') and the authorities will give him more trouble. As Trevor Johnston remarks in his review,

> being out and about in the city (or country) yet still sheltered enough to be able to speak your mind, is what the setting of the car has afforded all these filmmakers, bringing with it the implication that once you step outside the vehicle you're in an environment where words and behaviour must be kept within strictly defined and policed parameters.[44]

In this respect, the car *is* a heterotopia, affording an exceptional space for freedom of expression. However, Panahi is more constrained than most other filmmakers using this strategy because he has to direct from inside the car whereas they can direct from outside or another vehicle.

The DVD smuggler Omid plays a further key role. Firstly, he is the one who recognizes Panahi and that he is making a movie. Omid makes viewers aware that the film is scripted, relating the dialogue between the first two passengers to the director's earlier film *Crimson Gold* (2003). With carefully orchestrated character appearances and narrative twists, *Taxi* is not merely an observational document as it appears. Secondly, Omid's profession as a movie smuggler (known in Iran as a *filmī*) brings screen traffic into the picture, in particular the social practice of watching banned films bought from street vendors who sell pirated DVDs to car passengers and undertake home deliveries. In a context where the state tightly controls film distribution through regular channels, Omid claims to be providing a cultural service since he offers viewers in Iran rare access to foreign and banned Iranian films. It is on the DVD black market that banned work by Panahi, Akbari and others is found, a shadow economy that puts films into circulation while withholding financial remuneration from filmmakers.[45] In interview, Panahi has joked that 'not only did I not make any money, but when I want to give copies of my own films to my friends, I have to buy the DVDs. I don't even get a discount!'[46] Yet through these informal networks, local audiences can see his films, a matter of importance to Panahi himself, who has been accused of making films exclusively for international festivals. In the absence of official endorsement, piracy is a pragmatic alternative, turning Panahi and the DVD smuggler into veritable 'partners', as Omid hints in *Taxi Tehran*.

In other scenes, we follow Hana, who is making a film for her homework assignment which has to conform to certain rules to be 'distributable'.[47] The rules belong to the Ministry of Culture and Islamic Guidance's censorship guidelines.[48] One of them is to avoid exhibiting the dark side of realities (*siāh-namāyi*). Hana's experiences show how making a movie that can be legally shown in Iran can compromise the truth, since everyday reality is complex, with both 'light' and 'dark' sides. *Taxi* underlines the need for alternative outlets, a point that is reinforced when, in the absence of end credits, a title expresses gratitude to all those who helped anonymously with this 'undistributable' film, stamping its modes of production and circulation on the finished film.

Although not a road movie, Lebanese filmmaker Lara Zeidan's fictional short *Three Centimetres* is a variation on its tropes, using a ferris wheel ride in Beirut for an intimate conversation between four teenage girls, Suzie, Manal, Joanna and Tamara. Suzie confides in the others that she has had sex without compromising her virginity; the secret is not to exceed three centimetres. Advising Joanna how to overcome a recent break-up, Suzie then relates a scenario that is clearly homophobic. It provokes Manal to come out as gay herself, to her friends' disbelief since she does not conform to their preconceptions of gay people and has hidden this part of her life from them. Just then, a power cut brings the ferris wheel to a halt, suspending the girls in mid-air without any immediate prospect of escape from their tense exchange. The need to lead double lives links the two parts of the conversation, as it shifts from preserving virginity to homosexuality. In their different ways, Suzie and Manal are both attempting to experience freedom in a society where, in certain respects, they cannot be entirely free, due to expectations of staying a virgin before marriage, on the one hand, and homophobia, on the other. As Zeidan comments, Lebanon is 'not really a closed society' since it has both 'conservative' and 'open-minded' elements, sometimes in the same family and not necessarily related to religion; yet, as the society undergoes changes, young people often find themselves

> stuck between both, between being open-minded and not wanting to discuss things and not wanting to disrespect. There is this understanding that there are different ways of seeing things. And that's why some things stay hidden because sometimes you don't want to fight another's opinion but you still want to be what you want. So the way is just not to talk about things and lead a double life.[49]

As an undergraduate at the American University of Beirut, Zeidan visited the nearby ferris wheel at Luna Park and wrote her script when applying to the London Film School, unearthing it two-and-a-half years later for her graduation short. Situated next to the corniche, the Luna Park is a well-known landmark, purportedly the Middle East's oldest fairground, now almost abandoned, due to the growth of mall culture. As Zeidan reflects, the ferris wheel cabin was a useful dramatic set-up for her to tackle the conversation about virginity and homosexuality: 'It is a public space but very private; they are alone in the air and no one [else] is with them', imparting a sense of safety for the girls to express themselves about these topics.[50] Moreover, they are stuck together, especially when the power cut happens, so they cannot escape when they feel uncomfortable. Because of the cabin's surround structure, 'they all sit next to each other instead of facing each other',[51] an arrangement that enables them to talk more freely, recalling Kiarostami's insight about the car. While the conversation could have occurred in a car, the ferris wheel provides an even more dynamic setting. In the open air, yet enclosed, it transports us from the darkness at its base to its airy summit, where traffic clamour subsides into the calm sea. Integrated into the shots is a central pole, dividing Suzie and Manal, while different camera angles are achieved via a wheel that turns the cabin in different directions.

Like *20 Fingers*, *Three Centimetres* adopts the self-imposed constraint to shoot in one take. Although challenging, Zeidan reveals that, once everything was planned, this suited the ferris wheel set-up and made filming easier and more efficient for the crew since it took place at sunset, when light changes quickly. Carrying the camera on an easy rig, the cinematographer accompanied the girls in the cabin. Along with the focus-puller and sound recordist, Zeidan was three cabins away, communicating via walkie-talkie and watching the action via a monitor. The crew recorded a total of eighteen takes, of which the best, in terms of lighting and performance, was chosen for the final film. The single long take suited the story, building its intensity, as became apparent when an editor attempted an alternative version with two cuts; although those cuts were invisible, the intensity was lost. 'The constraint of one-shot let things happen', explains Zeidan, since the actors used both her script (which she had workshopped with them during rehearsals; they also substituted some lines) and on-set improvisation.[52]

While, within the story, the cabin's private/public space enables a conversation about intimate topics that are otherwise difficult to articulate, *Three Centimetres* itself contributes to conversations about hidden sexualities in the Middle East. The film has travelled worldwide, as well as being exhibited (without censorship) in Lebanon, at the Beirut International Women's Film Festival and Cinema al Fouad, the country's first queer film festival, and on the Beirut-based streaming platform Aflamuna. As Zeidan says, 'It puts on screen what is usually spoken in private'.[53]

Tactical insight #3: The road movie's foreground/background dynamics marries popular appeal with political consciousness

In the Argentine film *The Motorcycle Diaries* (2004), a dramatization of Ernesto 'Che' Guevara and his friend Alberto Granado's journey across Latin America, the focus diverts from the male buddies' story of adventure and sexual conquest to solidarity with the oppressed people whose struggles they witness on the road. Real people that the cast and crew met on the road are incorporated into the film, implying continuities between past injustices that revolutionized 'Che' Guevara and the present. Several road movies from the Middle East have also exploited relationships between foreground (the travelling characters in their vehicle) and background (the landscape and people that form their journey's backdrop) to generate political consciousness under the guise of an entertaining trip. Earlier examples include *Under the Bombs* (2007) which the Lebanese director Philippe Aractingi shot 'Dogme 95-style' during and in the immediate aftermath of the July 2006 War (also known as the Israel-Hezbollah War).[54] Its foreground story, of a wealthy Lebanese Shiite-Muslim woman travelling from Beirut to South Lebanon by taxi with a Christian driver to look for her missing son, is placed 'inside the chaos' of the real-life war.[55] The professional lead actors interact with actual civilians, soldiers and rescue-workers on location, who react spontaneously with authentic dialogue expressing their testimonies of the crisis. Through journeys that take characters out of their comfort zone and into contact with people and places they might otherwise never encounter, this use of the genre highlights the road trip's transformative power and allows a country or region's social hardships to be explored.

In academic studies, the turn to popular genres such as road movies in filmmaking practices outside Hollywood is often explained in terms of seeking international audiences. However, it can also be an attempt to reach domestic audiences. Realizing that films funded by foreign grants and aimed at festivals tended not to be successful with locals, Aractingi decided to make films that work at the box office, in order to attract the Lebanese audience first, then the international one.[56] Attracting audiences is essential to a self-sustaining film industry for which making popular genres has been embraced as a solution in the UAE as well, by the Abu Dhabi government-funded media company Image Nation. For the Emirati director Ali Mostafa, however, genre exploration is a self-imposed constraint rather than an externally, market-driven one and he sees it as part of his apprenticeship as a filmmaker: 'I felt I wanted to tap into all the genres as much as I can'.[57]

Directly inspired by *The Motorcycle Diaries*, Mostafa's film *From A to B* is about three wealthy young expats, Omar (a Syrian), Ramy (an Egyptian) and Youssef (a Saudi), on a road trip from Abu Dhabi to Beirut in honour of their high school friend Hady who died in the July 2006 War. The trio are performed by first-time actors, although two of them were previously known in Arab comedy: Saudi comedian Fahad Albutairi (who plays Youssef) and Shadi Alfons (who plays Ramy), a writer on the Egyptian TV show *Al-Bernameg* (discussed in Chapter 6). The film was mostly shot in Abu Dhabi, as well as Jordan and Lebanon. Jordan also acts as a substitute location when the buddies enter Saudi Arabia and Syria, the latter off limits because of the war. In fact, a journey of this kind across the Arab region, although once feasible, has become unimaginable due to regional turbulence. Starting as an escapist adventure, the story is set against the backdrop of these conflicts. Susan Hayward writes that 'Generically speaking, the road movie goes from *A* to *B* in a finite and chronological time'.[58] In *From A to B*, the initials stand for the characters' starting point, Abu Dhabi, and their destination, Beirut. If this implies a linearity, that is far from the case, as their journey has several disruptions, which are initially comic – wrong turns, arrest for suspected homosexuality and a crash (into a camel) resulting in a broken windshield – before becoming darker towards the end. The protagonists' Range Rover is itself a subject of comedy as its smashed windshield is patched up with tape by the only car-repairer that they encounter on the road.

Always rumbling in the background, regional politics takes a decisive step into the foreground when the buddies meet Shadya, a young Syrian who was Hady's girlfriend, and escort her to her hometown, Deraa. At the Syrian border, they are stopped by Syrian regime soldiers. Because he has a diplomatic passport (his father is a Syrian ambassador in Egypt), Omar is handled more gently. Eventually the group is released, but warned of the risks of driving in Syria with Gulf number plates, a reference to Gulf states' backing of Syrian rebels. It is Omar's first visit to Syria, the country of his heritage, although he never imagined it would be like this. After dropping off Shadya, the trio pass a place where civilians are identifying their dead. Seizing the chance for some real journalism (previously, he is shown attempting to report on the 'Arab Spring' from his bedroom), Ramy starts filming the scene. When armed rebels ambush them, we see a different attitude to Omar's diplomatic passport. Yousef waves it in the car, not realizing that this makes them more of a target. The trio are taken captive and interrogated in a scene that enacts further political alliances and rivalries. As a Saudi, Yousef is hailed as a friend, but Omar is under suspicion. Finally, they are released, urged to spread word of the suffering they have witnessed.

A latent homoeroticism pervades mainstream road movies where male buddies share intimacy on the road, 'cut off from any emotional ties except to each other'.[59] In *From A to B*, this manifests comically when the buddies are arrested for suspected homosexuality while camping in the Saudi desert; the incident is underpinned by knowledge that they are straight, making gay people the butt of the joke. In the experimental short film *Mondial 2010*, there is a shift to an explicitly gay couple, two young Lebanese men, Yousef and Ibrahim, who drive from Beirut to Ramallah. It shows an 'impossible journey':[60] these cities are geographically close, yet it is illegal for Lebanese nationals to visit Palestine, since it is occupied by Israel. As the director, Roy Dib, remarks, 'those impossibilities and constraints are a major element of why the movie was made and how it was made'.[61] Due to the travel restriction that prevents him from going to Palestine, he never met Palestinians living in Palestine until he participated in a teachers' workshop in Jordan. By asking some friends that he met there to film their cities as if he were visiting them, he obtained the rushes that he later transformed into *Mondial 2010*, whose story was dictated by footage that he acquired from a friend in Ramallah. As Dib elaborates, 'In filmmaking, the director [usually] has control, thinking of the image and the actors while writing', then supervising the shooting and editing but, with this film, 'first of all, I haven't filmed the footage, so I had no control over this. Second, I'm dealing with a city and a landscape that I don't know'.[62] In one scene, a group of people in a cafe are talking about the World Cup and address the friend who is filming by his name, Yousef. From this, Dib adopted the name Yousef for one of his protagonists and set the story during World Cup 2010; hence, the title.

Dib worked with a sound engineer, sound designer and two actors to create the dialogue and sound effects in similar spaces to those shown in the footage. For example, sound for the car scenes was recorded in a car. Although we never see the couple, the construction of cinematic space through sound and off-screen voices enables us to place the characters in the scenes and creates a convincing illusion that they really went on a road trip to Ramallah. Dib was influenced by one of Jean-Luc Godard's films on the Israel-Palestine conflict, *Notre Musique* (2004), in which he meditates on the shot/reverse shot. This classical Hollywood technique constructs conversation scenes from disparate shots of actors talking and looking off-screen. For Godard, it illustrates the dialectical relationship between image (documentary) and text (fiction) which he compares to the Palestinian Nakba and the Jewish exodus as two sides of the same story. This laid the basis for Dib's thinking about foreground/background dynamics: 'When we talk about Palestine, we tend to talk more about Israel, about what Israel is doing. So Palestine is on the third layer of the image, not the front layer.'[63] In *Mondial 2010*, he attempts to place Palestine in the foreground and Israel in the background. The only time we see Israelis is at a demonstration in which soldiers recede into the back of the image. In other scenes, Israeli settlements materialize in the backdrop.

Mondial 2010 further manipulates fields of foreground and background in its story of gay characters, identities that, if not exactly 'absent' in Middle Eastern cinema, have tended to be marginalized and stereotyped. It stages an 'impossible journey' in this sense, too, as characters that are 'not allowed to speak [their love] in public' are given a voice and brought into the foreground.[64] The story is told as if it were a video diary by Ibrahim, filming through the windshield from the passenger seat, next to his boyfriend, Yousef, who is driving. Their conversation on the road was 'built on small details' related to everyday difficulties faced by gay couples in the Arab world through which, Dib says, 'you get to understand much more' about their situation.[65] For example, they are afraid of reserving a hotel room with one bed; Yousef suggests booking one with two beds to 'avoid any trouble'. Later, they joke about a love bite that Ibrahim has given Yousef that might betray their relationship to others. When Yousef's friends discuss football at the cafe, Ibrahim teases his lover that he should reveal that they are gay and that they hate football, one of their motivations for leaving Beirut for Ramallah being that they could not stand World Cup festivities. Their relationship is hidden, even from friends, because of the lack of legal protections for LGBTQ communities in the region.

By ingeniously splicing together foreground and background, the film constructs the space of a gay road movie. It makes possible that impossible journey in the sense that cinema can take us to places to which we cannot physically go and can create an entirely new, imaginary space that has never existed in reality. Dib regards this imaginary space as 'a tool for politics', like the dialectic that Godard discussed in *Notre Musique*. While *Mondial 2010* is fictional, written in the popular genre of the road movie, it is also documentary, composed of commissioned footage that documents real places. The story builds towards a rooftop scene in which a Palestinian shows Israeli settlement-building in the surrounding area, 'Look how close it is to us. It is almost here', he says. Through him, the characters and we, as viewers, witness a city that is disappearing. Ibrahim is unsettled by the experience, since it does not fit the image of Palestine he had; it burdens him with the responsibility of witnessing. Dib explains, 'I wanted the focus of this queer road movie to shift from the body of protagonists to what they are seeing.'[66] We do not see the gay couple; instead, we see what they are seeing, diverting the gaze onto the politically contested territory through which they are travelling. Although it would have been possible to insert images of the protagonists, *not* being able to see them was a political decision for Dib, part of an 'intersectionality of causes. I'm not interested in doing a story about the drama of two lovers, about what happened in their relationship. I'm interested in using their story to tackle a wider society.'[67] In her essay, 'Film and the Visible', Teresa de Lauretis argues that films that merely represent gays and lesbians without altering conventional forms of seeing remain trapped within a heterosexual frame of visibility. By contrast, *Mondial 2010*, to borrow de Lauretis's words, 'create[s] a space for questioning not only what *they* see but also what *we* see in the film.'[68] The film's double taboo of a gay love story and filming in Palestinian territory makes screening in Lebanon risky, although it has been shown at festival openings (which are exempt from screening permits because attendance is by invitation only) and online by Aflamuna. In addition, it has screened internationally, including at the Berlinale where it won the Teddy Award for best LGBT-related film.

Conclusion

As adapted in the films in this chapter, the road movie, with its tropes of freedom and movement, vividly dramatizes the injustices of discrepant mobility in the region. Furthermore, discrepant mobility is not just a thematic concern; it underlies the conditions in which these films are made and distributed. Limits imposed on travel affect access to filmmaking locations and screening venues, as well the ease with which cast and crew can move to and from these spaces, depending on their citizenship status and the geopolitical situation. At the same time, the road movie has provided filmmakers with the creative impetus to overcome limitations on free speech and movement, a resourcefulness displayed in each of the case study films. As a private/public space, the vehicle allows filmmakers to engage with controversial subjects, pushing the boundaries of what is permissible to portray. Although it is usually enclosed, the outside world is glimpsed through its windscreens and side windows as it travels through politically contested landscapes, bringing those geopolitics into the story in a dynamic relationship between foreground and background. For similar reasons, the moving vehicle has been used as a logistical as well as a creative solution for filming in conflict zones, as seen in other chapters.

6

Humour

Humour disarms and invites you in to understand the people rather than just feel sorry for them.

Larissa Sansour[1]

Humour is present in films featured throughout this book – even the experimental short *Mondial 2010* (2013) which, as shown in the last chapter, charts a gay Lebanese couple's 'impossible' road trip to Palestine. Unable to make the journey himself, the director Roy Dib commissioned the footage from his Palestinian friends and created a story around it, matching dialogue and sound effects to the images. The film uses humour right from the opening credits in which Dib offers his thanks 'to everyone who participated in the film, with or without their knowledge (or mine)'. Dib explains, 'In all my work, I always use humour as a tool.' He needed humour in this film because we never see the protagonists: 'I wanted people to identify with them, to try to imagine their faces, to imagine who those people are, and to connect to them.'[2]

Scholarship on humour often focuses on why certain works are funny.[3] This kind of analysis has been seen as essential to the task of taking comedy seriously, often contrasted with the view, usually attributed to practitioners, that dissecting a joke destroys it and undermines its unconscious, intuitive sources of creativity. In my conversations with filmmakers, I was struck by the fact that they were not concerned with why works are funny but, rather, with the humour's purpose and intended impact on target audiences. For them, humour is one of the creative tools at their disposal. This chapter seeks to understand it from their perspective.

In this chapter, the word 'humour' describes both a cultural phenomenon and a creative tactic. 'Comedy' refers to genre, although it materializes in different modes, such as satire, black humour, romantic comedy and irony, and is not confined to films explicitly made as comedies.[4] As demonstrated in the chapter's case studies, filmmakers tactically adopt different comic modes according to their purpose and sociopolitical circumstances. Starting with satires such as the Syrian YouTube puppet show series *Top Goon: Diaries of a Little Dictator* (2011–12), we will see how this direct mode of humour mocks the powerful and punctures spectacles of power. Secondly, works by the Palestinian filmmakers Elia Suleiman and Basil Khalil, together with the Iranian director Mani Haghighi's black comedy *Pig* (2018), illustrate how situational absurdity is exposed in the surrealist mode. Finally, we turn to the indirect mode of irony in Ali Jaberansari's *Tehran: City of Love* (2018), which uses deadpan humour to veil expected emotions in stories of unrequited love in contemporary Iran, and Mahmoud Sabbagh's *Barakah Meets Barakah* (2016) in which the romcom genre serves as an ironic vehicle for non-provocative criticism of restrictions on public space and cross-gender mixing in Saudi society. Sometimes these modes overlap; for example, satire often employs irony, and surreal and satiric modes can blacken into dark humour. They form a spectrum that acts as an index of the range of freedom of expression enjoyed by the filmmakers.

As Geoff King states, 'Comedy, by definition, is not usually taken entirely seriously, a fact that sometimes gives it licence to trade in areas that might otherwise be off-limits.'[5] This licence to say the unsayable has allowed it to thrive in socially conservative and authoritarian contexts. A common explanation for the workings of humour under the region's authoritarian states is 'safety valve' theory, known in Arabic as *tanafas* ('breathing'), in which the breaching of customary constraints is permitted under certain circumstances. It suggests that the state *tolerates* some criticisms of its apparatus, while other areas (such as direct attacks on the president) are forbidden; this allows release of tensions that might otherwise find outlet in political action.[6] It is in this regard that Lisa Wedeen discusses Allayth Hajju's *Spotlight* (2001–) and *A Forgotten Village* (2008, 2010) as permitted television comedies under Bashar al-Assad's rule in Syria.[7] While useful, safety-valve theory attributes top-down control to the state, which it assumes is the main source of censorship. By itself, it is too limited for analysing the films in this chapter, which shows that filmmakers carefully calculate the effects of their humour through their tactical use of comic modes. This shifts the focus from state censorship to filmmakers' agency and chosen creative forms within the constraints.

Like the Arabic saying 'a knife that cuts both ways', comedy can be oppositional *and* affirm the status quo. Sometimes it can be both simultaneously, due to its ability to mean something different to different audiences. The philosopher Henri Bergson once said that 'laughter always implies a kind of secret freemasonry'.[8] The fact that humour requires a shared context in order to be understood, such as language and cultural references, can be turned to a filmmaker's advantage: to say things in such a way that those who are *meant* to understand do so. Naziha Arebi remarks that her documentary *Freedom Fields* has 'quite a lot of humour that Libyans might laugh at', but some of it might 'go over a certain age group's heads'.[9] Strategically preserving these layers of meaning at the editing stage enabled her to show the film in Libya and overcome age-related barriers of social disapproval. Comedy is one of the region's most popular genres, and where there have been objections to it, this has often been from parties other than the government. In Iran, some comedies approved for screening by the state have been subsequently removed from the theatres due to religious intervention, as happened to the satirical box-office hit *The Lizard* (2004) although it continued to circulate widely underground.[10] In Saudi Arabia, the satirical comedy *Tash ma Tash* (1993–2011), broadcast on state television during Ramadan, also provoked clerical ire, forcing the makers to relocate to Dubai after threats to them and their families; the show resumed from there on the Saudi-owned network MBC.[11]

Despite its domestic popularity, comedy is one of the least exportable genres. Hisham Fageeh, one of Saudi stand-up comedy's pioneers, is very aware of this constraint. In the early 2010s, Saudi stand-up began handling provocative topics with unprecedented candour in the kingdom.[12] At that time, there were no cinemas for alternative entertainment, 'so people went onto YouTube and I happened to be one of the people that showed up early on', Fageeh relates.[13] Working for the media company Telfaz 11, he produced the viral YouTube video *No Woman, No Drive* (2013). In it, he and fellow stand-up comedian Fahad Albutairi (who starred in *From A to B*, discussed in Chapter 5) sing an acapella version of Bob Marley's song 'No Woman, No Cry' in a parody of religious discourse that justified the women's driving ban, then official Saudi policy. Speaking of the Saudi comedy scene, Fageeh says 'there's an incredible group of people doing grassroots stuff in Saudi Arabia... There are things that work abroad, others that only work locally. When I speak to the world, if I'm too specific in my details, it will go over people's heads.'[14] While his material is in Arabic and deals with Saudi issues, he maintains a cosmopolitan outlook in a nod to international audiences.

One comment that is often made about humour is that it is untranslatable. In *Barakah Meets Barakah*, the jokes and punchlines were written with the Saudi audience in mind, then tailored to the international audience through English subtitles. Fageeh, who starred in and co-produced the film, also wrote the subtitles, underlining 'the importance of translating idiomatically because a lot of things are lost in translation', for example, slang and different dialects (the latter are a frequent source of comedy in the region).[15] He tried to write each character's subtitles differently to convey their colloquial style. Fageeh's comments emphasize the importance of audience targeting to humour creation: 'In production, it was "Let's do this for Jeddah, for Saudi". Then, in post-production, "Let's do this for the world".'[16]

Basil Khalil further reveals shifts that can occur as a film goes through the production process. In order to raise finance for his film *Ave Maria* (2015) in the West, he had to write the screenplay in English, then translate it into Arabic and Hebrew. In fact, he trained himself to write scripts in English, the language of screenwriting software. This has, he reflects, affected his style of comedy, which is not based on verbal puns, jokes and punchlines but, rather, 'embarrassing situations that anyone would identify with' – what is known as 'cringe comedy'.[17] In writing the script, he tried to make it as 'funny and as flowing as possible in English, without mentioning which language is being spoken', always conscious of what it will sound like in the other language, so that the translation has 'the same meaning, not word for word, but the same context, timing, humour'.[18]

These are some of the general constraints affecting filmmakers using humour. The next sections explore their use of particular comic modes in response to constraints.

Mocking the powerful: the satirical mode

Satire is the most politically explicit mode of humour. At one end of the spectrum, it often targets powerful figures and institutions, which makes it highly risky. At the other end lie more evasive and ambiguous forms of humour linked to practices of veiling, dissimulation, ritual politeness and indirection.[19] As we shall see, in films from Iran and Saudi Arabia, indirect humour still flourishes. However, like other creative strategies charted in this book, the region's humour is generally becoming more direct in its critical edge. Practices of dissimulation long prevalent in the region have created a division between what is appropriate to say in public and private. When such practices hold sway, jokes about rulers are mostly told behind closed doors, in private, between people who trust each other. The Internet and social media, particularly YouTube, have broken these walls by creating an alternative public space for sharing satirical laughter. The post-2009 uprisings destroyed them further. As Mohamed M. Helmy and Sabine Frerichs record in their first-person account of the 2011 Egyptian revolution, the president was openly ridiculed with songs and slogans.[20] Humour gave voice to the protestors' dissent and helped to break the fear and isolation of years of dissimulation, especially for the younger generation who were less conditioned, rallying their collective spirits in their successful toppling of the despot.

It was in the more open freedom of expression climate fostered by the Egyptian revolution that Bassem Youssef, then a cardiac surgeon, began his notorious satirical news show *Al-Bernameg* (2011–14). Initially uploaded to YouTube (under the title *The B+ Show*) the programme was later aired by Egyptian television channels, including ONTV and CBC satellite network. Like Jon Stewart's *The Daily Show*, it is a parodic send-up of current affairs programmes, with skits juxtaposed with real news footage and guest appearances. On *Al-Bernameg*, Youssef satirized the entire establishment – government, media and religious leaders. In one satirical attack on President Morsi, leader of the Muslim Brotherhood, he sported a gigantic graduation hat in parody of the one worn by Morsi during an honorary degree ceremony in Pakistan, exposing his vanity and his power's frail foundations, like the unveiled emperor in Hans Christian Anderson's tale. Youssef faced several court cases, accused of insulting Morsi (among others) and, when Sisi came to power in 2014, the military ruler proved himself to be even less tolerant of his satire than his Islamist predecessor by jamming broadcasts of the show. Following a legal dispute with CBC in which he faced a fine of around three million US dollars and a prison sentence, Youssef fled Egypt and now lives in exile in the United States.

Masasit Mati, the largely anonymous Syrian collective behind *Top Goon*, released their first two seasons on YouTube in 2011 and 2012, each consisting of multiple short episodes.[21] Their risky circumstances, in the midst of the Syrian crisis, influenced their choice of media: Internet video and home-made finger puppets 'easy to smuggle through checkpoints'.[22] These finger puppets move across a wooden stage against a black backdrop, filmed in an underground theatre. The puppeteers' identities and location are hidden, although they occasionally appear above stage with keffiyeh scarves concealing their faces. *Top Goon* openly satirizes the Syrian regime, without hedging or evasion. The group's director, known by the pseudonym Jamil al-Abyad, remarks, 'There are taboos and red lines you could not cross. We tried to break exactly these red lines and destroy them.'[23] Ridicule of the president is at the core of the series; he is the principal character in the form of Beeshu – a belittling nickname for Bashar al-Assad – with his long face, pointy nose, enormous ears and lisp. Other regular cast members are loyalist regime thug Shabih, George the Peaceful Protester and the Rose of Damascus.

Wearing a stripy nightgown and cap in the first episode, 'Beeshu's Nightmares', the president is caricatured as infantile, cowardly and insecure, needing to be lullabied to sleep by his reliable thug. The puppet doubles over with high-pitched wailing, haunted by his loss of popularity ('Why don't Syrians love me anymore? Why do they want to put me on trial?') despite not having massacred as many people as his father Hafez al-Assad did in Hama in 1982. The second episode, 'Who Wants to Kill a Million?' is a parody of the globally popular TV show *Who Wants to Be a Millionaire*, alluding to the tens of thousands killed by the Syrian regime's security forces at this point in the crisis. In a swipe at the neoliberal aspirations of the television game show as well as autocracy,[24] the cash prize is macabrely transformed into body count. Beeshu sets his sights on the million-body trophy, following previous contestants Hosni Mubarak, who attained '3,000 killed', and Muammar Gaddafi, whose score was 20,000 killed. When asked the final question, 'Will you manage to crush the protests and put an end to the Syrian revolution?', Beeshu hesitates, saying he would like to call a friend. 'You still have friends?' the presenter asks incredulously. Beeshu decides that he will crush the protests against everyone's will – and rages impetuously when told it is not the right answer.

Top Goon deconstructs Assad's charade, showing him to be propped up by regime-friendly media – a parody of Dunia TV, an independent channel

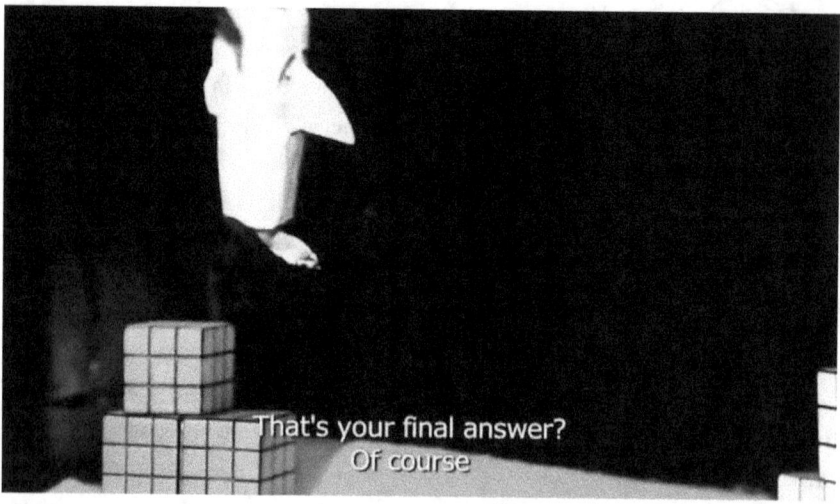

Figure 6.1 The episode 'Who Wants to Kill a Million?' satirizes Syrian President Bashar al-Assad with its macabre parody of the television game show *Who Wants to Be a Millionaire*. *Top Goon: Diaries of a Little Dictator* directed by Jamil al-Abyad © Masasit Mati 2011–12. All Rights Reserved.

virtually controlled by the Syrian government. With its provocative scripts, the series exposes the lies and propaganda upon which the regime has rested its authority, among which is its championing of the Palestinian cause that has formed the pretext for over forty years of emergency. Each episode begins with Beeshu feverishly repeating 'I am not crazy!' but implying the exact opposite. As if to confirm this, in December 2011, while the first season was ongoing, al-Assad appeared on the US network ABC denying all responsibility for killing protesters, insisting that Syria's security forces were not his forces and that 'No government in the world kills its people, unless it's led by a crazy person'.[25] The title *Top Goon* refers to Assad as the highest commander of Syria's armed forces, underlining his leading role in the killings, despite his denials.

In season one's last episode, a puppeteer whose face is masked by the Syrian revolutionary flag confronts Beeshu – 'I am the one who breathes life into you' – and rests the puppet on the stage. The lifeless figurine unmasks the president as a hollow character with strings pulled by external forces, removing the fear associated with him. By eroding Assad's personality cult and turning him into a diminutive finger puppet, *Top Goon* performs the function of 'reiterative resignification' that Amber Day ascribes to satire, 'gradually changing the pictures and associations that we have of particular people, concepts, or ideologies'.[26] The English words 'Freedom is coming' appear on the revolutionary flag, pointing to the satire's ultimately *regenerative* purpose of arousing international solidarity and morale-boosting for the Syrian resistance. Seasons one and two are English-subtitled throughout. Several years on, after the revolution's failure and Assad's reconsolidation of his power with the help of his Russian and Iranian allies, the words concluding season one read poignantly. Yet, as al-Abyad declares, 'Comedy strips things bare and gives you the strength to fight' and these Syrians show by their humour their refusal to become merely victims.[27]

Situational absurdity: a surrealist mode of humour

Filmmakers and critics alike often characterize humour in terms of nationality. For example, Leila Sansour initially reacted to a question regarding the presence of humour in her documentary *Open Bethlehem* (2014) by saying that 'Palestinians are often extremely humorous'.[28] However, she immediately related it to the 'bleak' and 'absurd' world of the Israeli occupation, which 'feed[s] the cannon on a daily basis for humour. People are humorous because they find themselves players in a surreal reality that unfolds in front of them all the time.'[29] Moreover, that dry, absurd humour, often identified as 'Palestinian humour' is, as, another Palestinian filmmaker Annemarie Jacir observes, 'typical of people all over the world when they're living in difficult conditions'.[30] In her study of Palestinian art and film, Chrisoula Lionis points to the failure of the Oslo peace process as the juncture that has led to the 'prominence of humour' in Palestinian collective identity and experience.[31] Such humour is rooted in a particular context, as Lionis suggests, but it is also somewhat universal, emerging as part of a response to, and commentary on, an ongoing crisis. I am calling this 'strange, situational humour'[32] surrealist because of its similarities to the Theatre of the Absurd and its occasional black comedy; these are features of surrealist aesthetics.[33] Absurdity is intrinsic to surrealism's bizarre juxtapositions, usually deployed for sinister, unsettling effects but also for humorously subverting normal expectations – for example, Méret Oppenheim's sculpture *Breakfast in Fur* (1936) which comprises a teacup, saucer and spoon coated in fur. For Larissa Sansour (Leila's sister), who uses both science fiction and humour in her work, these creative strategies encapsulate the occupation's surreal elements and absurdity in a way that mere factual documentation would not.[34]

In order to handle the occupation's everyday violence and humiliation, 'Palestinians have to have a sense of humour', Larissa Sansour explains.[35] Growing up in Bethlehem, 'I experienced this occupation first-hand so it's very defining of who I am... Humour is there as a self-defence mechanism to deal with such hardship.'[36] The Lebanese filmmaker Mounia Akl voiced a similar sentiment, 'In Lebanon, our status quo is sometimes absurdity'.[37] Although chronic hardships in Lebanon are different, there, too, a sense of humour is a way of managing in desperate times. In the documentary *For Sama* (2019), filmed under siege in Aleppo during the Syrian war (as discussed in Chapter 1), we hear jokes told by the director Waad al-Kateab's friend Afraa, who calls the siege a 'daily bombardment soap opera featuring all your favourite bombs'. These lighter moments are highlighted by the film's nonlinear storytelling which creates tonal shifts that, co-director Edward Watts claims, are 'true to conflict experiences, how light and dark sit side by side, the way people tell jokes in the worst of times to get each other through'.[38] In his essay 'On Humour', Sigmund Freud links the concept of humour as a defence mechanism to black humour through an anecdote. A condemned man is led to the gallows. 'Well, the week's beginning nicely,' he remarks.[39] According to Freud, this 'gallows humour' bespeaks a refusal to be hurt by adverse realities. In his economic model of the psyche, based on energy circulation and distribution, humour saves the expenditure of feeling caused by pain, which has a liberating effect. In today's well-being parlance, people talk of the defence humour provides against stress, as laughter is accompanied by release of pain-relieving endorphins. However, as well as *relief*, this humour's purpose is also *resistance*, as Freud's anecdote implies. Jacir explains, 'When your reality is so absurd that laws are designed to keep you marginalised and subservient, when there is a boot on your neck, you've got to find ways to resist. And laughing is one of them.'[40] Creators of this dark humour tend not to harbour illusions that the situation will change. Nonetheless, the very existence of humour gives a glimmer of that possibility.

Even when it is dark, humour is a way of lightening difficult subjects – again, not merely for the sake of relief. 'When you tackle topics that are usually heavy with humour, you keep asking the same questions but in fact you do them in a different way,' Dib says.[41] The need to reach audiences and establish channels of communication is an important factor. 'Neither do I like to produce films with no light in them,' Leila Sansour told me. 'I wouldn't want to inflict that on others.'[42] As her sister Larissa explains, humour is a crucial tool for forging bonds of sympathy and empathy, capable of (temporarily) overriding the power asymmetries of international news coverage that determine who gets to sympathize with whom:

> We know so much about America that whatever tragedy befalls Americans we feel closer to them. I think it's quite an important element that Palestinians never had. People [in the West] don't feel close to them; they feel close to the Israelis [because] they're more western. Also, they feel guilty about what happened in Europe so it's a closer subject than the Palestinians. People [in Palestine] are much more aware of what's happening internationally than the international world knows what's happening in Palestine. That's something very tragic in the dynamic of the colonizer and the colonized. The colonized always have an understanding of the oppressor that's oppressing them, while the person that's in power doesn't have to extend their mind that far.[43]

In news footage and war documentaries, Palestinians are often associated with tragedy, viewed as victims through a humanitarian gaze that calls upon viewers to feel sorry for and help them. Over the course of the Israel–Palestine crisis, which has been ongoing for over seventy years, this approach has become repetitive and fosters a sense of hopelessness. Humour presents a different perspective on adversity. Many films from the Middle East aimed at international audiences seek to challenge preconceptions about the region. Absurdist humour can offer a subtle way of doing this.

Elia Suleiman's films form an important benchmark for this use of humour. His gags are surreal, ironic and fantastical, often featuring his silent, deadpan persona E.S., played by himself. For example, in *Divine Intervention* (2002), E.S. meets his lover at a checkpoint. Their tryst is confined to a car, since the occupation prevents them from travelling between their cities. E.S. produces a red balloon and inflates it, revealing the smiling face of then PLO leader Yasser Arafat imprinted on it. The balloon sails over the checkpoint, distracting the soldiers who aim their weapons at it, while the lovers drive through unimpeded.

Suleiman's feature films up to *The Time That Remains* (2009) have been set in Palestine, usually in his hometown Nazareth or the West Bank, utilizing that 'reality as a backdrop, or even a set, speaking its own absurdities'.[44] In *Chronicle of a Disappearance* (1996), for instance, an Israeli police van skids to a halt and the policemen line up against a wall in perfect unison, then pile back into the vehicle, leaving as abruptly as they came. When he appears, Suleiman's onscreen avatar mutely observes the strange proceedings with an ironic distance. In contrast, *It Must Be Heaven* (2019), his most recent film to date, takes place in Paris and New York as well as Palestine and finds parallels for the occupation's absurdity in the 'state of exception everywhere', which he sees as the 'Palestinisation of the world as a whole'.[45] In one scene, French police roll through a cobbled street on Segways in a perfectly synchronized triad reminiscent of *Chronicle of a Disappearance*.

Producing these pleasurably comic images involves a great deal of hard work, as Suleiman reveals: the humour is created by the choreography and precision timing of the characters' movements, together with accentuated sound in post-production. His distinctive style and narrative structure come from compiling everyday observations in a notebook: 'If suddenly an image touches me – a movement, a choreography, a banality, something makes me laugh – I jot it down.'[46] After collecting these images, he builds successive tableaux, adding details as he goes along. His comic persona is integrated into the emerging narrative. In film history, early comedies consisted entirely of gags that formed the basis of one-shot silent films or were layered one after another into extended narratives before the rise of classical narrative.[47] Suleiman's work returns to the episodic mode of early silent movies. In *It Must Be Heaven*, there is a scene based on his attempts to finance his first feature. A Parisian producer (acted by Vincent Maraval, producer of the film we are watching) tells Suleiman's avatar that his latest script 'is not Palestinian enough' and throws him out of the production office. As Suleiman told me, 'They [the producers] don't want to let you say what you want to say. I was faced with a lot of rejections, mainly because of the narrative structure of the film and the humour.'[48]

The difficulties Suleiman experienced can be explained firstly by the fact that audience conditioning to narrative cinema has made sequences of gags without an apparent overarching 'story' seem deficient. His films inspire puzzlement in some critics and audiences who struggle to make sense of them narratively, as can be seen whenever anyone tries to summarize their 'plots'. Secondly, Suleiman's use of humour did not meet expectations of what a Palestinian film is, as he remarks: 'To producers at this moment in history, there is no way that Palestinians laugh. They only cry, they get beaten, they get tortured, they get arrested, so they are victims.'[49] Now, with four feature films behind him, he is at a stage in his career when he no longer encounters this particular hurdle. However, when *It Must Be Heaven* began screening at festivals, its global canvas provoked similar censure from audiences. As Suleiman retorts, 'A Palestinian has to stay in his own cage and should not talk about Paris or New York.'[50]

Struggling for ten years to raise funds for a feature, Basil Khalil made the short *Ave Maria* to prove that Palestinian comedy was commercially viable and could offer a different perspective: 'You can get misery for free on the news, why pay for it at the cinema?' he jokes.[51] In *Ave Maria*, five Palestinian nuns immersed in a daily routine of prayer and silence in their remote West Bank convent are startled by a family of Israeli settlers whose car breaks down and crashes into a Virgin Mary statue outside. One of the settlers, Moshe, asks to use the nuns' telephone for emergency services but, because it is the Sabbath, he cannot operate machinery and asks a young nun, Marie, to dial for him and even put the earpiece to his ear, which she refuses. The nuns hit upon a solution – purportedly in answer to their prayer to God. Led by Marie (who turns out to be an expert mechanic) they fix a vintage car owned by their deceased colleague, Sister Bernadette. Moshe's wife Rachel is initially reluctant to borrow the car because it looks distinctly 'Arab'. So the nuns refurbish it with a gaudy Virgin Mary statue on the roof and church music on the stereo, enabling the settlers to drive away without being shot at by the Israeli army. Although Khalil worked as an assistant on *Divine Intervention*, *Ave Maria*'s style is not arthouse like Suleiman's and the humour is more overt. As Khalil explains, 'the audience for Palestinian films is limited to people who have already bought into our cause. People go to see Elia Suleiman's films because they want to see Palestinian stories, not because they want to see a Palestinian comedy.'[52] Rather than 'preaching to the choir', his goal with *Ave Maria* was to reach people who might watch the film after reading the synopsis about nuns in Palestine and think 'this might be funny'.⁵³

Speaking about nuns as a source of humour, Khalil remarks, 'I think it's just the rigidity of it all in a world that is not rigid, but always changing. Also, you don't expect that from Palestine although it makes sense because that's where Jesus was from.'⁵⁴ Khalil himself comes from a Christian background; his father was an evangelical pastor and he was brought up with religious restrictions similar to those parodied in *Ave Maria*. For him, religion is an 'absurd, man-made concept': 'In Israel-Palestine, religion defines what rights you get as a human being. If you're Jewish, you get full rights; if you're not, you don't.'⁵⁵ Additionally, 'You don't get to choose your religion', since you are born into it, 'but you *do* get to choose the level of extremity'.⁵⁶ In *Ave Maria*, he sought to portray the absurdities of the extreme, from the Israeli settlers who believe that historic Palestine is their God-given land, to the Palestinian nuns in their vow of silence. Both groups are bound by 'absurd rules' and find themselves in an 'absurd situation' that forces them to break those rules.⁵⁷ The film's surrealist spirit is akin to the anthropologist Mary Douglas's notion of a joke as 'an anti-rite',⁵⁸ since it plays on the lack of logic behind society's accepted practices, revealing their arbitrary and socially constructed nature as well as implying that those practices could be changed for the better.

In a survey of the UK public's perceptions fostered by primetime television news, the Glasgow University Media Group reported that viewers often regard the relationship between Israel and Palestine as a conflict between two communities who merely cannot get along, which glosses over gross inequities.⁵⁹ Through its comedy, *Ave Maria* tackles the issue of co-existence. Rather than offering a fantasy of reconciliation in which two opposing sides resolve their differences, the nuns and settlers only cooperate because they want to get rid of each other, then resume their lives. As Khalil asserts, the film does not paint 'a rosy picture that everything is well at the end. If I was younger, I would have naively put it in, since that's what western audiences want'.⁶⁰ While developing the script, he felt it was ethically important to avoid this simplification: 'I had to make clear that they [the Palestinians and settlers] are not equal. They get along when they have to. I don't want to give the wrong impression' that all would be resolved 'if only the Palestinians would bend. I had to make sure I wasn't laying myself open to being appropriated to an agenda'.⁶¹

Ave Maria took four years to finance, facing some rejections from European funders until the Robert Bosch Foundation, which encourages co-productions between German and Arab producers, was willing to take the risk. Khalil recounts that it was initially also rejected by festivals since it was perceived as neither arthouse nor political enough and therefore did not meet their expectations. However, following its acceptance into competition at Cannes and Oscar nomination for Best Live Action Short, it had a highly successful release in theatres and online platforms. At the time of writing, Khalil had secured backing for his feature *A Gaza Weekend*, having demonstrated that there is an audience for Palestinian comedy and that gatekeepers of film funds and festivals 'dictating what is acceptable to be a Palestinian story' were wrong.[62]

The Iranian cinema that is exported to the world, epitomized by Abbas Kiarostami's work and social dramas by twice-Oscar-winning director Asghar Farhadi, is not known for comedy. These internationally acclaimed movies have a 'serious, sad, or downright tragic' tone[63] that has fostered certain images of Iran that affect how its films are judged abroad. But, as elsewhere in the region, comedy is hugely popular within Iran and humour is a way of coping with daily hardships and absurdities. It is abundantly present in Iranians' use of the social media app Telegram to share political jokes, including about the president. Even the Iranian art cinema known abroad has undercurrents of humour. For example, in Jafar Panahi's *Offside* (2006), girls disguise themselves as boys to attend a World Cup qualifier due to a law that forbids women from going to men's football matches. Guards catch and confine them to a barricaded area outside the stadium, where comic exchanges ensue between the streetwise city girls and naïve rural soldiers whose protectiveness expresses moral views about cross-gender relations. One girl begs to go to the toilet. As the stadium lacks women's toilets, a soldier chaperons her to the men's, crafting a mask from a football star's poster and tying it with a shoelace around her head to conceal her gender. She is an accomplished footballer herself, she tells him en route, although she has to undergo this charade just to watch a men's match. The surreal humour playfully illuminates the absurdity of practices that exclude women on this gendered basis. Panahi made *Offside* before his twenty-year sentence banning him from filmmaking although it, too, was banned. Nonetheless, it has been guaranteed a local audience on the black market and has become his most popular movie in Iran.[64]

The director of *Pig*, Mani Haghighi, related to me that a journalist once asked him if he thought Panahi was a charlatan 'making a living out of his oppression.'[65] He disagreed. At the same time, the idea of filmmaker obsessed with becoming a victim or martyr interested him and laid the basis for his story. In *Pig*, a serial killer is intent on beheading Iran's prominent filmmakers and carves the word *khuk* ('pig') onto their foreheads as a signature of his work. A blacklisted filmmaker named Hasan wonders why the killer has not yet targeted him, narcissistically believing that he deserves that honour as a big-shot director himself ('Don't worry', his mother reassures him, 'the killer is saving the best to last'). Some real-life directors are written into the story as victims – Rakhshan Banietemad, Ebrahim Hatamikia, Hamid Nematollah and Haghighi himself, whose severed head turns up on the pavement in the opening. *Pig*'s black humour is, by turns, macabre, absurd and ironic. Its storyline has led some international reviewers to interpret it as a satire of state censorship.[66] In fact, *Pig* alludes to the Iranian government's killings of prominent writers and dissidents sometimes known as the 'Chain Murders' (1988–98). Ironically, however, 'not a single frame of the film was censored. And the script was approved in one day', Haghighi recalls. 'I was astonished because it clearly makes obvious reference to the murder of intellectuals by state operatives. But it wasn't explicit – that was the main thing.'[67]

In *Pig*, the murdered filmmakers represent diverse sociopolitical views, as emphasized in a scene with a *New York Times* journalist who interviews Hasan about the killings. 'What could have been the common factor that led to their murder?' he asks. When Hasan exclaims, 'These people simply hate us!' the film prompts us to think about who 'these people' – the enemies of free expression – might be. It suggests that state censorship is not the sole culprit. Haghighi says that *Pig* was motivated by a general malaise that freedom of speech is universally not as valued as it once was, citing the Enlightenment saying, 'I disapprove of what you say, but I will defend to the death your right to say it'.[68] On social media, members of the public are 'emulating and replicating the tropes and strategies of state oppression', he explains.

> As an example, right now I'm in pre-production for my new film and we're working with an actress who was recently charged by the state for slander against the police. She wrote something in her Instagram account about the way security forces treated protestors and so she was brought in, questioned, tried, charged and there was a verdict against her. They didn't prevent her from acting. They just gave her a sentence of some kind. When we announced we were working with her, there was this huge [uproar] on social media where people were asking, 'How come she gets to act now, hasn't she been charged with some crime?' And it was them, not the state, who were demanding her removal from my cast.[69]

Compared to this 'mob justice of "The People"', Haghighi claims, 'state censorship is nothing'.[70] Or, at least, it is easier to handle since, once a script or film is submitted, filmmakers can enter into negotiations with the authorities:

They call you in, they give you a list of things that they're unhappy with in the film, you have meetings with them and you try to convince them that they're wrong. I usually succeed. And that's the end of state censorship for me. In more extreme cases, like Jafar [Panahi], he makes his film, he puts it on a flashcard and sends it by DHL to the Berlin Film Festival and they screen it.[71]

However, this is not to underplay the 'very real and very dangerous problem' posed by state censorship, which Haghighi recognizes.[72] As shown in other chapters, not all filmmakers can count on a smooth passage through this process, and many have been prevented from working in Iran altogether.

Pig's acerbic humour culminates in Hasan's attempt to restore his reputation by staging his own attempted murder. He posts it on Instagram, where it gains instantaneous 'likes'. The film's title refers to the murderer, who sports a pig mask. Unlike the comic levity of animals behaving like humans, as we saw in *The Wanted 18* (in Chapter 3), the human turned animal betokens a darker humour.[73] When I put this to Haghighi, he concurred: 'It's sinister, yes – like behaving like a pack of wolves'.[74] The human–animal transformation in the film, however, is into a pig – a provocative choice since Islam deems this animal *harām*. This did cause some trouble from the Ministry of Culture and Islamic Guidance, but Haghighi persuaded them to let him keep it, arguing that 'nobody eats a pig in the film'.[75]

Deadpan comedy and romcom: the ironic mode

The films in this final section take the situational humour that arises from real-world observations and construct ironic scenarios that are more ambiguous. Linda Hutcheon asserts that in irony 'the said and the unsaid must play off against each other'.[76] Since it works by inference of another meaning, irony has a certain degree of indirectness and therefore lends itself to being strategically adopted in circumstances where a more direct approach might be risky or controversial. In *Tehran: City of Love* (first discussed in relation to psychogeography in Chapter 4), the director Ali Jaberansari wanted to experiment with the form of deadpan humour, a choice that arose both from his own enjoyment of this genre and censorship restrictions in Iran: 'When you're working with constraints, you find out how am I going to say what I'm going to say with all these constraints.'[77] He refers to Elia Suleiman as a director whose use of humour has a similar function of highlighting situational absurdities but, as *Tehran: City of Love* is deadpan rather than surreal, he acknowledges the Finnish director Aki Kaurismäki as his most direct stylistic influence.[78]

Like Kaurismäki's characters, *Tehran: City of Love*'s protagonists are misfits who are socially awkward and unable to communicate their feelings. Suffering from unrequited love, they are engaged in a Sisyphus-like search for happiness, seeming to find it and at that moment losing it again.[79] Although *Tehran: City of Love* does not have the overtly political aspects of Kaurismäki's cinema in which characters are crushed by capitalist forces, it uses its deadpan humour to comment on Iranian society, particularly its dating culture. As a comic mode, deadpan can be traced to silent cinema, encapsulated in Buster Keaton's expressionless performance in *Steamboat Bill, Jr* (1928) when he stands in front of a house whose detached façade collapses around him. It is a comedy of understatement, where actors remain tactically 'poker-faced' and refrain from conventionally dramatic vocal and bodily gestures. 'Expected emotions'[80] are drained away from 'an emotionally heightened moment' which produces 'a sense of ironic distance from the effective demands such a moment seems logically to make'.[81] In his directorial style, Kaurismäki declares he has 'an iron law' – 'I do not want acting in my movies. The performer should definitely play, but so you cannot tell. He should not wave his hands about or cry.'[82] As Michael Lawrence argues in his analysis of Kaurismäki's films, deadpan performance 'present[s] a mask that obscures the emotions we assume to be there'; it renders those emotions 'oblique' or 'ambiguous' and prevents them from being 'quickly' or 'easily legible'.[83] Yet, the emotions that the character struggles to articulate can be inferred.

Tehran: City of Love makes use of the ambiguities of deadpan performance. Jaberansari asked his actors to watch Kaurismäki's films to prepare for their roles, although this was difficult as not many of them are translated into Persian; in particular, they viewed *La Vie de Bohème* (1992), *Drifting Clouds* (1996) and *Take Care of Your Scarf, Tatiana* (1994). Directing actors in this style involved instructing them to keep their hands down and maintain expressionless faces, which was challenging since it ran counter to their previous training and expectations of dramatic performance (especially for the amateur actor who plays Hessam, the bodybuilder). The ironic ambiguities of deadpan performance extend to the manner in which lines are delivered. In Kaurismäki's films, the characters speak absurd dialogue in 'literary Finnish with a serious voice, devoid of emotion, slang intonation and contemporary phrasings,'[84] which lends a comical strangeness. Although the dialogue in *Tehran: City of Love* is more realist, the main characters speak in a similarly sparse, clipped Persian, unlike how most Persian speakers talk in reality.

One predecessor for deadpan humour in Iranian cinema is *Risk of Acid Rain* (2015), whose cinematographer, Mohammad Reza Jahanpanah, was hired by Jaberansari for his film. Although deadpan humour is largely expressed through performance, camerawork plays an important role in generating levels of 'discrepant awareness'[85] between the audience and characters who, as discussed in Chapter 4, lack self-knowledge about their desires. The camera calls attention to the disparity between the characters' reticent façades and expected emotions by adopting a certain distance from them in long takes and static framings. At the same time, it remains close enough to imbue the humour with empathy, which invites us to laugh at the characters' awkward situations and naivety, but not at their distress.[86] In this respect, *Tehran: City of Love* has elements of melancholy and pathos that distinguish it from the cringe comedy of *Ave Maria*.

When new male clients arrive at the beauty clinic where she works, Mina, a plump receptionist, scribbles a star next to their name and telephone number in the appointments diary and later calls them on her smart phone, impersonating a woman with model looks. She arranges dates with them, sending pictures via her Telegram app, then stands them up. In Tehran, cafés form one of the few meeting places for dating couples. Because love and affection are not displayed publicly, lovers behave with distance and reserve towards each other in these public places. Sitting discreetly at a table on her own, Mina uses a café as a place to lure men, forming a humorous commentary on the dislocations of modern dating. When, finally, she meets Reza, a man who likes her for who she is, not her sexy virtual avatar, she initially behaves cautiously – shy, hesitant and uncertain of his attentions. Her newfound happiness is fleeting, as he later reveals he is married. As if to compensate for the news, he sends her a giant teddy bear by courier. As seen in Chapter 2, post-revolutionary Iranian cinema has often used proxies, such as children, to express desire between men and women. The gargantuan soft toy appears as a comic stand-in for Reza, as we follow Mina attempting to hail a taxi with it hoisted on her back and then sitting next to it at a bus shelter. The film lingers on her and the teddy bear seated together, highlighting her inscrutable expression.

When another character, the professional mourner Vahid, is abandoned by his fiancé, his friend tells him, 'No girl is going to put up with this lifestyle of yours'. To give him something more 'upbeat', he gets him hired as a wedding singer. Accustomed to singing at funerals, Vahid's doleful voice is clearly not suitable for weddings. Nonetheless, he enthusiastically throws himself into his new job when he falls for a female wedding photographer. From legal, sex-segregated weddings, he progresses to illegal, mixed-gender parties. His revived spirit is dashed, however, when he is arrested in a police raid. Editing is essential to the film's deadpan irony here, through an impeccably timed cut juxtaposing an unusually exuberant Vahid on stage with his usual reticent self in a police car. The ellipsis highlights the contrast and, moreover, *implies* that the law has been broken, without showing the events.

As mentioned in Chapter 4, Hessam is a personal trainer at a gym who is coaching a young client, Arshia, for a championship. During the time they spend with each other, Hessam's inchoate feelings for Arshia grow. In one scene, at a traffic jam, two young women in a nearby car joke to Arshia, 'Does your friend have a sore neck?', since Hessam has not turned sideways to look at them. Later, Hessam invites Arshia to his home one night to watch videos of former championships. As the two men sit together on the sofa, Hessam turns sideways to look at Arshia with an expressionless gaze that the camera lingers on. For viewers with a higher level of awareness than the character, the gesture carries connotations of desire. Arshia feels Hessam's gaze upon him and returns the look. We do not see what, if anything, happens between them, leaving the possibilities to viewers' imaginations. After this, however, Arshia discontinues his training with Hessam on pretext of quitting the championship. Discussing Kaurismäki's film *The Man without a Past* (2002), Jonathan Romney remarks that 'Few recent films have depended so much on their stars' facial architecture'.[87] The same could be argued of *Tehran: City of Love*, where the amateur actor Amir Hessam Bekhtiari's blank, large-boned face veils his character's homoerotic feelings and carries much of the story's unspoken subtleties about unrequited gay love.

In the ironic mode, contradictory possibilities can be held together at the same time. One way that filmmakers do this is by putting the entire film or particular scenes into the cinematic equivalents of quotation marks, implying that those scene(s) should not be read at face value.[88] For example, the Saudi romcom *Barakah Meets Barakah* begins with this title: 'The pixelation you will experience during this film is totally normal. It is not a commentary on censorship. We repeat, it is not a commentary on censorship.' Coming before the audience's encounter with the 'main text', it emphasizes that what is being said is 'both meant and not meant'.[89] Since the film was made at a time when there was no theatrical cinema exhibition in Saudi Arabia, the director Mahmoud Sabbagh applied for a TV shoot permit to the Ministry of Culture and Information (the body responsible for broadcast, print and online media regulation). Saudi Arabia has a reputation for heavy censorship. However, Sabbagh was only required to submit a synopsis, not a full script.[90] As a journalist, he was already cognizant of realms of permissibility. Furthermore, as he stresses, 'People tend to forget or don't know that there is a strong critical culture in Saudi Arabia – in journalism, caricature, even in civil society.'[91]

Barakah Meets Barakah explores restrictions in Saudi society from the perspective of the country's millennial generation, to which Sabbagh and the two lead actors Hisham Fageeh and Fatima al-Banawi belong. It is set in Jeddah, where Barakah, a lowly municipal employee whose job is to enforce public space regulations, falls in love with Bibi, an Instagram star and adopted daughter of a wealthy family. When the couple attempt to date, they find the simple matter of even sharing a moment together laden with challenges, as unrelated men and women have few opportunities to meet in public. Traditions of gender segregation, prevalent throughout the region, are more extensive in Saudi Arabia and the Arabian Gulf, manifesting in separate areas for men and women in many public places, with black coverings required for women and white robes for men. Moreover, Fageeh claims, because of market-led urban planning, corporations have acquired land in the heart of cities: 'Civic identity was a big sacrifice for this [millennial] generation.'[92] Social media forms 'a big part of our identity because it creates a virtual public space to our non-existent public space.'[93]

The genre of romantic comedy, with its typical narrative of 'boy meets girl' and diverse obstacles that thwart their union, forms a perfect vehicle to express these concerns. The couple first meet when Barakah receives a complaint about mixing on a beach and stumbles upon Bibi modelling in a photoshoot for her mother's boutique. At an art gallery, one of the few public spaces without gender segregation, they run into each other again. They exchange a few thoughts on conceptual art (Saudi Arabia has a vibrant arts scene and many works are displayed in the film) before somebody announces the religious police's arrival and Bibi hastily exits.[94] When the couple review their options for meeting-places, a comic montage displays them in typical settings for dates – a restaurant, a beach, a car – but, each time, the action freezes and religious police break up their trysts.

From the outset, Barakah and Bibi are a mismatched couple, a staple of the romcom genre where such 'incompatibility may arise from social status, wealth, conflicting lifestyles and attitudes, or even purely their differing expectations of relationships'.[95] The film uses their differences to complicate its picture of Saudi society and highlight a neoliberal structure of access. Despite living in Saudi patriarchy, Bibi is in some respects more powerful in terms of her wealth and access to the beach; the lower-class Barakah lives on the other side of Jeddah, in one of its old, ramshackle neighbourhoods. In courtship, Barakah is gauche and naïve – in typical romcom fashion, a male needing experienced female guidance.

Figure 6.2 Romantic comedy's boy-meets-girl format is transformed into a vehicle for exploring gender segregation and other restrictions on interacting in public space in Saudi society. *Barakah Meets Barakah* directed by Mahmoud Sabbagh © El Housh Productions 2016. All Rights Reserved.

When he presents Bibi with an underwear thong in a heart-shaped box, she is horrified and teaches him that flowers are the perfect romantic gift. The film underlines that Barakah's comic immaturity owes to his lack of love life, itself due to restrictions on cross-gender mixing.

Going back to early 'screwball comedies', such as *Bringing Up Baby* (1938), romcoms have debated society's changing attitudes to gender roles through the recurring theme of gender reversal. Barakah participates in an all-male amateur theatrical troupe, rehearsing for a production of *Hamlet*. In the film's opening, dressed in traditional male Saudi attire, a white *thawb* (long garment) and *ghutrah* (headdress), he enters a women's clothes shop and bemusedly holds up a frilly pink push-up bra which is, we later learn, to accompany his Ophelia outfit. Crossdressing is part of theatre tradition. In Shakespeare's time, men performed female roles; likewise, in contemporary, Saudi Arabia, men and women generally perform on different stages.[96] In another gender reversal, Bibi dons a moustache, *ghutrah*, waistcoat and pantaloons for her mother's costume party and drives off in an open-topped car – a transgressive act, since this was when the ban on women driving was still in force. While crossdressing is a common source of comedy, frequently located in the incongruous 'breach' of gender norms, its purpose in *Barakah Meets Barakah* is to play around with and question the gender binaries that underlie such restrictions. Even the film's title is pun on a unisex name – Bibi confesses that her birthname is also Barakah, which means 'blessing' in Arabic.

Saudi society was not always so restrictive, Barakah reflects. In two sequences, present-day photographs are juxtaposed with those from the 1960s and 70s, when cinemas flourished, airline stewardesses wore miniskirts and his unmarried parents dated relatively freely. The turning point was in 1979, when Islamic militants laid siege to Mecca's Grand Mosque in an attempt to topple the monarchy. As a result, the reigning King Khaled conceded more power to religious conservatives, which led to stricter application of Sharia law and changes throughout Saudi society, including the banning of movie theatres and greater restrictions on women's rights. Addressing his father, Barakah declares that the older generation surrendered the younger generation to the conservative forces that took hold of society, and 'didn't defend our generation's rights' to the more open society that existed in the past. Communicating these points from his nostalgic perspective helps the film retain a degree of ironic detachment. Yet, his perception that Saudi society used to be more liberal evokes the possibility of change: it can be like that again.

At film screenings and discussions, the filmmakers have presented their film as part of a conversation about social change in Saudi Arabia; as al-Banawi puts it, art is a 'soft weapon for addressing these issues', 'a platform that enables dialogue'.[97] They are equally concerned about what form dissent should take and not being provocative, carefully weighing up the effects of their freedom of expression on the wider industry as well as their personal safety in Saudi Arabia. As Fageeh says, 'You have to plant seeds towards real, tangible optimism... If we were to make a movie that was tending towards our provocateur nature, we would have prevented a lot of people from creating movies but now we have two movies in the pipeline and many more.'[98] The use of the romcom genre, with its 'gentle tone'[99] that more often upholds dominant ideology, may be seen in this light, for when it *does* challenge, its manner is restrained and nuanced. Along with irony, it enables the filmmakers to achieve the delicate balance needed for exploring controversial subjects without seeming provocative.

The film's significant impact proves the success of their approach. As intended, it has instigated debates among Saudis.[100] The Saudi government selected *Barakah Meets Barakah* for the country's foreign-language Oscar entry in 2017, conferring an official endorsement even though it was independently produced. Moreover, in 2017, Crown Prince Mohammed bin Salman gave a speech that reiterated Barakah's sentiments, stating that Saudi Arabia 'would soon return to the "moderate" form of Islam present in the kingdom before the unleashing of "extremist ideologies" after 1979'.[101] The lifting of the bans on cinema exhibition and women driving in 2018 are part of this apparent attempt to return to a more moderate past. Sean Foley argues that these changes should not be seen merely as the monarchy's top-down decisions but instead as indicating the influence of debates in artistic forms 'occurring "beneath the surfaces of power"'.[102] This makes films such as *Barakah Meets Barakah* into engines of this social change. Yet, there are strategic reasons behind these developments, too, intended to 'oversee a transition to a less oil-dependent economy'.[103] Ahd Kamel, another Saudi filmmaker, believes that the relaxing of rules on driving and entertainment will make people's lives less hard. But other than that, she says, 'I don't think it's a reform in any shape or form.'[104] A joke circulated amongst her friends when the Saudi monarchy announced the decision to allow women to drive: '2017 was the year they discovered women'.[105]

Conclusion

In this chapter, I have sought to analyse humour from practitioners' perspectives, exploring its purpose and the different comic modes they adopt, depending on their sociopolitical circumstances. These range from direct satire to the indirectness of irony, reflecting the realms of permissible speech. Humour enjoys a certain licence to say the unsayable but, as emphasized throughout this chapter, it is used to circumvent multiple constraints, not just state censorship. The pressures on freedom of expression come in a variety of forms. Religious authorities, public opinion, funders and festivals as well as governments all place limits on what filmmakers are allowed or expected to say in their bids to be humorous.

Writing this chapter also made me acutely aware of gender imbalance. Unlike most other chapters in this book, where male and female filmmakers are equally represented, works by male directors or performers have dominated. Although women also incorporate humour, as testified by plentiful quotes from my female interviewees, fewer of them have chosen to foreground this strategy in their work. Speaking of US satire, Amber Day asserts that male satirists are more able to mock the powerful because they possess some power in the first place, suggesting that there are greater constraints for women undertaking comic strategies internationally.[106] 'Being male, I have a privilege', Fageeh observes, while his co-star al-Banawi 'has more reason to be more anxious'.[107] As King writes, 'The dominant norms of many cultures give women less licence than men to depart from prevailing inhibitions, especially in public forms such as performance.'[108] This can be seen in the music video *Hawages* (2016) directed by

Majed Alesa, which followed *No Women, No Drive* in demanding women's right to drive in Saudi Arabia. It begins with three women getting into a car driven by a young boy, referring to male guardianship laws that grant greater authority to male minors than to adult women. Subsequently, the women perform various activities, including basketball and skateboarding, traditionally forbidden to them. They all wear a *niqāb* that covers their entire body apart from their eyes, concealing their identities.

7

Stories within stories

Storytelling has the power to seize our attention. The traditional Arab oral storyteller, known as *al-hakawati*, drew stories from a repertoire collectively owned by the community and wove them together in different ways for different audiences. They would tell one story after another with variations, embedding them within a frame story that contained all the tales.[1] Stories within stories feature in both Arabic and Persian traditions. As Orkideh Behrouzan notes, 'Epic Persian literature, Islamic and Zoroastrian scripture, even the Koran itself, can be read as a series of collected short stories.'[2] One of the best-known examples is *The Thousand and One Nights*, which contains Persian, Indian and Arabic folktales compiled by multiple scribes and editors.[3] In the frame story, following betrayal by his former wife, King Shahriyar resolves to marry a virgin every night and kill her the next day. To avoid execution, his newly wed, Scheherazade (Shahrazad in Persian), tells him stories night after night.

Conventional film narrative is built around a single main character or pair of protagonists in three acts leading to a definitive ending.[4] In contrast, stories within stories have an open-ended, rhizomatic character that is 'additive' and 'aggregative' like oral culture in general.[5] While a frame story delimits the text, it guarantees neither a particular internal structure nor a fixed number of protagonists nor closure, as the storytelling could go on and on. This chapter, with its case studies – the multi-strand fictional narrative *Tales* (2014), collective documentary *Profession: Documentarist* (2014) and theatre documentary *Queens of Syria* (2014) – explores how filmmakers from the region have adopted a stories-within-stories technique during crisis conditions. The flexibility of this form makes it useful for filmmaking in crisis, since stories can be added or subtracted depending on changing risks and circumstances; it also lends itself to collective authorship. Furthermore, while international mainstream media often promote one-dimensional views of the region, ranging from misunderstandings about veiled women to 'view from above' reporting on political tensions and conflicts, this strategy unfolds a multiplicity of different perspectives. It is one way that the filmmakers attempt to do justice to the complexity of everyday life during crises, when a singular viewpoint would be insufficient.

As María del Mar Azcona writes of the multi-protagonist film, a transnational multi-strand narrative genre that, she argues, has risen since the end of the twentieth century, 'By easily moving between different characters and storylines of similar narrative importance, these texts refuse to offer a monolithic view of events but rather favor the portrayal of several, and sometimes contradictory, points of view.'[6] Stories within stories reveal fragments of lives ranging along a cross-section of society. This form of storytelling is close to anthropology since it is deeply embedded in the social contexts of people's lives, attempting to convey nuances of 'life as lived' in a community.[7]

Storytelling itself emerges from crisis, as both filmmakers and their characters turn to stories to work through painful and difficult experiences, improve social conditions and, especially in *Queens of Syria*, to galvanize international attention to their predicament. Although some hold it responsible for propagating Orientalist images of the Middle East,[8] *The Thousand and One Nights* epitomizes this aspect of storytelling as creative therapy and changemaking. Already in a dangerous situation, Scheherazade takes a gamble and harnesses the power of storytelling to create change for herself and others by altering the king's perception of women. In fact, fatal risk presides over many of her tales, together with recourse to stories as a means of delaying or eluding that violence, suggesting that, through the act of storytelling, those facing crisis gain the agency to speak out and become survivors, rather than merely victims. As the narrative unfolds, characters detach themselves from the story in which they first appear to tell their own tales in their own voices.[9]

In this chapter, I analyse how filmmakers use stories within stories, and the role this strategy plays in freedom of expression more generally before focusing on the case studies, which are all directed by women. Steeped in the politics of voice, *Tales*, *Profession: Documentarist* and *Queens of Syria* largely tell women's stories, using their embedded tales as a strategy for narrating women's inner, private lives, their traumatic histories, hopes, anxieties and challenges. Turning away from dramatic events taking place in the public arena, they dwell on the interior spaces of homes and relationships, exploring the everyday effects of crises upon civilians.

The story within a story as a *mise en abyme*

Inserting a story within a story is a technique known in literary theory as *mise en abyme*. For Lucien Dällenbach, the *mise en abyme* functions as a mirror, making the work 'an internal play of mirrors'.[10] The frame and inner stories reflect and illuminate each other. This can have a 'subversive intent', as seen in Shakespeare's *Hamlet*, in which Hamlet commissions a theatrical troupe to perform *The Mousetrap*, a play within a play that illustrates the murder of his father in order to implicate his uncle.[11] In *Cinema 2*, Gilles Deleuze uses the term 'crystal images' for types of *mise en abyme*. One form that they take is a work within a work in which the reflecting work can be from another medium, such as a play, or it can be a film within a film, contemplating 'the process of its making or of its setbacks in being made'.[12] It might seem 'inevitable', Deleuze writes, 'that cinema, in the crises of the action image ... having no more stories to tell, would take itself as its object and would be able to tell only its own story', yet filmmakers internationally have found in the film within the film a means of creating 'special' images.[13] If such techniques are present, they are often not merely self-referential but are there for a reason.

Several directors from the region have used the film within the film to document crisis and the constraints of making their films in creative ways that go far beyond standard 'behind the scenes' features. For example, Abbas Kiarostami's *And Life Goes On* (1992) and *Through the Olive Trees* (1994) were both made in the aftermath of the Koker earthquake and use the film-within-a-film technique to revisit the region that was the location of his earlier film, *Where Is the Friend's House?* (1987). Fictional stand-ins are used for the director in the latter two films, art and life mirroring each other in an infinite regression. Mohamed Al-Daradji's documentary *War, Love, God & Madness* (2008) is about the making of his film *Dreams* (2006) in the risky, chaotic conditions of occupied Iraq, as director and crew members battle against time pressures and the worsening spiral of security that leads to their kidnapping and torture. In *The Immortal Sergeant* (2014), Ziad Kalthoum records the making of Mohamed Malas's *Ladder to Damascus* (2013) during the Syrian uprising, when the shoot was disrupted by explosions, attempts to halt filming and the crew members' traumatic breakdowns.

Historically, the story within a story has functioned as a way to avert censorship. For example, the Syrian director Duraid Lahham's satire *The Report* (1987) features a dream in which a balance hangs lopsided in a courtroom, an indirect critique of official corruption.[14] The dream affords a certain protection: not only is it unreal, but the scandalous content is buried deep within the work, where it can pass unnoticed. This use of the story within a story to deflect censorship persists today. In Asghar Farhadi's *The Salesman* (2016), Arthur Miller's *Death of a Salesman* is the play inside the film that the protagonists Emad and Rana are performing as part of an amateur drama group. Through its parallels with the film, the play illuminates the married couple's dynamics, especially after Rana is assaulted by an intruder into their flat, a scene that remains unshown, partly to avoid censorship and partly to implicate the audience in speculation around what happened between Rana and her attacker. As Nacim Pak-Shiraz says of another of Farhadi's films, *The Separation* (2011), 'attaining the very truth of the events themselves becomes impossible'.[15] She writes, 'In Shi'i and Sufi thought, truth is multi-layered. It has a *ẓāhir*, outward or exoteric, and *bāṭin*, internal or esoteric, meaning.'[16] Applying this logic, the story within a story holds further layers of meaning that are necessary to unpeel in order to reveal the complete picture. However, as Farhadi's films intimate, attaining 'the whole truth' is impossible, even by viewers who have a greater range of knowledge over the narrative events than any of the characters. All we can grasp are fragments of the truth, like the poet Rumi's saying, 'Truth is a mirror that falls from the hand of God and shatters into pieces. Everyone picks up a piece and believes that that piece contains the whole truth, even though the truth is left sown about in each fragment.'[17]

However, circumventing censorship is not always the primary purpose of the story within a story. We can see this in Mohammed Rasoulof's *Manuscripts Don't Burn* (2013) which is such a direct indictment of Iran's security apparatus that it has been called 'the most inflammatory Iranian film ever made'.[18] In his earlier career, Rasoulof was known for making cryptic, allegorical films such as *Iron Island* (2005) and *The White Meadows* (2009). His arrest in 2010, along with Jafar Panahi, on charges of filming without a permit, led him to change his approach. Like Panahi, he was sentenced to six years in prison and a twenty-year filmmaking ban (although, also like Panahi, his prison sentence has not yet been enforced). As Rasoulof declares, 'I used to think that the best way of evading the pressure exerted by the all-consuming and powerful government institutions was those artistic devices that are prevalent in our culture: namely, metaphors and indirect references.'[19] However, after his arrest, he felt it was no longer necessary to use those strategies since 'my new circumstances meant that I no longer required them.'[20] Like Panahi, he has continued filmmaking despite his ban and his films have become much more direct.

Manuscripts Don't Burn has the appearance of a thriller. Its outer story is that of two hitmen driving around Tehran, exchanging mundane remarks and running everyday errands. The hitmen hunt down two dissident writers to retrieve copies of a manuscript they possess and then kill them. The manuscript has been written by a third author, as a memoir of an incident years earlier when a delegation of Iranian writers were travelling to Armenia and their driver attempted to crash the bus. It makes direct reference to an actual event in 1996 that was part of a programme of political assassinations known as 'the Chain Murders' carried out by Iran's Ministry of Intelligence. 'The Chain Murders' came to light during a period of greater press freedom in 1998. Like Hamlet playing a cat-and-mouse game with the state, Rasoulof revives this incident in the Ahmadinejad era, when freedom of speech was drastically curtailed, especially after the 2009 Green Movement.

By necessity, the film was shot underground, on a low budget; despite this, it looks polished with its blue- and grey-hued cinematography, lacking the low-tech appearance of many other underground films. For security reasons, only Rasoulof's name appears in the credits (as writer and director, although he also has an uncredited role as one of the hitmen, Morteza). He wrote the script with production limitations in mind, and shot half the film in Iran and the other half in Germany, with some scenes filmed in multiple locations across the two countries depending on what could be replicated elsewhere (the interior story of the writers) and what had to be in Tehran (the outer story of the hitmen's rounds). Rasoulof reflects that 'Ultimately, these limitations resulted in small bursts of creativity and ingenuity from which I feel that the film benefitted structurally'.[21] The result is the story-within-a-story structure. The title *Manuscripts Don't Burn* comes from the Soviet writer Mikhail Bulgakov's novel *The Master and Margarita* (1966). It epitomizes the idea that stories cannot be completely destroyed, however much trouble they give to beleaguered writers or governments who try to ban them. Stories have a way of coming to light: a leitmotif of many films in this chapter.

Although many constraints on filmmaking were already in place before the 2009 protests in Iran, after these events the state hugely increased the restrictions. As Shirin Barghnavard, one of the co-directors of *Profession: Documentarist*, explains, 'That was the first time that the state found out the power of documentary films because people were documenting the events on their cellphones. Previously you only needed a permit for shooting and screening feature-length fiction films; suddenly, new rules applied to documentary and short films', which now require both shooting and screening permission.[22]

Despite the fact that short films are now subject to censorship in a way they were not before, constructing a feature film from a series of shorts has remained a creative way of defying the authorities. Rasoulof's *There Is No Evil* (2020) consists of short stories exploring characters involved in the state's machinery of capital punishment. Mindful of his filmmaking ban, his production team applied for licences to make four short films in different provinces, without giving his name on the forms.[23] As we will see in the following case study, Rakhshan Banietemad, while not operating under a filmmaking ban, was a pioneer of this strategy in *Tales*.

Tales: a feature composed from short films

Tales consists of seven intersecting stories featuring characters from Banietemad's fiction films from the previous two decades. It imagines how these characters are faring under the hardships of Ahmadinejad's second term of presidency when it was made. Knowledge of their backstories in the earlier films – *Under the Skin of the City* (2001), *Off-limits* (1988), *Gilaneh* (2005), *The Blue-Veiled* (1995), *Nargess* (1992) and *Mainline* (2006) – compensates for the characters' brief screen time and adds significant depth to the narrative.[24] As Zahra Khosroshahi comments, 'not only do these past characters reappear, but they also join to be part of the same story'.[25] On the surface, *Tales* seems like other multi-strand narratives that have arisen since the end of the twentieth century, known by different labels such as ensemble and mosaic films,[26] network narratives,[27] multi-protagonist films[28] and kaleidoscopic storytelling.[29] These films often have multiple, intersecting storylines that follow a range of characters loosely linked together by a shared location (such as a city or neighbourhood) and a circumscribed time-frame or event, emphasizing chance and coincidence. This kind of multi-story pattern is associated with the American independent director Robert Altman (*Short Cuts* (1993)), but it has also been used in Hong Kong by Wong Kar-wai (*Chungking Express* (1994)), in Mexico by Alejandro González Iñárritu (*Babel* (2006)), in Egypt by Ahmad Abdalla (*Heliopolis* (2009)), in the UAE by Ali Mostafa (*City of Life* (2009)) and in Iran by Ali Jaberansari (*Tehran: City of Love* (2018)) as well as in many other places. However, what distinguishes *Tales* is the constraints under which it was produced.

Before *Tales*, Banietemad had made her fictional features via the state-sponsored Farabi Cinema Foundation, which is directly supervised by Iran's Ministry of Culture and Islamic Guidance (MCIG). This ensconced her firmly within the system, although during this time she was able to make socially and politically challenging works through constant negotiations with the authorities, as well as numerous documentaries.[30] Her documentaries are sources of inspiration for the social issues that she treats in her fictional narratives, grounding them in concrete realities.[31] However, 'Under the Ahmadinejad government', she declares, 'I boycotted film-making. I didn't accept the new management of the ministry of arts and culture, and I didn't want to make films under such conditions.' For this reason, Banietemad states, '*Tales* was made up of shorter films, which meant it didn't require a license, and as a result was made independently.'[32] Later, when reformist president Hasan Rouhani was elected, she joined these short films together in order to release the work as a feature. Not only did her chosen creative strategy give her greater freedom of expression, she suggests that it was necessitated by the crisis in Iran's film industry during Ahmadinejad's presidency, leading her to produce her first truly independent fictional work.

The crisis conditions of the film's production, amidst Western sanctions, hyperinflation and greater restrictions on freedom of expression, are reflected in the storylines which foreground the everyday impact of these broader social, political and economic phenomena. Through its multi-story structure, *Tales* explores a cross-section of Iranian society in the aftermath of 2009, with the aforementioned crises acting as an event-frame that connects disparate characters. Their tales are linked by transitional scenes in which a character from one story crosses paths with characters from the next, and a frame story of an unnamed filmmaker struggling to make a documentary in these circumstances. Indeed, the stories are so well interwoven, using continuity editing techniques to bridge the different episodes (as is common in multi-strand narrative),[33] that it is hard to imagine that they began their life as independent shorts.

The filmmaker's documentary forms a film within a film, another story within a story that encapsulates the characters' experience of crisis. In one scene, he boards a minibus to film workers demanding their rights after their factory's closure and the owner's departure without paying them. Among the mainly male workers is a woman named Tuba (whose backstory viewers may know from *Under the Skin of the City*), who emerges as their spokesperson. Despite her chronic cough, a result of her constant exposure to factory dust, she gives a heartfelt speech on how she and her co-workers have been affected by the economic and political situation: 'The high prices are breaking us... To get any kind of job you need to pull the right strings.' Worried that she will cause trouble, her colleagues urge her not to make these political statements on camera, yet she persists. 'It's a year since they arrested my boy,' she remonstrates, alluding to the 2009 protests in which, the film implies, her son participated. Additionally, she mentions drug abuse by Iran's youth, thankful that her son never became a heroin addict. In despair that anything can be changed, she concludes by looking into the camera and exclaiming, 'Who watches these films anyway?!'

This line is a reprise of Tuba's words in Banietemad's previous films *Under the Skin of the City* and *The May Lady* (1998). As both Zahra Khosroshahi and Maryam Ghorbankarimi point out in their contributions to an edited book on Banietemad, its origins lie in an utterance by Mehri, a protagonist of Banietemad's documentary, *To Whom Do You Show These Films?* (1993).[34] While this might be seen as part of the 'self-referential intertextuality' that Ghorbankarimi identifies throughout Banietemad's work, the filmmaker herself states, 'for me, cinema is a tool and device, not the endpoint'.[35] A concern with social conditions and cinema as an impact tool forms the context within which the film within a film appears in *Tales*.[36] Most of the scene is shown in one apparent long take (with cuts disguised by people passing in front of the camera) through the viewfinder on the filmmaker's camcorder. The camera point of view emphasizes the power of cinematic storytelling to capture people's everyday struggles and render them with a sense of immediacy. But, as Tuba's line highlights, a film's ability to bear witness and create social impact is questionable if it cannot be distributed and reach an audience – even then, the path to change is not guaranteed. Sure enough, the camera is detected by one of the authorities who approaches the minibus; the recording halts abruptly and *Tales* shifts to the next story, implying the camera's confiscation.

In the film's final scene, the filmmaker has regained his camera, although the footage has been seized. He nonetheless affirms his desire to keep shooting, since 'no film will ever stay in the closet. Someday, somehow, whether we're here or not, these films will be shown.' His words articulate a well-known saying in Iran that a film's raison d'être is to be exhibited to an audience, whatever obstacles beset its production and release. Although unable to be screened during Ahmadinejad's presidency, *Tales* did not remain in the closet. Its stories were retrieved and assembled into a feature that finally obtained screening permission when Rouhani came to power. Even then, its theatrical release in Iran was obstructed for another two years by pressure groups who accused it of portraying a negative view of the country, as Banietemad recalls: 'The main cinemas that belonged to government institutions in Tehran and other cities boycotted the film and prevented its screening. They even blocked me from attending Q&A sessions and other events. At the end, without any publicity, and without any television or radio advertisement, and very few exhibiting slots, the film was screened.'[37]

Profession: Documentarist: collective filmmaking

Profession: Documentarist is a collective film comprising seven stories by seven Iranian female documentary makers who came of age after the 1979 Revolution. These are autobiographical stories in which the women talk about themselves and their profession, 'living in a country where documentary makers face a lot of limitations', as Barghnavard, one of the seven, explains.[38] With the introduction of new rules requiring both shooting and screening permits, conditions for documentary makers in Iran worsened after the 2009 protests. The risks also increased, as attested to by the persecution and arrests of several filmmakers alleged to be working with BBC Persian.[39] These factors added to general difficulties faced by documentary makers, who 'are more marginalized, seen as more specialist than mainstream', says Barghnavard. Although the form is gaining more recognition as a creative art, 'by choosing to become documentary makers, you have chosen not to be seen or heard a lot'.[40] *Profession: Documentarist* arose from this post-2009 crisis. Feeling depressed and weighed down by the difficulty of making feature-length documentaries on their own, the group of filmmakers, who were already friends, arrived at the solution of making a film collectively: a shared creation through which they could support each other and gain solidarity to move on.

In its collective mode of production, *Profession: Documentarist* salvages a historical tactic from earlier filmmaking cooperatives that include Third Cinema practices in decolonizing nations, alternative filmmaking collectives in the United States and UK in the 1960s and 1970s and Black Audio Film Collective in Britain in the 1980s and 1990s. As Helen Michiel and Patricia Zimmerman note, there is a 'history of media collectives responding to social and political crises' going as least as far back as the 1930s when the US Workers Film and Photo League 'represented left-leaning film makers and writers' responses' to the Depression and its effects on ordinary people, offering an 'alternative view to newsreels' through short films shown outside commercial venues.[41] In cooperative filmmaking, several filmmakers collaborate in one project, sharing common goals and collectively making production decisions. Instead of the authority of one director/producer, creative responsibility is distributed more equally and roles are often rotated. The productions are usually small-scale, often financed by the collective's personal resources.

This is exactly how *Profession: Documentarist* was made. From conceiving the stories through to script development, research, shooting and post-production, every stage of the production process was performed collectively by the women themselves, apart from cinematography and sound design. Although they realized the film's potential interest for foreign co-producers, the collective shared the cost themselves without applying for any external funding, since 'the subject is sensitive and by getting money from global organisations, we might be placing ourselves in greater danger'.[42] They wanted to avoid a common accusation levelled against filmmakers, of using Western funds to act against Iran's interests. Barghnavard believes this is contrary to how they made the film, suffusing it with 'love for our country, for our memories, for the society', despite also being critical of the system.[43] Nonetheless, the costly nature of filmmaking made this abjuring of external funding hugely challenging. The cinematographer (Barghnavard's husband Mohammad Reza Jahanpanah) and sound designer worked pro bono on promise of shared revenues from the film, although that did not amount to much because of its limited distribution. Even while engaged in it, the collective was aware that this way of working lacked long-term sustainability.

Initially, there were ten filmmakers for ten episodes, but they were reduced to seven during the challenging two-and-a-half-year process. 'There were arguments', Barghnavard recalls, and some filmmakers left.[44] Consequently, the number of stories fluctuated, and their order was also not fixed in advance. In the edit, the collective experimented with different sequences, including ending with Barghnavard's story which, as we will see in the analysis below, has a bitter tone. Instead, they ultimately chose to conclude with Nahid Rezaei's more optimistic episode. However, the stories could easily have been in a different order, like the multi-strand tales in oral storytelling. As in other community projects, the filmmakers regarded the collaborative process of filmmaking as more important than the outcome.[45] Not everyone was satisfied with the final product, Barghnavard says, yet 'in the end, we decided to accept this as it is... It wasn't only about filmmaking; it was about friendship'.[46] The act of making the film together was 'an excuse to meet frequently' and discuss their sorrows and it 'gradually became a therapy'.[47]

Profession: Documentarist builds a kaleidoscopic view of crisis through the filmmakers' different perspectives in their respective episodes. Each episode is titled with the filmmaker's first name, and features her voice-over narrating her story, thoughts and concerns. The use of first names and first-person voice is characteristic of the film's intimate, confidential tone, while the changes in narrative voice for each story recall *The Thousand and One Nights*. Many stories are told through autobiographical documents, such as family photographs and home movies, that transform into dynamic frames within the frame, generating further *mise-en-abyme* effects. As Farahnaz Sharifi says in her segment, home videos are 'full of things you're only allowed to do at home'. Despite the state's attempts to intrude into private space and politicize women's bodies, this was resisted by the Iranian population and so the home has 'remained a "state-free" site, a "release valve" for public tensions'.[48] The home-movie footage reveals women's parallel lives in their homes – dancing without *hejāb*, among other things – and makes their experiences visible in a way they can never be in MCIG-approved cinema.

Barghnavard's opening story, 'Shirin', reflects on experiences of war.[49] It begins with sounds of missiles and an animation of Tehran's distinctive cityscape illuminated by white flares in the night sky. We realize that this is a videogame, in which you play a US soldier invading Iran. At first, the marines lie in ambush, then the 'camera' takes their point of view as they advance and blow up Gisha Bridge. Through their weapon's viewfinder we see 'an enemy' on the other side. Shirin's voice-over personalizes the landscape targeted for destruction, identifying the neighbourhood where she lived during her childhood: 'This is my hometown, Tehran. The place I grew up.' It inverts the videogame's usual point of view and generic images with the experience of an 'I', offering an intimate tale that gives a sense of what it feels like to be inside these events in a way that cannot be captured from outside. The film's camera then moves out to show the videogame is playing on a monitor, another frame within a frame.

The videogame is a product of political discourse about an imminent war with Iran. 'That was a very real issue at the time and has also recurred now,' Barghnavard comments, referring to tensions that resurfaced during President Trump's era. 'We are constantly faced with domestic and international issues imposed on us.'[50] The film abruptly cuts from the appropriated video game to archive footage of the Iran–Iraq war, another barrage of sounds and images of violence. The shift from iconic animated images to indexical found images serves to remind viewers that Shirin's generation already experienced a war, and that what can start with a game can easily transform into a reality where loved ones are lost. Using photographs of her as a child, just five years old when the war started, the story recounts its effects on civilians through aerial bombardment and internal displacement. The Gisha neighbourhood bombing shattered all the windows in her house: 'the war had reached our front door'. Thereafter she

Figure 7.1 Shirin's voice-over lays the nuances of her lived experience over a videogame of US soldiers invading Iran, deploying a story-within-a-story strategy. *Profession: Documentarist* directed by Shirin Barghnavard, Firouzeh Khosrovani, Farahnaz Sharifi, Mina Keshavarz, Sepideh Abtahi, Sahar Salahshoor, Nahid Rezaei © *Profession: Documentarist* collective 2014. All Rights Reserved.

was evacuated to northern Iran, which was safer. There she met her first love, a boy who was later killed in the conflict. Having layered speculation of a future possible war with the legacy of a past war, the film captures images of Tehran in the present day. It suggests that the scars of war remain as undercurrents under the surface – 'hidden, subtle and mute'.

When, in 2003, Iraqis faced another war, the 2003 US-led invasion, Shirin was in Perth and captured the anti-war rallies there. It was safe for her to film demonstrations in Australia; however, when the 2009 Green Movement happened in Iran, and people documented it as citizen journalists with their mobile phones, she was fearful and did not record it herself. Shirin's story is about a documentary filmmaker's capacity for documenting violence, something to which she is averse. This is not only because of the risks: 'I cannot tolerate any violence,' she reflects. 'But sometimes it imposes itself on you and you are inside it. In those situations, I am not the kind of person who can take their camera and record the violence.'[51]

In another episode, Firouzeh relates her anxieties about returning to Iran after trips abroad. One time her name was announced over Tehran airport's tannoy and an official came over to her and took her passport. Although her passport was returned, the incident unsettled her. She hears of friends who have been taken from their homes and detained, and fears the same may happen to her. Farahnaz in her segment discloses, 'We Iranian documentary filmmakers have movies that can only be made in our minds. Sometimes we tell them to each other.' She tells us about one such film she wanted to make about the popular Iranian singer Googoosh since, after the 1979 revolution, solo female singers were banned from singing in public. In other stories, Mina contemplates leaving Iran while another filmmaker, Sepideh, interweaves the story of the 1979 revolution with her family history. Sahar's story centres on the window in her home that overlooks a prison. It likens her own home to a prison and expresses her longing to live somewhere she would not need to conceal herself but could do everything in the open. In the final episode, Nahid, the eldest of the filmmakers, focuses on personal and professional strategies to overcome these limitations, documenting the collective who made the film we are watching. With her, we enter the House of Cinema, the filmmakers' guild where they gather to watch each other's banned films. Her story ends with celebrations of the 2013 election result, which brought Rouhani to power, and shows Nahid out on the streets, filming.

The collective knew it was 'pointless' to apply for a screening permit since their film did not abide by censorship rules, featuring women singing among other things.[52] With this, they accepted that screening possibilities within Iran were limited. So they self-distributed the film, hiring a 400-seat cinema in a private school for the invitation-only première. Later, *Profession: Documentarist* was exhibited at galleries and other private venues. It was also selected for screening at the House of Cinema's Celebration of Iranian Cinema. While the collective was careful not to draw attention to the film in Iran, they submitted it to as many international festivals as they could and therefore it was more widely seen abroad. 'I think any filmmaker makes films to be seen,' Barghnavard says, utilizing the same saying that occurs at the end of *Tales*. 'It used to be said that "at least we documented it; though there's no space to show it, perhaps it can be shown later". But now, we *have* to show it – if not here, then somewhere else.'[53]

Queens of Syria: sharing other people's stories

Queens of Syria is a documentary about Syrian refugee women in Jordan who perform their own interpretation of Euripides's classical Greek play *The Trojan Women* (415 BC). These women, who had fled the Syrian war, had never acted previously. The play dramatizes the plight of women whose city was destroyed by the Greek army, resulting in their captivity and forced exile. It has continually lent itself to contemporary parallels since it deals with war crimes against civilians, displacement and sexual violence against women in conflict.[54] Charlotte Eagar, one of the executive producers of the British company, Refuge Productions, that instigated the project, has spoken of how she saw it as an 'opportunity' to make powerful drama and highlight the Syrian refugee crisis: 'because the amateur cast are playing out experiences very similar to their own, even though they are not professional actors, they can give very powerful performances'.[55]

However, contradictions can exist between the emancipatory potential of 'giving voice' and how this is managed by media professionals.[56] Yasmin Fedda was very aware of this when she was hired to direct the documentary. A Palestinian by background, with a Syrian grandmother, she now lives in Britain, although she grew up in Kuwait and lived in Syria at various times, making her previous films there. Fedda was not interested in the fact that a British production company conceived the idea, but rather in what happened in the workshops leading to the performance, the Syrian women involved and their journey over that two month-period. The producer Itab Izzam recruited women to take part, visiting community centres and refugee drop-in places to convince them. 'She would just say, "Just come for a day"', Fedda recalls.[57] The women came, not knowing what to expect or even understanding what the project was. Knowing this, and informed by her own background in anthropology, which had taught her to be sensitive to people's stories, Fedda felt that an observational approach would be productive: 'Spending a long time in the room and not imposing my ideas was a starting point, and giving it the time to see what would happen.'[58] She gained the women's trust by being continually around, as they became used to her and her camera.

Although we follow the theatre production through workshops and rehearsals, *Queens of Syria* is more than just a behind-the-scenes documentary. It gives us deeper access to the women's stories and their perspectives by documenting their creative process and debates about the play as well as taking us into some of their homes. Initially part of trust-building during the filmmaking process, these more intimate, domestic scenes were integrated in the edit. One of the women we see at home is Maha, who talks about her fear and exhilaration of going on stage, as it will be her first time speaking in public. Otherwise, she feels, her everyday horizons are low: 'I live on a floor with two foam mattresses. What can I dream about?' Later, she recounts losing this meagre home, as its roof flew off in a storm, rendering her family homeless again, in an anecdote made more tangible to the audience by already having witnessed her lodgings.

While the film has a linear structure, tracing the production's creative development and its realization on stage at the end, this is broken up by scenes from the stage performance interspersed throughout. Fedda explains, 'we had really limited funds, it was just me filming'; therefore, 'we couldn't really show the whole play' from just one angle.[59] Listening to the stories in the workshops, then seeing them transform on stage, she realized that she could interweave them. This lends the film a stories-within-stories structure, as it shifts back and forth between the workshops and the actual performance. The different versions of the stories are distinguished by background – variegated colours for the rehearsal room, black for the theatre and white for videos projected onstage – and costume, as the women exchange their coats and headscarves for black abayahs and veils that, fittingly for a Greek tragedy, frame their faces like masks.

In the film, the theatre director Omar Abu Saada is shown creating a new script with the women, inspired by Euripides's play yet containing 'their stories, thoughts and experiences'. In other words, they use *The Trojan Woman* as a frame narrative. The women are startled to find parallels between their experiences and the play, which they interpret as a reflection of their reality: 'It's not just in Troy. This has happened for real. It's happened to us even,' Maha says.[60] When she recites a line from the play, 'Tragedy is living a painful present while your soul yearns for happy past', she pauses, as its weighted correspondence with her own life sinks in. The play moves the women because they recognize the difficult circumstances that its characters undergo; it becomes a vehicle for articulating their own stories and sentiments. That the play belongs to a publicly owned cultural repertoire perhaps makes it easier for them to insert their stories into it, turning their experiences into something more universal. Moreover, it allows the women to speak with greater freedom about themselves through 'an element of depersonalization', switching between first and third person.[61] As Fedda remarks, 'There was the chorus, and personalities from the play to break the themes of what everyone was talking about. Using the Greek play in 2013 made people more able to express their stories, because there was a slight remove; it made them feel that it was not just them, that there was a higher purpose.'[62]

The fact that the women can 'cloak' their experiences in this way might suggest that the play works as an allegory for the contemporary regime. This is certainly how some adaptations, for example Shakespeare's plays, have functioned historically in Syria.[63] However, in neither the film nor the stage performance does the play serve a purely allegorical role, since the form of expression is both direct and indirect. In a technique that I prefer to call 'double-voicing', sometimes the women channel their own experiences through their characters; at others, they speak as themselves. In fact, at the beginning, Fedda told me, some women 'didn't see it as a play, they saw it as a platform to share their stories'.[64] Several had to negotiate being on stage with their families since, according to their conservative social customs, acting is not seen as proper behaviour for women, so they preferred to think of it as 'sharing', which made it more acceptable. On the other hand, some women are seen having fun with acting, as in one backstage scene where they express their inner divas. While sharing, they would be affected by the power of each other's stories, which they regarded as belonging to collective experience.[65] Asserting individual authorship did not concern them. At home in her kitchen, one of the women, Fatima, reveals her identification with Queen Hecuba, a high-ranking woman who 'lost everything she owned'. For Fatima, her house was her kingdom, despite being small, and she was 'the queen' of it.[66] Although the play features a number of characters, Hecuba's perspective on loss of home, family members and status resonated the most, inspiring the film's title, *Queens of Syria*. The women speak Hecuba's lines in unison when she buries her grandchild; their chorus of voices evokes a multiplicity of stories similar to these experiences.

As Fedda revealed, the women were always negotiating what stories they would share in the play or the film, aware of the different risks accompanying these media.[67] While the play was due to be performed for only two days in Jordan, the film could potentially be shown anywhere – even, via satellite TV, in Syria. These constraints on free expression are reflected in the film, which begins with the women rehearsing their lines covering their mouths with their hands. The women saw the play and the film as a way of telling the world about their struggles, which they felt had been unheard due to media underreporting. Some of them wanted to be *more* direct, so upset were they at what had happened to their families. 'We can't be afraid in our country and out of it,' one says. However, another cautions, 'People will understand that we're anti-regime. Even if we don't say it directly, people will understand that we're against Bashar.' Having grown up in a dictatorship, the women know that Syrians are well-versed in this 'cloaked' manner of speaking. Many of the women become reluctant to participate or talk about their experiences in the play since they fear repercussions for their families in Syria or for themselves should they return while Assad is still in power. They debate with Omar about whether they will reveal their names, and some of them opt to wear a *niqāb* to conceal their faces. As time goes on, the group gets smaller; a weekly countdown shows participant numbers dwindling from sixty to twenty-five.

These constraints likewise affected the making of Fedda's film. Early on, almost half the women declared that they did not want to appear on camera. Although many changed their minds later, this put the documentary in jeopardy and Fedda briefly contemplated animating it to overcome this constraint.[68] Several faces are blurred to preserve anonymity, a mark of the ingrained fear that comes from living in 'a dictatorship run on fear', even when the risks had subsided for some: 'the fear was there, so you have to be sensitive to that reality', Fedda explains.[69] Although the atrocities that the women relate in their stories were mainly carried out by the Syrian state, there are only a few mentions of Assad in the film and the stage performance itself contains no direct references to the regime. As Fedda states, some audiences, particularly Syrians, will 'understand that, if there was an incursion, it's most likely it's a regime unit or an affiliated militia'.[70] However, these meanings are not so legible to international audiences, as she discovered during screenings when she was asked, 'What about ISIS?' Before 2013, by which time the woman had left Syria and taken part in the play, ISIS was not active in Syria. Yet, due to dominant media narratives about Syria, ISIS is imagined to be the bigger threat which, as Fedda stresses, is 'a complete misunderstanding of the causes of the crisis'.[71]

As this shows, there is censorship of different kinds in how stories are shared. 'Some women's stories had really strong parallels with the play but, because they were so strong, they were too sensitive to go in the film,' Fedda notes. It is striking that there are no stories about sexual violence, a prominent theme in *The Trojan Women*. Moreover, Fedda exercised her own self-censorship, removing material 'because the situation was fragile or had changed after filming', possibly putting the women at risk.[72] This was based partly on her own knowledge of what would be sensitive in Syria and partly on checking with the women whether scenes she was planning to include were acceptable. One of the women whose situation changed was Huyam, an activist in the revolution who had powerful stories to share. She quit the production, because her family was against her performing on stage and thought it might endanger her fifteen-year-old son who had been imprisoned in Syria. When Fedda rang her afterwards, Huyam urged her to use her story. By then, she had learned that her son had been executed: 'Her position had changed horribly,' Fedda recalls. 'She had censored herself at the time, then decided she didn't want to be censored anymore.'[73]

Aside from political sensitivities, there were social constraints that caused difficulties. For example, a woman who blows a kiss backstage on the opening night got into trouble with her family because of expectations around how married women should behave. The scene appears in the version of the film

Figure 7.2 A group of Syrian refugee women rehearse their version of *The Trojan Women* with their hands covering their mouths, pointing to constraints upon their free expression. The same constraints impacted upon the film. *Queens of Syria* directed by Yasmin Fedda © Refuge Productions 2014. All Rights Reserved.

broadcast by BBC Arabic. Although it is a beautiful moment of lightness, Fedda decided to excise it from the Middle East theatrical version, while retaining it for the international festival version. The necessity for three versions of the film encapsulates the multiple constraints under which the documentary was produced. On stage towards the end, we see the women perform the same lines that they rehearsed at the beginning, with their hands cupped over their mouths: 'I have reached the end of my sorrows. I shall leave as my city turns to dust.' The repetition underscores how far they have come on their journey. As Fedda remarks, the film could have ended 'with women coming off stage, crying and emotional', yet she felt she needed 'to leave the audience with a moment to pause and reflect, because it was hard for them to go on stage and tell their stories'.[74] Instead, the film concludes with empty shots of the rehearsal room and corridors of that building to emphasize the significance of the process for the women. For its duration, the project had created a sense of purpose and freedom that they had not experienced before, along with many friendships. It gave them a chance to talk about their experiences and process the trauma that it opened up through drama therapy. When it ended, it left many feeling bereft since it wasn't going to be a regular part of their lives anymore.

In 2016, Refuge Productions brought some of the women to the UK to perform another version of the play, which emphasized themes of motherhood and migration. The accompanying brochure depicted women in Afghan-style burkas, which is not how Syrian women dress, branding them with a generic, Orientalist image of female victimhood. While the UK stage play gave the women another opportunity to get their stories heard and was an empowering experience for them, it returns us to ethical problems around how stories are shared. While the women in *Queens of Syria* are victims of violence, the documentary never shows them as *merely* victimized. Moreover, as Fedda remarks, 'Though they talked about their experiences and their children, it was them as a person, not just as a mother, through their relationships to others. I think that was important because it gives them a sense of worth – that they're not just a wife or mother.'[75] As part of her own ethical documentary practice, she has kept in touch with the women, some of whom have migrated to other countries, such as Germany and the United States, yet 'they are not in easy conditions still'.[76]

Conclusion

The films featured in this chapter have all adopted stories within stories, an influential template for which is *The Thousand and One Nights*. We have seen how filmmakers have used this technique for storytelling from multiple perspectives under crisis conditions and documenting production constraints, as well as how it functions as a resourceful means of circumventing censorship. Moreover, in the case-study films centring on female stories, the technique provides intimate tales of 'life as lived' in particular communities, for the most part challenging dominant cultural representations of Middle Eastern women and politics in the region. As shown especially in relation to *Queens of Syria*, there are issues of risk and ethical practice around how stories are shared that affect which stories are told, how they are presented and where they can be distributed. Unlike the resolute closure of conventional film narrative, these women's stories are unfinished and their telling has ongoing repercussions on their real lives. At the same time, these films testify to a determination to get stories heard or shown somehow.

In the web 2.0 era, people can upload their stories onto video-sharing websites or social media, or appropriate stories from this online storytelling database, as we will see in the next chapter on archival strategies. Among other films, we will consider the ethics of *Silvered Water, Syria Self-Portrait* (2014) which is largely composed of YouTube videos. Its authorship is attributed to '1001 Syrians' – a kind of *Thousand and One Nights* for the digital era, with a story-within-a-story structure created by embedding these online artefacts. Through these video fragments, the film gives visibility to a multiplicity of storytelling perspectives in which protesters 'tell' their stories under life-threatening circumstances and it even has a Scheherazade-like storyteller.

8

Archival strategies

Being Lebanese, with my history, I always think that anything I have can disappear forever in some twist of history.

Rania Stephan[1]

On 4 August 2020, as I was writing this book, a catastrophic explosion of ammonium nitrate stored at Beirut's port destroyed much of Gemmayzeh and Mar Mikhael, the city's hubs of art and nightlife. Among the devastated buildings was the Arab Image Foundation (AIF), founded in 1997 to safeguard the photographic heritage of the Middle East in the wake of recurrent crises and state neglect. Although their premises and equipment were severely damaged, the AIF's methods of protection saved their collection – a testament to their valuable work and ethics of care in archiving other people's images.[2] Archives in the region are frequently in a poor state or non-existent due to ravages of conflict, censorship, looting and other disasters as well as negligence resulting from underfunding and inadequate preservation. These conditions intensify gaps and occlusions: records are never made, distorted, lost, discarded or degenerate over time. But as filmmaker Mariam Ghani says, 'archive fever is most likely to break out when your history is being erased'.[3] Archival strategies arise out of these crises, as a form of creative resistance for those whose histories are contested and unevenly represented.

An archive is a place where documents (including photos, videos and other objects) are stored, usually organized according to principles of collection and access. While some archives are 'official', controlled by governments, universities and corporations, others might be classified as 'unofficial', such as home movies, home video collections and online user-generated materials, although these are increasingly reshaping what we understand as archival.[4] Whether official or unofficial, archiving is never ideologically neutral or comprehensive. For Jacques Derrida, archives don't just preserve the past; they interpret and 'produce' it through their classificatory systems and judgements about which documents are kept and which are excluded.[5] As Beirut's port explosion shows, archival documents are vulnerable to loss and ruin. In fact, Derrida suggests that the desire to archive is haunted by the threat of destruction, 'introducing, *a priori*, forgetfulness and the archiviolithic into the heart of the monument'.[6]

In salvaging fragments from archives that give visibility to a past at risk of being forgotten or wiped out, filmmakers share the sensibility of historians who critique official history's grand narratives, shifting the focus onto ordinary people's 'microhistories' and untold perspectives voiced through unofficial documents.[7] The strategy holds many possibilities for articulating desires and critical standpoints marginalized in mainstream accounts. In their purest form, archival strategies enable expressive filmmaking without recourse to a camera and on-location filmmaking. Their domain is postproduction: the assemblage of recorded materials, mediated by editing, sound, subtitles and special effects, rather than production of raw images. For this reason, archival strategies lend themselves well to working within constraints, as well as offering ways to overcome them.

The case studies in this chapter, Rania Stephan's *The Three Disappearances of Soad Hosni* (2011), Ossama Mohammed and Wiam Simav Bedirxan's *Silvered Water, Syria Self-Portrait* (2014) and Yasmin Fedda's *Ayouni* (2020), are made entirely or in a large part from archival moving images. Before looking at these films, the chapter briefly contextualizes their archival strategies in relation to practices of appropriation and postproduction in film and art history. Unlike witnessing on the spot which emphasizes immediacy (as explored in Chapter 1), archival strategies take place at a temporal and spatial remove from events. The filmmakers' roles are similar to that of a historian or curator, collecting, rearranging and preserving existing materials to tell new stories about the past in ways that resonate with the present. Yet, as members of the Pad.ma online video archive remark, 'Historians have merely interpreted the Archive. The Point however is to Feel it.'[8] At the same time, archival strategies prompt questions around what materials can be found, what can be used and how they are deployed, leading me to emphasize an ethics of care that manifests to varying degrees in the case study films.

The film medium is itself an archive, 'by virtue of its indexical and recording properties'.[9] As artefacts, films become part of archives or are incorporated into other films. Archival footage frequently provides documentary 'evidence' of the past, as in *Little Gandhi* (2016), which uncovers the forgotten history of the Syrian uprising's peaceful origins, or *Coup 53* (2019) which tells the story of UK and US covert operations to overthrow Iran's democratically elected Prime Minister Mossadegh in 1953. Nowadays, filmmakers often produce films from personal archives consisting of hundreds of hours of footage stored on their digital hard drives, as was the case in *For Sama* (2019) and *5 Broken Cameras* (2011) (discussed in Chapter 1). Their purpose may be creative as well as evidential. To distinguish the archival strategies in this chapter from more general use of archival evidence, it is helpful to invoke Jaime Baron's emphasis on the 'foundness' of found footage, consisting of a perception that the images come from another time and context of use: 'this sense of "foundness" is integral to the experience of the archive effect'.[10] In this reading, a film like *For Sama*, at least at the time of its release, is not primarily perceived as archival although this may change over time. In this respect, an additional factor suggested by Adrian Danks – 'whether or to what extent the footage's recontextualised materiality is recognised or insisted on' – serves to narrow the field of what I am talking about.[11]

Precursors of this strategy are scattered through film history. Radical possibilities for repurposing archival footage were shown by 1920s Soviet filmmakers in their use of dialectical montage. For example, Esfir Shub's *The Fall of the Romanov Dynasty* (1927) subverts the intended meanings and ideological functions of Western and Russian imperial news footage which it appropriates to narrate the 'glorious' birth of the Soviet Union, creating new connections by juxtaposing disparate fragments. Marginalized groups have also used found footage to uncover and inject new meanings into dominant texts, a strategy that, according to Paul Arthur, can be traced back to the 1960s, expressing a 'desire to reformulate tropes of historical narrative' and undertake a 'micro-political critique of historical exclusion or distortion'.[12]

By redefining the concept of creation, these practices provoke questions about boundaries between the appropriated document and its creative interpretation: where does one end and the other begin? One answer to this lies in what Baron calls 'intentional disparity', since filmmakers are incorporating the footage in ways unlikely to have been anticipated by the original producers. Even if the original producers' intentions are unknown, viewers reach 'probable conclusions' about the found footage's intended context of use and reception, which shape how we understand its recontextualization.[13] The degree of intentional disparity varies, ranging from very high at one end of the spectrum, as we will see in *Three Disappearances* and *Silvered Water*, to fairly low, when the footage's original purpose does not appear to conflict with its purpose in the film. However, there is always *some* discrepancy between the 'intentions' of the found footage and those of filmmakers appropriating it; whenever objects enter an archive or another context of use, they are 'inherently decontextualized', that is, 'detached from the conditions and situations in which they were produced'.[14] As Nicolas Bourriaud says, 'To use an object is necessarily to interpret it… We never read a book the way its author would like us to.'[15]

In 2001, Bourriaud adopted the term postproduction for a contemporary trend of making artworks from pre-existing cultural products.[16] Although he describes mostly Western artworks, this chapter's case study films use similar tactics in different contexts. Postproduction is about 'inventing protocols of use', creating original pathways through pre-existing materials and reassembling them into 'a new whole'. The artist Marcel Duchamp's ready-mades are an obvious forerunner. The creative use of archives can, further, be linked to techniques of collage and assemblage in Cubism, Dada and Surrealism as well as acts of *détournement* (subversions of a pre-existing work's intended meaning or usage) advocated by the avant-garde collective Situationist International.[17] The strategy has also been influenced by cultures of sampling and remixing, exemplified for Bourriaud by the DJ and computer programmer, 'both of whom have the task of selecting cultural objects and inserting them into new contexts'.[18] Furthermore, the Internet has generated and given access to new archives, including those hosted on social media platforms, and has led to widespread practices of repurposing known as mash-ups.

As seen in the Iranian Green Movement and 'Arab Spring', user-generated videos on social media form a vast content library documenting crisis from many perspectives. As micronarratives of events, they expand the arena of the visible and what we count as historical. Unlike traditional archives, anyone can post items for anyone else to access. On the one hand, these electronic archives are treasure troves of material; on the other, their sheer volume is a nightmare to sift through. In 2020, it was reported that over 500 hours of video were being uploaded to YouTube every minute.[19] YouTube has been hailed as 'a public, complex and heterogeneous digital archive of recorded virtual memories'.[20] However, archives are not just deposits of live memories; they are better understood as external supplements to memory, helping to retell the past in the present. As Derrida reminds us, 'The archive… will never be either memory or anamnesis as spontaneous, alive and internal experience. On the contrary: the archive takes place at the place of originary and structural breakdown of the said memory.'[21] Moreover, not everything is shared online, for numerous reasons, among them security risks and Internet speed. Zaheer Omareen, a Syrian filmmaker, told me that he knew several activists afraid to upload their videos because their faces were visible, compromising their safety while still in Syria.[22] Many terabytes of recordings remain tucked away on people's hard drives or mobile phones.

Electronic archives such as YouTube have their own curating practices shaped by powerful interests, including market forces, that affect search engine results and access to content. Search results are ranked according to matches between search terms and uploaders' textual descriptors of content, and large corporations tag themselves to their uploaded videos to ensure their visibility.[23] Descriptors have variable precision; as anyone who has performed a Google search in different languages will know, each search turns up different results. Moreover, videos are frequently removed by tech companies for breaches of copyright and community service guidelines. As Baron writes, 'On the Internet, things appear and disappear all the time.'[24] So far, Syria is the most documented conflict, yet it, too, may become an empty record. Since 2017, under pressure from the US-led coalition fighting ISIS in Iraq and Syria, social media giants have been algorithmically suppressing 'extremist' content.[25] Numerous videos have been deleted, including substantial footage from early peaceful protests, along with videos of human rights violations that conflict monitors consider valuable documents for future justice. Although some content has been restored through appeals to YouTube, other deleted videos may be lost forever as many videographers have been displaced or killed in the conflict.[26] It is not only the Syrian crisis that is at stake. Tech companies are setting rules about which 'images should be passed to future generations' and which should be consigned to oblivion, thus shaping our memory of events.[27] This is contrary to the perception, fostered by tech companies themselves, of social media platforms as a creative commons, and certainly at odds with people risking their lives to film and upload images.

Even if videos have been uploaded online for public consumption, often anonymously and without remuneration, recirculating them still raises legal and ethical challenges. Many filmmakers raid electronic archives without seeking permissions. As Joshka Wessels recounts, videographers don't appear to have any rights when their uploaded YouTube footage is recontextualized without consent by other parties who, in turn, justify their actions by saying it was impossible to contact the anonymous creators.[28] Amid wider concerns about ownership of this material, YouTube footage from the Syrian crisis has become the site of bitter conflicts over copyright, evoking the post-Marxist critique of the exploitation of digital labour.[29] According to this interpretation, exploiting and editing others' footage for free, without consent or financial rights, while enjoying all the reputational value and sales profits oneself is 'purely extractive' behaviour.[30] It becomes particularly ethically complex when the work is a record of other people's suffering. For Abounaddara, a largely anonymous filmmaking collective from Syria, what is at stake here is the appropriation of these images in ways that deprive Syrians of dignity, transforming them from revolutionaries into victims that merely arouse 'sorrow or disgust'; it denies them 'the right to represent the crimes committed against them in a way that is compatible with their own political project'.[31]

Jon Dovey argues that there should be at least an implicit contract between image-makers and filmmakers who use their content – for instance, proper credits and arrangements for image-makers to share benefits and rewards.[32] In another vein, the collective Pad.ma offers an ethical approach that transcends legal claims of copyright and 'narrow ideas' of authorship by recommending that we treat archives with 'Intellectual Propriety' rather than as 'Property'.[33] Intellectual propriety acknowledges that archivists are entrusted with other peoples' memories and transmit public knowledge. It extends care and responsibility in preservation methods to the context and content of archival documents. In the case studies, we will see how this ethics of care plays out in different ways: one fundamental concern is to safeguard the security and dignity of people appearing in the videos, especially given that some of them may be dead or still living in conflict zones; another is political agency over the historical narrative.

Online videos have been curated into archival projects by activists striving to build their own permanent record of testimonial images, rather than leaving them to the mercy of tech companies, algorithms or governments that might destroy them or distort the historical record. For example, Syrian Archive gathers and curates materials from elsewhere on the Internet on its own server; it is dedicated to mass-archiving, verifying, annotating and publicly storing evidence for accountability and justice – although without guarantees that it will be used in court – as well as counteracting revisionist or simplified narratives.[34] Other collectives commemorate creative resistance, such as Creative Memory of the Syrian Revolution which archives Syrian artworks in the name of solidarity with the Syrian people,[35] or Mosireen whose *858: An Archive of Resistance* compiles footage from the Egyptian Revolution as a resource for future uprisings. Unlike Syrian Archive, 858 does not seek to document crimes and appeal to an absent law; rather, its aim is 'narrating our version of the story'.[36]

In contrast to these collective endeavours, the feature-length films that form this chapter's case studies belong to an authorial cinema. They are made by filmmakers, not necessarily activists, who imprint their distinctive vision and personality on the material. They work in a different country from the subject matter they are dealing with, and their use of archival strategies is facilitated by the fact that they do not require on-location production. As Fedda, director of *Ayouni*, explains, the risks she faces are lower than those of people witnessing on the ground and so she sees her role as amplifying their voices.[37] Whereas 'witnessing' videos capture the immediacy of unfolding events, the feature films that appropriate them take a broader view, curating the sounds and images to construct a memory of these conflicts that will endure in their aftermath. Yet by drawing on archives, films are conditioned by their limits. For example, Ali Samadi Ahadi's *The Green Wave*, whose use of animation was discussed in Chapter 3, also uses social media archives and was shaped by what was available on the Internet. Despite the fact that Iran has one of the world's most active social media populations, text-based activities such as blogging and tweeting are more prevalent there than video-uploading due to the government's periodic blocking of YouTube (including during the 2009 protests) and speed-limiting of the Internet. As a result, Samadi's team had limited video material, a constraint that led them to use animation as a creative strategy to bring to life character-driven stories based on blog entries. As well as extending the lifespan of materials that may not endure on the Internet, films such as this perform a vital service of cultural translation, since they give visibility to documents that might otherwise be invisible to outside audiences unlikely to find this footage themselves or watch it without subtitles.

Mohammed Ali Atassi has argued that videographers and filmmakers 'belong to two different worlds' and that, by extension, film theory's tools are not meant for analysing videos on the Internet.[38] Although I respect the grounds on which he makes this claim – namely, that videographers and filmmakers are working in different contexts – I take a different perspective. Digital video is often claimed to be 'something else', even if it is 'descended' from film and contains cinematic layers in its shots.[39] At the same time, the rise of newer technologies has inspired the rethinking of cinema. Intermediality, the study of relations between different media, suggests that cinema, along with any other medium, has always been mixed and impure. Although known (erroneously) as a theorist of cinematic specificity, André Bazin recognized this in his essay 'In Defense of Mixed Cinema' (1951).[40] Shifting media technologies and aesthetic practices have exposed cinema to change throughout its history, making it evolve and adapt into new forms. Claims for a 'historical break' return us to an essentialist position of media purity rather than this more historicist view of media impurity.[41] The use of archival footage is itself a hybrid and impure strategy in which contents of newer media are found in an older one, or vice versa. We can see this in *The Green Wave*, which is composed of many different media, as well as in this chapter's case studies.

Another way of telling: *The Three Disappearances of Soad Hosni*

The Egyptian film star Soad Hosni died in 2001 after falling from a London high-rise apartment in what were rumoured to be suspicious circumstances. *The Three Disappearances of Soad Hosni* is a fiction film constructed from VHS clips from her long career, which spanned from 1959 to 1991. Its Lebanese director, Rania Stephan, physically procured videotapes of Hosni's entire oeuvre, then digitized them. Although several of Hosni's films have a digital afterlife on YouTube, older VHS technology was the only way of salvaging her complete body of work and many original negatives in Egypt's National Film Archives have been lost or destroyed due to 'inadequate storage facilities and two major fires'.[42] The materiality of media becomes tangible when they are duplicated and reformatted, as they are in movies with archival footage, resulting in loss of resolution. Laura Marks suggests that archival fragments retain the trace of their material history, like the train of a lady's gown that 'sweeps up and carries along debris as she passes'.[43] In *Three Disappearances*, the ageing VHS images are fuzzy, streaked with tracking lines and static resulting from damage to magnetic tapes. White spots, squiggles and colour splodges inherited from original film negatives further add to their textures, lovingly preserved in Stephan's movie, as she remarks: 'Everything comes from VHS… every breath, phrase, image, scratch, the music; everything comes from the body of films of Soad Hosni.'[44] Her film makes expressive use of the 'poor' image, part of a longer history of archival strategies in experimental cinema; it also forms a precursor to appropriation of online archives in films such as *Silvered Water*, as we will see.

Three Disappearances was created entirely in postproduction, a method adopted partly because of Stephan's artistic training but also, she says, as 'an aesthetic and moral choice' not to submit to production and permit procedures.[45] She works 'under the radar' in a small-scale, artisanal way that gives her creative freedom, although it comes with financial and other constraints. In Lebanon, her work has largely been shown in galleries, which are exempt from screening permits, and it has been exhibited in museums and in some theatres worldwide.

Stephan calls herself 'a sculptor of images'.[46] The images are 'matter' that she works with, and ideas are shaped 'through the materiality of the images' in the editing process. 'It's not like I sit down and wait for the idea to come,' she told me. 'You have to go inside the image and feel it.'[47] For her, editing is not merely a technical process or rational construction of story, it is also a sensual and physical relation: 'When you edit you experience the image over again. It's completely tactile – the way you sit in front of it, the way you receive it through your eyes, your ears... Sometimes I edit without thinking. It's about how images resonate with each other, the underground layers that come through.'[48] This applies to *Panoptic*, a film that Stephan edited (discussed in Chapter 4), as well as her own films in which sound and image are lent equal importance. 'I often edit with my ears,' she says.[49] While inspired by experimental cinema, her use of sound is similar to that of a DJ, 'copying and pasting together loops of sound'.[50] She constructs her soundtrack from existing dialogue and music, building new scenes from extracts and layering together sounds and images from different films.

In *Three Disappearances*, Stephan 'reshuffles' Hosni's body of work into a new fiction.[51] It is structured as a flashback of Hosni's life. In a prologue, Hosni lies on an analyst's couch, trying to remember her past. 'A tragedy in three acts' follows, consisting of a montage of clips from her different film roles that unfold her memories and dreams. Stephan's editing turns Egyptian popular cinema into a dream-like avant-garde work reminiscent of surrealist practices. In Act One, Soad is a young actress whose sensuality embodies the secular spirit of pan-Arab nationalism; she is a self-declared 'child of the [1952] revolution'. In the second act, she undergoes one marriage after another, as she did in real life. By Act Three, she is a mature actress. The dream has turned into a nightmare, filled with tears, divorce, death and torture, the trauma of these events enhanced by video static that forms part of the editing rhythm. Here, Hosni dreams of falling from a construction site and finally identifies her own dead body at a morgue. Principles of continuity editing, such as eyeline match, are used to join together and construct a story from disparate clips.

The film recounts not just Hosni's life, but also Egypt's modern political and cultural history. Tonally, it moves from the optimism of pan-Arab nationalism, which peaked in the 1960s, a time when social change seemed a real possibility, to the dark years of Mubarak's brutal dictatorship (1981–2011). The structure reflects the historical vantage-point from which Stephan made the film; it was completed in early 2011, coincidentally just as the Egyptian Revolution started and protesters were singing Hosni's song 'I'm going down to the square'. It starts portentously with footage of the Cairo fires on 26 January 1952 which were anti-British protests that have been likened to the 25 January 2011 'Day of Rage' against police brutality.[52] These political events can be referenced in *Three Disappearances* precisely because it is built from popular clips: cultural artefacts that are 'materializations'[53] of historical and ideological narratives. The film charts Egyptian cinema's golden age and its decline, hastened by removal of state support for the industry which soon after lost its dominance of Arab popular culture to regional satellite TV networks.

In contemporary archival film practices, Baron identifies 'a desire to find and "collect" the contingent synchronicities that occur across sources previously unrelated to one another'.[54] *Three Disappearances* assembles similar gestures and actions from Hosni's films, revealing textual and cultural patterns. In one sequence, drawing on snippets from *Al-Karnak* (1975) where Hosni plays a student political activist who undergoes torture, state brutality and domestic violence are juxtaposed. This lends the film to an allegorical reading, like the one proposed by Catherine Russell, centring around Hosni's fall in which she embodies both the failure of utopian ideals and the fading of a female star, valued only for her appearance and subject to 'the obsolescence intrinsic to commodity capitalism'.[55] However, *Three Disappearances* is open to many different interpretations. It is also, as I have suggested, another way of telling Egypt's modern history. Due to present-day censorship, Hosni's early films cannot be shown in their entirety on Egyptian television: 'even a kiss is now forbidden'.[56] As Bourriaud remarks, art has an ability 'to give shape and weight to… what is disappearing before our eyes'.[57] Through its archival fragments, *Three Disappearances* renders visible these 'disappearances' that have profoundly altered the media and political landscape during Hosni's career.

Preserving the stories of the multitude: *Silvered Water, Syria Self-Portrait*

Silvered Water, Syria Self-Portrait contains YouTube videos shot on mobile phones by anonymous videomakers during the early years of the Syrian revolution and war, footage taken by Wiam Simav Bedirxan, an amateur Syrian-Kurdish filmmaker from the besieged city of Homs, and an exchange of letters between her and her co-director Ossama Mohammed. In the credits, Mohammed acknowledges the film's collective authorship, attributing it to '1001 Syrians, Wiam Bedirxan and me'. He selects and arranges this material to relay stories within stories, *Thousand and One Nights*-style, told by diverse actors – activists, armed rebels, jihadis, regime soldiers and torturers – who filmed the images. A veteran filmmaker previously known for his poetic experimental cinema made under Syria's National Film Organisation, Mohammed left Syria for France in May 2011, believing his life was in danger after protesting against the regime's detention of activists. *Silvered Water* was inspired by the YouTube videos he saw online, 'Watching from far away, I had the feeling that my internal time had become corrupt. I wanted to save myself and my humanity.'[58] The strategy of using online archives enabled Mohammed to overcome the constraints of distance and exile. Maisoun Assad, another Syrian exile in Paris, helped him find the footage online and later became the film's editor. The film's subtitle, *Syria Self-Portrait*, epitomizes its archival strategy: assembling a multitude of user-generated videos that together constitute a 'self-portrait' of Syrians' collective suffering.

In his voice-over, Mohammed contemplates the YouTube videos from afar, making personal associations. For him, 'Syria's 2011 revolution was a revolution of images', heralding a new kind of cinema liberated from standard conventions of quality and artistic unity.[59] He offers a poetic reading of this amateur footage, as Lebanese artists Ali Cherri and Rabih Mroué have also done in their work.[60] However, more than any other film about the Syrian crisis, *Silvered Water* has attracted severe criticism. Since an emphasis on graphic violence contributes to local and international powers' sensationalist narratives of the Syrian conflict as sectarian and barbaric,[61] *Silvered Water* has, firstly, been lambasted from this perspective. Its graphic imagery has been called Orientalist, even judged as such merely by its references to *The Thousand and One Nights*, and unfavourably contrasted with Abounaddara's ethical practice of avoiding direct depictions of violence. Abounaddara themselves have raised questions about the dignity of the people who appear in the videos.[62] Secondly, critics have contested *Silvered Water*'s interpretation of the mobile phone videos as a new form of cinema, arguing that this footage's purpose was simply to document, without any cinematic or expressive purpose.[63] Thirdly, although Mohammed credits the film to '1001 Syrians', it has been argued that his voice-over dominates the footage and 'paradoxically silences the voices of the Syrians that Mohammed himself wishes so much to be heard'.[64] This lays the film open to charges of extractive labour discussed earlier: the exploitation of amateur footage as 'raw material' by a professional filmmaker not responsible for its production who benefits by turning it into an artistic commodity.[65]

While these arguments have gained traction among some critics, I want to show how Mohammed's approach shares some common ground with the amateur creators and activates this footage's long-term significance. As emphasized earlier, when archival fragments are repurposed in a film, they are recontextualized. Removed from their original context, the videos in *Silvered Water* are layered with subjective associations and suffused with poetic ambiguity. Their original 'intentions', however, can be perceived beneath, like a palimpsest.[66] For example, in one of many videos showing the aftermath of an attack, the camera phone is dropped in the chaos, capturing sounds of screaming and partial glimpses of skin and fabric, a person lying on the ground and trails of blood. We have just been jolted into the embodied experience of a terrified Syrian protestor, filming their surroundings at that instant. Although the unsteady, pixelated images result from the urgency under which they were recorded and are *probably* not intended by the filmer as expressive qualities, it is precisely these that interest Mohammed as signs of a new cinema and that invite us, as viewers, to reconsider the footage. Some images are repeated or slowed down, with the original sound removed and the director's voice-over laid over them – established techniques in archival movies that emphasize intentional disparity, often to reveal hidden subtexts.[67] Despite their differing outlooks and backgrounds, Mohammed finds common cause with the videographers since his purpose, too, is to commemorate martyrs and preserve moments for others to see, although by a different route.

In the videos, many people, unknown to each other, documented their experiences in an uncoordinated manner and uploaded their footage online. In *Silvered Water*, we obtain a 'god's eye view'[68] of this multitude: their stories are gathered together in a mosaic structure, like *The Thousand and One Nights*. The film itself acts as an archive, creating not a single story but a multi-strand narrative of that time. Mohammed told me that the first YouTube video he watched – of a '"Teenager boy" in the back of a pickup car, bending over the body of his father, raising his head to the sky and sobbing' – was what prompted him to make the film.[69] This video forms one of many recurring images, along with that of a newborn baby having its umbilical cord cut and a teenager in prison, one of several schoolboys from Dera'a arrested for writing anti-regime graffiti whose brutal treatment in custody was a catalyst of the revolution. A signifier of birth, the newborn baby implies causal links between stories. As Mohammed puts it, 'The story of the boy who got arrested gave birth to demonstrations [which] gave birth to a new cinema and to the anonymous filmmaker. The first demonstration caused the first massacre [which] causes a funeral… and gives birth to the rebellion of the first soldier, Spartacus.'[70] Although not a linear timeline, *Silvered Water*'s sequencing reflects the cycle of protests, outrage and grief in video content uploaded by the Syrian opposition: street demonstrations, followed by funerals, more demonstrations, bombings and other war crimes. 'Spartacus', the video of soldier Walid Qashami announcing his defection from the regime army, is important to the revolution's chronology since he was the first army defector (he later disappeared in 2013 and is still missing). Speaking to camera, he holds up his military ID in defiance of the regime and testifies how he was ordered to fire on peaceful protestors under the pretext that they were an armed gang, setting the pattern for many defector videos that followed. Combining oppositional footage with videos by regime agents, who recorded themselves carrying out atrocities or at leisure, *Silvered Water* offers prismatic micro-histories of the conflict that differ from either official regime or international media coverage. Contrary to claims about the film's attempted appeal to Western audiences, this structure is only apparent to those familiar with the events or who have studied them closely.

The selected footage reveals patterns that the filmmakers-turned-curator has found within the YouTube archive, establishing their own coherence on these

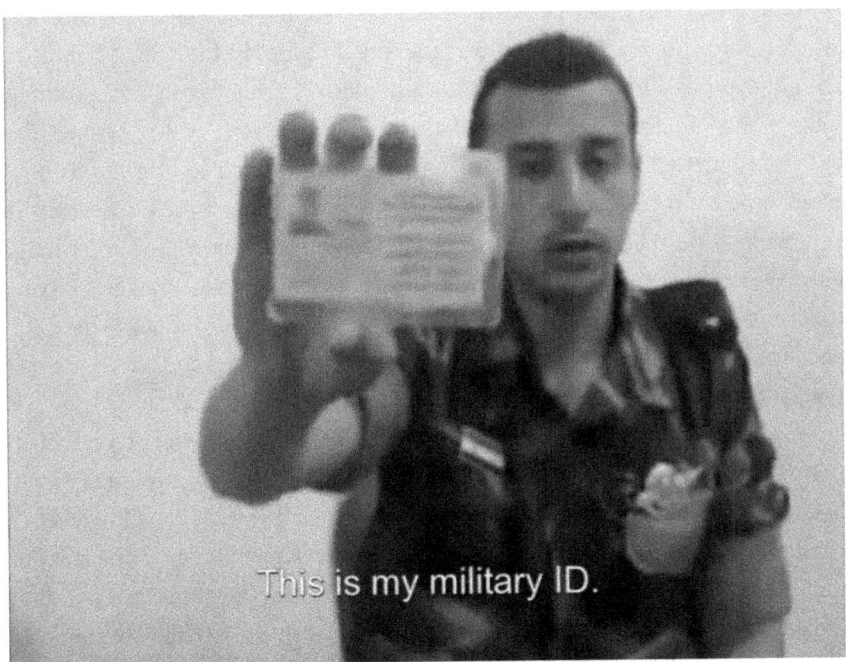

Figure 8.1 A mosaic composition of YouTube clips presents stories of the multitude during the early years of the Syrian revolution and war, including a video by the first Syrian army defector, Walid Qashami. *Silvered Water, Syria Self-Portrait* directed by Ossama Mohammed and Wiam Simav Bedirxan © Les Films d'ici and Proaction Film 2014. All Rights Reserved.

previously unrelated fragments. As in *Three Disappearances*, the patterns express synchronicities inconceivable by the image-makers themselves, including patterns of human behaviour. For example, in one sequence, people poignantly attempt to bring home dead bodies lying on the street by pulling them in with a rope, since it is too dangerous to venture out themselves – an effort to bestow dignity with last rites. As Baron mentions, digital archives and search engines have created unprecedented opportunities for filmmakers to aggregate hundreds of unrelated videos into a 'chorus' of voices speaking of human pluralities.[71] It is precisely this chorus that *Silvered Water* evokes with its '1001' references.

Mohammed sought ways 'to compose a character of the anonymous image-maker' who is 'the "Hero of this time"'.[72] However, he says, 'it was not easy to build a cinematic personage, from and with huge numbers of defiant images of Syria, or tragic Syria'.[73] Amidst the chorus, the voice of the opera singer Nouma Omran can be heard humming and sighing on the soundtrack. Mohammed regards her as the film's 'hidden narrator', a Scheherazade figure whose voice later 'merges and becomes one with that of Simav'; in a powerful sequence, Nouma's lyrics and Simav's voice-over echo each other. Credited as co-director, Simav is introduced around a third of the way through the film. She personifies the anonymous filmmaker. The film's title derives from her name, meaning 'silver water' in Kurdish; it also alludes to silver nitrate, which formed the basis of film stock. Simav, then, becomes the storyteller. The film recalls how Mohammed and Simav met online. 'Are you Ossama Mohammed?' she asks. 'If your camera were here in Homs, what would you have captured?' 'Everything', he answers. Simav travels 500 miles to obtain a camera, then smuggles it back to Homs. Her footage has been regarded as commissioned footage, since 'the encounter between the two allowed Mohammed to have eyes and hands in Syria that he could, to some extent, control from a distance'.[74] It is certainly true that he originated cinematic devices such as their exchange of letters (conducted, like Mohammed's voice-over, in poetic, standard Arabic) but, although Simav had no previous experience of filmmaking, her footage makes startling creative choices that distinguish it from the rest of the movie. She narrates the story of besieged Homs and the school that she opens, and accompanies a small boy, Omar, gathering roses for his father's grave – a beautiful act that recomposes the film's painful world. If anything, her footage has even more of a collecting tendency than Mohammed's selection of YouTube videos. What she collects are heart-rending images of starving, wounded cats and dead children – all innocent victims of regime bombings.[75] If the world doesn't care about Syrian people's suffering, these sequences seem to say, maybe it will care about cats.

As Derrida noted, death haunts the archive. In *Silvered Water*, we look at these '1001' stories, 'each a metonymic fragment'[76] of the larger archive from which they came, and see lives lost and destroyed, people who may now be dead, victims of a genocide who can never be brought back. *Silvered Water* is haunted by the pathos of this loss, even as it tries to preserve the victims' memory in film. It recalls what Bazin calls 'the mummy complex' implicit in film and photography; the 'desire to preserve objects against the ravages of time' is a defence against death, compelled by the irrational belief that we can.[77] Several years after the revolution, many of these videos have disappeared from the Internet, for reasons discussed earlier. With its archival strategy, *Silvered Water* has accrued a historical value, since it enables these stories to be replayed in a thoughtful manner. The significance of this footage has also changed over time, from documenting creative resistance to being a record of the past, perhaps a pledge of justice for the future. As Enrico De Angelis remarks, for the videographers, '[t]he photographic act becomes the last resource against the danger of oblivion' which would erase the memory of the victims forever.[78] This is what Mohammed recognizes when he claims that 'aesthetic and ethical criteria are the same; Syrians were resisting violence with beauty. The criterion of beauty is to rescue the tale of the victim from oblivion. Beauty is when you retain justice somewhere, even if this somewhere is in the future.'[79]

Intimate access to memories of the disappeared: *Ayouni*

In the documentary *Ayouni*, the protagonists are the lovers Bassel and Noura and siblings Paolo and Machi. Bassel Khartabil Safadi, a Syrian open-source software developer and activist who established Creative Commons Syria, was disappeared by the Syrian regime in 2015. Father Paolo Dall'Oglio, an Italian Jesuit priest, lived for over thirty years in Syria, where he turned the Deir Mar Musa monastery into a centre for interfaith dialogue. After his expulsion by the Syrian government in 2012, he smuggled himself back into the country to negotiate hostages' release in Raqqa, where he himself was kidnapped, presumably by ISIS, in 2013. *Ayouni* follows Noura and Machi in their search for their missing loved ones, giving the disappeared voice and visibility through its archival strategies.

Ayouni's British-Palestinian director, Yasmin Fedda, did not set out to make a documentary about enforced disappearance. She had filmed with Paolo previously, between 2004 and 2010, then began filming him again when he became active in the Syrian Revolution; his kidnapping dramatically changed her film's course. Meeting many Syrians who knew people who had disappeared led her to understand that forcible disappearance was being used as a systematic tactic, in the vast majority of cases by the regime.[80] As mentioned in previous chapters, it has also occurred in Lebanon, Egypt and Iran. An international crime deployed in many contexts over the last century, enforced disappearance is an attempt to make people vanish without a trace and silence them, leaving relatives in a painful state of uncertainty about their loved ones' fate and whereabouts, unsure if they are alive or dead. In Syria, as elsewhere, activists are often the targets, particularly those who stand up for free speech.

What makes disappearance peculiar as a crime also poses a problem for filmmaking: how does one resurrect bodies that are absent and invisible, and convey the void of forcible disappearance to audiences? *Ayouni* has parallels with films from Argentina and Chile addressing enforced disappearance. There is no closure as such, since people are still missing and families continue to seek justice. But those films are mainly about the medium to long-term past.[81] 'There's a passage of time and a different kind of reflection,' says Fedda. In Syria, 'we're still in the middle of it... People are still being detained and disappeared'.[82] So in *Ayouni* reflection can only be 'very close to the moment'.[83] As we will see, the film works creatively within these constraints by using its archival footage to narrate the story in the present tense.

One of Fedda's aims was to try to understand forcible disappearance 'in an intimate way, rather than a statistical way [that just] talks about it as a crime. It *is* a crime, but [I wanted] to go behind what happens.'[84] Although she personally knew Paolo and Bassel, it was only later that she met Machi and Noura. Through meeting them, she came to grasp the phenomenon through relationships:

> When I understood that was our key to unlock it, I also understood that was how we needed to build the film. And I also realized that I had my own footage of Paolo that I'd filmed from the past [and] I had access to Bassel and Noura's footage that their friends had filmed and that they had filmed [which] could bring the disappeared, Bassel and Paolo, to life in their own voices. We could create a presence through our edit, so that we live with them a little bit. So that was our way to bring that presence back.[85]

Roughly half of *Ayouni* is composed of different types of found footage (in addition to Bassel and Noura's personal archives, this includes YouTube videos of the revolution and television archive material), while the other half is shot by Fedda herself. While, as high-profile activists, both Paolo and Bassel had become global icons, *Ayouni* remembers them as people known and loved by their closest ones. Fedda attempts to use the footage to tell her protagonists' story 'through their eyes', in the present tense, eliminating voice-over which, as seen in *Silvered Water*, often imposes other meanings; instead, the film retains the original audio-visual qualities, as a way of giving back 'voice' to the images.

Bassel and Noura's personal archives can be classified as 'home mode' records, in the sense that they were, like home movies, intended for private rather than public communication.[86] Filmed by themselves or their friends, the footage contains a special intimacy, as in a cafe scene when they have just got engaged. Bassel and Noura are then at their closest and happiest, laughing and joking about when they first met. They are even sharing the same chair; they couldn't be closer. As Fedda says, these moments transport viewers into their lives, enabling them somehow to relive what the lovers were feeling.[87] Like footage of the uprisings uploaded to YouTube, they narrate from the micro-historical perspectives of people inside these events. But while most of those YouTube videos are intended for public consumption and document public events, home mode activities are private, intimate and personal, filmed in domestic and interior spaces. Increasingly, 'with the advent of analog video and then digital cameras, moments that previously might not have been preserved on film... are now recorded and retained', among them intimate occasions and moments when the filmer records themselves alone.[88] This proliferation in the recording of private

Figure 8.2 Bassel and Noura's personal archives tell their story through their perspective to foster a more intimate understanding of forcible disappearance. *Ayouni* directed by Yasmin Fedda © Banyak Films and Hakawati 2020. All Rights Reserved.

lives is what enables present-tense narration in *Ayouni* and what distinguishes it from many previous documentaries about enforced disappearance that are retrospective accounts of what happened. As Fedda says, we are now in a unique position compared to over thirty years ago when people were not filming as much – access to personal video archives is 'such an opportunity to tell those stories more fully or in a different way, not only by someone explaining to us but by feeling it with them'.[89]

These personal archives come with further ethical challenges intensified by the currency of events, posing this question for Fedda: 'How do I make sure people are safe when I put this out?'[90] As she did for *Queens of Syria* (discussed in Chapter 7) she negotiated with individuals involved before making the work public, because of potential repercussions: 'As a filmmaker it's really important to constantly have those conversations, that you're clear with everyone what you're doing,' she stresses.[91] The use of other people's private communications in a film has distinct ethical implications since it transfers artefacts from a private to a public context of reception for which they were never intended.[92] For example, the day after her engagement party, Noura filmed herself wearing her engagement ring, curled up alone on her bed at home. This intimate video, meant for Bassel's eyes only, gives us a sense of entering a private moment. Found in a hard drive that Fedda obtained from Noura, it was used with her permission.

Watching *Ayouni* is like jacking into other people's memories, reminiscent of science-fiction films such as *Mnemophrenia* (2019) or *Strange Days* (1995) where characters access recorded memories via a headset. In this case, there is no headset – just the film itself. As Fedda suggests, filmmaking is a 'memory-making machine' for events we have not experienced first-hand.[93] Although she was not there when footage of Bassel and Noura was shot, watching it repeatedly during the edit turned it into, not a lived memory exactly, but something familiar that acts like a memory:

> [W]orking with footage shot by someone else, actually Bassel himself, it's really strange watching it again and again because you feel so present, yet you're not... I mean, when I watched that material, I could feel Bassel there, I could feel Paolo there. I understood that, sometimes, there are just these tiny fragments, that little clip we had of someone, [that] gave us something about these people's lives and voices.[94]

Although it was not Fedda's intention, *Ayouni* has become a memory for Noura, preserving her relationship with Bassel.[95] As Ghani writes, 'A film archive is...

full of flickering images of things and people long lost.'⁹⁶ *Ayouni* uses its archival footage to evoke memory, as when Noura is shown alone in the kitchen, waiting for a pan of water to boil, and smoking on the balcony. Like a fleeting memory, a brief snippet of the footage of Bassel in the café materializes, then vanishes, replaced by a black screen; as viewers, we, too, are made to feel loss, as Bassel is taken away from us.

Scenes like this activate the metaphoric potential of the film's title. Literally meaning 'my eyes' in Arabic, *ayouni* is also a term of endearment between lovers and siblings. Bassel, the beloved, disappears from Noura's vision. On a black screen, the words of a poem by Dunya Mikhail appear, read in Fedda's off-screen voice: 'If the world were flat/like a flying carpet, our sorrow/would have a beginning and an end.' Similar to Middle Eastern oral storytelling, where poetry is inserted into prose narrative,⁹⁷ *Ayouni* is punctuated by intervals of poetry to create a respite from the stories and pause for reflection upon their meaning.⁹⁸ But while poetry is often an indirect mode of telling, Iraqi-American poet Mikhail's work was chosen for *Ayouni* because of its straightforwardness.⁹⁹ It offers a lucid way of imagining what it is like to lose someone through its simple, cosmic metaphors.¹⁰⁰

While archive footage, along with poetry, forms a creative solution to the problem of representing disappearance, reliance upon it also becomes a constraint. Through an interview that Noura gives, we learn that she and Bassel got married in prison. The film does not show us their secret wedding nor does it tell us that Noura visited Bassel in prison regularly for two years before he finally disappeared in 2015. The complex circumstances behind this were that Bassel was initially disappeared, then reappeared in a civilian prison, managing to get word out to his family via another prisoner.¹⁰¹ There, Noura was able to visit him, both as a human rights lawyer specializing in political prisoner detention and as his partner. As part of the #FreeBassel campaign, Noura took letters to Bassel and posted his replies online. Despite trying out experiments with filming their letters, these events were eventually excluded from the film because they did not 'fit' its emotional arc, the crew were not there to document them and there was no archival footage.¹⁰² Cinema, documentary filmmaking in particular, is always constrained by what can be presented as a counterpart to experience, although this can conflict with actual events, since Bassel did not vanish from Noura's eyes in the abrupt and final way that the film suggests.

In one scene in *Ayouni*, Bassel films a person demonstrating how to shoot with a hidden phone camera by inserting it under his shirt, where it acts like another 'eye' during protests. Part of Bassel's work involves uploading witness footage online to ensure that it is disseminated to the world: 'Otherwise there'll be massacres happening without anyone knowing about it,' he says in the film. In their different ways, both Bassel and Paolo use their platforms for witnessing, evoking another connotation of the word *ayouni*: 'seeing'. However, as seen in Chapter 1, witnessing is usually carried out by someone there at the time, filming and sharing in the hope of bringing about change. This raises questions about the value of archival strategies that give access to knowledge after events have passed. Does a film like *Ayouni* 'position us as belated witnesses', as one audience member asked during a Q&A?[103] Fedda answered, 'Even if you are belatedly witnessing, you still are.'[104] Not forgetting the disappeared is part of the long-term value of films such as *Ayouni*, which turns private memories into public knowledge; for relatives and those who are detained this is an important basis for solidarity. Moreover, Fedda believes the film can play a role by encouraging people to report disappeared family members (since many disappearances go unrecorded) and put pressure on authorities: 'It's a very slow, long process but if we can plant the seeds for justice and accountability', families may eventually obtain answers to what happened to their loved ones; along with legal frameworks, it can be 'one little piece in that larger struggle.'[105] Finally, since enforced disappearance is not just a Syrian issue but one with 'international reach and resonance', this lends the film potential to inspire conversations about other histories of the disappeared, and it has been subtitled into seven languages for this purpose.[106]

Conclusion

In this chapter we have seen how archival strategies are driven by contested histories and even the threat of the destruction of archives themselves. I have argued against the idea of a digital break by emphasizing the character of archival strategies, which mix different media. Since archival films are mainly created in the edit, they offer ways of working within constraints, such as limited access to locations, making them amenable to filmmakers working abroad. Through assemblage and mediation of material artefacts, filmmakers can construct alternative historical accounts that counter dominant narratives and may endure longer than the artefacts themselves. Their archival strategies give these artefacts an afterlife, lending them an ongoing power and testimony for belated witnessing by new audiences. As this chapter has stressed, especially in relation to *Ayouni*, archival strategies have a value in communicating knowledge after events have passed, since they offer thoughtful reflection on those events and can play a part in struggles for justice and accountability.

As Derrida suggests, the archive is not merely a record of the past but an undertaking for the future since it poses 'the question of a response, promise and of a responsibility for tomorrow'.[107] An ethical responsibility is invested in the archive, partly because it is an attempt to battle disappearances of different kinds. Further, appropriating materials produced by others and transferring them to another context of use require an ethics of care over the dignity, safety and political agency of people who appear in them. The films in this chapter are conditioned by limits of the archive itself: 'since it is impossible for every – or any – single event to be recorded from every possible angle, there will always be missing pieces in the histories we were able to tell'.[108] But these films (and this book itself) form a collective archive of the times of crisis in which they were made.

9

Sci-fi dystopia

The period following the Green Movement protests in Iran and the 'Arab Spring' has been a rollercoaster ride of euphoria and despair. Hopes for a better future have faded as the situation has worsened economically, politically and socially in many parts of the region, manifesting in resurgent dictatorships, civil wars, the rise of extremist groups, rampant inflation, high unemployment and the ongoing colonization of Palestine. Science-fiction dystopia often extrapolates from present tendencies and projects them into the future, acting as 'the canary in a cage... warning us of terrible sociopolitical tendencies that could, if continued, turn our contemporary world into the iron cages portrayed'.[1] As reality overtakes fiction, many citizens in the region already have a sense of living in dystopias, seemingly making redundant the need to *imagine* them.

Science fiction, however, is more than a predictive genre; it emerges from crisis, being 'predominantly found in the great whirlpools of history'.[2] Moreover, as Michael Gordin, Helen Tilley and Gyan Prakash suggest, 'utopias and dystopias are histories of the present' – practices used by historical actors to understand their contemporary environment.[3] In this chapter, dystopia designates both a sub-genre of science fiction and a perception of unliveable conditions. The term comes from the Greek *dus-topos*, designating 'a diseased, bad, faulty, or unfavourable place'.[4] It evokes its apparent opposite, utopia, which has a double meaning: both 'no place' from the Greek *ou-topos*, and 'a good place', an earthly paradise, from the near-identical *eu-topos*. In their imagining, utopia and dystopia are implicated in each other, shown by the 'dystopian transfiguration' of utopian hopes of the uprisings in subsequent counterrevolutions and repressions.[5]

Darko Suvin describes science fiction as the art of 'cognitive estrangement', 'a creative approach' that dynamically transforms the author's environment, using 'imagination as a means of understanding the tendencies latent in reality'.[6] It creates an alternate reality that is a cousin of the one in which we are living. Totalitarian states are a staple of dystopian fiction, including classics such as *We*

(1924), *1984* (1949) and *The Handmaid's Tale* (1985); the popularity of the latter soared in the United States after Donald Trump's election in 2016, indicating the topic's wider salience. With its themes of thought control, surveillance and rewriting the past, *1984* exemplifies the genre's preoccupation with freedom of expression. Science fiction's 'estranging devices'[7] have, moreover, historically provided cover for sociopolitical commentary. As Ian Campbell writes, Arab science-fiction novelists such as Ahmed Towfik have 'learned to conceal their critique under layers of story in order to provide plausible deniability in the face of scrutiny by their regime'.[8]

Science fiction is a burgeoning strategy in filmmaking from the region, as recognized by a growing body of scholarship.[9] However, the case studies in this chapter – Ali Ahmadzadeh's *Atomic Heart Mother* (2015), Johanna Domke and Marouan Omara's *Dreamaway* (2018), Larissa Sansour's *Nation Estate* (2013) and Mounia Akl's *Submarine* (2016) – defy genre or are genre-blurring rather than fully embracing sci-fi dystopia. By taking on hybrid forms, they expand the dystopian imagination's creative and critical possibilities. The films' unconventional approaches also relate to ways in which science fiction's poetics of estrangement have developed in the Middle East, where it has strong affinities with surrealism, magic realism and fantastic tales such as *The Thousand and One Nights* which, as discussed in Chapter 7, has Persian, Arabic and Indian provenance.[10] The Arabic and Persian words for science fiction, *khayāl 'ilmi* and *dāstān takhayli 'ilmi*, respectively, derive from the Arabic word *khayāl*, meaning 'spirit', 'vision', 'fantasy' and 'imagination'; they stress otherworldly realms 'outside normal reality' much more than the English equivalent.[11] While Suvin excludes fantasy from his definition of science fiction, insisting that science-fiction worlds are possible rather than impossible, the fabulous and the oneiric are indispensable elements of Middle Eastern science fiction.

As we will see, dreams serve important functions in this chapter's films, acting as both a protective shield for sensitive subject matter and a means for moving fluidly between reality and fantasy. Laura Marks writes that 'Many Muslims take dreams and visions seriously as signs of a reality more real than material reality and greater than individual imagination'.[12] This is true not only of Islamic but also other Eastern philosophies in which dreams are held to emanate from exterior environments. A linguistic reflection of this thinking can be found in the fact that the English phrase 'I had a dream' literally translates as 'I saw a dream' in Persian, Arabic and Indian sub-continental languages, contrasting with the concept of the dream as a product of an individual psyche in much of Western thought and Freudian psychoanalysis.[13]

In these case studies, it is the often-unbelievable strangeness produced by the external environment that acts as a stimulus to the filmmakers' creativity. While Campbell characterizes Arabic science-fiction literature as allegorical, sociopolitical commentary in the films works through surreal crossovers between reality and fiction rather than hidden subtexts. In this sense, they are like a pointing finger, which C.S. Peirce classifies as a type of index: 'The index asserts nothing; it only says "There!" It takes hold of our eyes, as it were, and forcibly directs them to a particular object, and there it stops.'[14] Furthermore, for these filmmakers, the motivation for adopting science-fictional strategies is not just to overcome state censorship but also other limitations. They turn these limitations into an advantage by making use of 'found' dystopias or alternate realities on their doorsteps, such as polluted cityscapes and desert landscapes.

The Middle East has frequently lent its landscapes to Western science fiction, turning deserts into a mainstay of the genre's iconography. George Lucas shot *Star Wars: A New Hope* (1977) and its immediate sequels in Tunisia, where he found a location for the alien desert planet Tatooine. *Star Wars* itself was influenced by Frank Herbert's novel *Dune* (1965), set on Arrakis, an inhospitable desert planet that holds spice, a commodity essential for intergalactic space travel that alludes to Western power struggles over Middle Eastern oil.[15] In Western productions, the desert functions primarily as a visual backdrop – a *terra nullius* (nobody's land) indicating that science fiction's otherworldly settings are often colonial spaces. As John Rieder has shown, science fiction has roots in colonial narratives in which explorers encounter their cultural past in the form of technologically-backward 'natives'.[16] Science-fictional estrangement can take the form of an Orientalizing gaze that sees the colonized as strange and inferior. Some films in this chapter play on the desert's strangeness, although they do not present it as a *terra nullius* and their intercultural encounters are often narrated from the perspective of its inhabitants.

The first part of this chapter focuses on 'weird and eerie' forms of estrangement, expanding upon Farshid Kazemi's argument that there is a new breed of Iranian films that evoke and critique 'the menacing environment of post-2009 Iran'.[17] I apply this more broadly to point to science-fictional strategies that have emerged in the economic, political and social downturn of this period. As terms defined by Mark Fisher, the weird and eerie are modes 'found at the edges of genres such as horror and science fiction', and share 'a preoccupation with the strange'.[18] While the weird consists of the presence of a strange entity that '*does not belong*' here, making us question how we make sense of the world,[19] eerie feelings arise from mysterious absence or unexplained presence, provoking questions about agency and unseen forces that rule our world.[20] Fisher implies that the weird and eerie are largely absent from mainstream science fiction because of their ambiguity. Inspired by the weird and eerie in real life as well as in art, the films *Atomic Heart* and *Dreamaway* furnish us with means for speculation on their sociopolitical implications while keeping their purposes fairly ambiguous.

In films featured in the second part of the chapter, *Nation Estate* and *Submarine*, the goal of illuminating local and wider political and environmental issues is achieved by building alternative worlds projected into the future or parallel present. As discussed in this book's introduction, many Middle Eastern filmmakers get frustrated by assumptions that they are merely dealing with local concerns and therefore that their work is not relevant to their international audiences' daily lives. The use of science fiction enables them to tell 'universal' stories that reflect on unfolding local realities yet that transcend regional geography and specific events. In a reversal of developmental narratives, these filmmakers' use of science-fictional strategies reveals the Middle East as a crucible of changes lying in store for the rest of humanity.

Weird and eerie estrangement: *Atomic Heart* and *Dreamaway*

Atomic Heart opens with a riddle: 'This film is about one of the most important characters of our time./ This is a film about me./ About one of my dreams whose events occur on the night the subsidy payments were distributed./ I will never tell you who I am or what my name is/ and you will never find out.'[21] A dystopian tale set in Tehran by night as two women in their late twenties, Arineh and Nobahar, drive home from a party, the film has two parts which, according to the director Ali Ahmadzadeh, are reality and dream, respectively, with a stranger in the second part who becomes increasingly menacing.[22] In his Lacanian interpretation, Kazemi proposes instead that the film's first part is fantasy and the second part is reality, stripped of its 'fantasmatic supplement', thus turning into a traumatic, 'nightmarish surreality': 'The nightmare is not only related to the fears and anxieties of a possible nuclear destruction of Tehran, but more precisely, to the totalitarian nightmare of the Islamic Republic', embodied by the stranger.[23] Kazemi highlights similarities to the films of David Lynch, an exemplar of 'weird' cinema, particularly the two-part structure of *Lost Highway* (1997) and *Mulholland Drive* (2001), and cites as another 'influence' Mikhail Bulgakov's novel *The Master and Margarita* in which the devil figures as a totalitarian allegory.

Although these resemblances are striking, Ahmadzadeh told me that his main sources of inspiration were his own life and the city of Tehran, not these international artworks.[24] In my reading of *Atomic Heart*, the environment *itself* produces a Lynchian strangeness, which is enhanced by science-fiction tropes. The first part focuses on the life that the protagonists are leading, which has utopian moments, then the second is its dystopian transfiguration, plunging us into a dark and depressing world that portends a terrifying future. Nevertheless, the two parts are intimately related, like a Moebius Strip on which we travel on the underside and overside, because the dictatorship projected as a dystopian possibility *is* the fictional world in which the characters already reside.[25] We meet Arineh and Nobahar when they are emerging from a party, intoxicated. They belong to a modern, youthful and anarchic subculture from the generation born after the Islamic Revolution that likes to party, drink and take drugs. Two important features of this modern, urban, middle-class youth are that it is steeped in Western pop culture and that it rejects the Islamic Republic's rules although, as we will see in the analysis below, its confrontation with the ruling power is more nuanced than a straightforward opposition.

Its focus on this generation links *Atomic Heart* to Ahmadzadeh's previous feature, *Kami's Party* (2013), which was made underground during the Ahmadinejad era since it failed to get either shooting or screening permits. *Atomic Heart* was made at the beginning of Rouhani's presidential term and *was* granted a shooting permit. Even so, as Ahmadzadeh remarks, the group's anti-regime attitude 'cannot be easily shown, but it can be hinted at' and therefore he decided to use 'the logic of the road movie' to overcome those restrictions.[26] *Atomic Heart* is mostly set inside a car as Arineh and Nobahar drive around nocturnal Tehran, meeting other characters along the way – including, in the first part, their friend Kami whom they invite for a ride after finding him walking alone wearing sunglasses although it is night. As we saw in Chapter 5, where the road movie is discussed at length, the car affords creative and practical possibilities surmounting (among other things) the difficulties of depicting women realistically due to compulsory *hejāb* in Iranian cinema. In addition, Ahmadzadeh uses the road movie – a genre of freedom, rebellion and escapism – to show his characters' unconventional lifestyle and desire for utopian transcendence. We see them stoned and breaking the law in numerous ways. As a private/public space, the car grants the characters a degree of free expression, where they can banter on eclectic subjects from theme tunes of children's programmes to the cultural history of toilets.

From a high vantage point overlooking the city, Kami recalls a dream in which an atomic bomb exploded in Tehran and its fireball kindled his cigarette to the sounds of Pink Floyd's *Atom Heart Mother*. As a reflection of the environment, the dream illuminates latent elements in reality. It signals apprehension over Iran's nuclear programme and portends the reversal of utopia into dystopia that occurs soon after during a car crash on Valiasr Street. Once a two-way thoroughfare, Valiasr Street was turned into a one-way street after the 2009 protests in an attempt to prevent crowds. Unaware of, or ignoring, this new urban layout that is a form of social control, Arineh drives the wrong way and collides with another car. Arineh and Nobahar's behaviour changes after this turning point, highlighting the politicization of their bodies and the double life in the Islamic Republic in which one self is displayed in private and another in public. They start dissimulating, tucking their hair into their headscarves before getting out of the car and talking to the other driver.

When a policeman gets into the car, the film stages a confrontation between these rebellious characters and the regime, which invades private lives through its security apparatus. Although Ahmadzadeh identifies with the youth, he bestows his own surname upon the policeman to impart similarities between the regime and the counterculture. Their conversation turns to the Hollywood film *Argo* (2012) on which Lieutenant Ahmadzadeh seeks Arineh's opinion. Gesturing to the way that Iran (and the Middle East more generally) is frequently misrepresented in Western media, Arineh asserts that *Argo* depicted Iran 'in a bad light'. Her words echo the criticism *siāh-namāyi* ('showing the negative aspects') frequently levelled at filmmakers who offer critical perspectives on their country. The policeman replies, 'Despite your looks, you are sometimes with the Islamic Republic.' As the director reflects, the dialogue is 'a kind of a dialectic' in which 'you could hear the voice of the police in the youth and the voice of the youth in the police'.[27] They share concerns about how Iran is perceived by the outside world. The scene moreover serves to distinguish *Atomic Heart*'s complex dystopic vision from simplified portraits of Iran as a 'bad place'.

Although the stranger appears about thirty minutes into the film, Ahmadzadeh regards him as the central character.[28] He suddenly jumps into the frame after the accident, displaying his quality of appearing and disappearing mysteriously, like a being from another dimension exempt from our world's physical laws. Upon his arrival, the film's colour palette and lighting darken and turn colder, creating nightmarish sensations after the first part's more inviting, warmer colours. Initially, the stranger seems benevolent, paying damages to the other driver as the protagonists cannot themselves obtain cash from ATMs on the night of the government's subsidy distribution. He is played by Mohammad Reza Golzar, a superstar in Iran, chosen for his good looks and ability to embody this ambivalence: both attractive and diabolical, ordinary and supernatural, benign and repressive. As hinted in the opening riddle, his identity remains ambiguous and nameless, resisting reduction to a single meaning because the film is oneiric and speculative – not a simple allegory. Ahmadzadeh explained that he wanted this character to have 'several layers, but much of it related to the dictatorship in power', that is, the Islamic Republic.[29] While writing this character, he was partly thinking of Ahmadinejad, yet the stranger is not only that; many of these types exist in society and government.

The first part's triangular set-up – the two women in the front seat and Kami at the back – is repeated in the second part, with the stranger on the backseat. The car, already a claustrophobic space permitting only tight framings and limited camera movement, becomes a trap. The trio's conversation becomes increasingly bizarre, interrupted by the stranger's mobile ringtone, its piercing notes reminiscent of soundtracks evoking alien presence in science-fiction films, immediately creating an eerie atmosphere without any elaborate special effects. The stranger recounts setting foot in Lebanon and Syria, declaring, 'I am in Syria now!' The spatial paradox of being in two places at the same time provokes unsettling sensations, like the scene in Lynch's *Lost Highway* where the Mystery Man tells the protagonist Fred at a party that he is at Fred's house, even handing him a phone to prove it. *Atomic Heart* uses this weird motif to allude to Iran's expanded influence in Syria and Lebanon through Hezbollah and the dystopia of resurgent dictatorships after the failed uprisings. 'I'm real good friends with Bashar!' the stranger goes on to claim. His relationship to dictatorial figures is reinforced when he takes the women to the same vantage-point where Kami narrated his dream. In the headlights, a man in a dark suit turns around, revealing a striking resemblance to Saddam Hussein, the Iraqi dictator who died in 2006. Fisher writes, 'It is the irruption into *this* world of something from outside which is the marker of the weird.'[30] The dead dictator's appearance from beyond this world marks a weird moment. All three characters in the car stare at him in disturbed disbelief, although once he climbs into the backseat, he and the stranger immediately converse in an alien language, with the reanimated Saddam speaking in distorted, synthetic vocals through a vocoder, which enhances the scene's weirdness.

The stranger reveals himself as an agent from another world, assigned to Earth on a two-year mission, when he takes Nobahar and Arineh down a tunnel to a door marked C-27 in luminous orange.[31] 'This door is the gateway between our world and yours,' he claims. 'Weird' science fiction often 'opens up an *egress* between this world and others', creating exchanges between these different worlds.[32] The stranger tries to persuade the women that the other world is 'much better than here' in order to transport them there: 'Our doubles lead their lives there with no wars, no diseases.' For him, this parallel world is a utopia; however, as he is someone who admires and consorts with dictators, we can infer that it is a kind of dystopia, similar to Nazi utopias of social engineering. In *What is Philosophy?* Gilles Deleuze and Félix Guattari distinguish between 'different types of utopia'.[33] Among these types are 'authoritarian utopias, or utopias of transcendence' that they contrast with 'revolutionary, libertarian utopias' which are immanent because they respond to our real conditions of existence and contemporary struggles. Through the science-fiction trope of an egress between worlds, *Atomic Heart* evokes authoritarian utopias: both government rhetoric promising to take citizens to a better place and, some might argue, the Islamic vision of paradise. That promised utopia serves as a fantasy for the populace since, Ahmadzadeh remarks, 'behind that door, there could also be another dictatorship'.[34]

Despite obtaining a shooting permit, *Atomic Heart* was not approved for screening in Iran for three years until the time of the 2017 election, when it was granted a two-week theatrical run. After the election, which returned Rouhani to power, screening permission was again withdrawn. Ahmadzadeh's experiences with state censorship indicate that harsh restrictions can remain under both 'moderate' and 'hardline' presidents which, according to him, is because the same repressive apparatus is pulling the strings.[35] The censors demanded thirty minutes of cuts altogether, including the scene with the policeman. The words of Mohammad Beheshti, former head of the Farabi Cinema Foundation, illuminate why this scene was judged particularly sensitive: 'when a film-maker introduces a miscreant, a police officer or teacher … it has to be clear whether he is criticising an individual or the system as a whole. If the latter, then he must be stopped.'[36] As a solution to these restrictions, during his negotiations with the censors Ahmadzadeh proposed voice-over narration.[37] So, in the version shown in Iran, the stranger narrates the story, permitting events and characters, including the policeman, to pass as his dream and therefore not 'real'. With this alteration, Ahmadzadeh gave audiences the chance to see *Atomic Heart* in theatres in Iran (albeit briefly) without further interference by the authorities and in a manner that remains true to the importance of dreams within the film.

As its title suggests, dreams are also prominent in the fiction–documentary hybrid *Dreamaway*. In its opening, a strange humanoid creature, later revealed as an inflatable black monkey, ambles across a rocky desert, followed by seven individuals in party outfits. These seven characters are employees of the Sunrise Hotel in Sharm el-Sheikh, an enclave between the Sinai Desert and Red Sea coast, once a busy tourist spot. We watch the entertainment team welcome non-existent guests with a club dance by the swimming pool. 'Wakey, wakey, Sharm el-Sheikhy' comes a voice from the PA. The empty pool is surrounded by sunbeds that masseurs deck artistically with towels and wait around hopefully. Rami, a living statue in black-and-gold make up, performs without anyone to appreciate his art. At night, Taki the DJ plays his set to an empty dance floor apart from a cleaner mopping it. Virtually the only people at the resort are its employees, continuing their routines in the near absence of guests. The desert's otherworldliness, the eerily empty town and focus on its last inhabitants evoke a utopian dream that has petered out. *Dreamaway* is reminiscent of J.G. Ballard's science fiction set in present-day resorts and suburbia where he locates the seeds of the future.[38] Sharm el-Sheikh's Ballardian qualities also reside in the fact that its community is shaped by intercultural encounters with Western tourists, yet is now increasingly cut off from the outside world as fewer flights operate, leaving employees struggling to adapt and survive, and hoping that life will return to normal.

The demise of Egypt's petroleum economy has made it dependent on tourism; however, since the 2011 revolution, there has been a fall in both tourism and foreign investment, linked to political developments. Egyptian filmmaker Marouan Omara and German filmmaker Johanna Domke, who began their cross-cultural creative partnership with their documentary *Crop* (2013), were interested in how young Egyptians were drawn to Sharm el-Sheikh not only to make a living but also to find freedom and explore their identities in this city where East and West meet.[39] From 2013, Domke and Omara began going there to research and film material, although their main shoot took place in 2016. By then, Sharm el-Sheik, already declining due to the wider economic and political situation, had been turned into a ghost town by the 2015 bombing, claimed by ISIS, of a Russian passenger aircraft above the Sinai Peninsula. Inevitably, this changed the film, but not its concept, since the filmmakers were less interested in the tourists than the employees whose labour continued, despite reduced wages, since work elsewhere was scarce. In fact, the deserted town sharpened the contrast with the workers' dreams and supported underlying themes of alienation.

The filmmakers did not get the permits to shoot a documentary, which was their original intention. As Omara explains, there were 'a lot of constraints from the political side'.[40] Politically, documentaries are perceived as 'problematic films' in Egypt and fiction is preferable, although the type of fiction and topics are also subject to approval.[41] Since Sharm el-Sheik is in the Sinai Peninsula, which is under military jurisdiction, 'it's a very sensitive place to film', necessitating permits from the army as well as numerous other permits (including from the cinema syndicate and Ministry of the Interior) required for filmmaking in Egypt.[42] Additionally, the filmmakers knew they would be followed, as can happen for any film production in Egypt but especially for international co-productions like this: 'It was really complicated and we had to be very careful while shooting it,' Omara recalls.[43] The story of how they were followed is like a dystopian comedy/thriller in itself, as their production company devised several strategies to dodge surveillants from the censorship bureau and secret police. One strategy was to announce the film shoot publicly in Sharm el-Sheikh to make it 'as explicit as possible, so there was no suspicion of any kind of secrecy from our production team'.[44]

These constraints led to creative decisions that resulted in *Dreamaway*'s hybrid form. 'Our choice was, okay, if we're not allowed to shoot a documentary, then we'll shoot a fiction', Domke explains.[45] The filmmakers wrote a fictional script that was accepted and earned the requisite permits. Because they had already planned to incorporate fictional elements (as discussed below), they had no problem re-classifying their work as fiction. Not being able to shoot a documentary clarified their approach to the filmmaking process: 'it was a restriction that we could use creatively to design our film,' Domke asserts.[46] The filmmakers posted a casting call in Sharm el-Sheikh seeking participants to create and play roles based on their 'true stories', to which three hundred people responded and from which they selected seven main 'characters'. Making a fiction film reflected how the filmmakers saw Sharm el-Sheikh as a stage on which resort employees continually reinvented themselves, since they met new tourists weekly. Whenever the filmmakers returned they would find their protagonists with 'a different haircut and style and even a different name', working in an entirely different field.[47] In many respects, the city itself was stranger than fiction, populated by a pink dinosaur and other fake animals, and filled with surreal scenes of empty hotels and employees performing to absent guests: 'We didn't even plan that. It was like that – happening in front of our eyes. We thought this is hilarious!' Domke recollects.[48]

Another constraint that the filmmakers faced also drove them towards using fictional elements. When they began visiting Sharm el-Sheikh, they found employees willing to tell their stories and divulge their secrets. But as soon as they revealed they were filmmakers, their interlocutors became more cautious, apprehensive that for religious or other reasons their families would disapprove of the different personalities that they adopt in Sharm el-Sheikh. Therefore, the filmmakers introduced role-playing to blur boundaries between reality and fiction, and to act as a 'security shield' protecting their participants.[49] This was an important ethical consideration since their film is about real people, not just fictional characters, and has repercussions on their lives. The fictionalization and role-playing were creative ways of overcoming this limitation so that their participants could simply say to others, 'We're acting'.[50]

Dreamaway is punctuated by scenes of the inflatable black monkey touring the city on a pick-up truck, enticing the characters to follow him and reveal their dreams and aspirations. Omara explains that the monkey 'came from the same world of Sharm el-Sheikh, of alienation and sci-fi absurdity'.[51] It is introduced with an alien-eerie soundtrack and speaks through an amplifier with an uncanny human voice. The filmmakers were drawn to the monkey aesthetically before beginning the production; however, its manner of deployment was decided much later, as part of their process of working with their actors. While fictionalizing their roles gave participants some security, they were still not confident acting on camera. The playful monkey scenes helped as a strategy of free expression. 'If you deconstruct what the monkey is doing, he is just doing an interview,' Omara says. 'We decided, instead of just putting this interview in a normal set-up', the monkey 'could liberate them [the participants]' to talk about subjects 'that might be a bit sensitive to them without too much seriousness around it'.[52] For Omara, the monkey additionally embodies the hopes and dreams of Sharm el-Sheikh that the characters are chasing. The city is like a 'paradise' to them where they believe their dreams will be realized, that they will become rich, marry foreigners and emigrate to Europe, although their actual experiences are often filled with 'harshness and disappointments'.[53] During the film, the monkey changes from a hopeful to a demanding figure: 'Why are you dragging me and asking all these questions?', Alaa the masseur entreats. Finally, the monkey's truck speeds away into the night, leaving the characters' world and leaving *them* behind *in* that world. In this respect, Domke comments, it

> reflects our role as directors, because we're actually like this fantasy figure for them that comes to town and attracts them and drags them into the process of making a film and we represent hope for them that we will change the situation. We told them very clearly we will not be able to bring them to Hollywood, even though they had hopes for it. But that's actually what you are always inclined to do as a filmmaker: you engage in other people's lives and then you have to leave them.[54]

Figure 9.1 A large, inflatable black monkey, found within the absurd sci-fi-like world of Sharm el-Sheik, became a playful tactic of free expression, encouraging the characters to speak about their dreams and longings as they follow him in his truck. *Dreamaway* directed by Johanna Domke and Marouan Omara © Monokel, WDR Westdeutscher Rundfunk, Fruitmarket Kultur und Medien, Fig Leaf 2018. All Rights Reserved.

Dreamaway visualizes its characters' dreams through scenes shot as if they are fantasy moments. Often these are about aspects of life that they miss, no longer happening due to the resort's dire situation, itself a reflection of wider economic and political trends. When Alaa borrows his friend's studio for a private massage, apparently requested by a hotel guest, a surreal cut turns the woman being massaged into a mannequin with a disjointed arm, raising doubt about the 'reality' of this incident. In Egypt, men are not allowed to massage women in hotels, and vice versa; breach of this law can result in a prison sentence. By filming the massage in this way, *Dreamaway* navigates around this problematic area, and opens up a space of speculation, making us wonder to what extent its characters' stories are real or invented. In another scene, DJ Taki plays at a nightclub filled with revellers dressed in flamboyant circus outfits. The heady sequence is filmed impressionistically so that we infer it is his subjective perspective, catching glimpses of a trapeze artist spinning overhead, a flamethrower tossing a flame and a flourish of a can-can dancer's skirt. It ends with a spotlight on Taki in the crowd, as if he imagined it. Domke revealed that this was real footage shot several years previously, during the film's research stage, reflecting how Sharm el-Sheikh was then.[55] However, its eerie insertion intimates the character's longing for those better times along with the invisible global forces that have led the resort and its employees to be abandoned.

The lack of people is a motif familiar from post-apocalyptic science-fiction films. According to Fisher, eerie feelings are usually short-lived in such films, since their plots explain why the cities have been depopulated. Enigma is what sustains eeriness; it revolves around 'two questions – *what happened* and *why?*'[56] By provoking these questions of agency, the eerie summons 'the forces that govern our lives and the world', including those usually hidden from our sense perceptions, such as global capitalist forces.[57] *Dreamaway* does not offer any explanations about what happened and what made the tourists leave. It opens a space of speculation in which the eerie thrives. Without saying anything explicitly, its surreal portrayal of a resort devoid of guests and employees expending labour almost nobody needs is a glimpse into contemporary Egypt's dire economic and political realities.

Omara was apprehensive when *Dreamaway* was completed because it dealt with many sensitive topics: 'I was expecting it to be not even be allowed to be shown in Egypt with all these creative approaches that we did. It was a surprise that all this abstraction and the creative craziness allowed the film to be shown without a problem.'[58] The production team member whose job was to obtain permits was told: 'We are not happy with the film, but we cannot find anything against it.'[59] The creative choices taken in *Dreamaway*, not least its science-fictional tropes, enabled it to be seen widely in Egypt, at festivals in cities across the country and theatres in Cairo, where the participants attended to present the film and even took their families.

Parallel world-building: *Nation Estate* and *Submarine*

The films in this section move into more straightforward genre territory in that they are explicitly presented as science fiction/dystopia. However, the fact that they are made by filmmakers from the region means that their use of the genre is never straightforward. As Larissa Sansour remarks, science fiction is associated with progress and the Western world, rather than the Arab world.[60] In her work, science fiction is a way of overturning stereotypes about the Middle East, Palestine and herself as a female artist from the region. In this respect, it is like the use of humour, discussed in Chapter 6. Sansour declares, 'Any form that is not associated with your gender or the region that you come from – anything unexpected – is quite important for my work because I like challenging clichés of what I'm supposed to do.'[61]

Sansour's art background forms the context in which she makes her short films which are designed for both gallery and theatrical spaces. Her early films such as *Land Confiscation Order* (2007) document people and places in the West Bank that she was afraid would disappear under Israeli annexation. However, she found this approach did not work for her target audiences in the West who could not believe that Israel, which presents itself as 'the only democracy in the Middle East', could carry out such human rights violations. When reality was more surreal than fiction, turning to the fictional realm was a way, she explains, to 'speak more honestly and more directly about, or touch upon different dimensions of, what's really going on'.[62] Science fiction, which Sansour first ventured into with *A Space Exodus* (2009), allowed her to translate her personal experience of Israeli colonialism; in her words, the genre serves as 'a more universal language that everyone knows'.[63]

Furthermore, science fiction's alternative world-building offers Sansour a framework in which to reset the terms of well-worn debates.[64] This is exemplified in *Nation Estate*, where the future Palestinian state is a skyscraper in which each floor contains a simulacrum of its former cities and landmarks. A traveller, played by Sansour herself, 'returns' to Palestine via an underground train called Amman Express. The lengthy, convoluted trip that West Bank Palestinians undergo from Jordan after trips abroad (because they are not Israeli citizens, they cannot fly to Ben Gurion, Israel's main airport) has become a swift, smooth journey through a tunnel. After passing security checks (a fingerprint- and eye-scan), the traveller emerges into a pristine building, itself a technological marvel with efficient transportation, cavernous halls and interactive screens, giving viewers an initial impression of progress and comfort. Gone are the roadblocks and checkpoints that, as we saw in Chapter 5, seal off Palestinian cities from each other; intercity travel is made hassle-free by a single mode of public transport, an elevator that the traveller takes to Bethlehem floor. Walking past life-size replicas of Manger Square and the Nativity Church, she enters her apartment where she tends an olive tree growing from the floor.

Nation Estate's world can be described as an 'arcology', a concept that the futurist Paolo Soleri coined from the words architecture and ecology.[65] A self-contained community, an arcology is usually designed to be isolated from the world and capable of surviving catastrophes. Soleri envisaged a form of utopian, sustainable living, with inhabitants cultivating their own crops indoors and relying on walking or public transport to access their work, public spaces and residential areas, all located close to each other to avoid the need for cars. As an arcology, the skyscraper in Nation Estate has utopian dimensions, expressing Palestinian yearning for an independent state and journeys free of obstacles.

Because the Palestinian predicament is suspended between projection of a future state (which we can call utopia) and past disaster – the historical and ongoing dispossession known as the Nakba – Sansour believes it is suited to science fiction.[66] Within Nation Estate's futuristic skyscraper, Palestinian national and cultural symbols proliferate. In the atrium, a huge Palestinian flag hangs vertically, 'reminiscent of an altar'.[67] Cacti in tall vases are arranged in lines (for generations Palestinians used sabr cacti to create fences around their lands). When the traveller prepares a meal in her apartment, she reheats futuristic sensor boxes containing traditional Palestinian food – tabouleh, falafel and marmaon – and decants it into porcelain plates imprinted with a keffiyeh pattern, a symbol of resistance. The olive tree in her apartment stands for connection to the land, while the key icon on the door represents the right of return. All these symbols are dearly valued by Palestinians, for whom they are an important means of transmitting memories and traditions, signifying national belonging, especially in the diaspora. However, Sansour approaches them from a different angle, suggesting that Palestinian resistance has stagnated, unable to move beyond these symbols: 'I wanted to house these symbols in a museum-like structure' so that they appear 'as artefacts rather than living things'.[68] In this dystopian future, Palestine has disappeared and a mausoleum of symbolic relics remains.

It becomes increasingly clear that this utopia is in fact a dystopia, that the aspiration for statehood has turned into a caged nightmare. Along with close-ups of the traveller's anxious eyes and her breathlessness, early indications of the building's dystopic character include its prison-like structure and its atomized, alienated society, manifested in two people dressed in similar grey outfits to the traveller that she encounters in the lift and who merely nod at her, suggesting uniformity, group discipline and fear to speak. The building does not support any public social or cultural interaction; there are no crowds or collectives, and no unrest stirs. Grey watchtowers can be glimpsed through windows but in fact the whole building is a sentient surveillance machine with biometric security technologies installed in its doorways and elevator adverts that remind passengers to validate their passports for travel. Bathed in light, aimed at maximum visibility and control of the population's mobility, the sterile, white atrium epitomizes what Helga Tawil-Souri calls the 'sublime essence' of surveillance, with 'God-like capabilities: all-knowing, all-seeing, all the time, everywhere'.[69] As in contemporary Palestine, surveillance operates through a hybrid of high- and low-tech tools, and 'hides the more ominous practice of colonialism'.[70]

In the final scene, the traveller adjusts her apartment's window settings to reveal the outside landscape, with Jerusalem's Dome of the Rock visible in the distance although from its hyperreal appearance we can infer it is a digital backdrop.[71] She stands looking out, feeling her pregnant belly apprehensively, as the camera rapidly pulls back, revealing not only that Palestinians must live in this totally enclosed environment, segregated in numerous apartments, but they are also surrounded by a gigantic concrete wall. Outside there is nothing but a desolate wasteland. Although the skyscraper is nominally in the West Bank, the landscape is ambiguous and could be anywhere, suggesting that the 'real' Palestine has ceased to exist except in this virtual form.

Nation Estate's futuristic dystopian setting alludes to realities playing out in Palestine today and forebodes what may happen if present policies continue. It powerfully reflects on land confiscation, drawing on Sansour's own experiences: 'Whenever I go back to Bethlehem you can see that there is, first, the wall circling the city and then there are the Israeli settlements coming closer and closer, like an army. This is happening all over Palestine.'[72] Moreover, as shown by 'a more technologized and distant surveillance'[73] since Israel's 2005 withdrawal from Gaza, the colonizer's physical presence is no longer required. Surveillance of Palestinians can be undertaken remotely – for example, by walls equipped with cameras and radar.[74] As well as commenting on surveillance systems already in place and their direction of travel, the isolated skyscraper satirizes the so-called 'peace process'. A featured advertisement in the lift states that the week's water supply is 'supplied by Norwegian Fjords, proud supporter of the Pipes for Peace Program', indicating the skyscraper is still dependent on foreign aid because of Israel's control of water resources in Palestine. The 'peace process' contemplates all kinds of 'solutions' to the Palestinian question, even including the building of artificial islands – everything, it seems, except the lifting of the occupation itself.

Like Sansour's other science-fiction films, *Nation Estate* uses green screens and CGI to build its alternative world. Her team added futuristic features to the Copenhagen Metro (where scenes were shot at 4.00 am when the place was deserted), and recreated landmarks such as the Dome of the Rock and Nativity Square from high-resolution photographs. These visual effects exponentially increase Sansour's budgets, posing another challenge because it is not easy to raise these kinds of funds for experimental art films.[75] However, directing glossy, high-budget productions is another way in which she seeks to subvert expectations of her as a Middle Eastern filmmaker.[76] CGI also enabled her to overcome constraints of shooting in Palestine. Aside from difficulties of taking her whole team there and then finding a producer to secure locations and permits, one risk that Sansour did not want to gamble on was having expensive equipment and footage confiscated by Israeli officials during border inspections.[77] Therefore, she opted for the more secure (though also expensive) solution of reconstructing Palestine through computers – fittingly for a story about a simulacral Palestinian state.

The keffiyeh-printed porcelain plates into which Sansour's character pours food in *Nation Estate* became the starting-point for her next film, *In the Future, They Ate from the Finest Porcelain* (2015). In this, a futuristic resistance leader deploys spaceships to drop the plates into the ground as artefacts testifying to her people's existence for future generations. Its premise is an ironic appropriation of Israel's use of archaeological digs to prove its claims to historic Palestine. The crux of this strategy is the Zionist slogan, 'a land without people, for a people without a land'. In this colonial imagination, Palestine figures as a barren desert: a *terra nullius*. *In the Future* questions this rewriting of history through its dreamlike desert landscape in which Palestine's past, present and future manifest in the same space. It takes the form of a dialogue between the resistance leader and her psychiatrist; the landscape appears to be an externalization of her inner states, blurring real and unreal with the purpose of unravelling the processes through which memory and historical narrative are constructed. As part of the project, Sansour actually buried some porcelain plates in Palestine. She concealed their site coordinates in bomb-like contraptions modelled on her spaceships, which have been exhibited alongside the film: anyone who collects these objects can deduce the porcelain's location.[78] What was a prop in *Nation Estate* and later a plot device in *In the Future* steps out of the boundaries of fiction to intervene into reality, illuminating from another angle the crossover between reality and fiction in this chapter's science-fictional strategies.

In Sansour's subsequent film, *In Vitro* (2019), Palestine is 'a microcosm and accelerated state' of wider ecological disaster since climate change is happening faster there due to Israel's control of water resources.[79] Mounia Akl's fictional short, *Submarine*, too, can be classified as an ecological dystopia, a sub-genre that has existed at least since the 1970s and that has (re-)emerged in the region and internationally amid renewed awareness of environmental crises we are collectively facing.[80] In its dystopian world, uncollected rubbish piles up everywhere. People wear face masks to protect themselves from air pollution and diseases produced by accumulated trash. Lebanon has become an unliveable place and its rulers have fled abroad. Over a loudspeaker, a mass evacuation is announced, as the population pack their suitcases and prepare to leave, too; only the protagonist, Hala, resolves to remain.

Submarine was inspired by the 2015 waste management crisis (known as the 'trash crisis') in Beirut and Mount Lebanon after the Namaah landfill site became overfull and was closed. In the absence of contingency plans, the private waste management company sub-contracted by the government suspended rubbish collection, resulting in large-scale dumping and burning of waste on the streets – a huge risk to public health and the environment. As Akl recalls, 'People were living in their own trash' which was 'environmentally and visually shocking'.[81] Although municipal waste collection resumed shortly after, rubbish was simply disposed in locations around capital, 'dumping "elsewhere" out of sight' rather than solving the problem.[82] Thousands of people poured onto the streets to protest, their demands expanding from solutions to the trash crisis to other innumerable problems afflicting Lebanon. The protests evolved into the grassroots 'You Stink' civil society movement which took 'ownership of garbage management and disposal' themselves.[83] For protestors such as Akl herself, the trash crisis was a symptom of 'everything that's wrong in the country', part of the long-term legacy of the Lebanese Civil War (1975–90) which left the country with a sect-based system of power-sharing and free market economy leading to continual political instability, dysfunctional government and private sector profiteering and corruption.

As Christine Mady suggests, random garbage is often a sign of 'urban malfunction' and '[i]f it endures, it signals a crisis'.[84] The lack of waste management is an everyday crisis that points to wider instability. Akl states that she 'wasn't interested in making a documentary about the garbage crisis'; instead, the genre of dystopia became a creative way to 'witness' it because 'for me that garbage crisis represented so much more than just a garbage crisis', evoking 'the cracks of our society and not just our government'.[85] Moreover, it enabled her to make a film resonating with wider ecological issues, using Lebanon as 'a microcosm of the world'.[86] Science fiction/dystopia's extrapolation of present trends served her purpose well since 'imagining the worst-case scenarios can sometimes awaken desires to do something'.[87] Akl recalls that, during the trash crisis, Lebanon's Ministry of Tourism released images of the country's most beautiful landscapes in an attempt to deflect from the disaster; the sci-fi genre appeared to solve the difficulty of tackling realities unpalatable for the Lebanese government.[88] Despite this, *Submarine* was censored when it was due to have its Lebanese premiere at the Beirut Days Festival. General Security (the government body responsible for media censorship in Lebanon) claimed that the film did not represent Lebanon's reality. As we have seen earlier in this book, this reaction is typical of censors who assume that a film's purpose is to promote and affirm allegiance to the country without countenancing, as Akl puts it, that one can 'be critical of it, while loving it'.[89]

Submarine was shot during the trash crisis, and Akl changed the script as the situation evolved. One of its locations is a real garbage dump at Beirut River, one of the sites around the capital where waste was thrown. As Akl recalls, 'the garbage started disappearing from the streets of the city, but it was all dumped there and it was flowing into the river'.[90] This landmark is incorporated into the film in a scene when Hala walks past a mountain of uncollected rubbish: an entangled mesh of tyres, plastic bottles, bags and cardboard boxes. Even as they purport to raise environmental awareness, eco-disaster films often exert a huge environmental impact; indeed, any 'typical big-budget movie will consume immense amounts of resources and produce, as a result, comparable waste'.[91] *Submarine* creatively works around these problems through its use of an actual dump, which points to a dystopian reality beyond the film as well as minimizing environmental damage by not altering the location for the purposes of the production. Nonetheless, filming there was hazardous since waste fumes caused breathing difficulties; therefore, the crew arrived equipped with masks and shooting was limited to four hours. Other scenes were shot in the city of Tyre (known as Sur in Arabic), where the garbage crisis was recreated with the residents' cooperation, another instance of care towards the biophysical environment. 'The people of Sur were helpful,' Akl says, 'because they read the script and understood that the film was made to change the situation.'[92] They became part of the team, although Sur itself had not been affected by the crisis.

It was during her location scouting that garbage began to fascinate Akl as a marker of cultural identity. From a distance, waste seems an indistinguishable mass yet closer up these objects reveal themselves as 'what people have left behind'.[93] Garbage, therefore, tells stories about who we are. Wendy Faris suggests that magic realism, like surrealism, constructs 'magical images' from 'ordinary objects' that exude an 'aura of surprising craziness' yet, while surreal images remain enigmatic, magic realist ones 'tend to reveal their motivations – psychological, social, emotional, political – after some scrutiny'.[94] *Submarine* creates magic realist images from garbage with these kinds of intentions. Like other science fiction/dystopias, it also deploys what David Desser calls a '*politicized production design*' in which spatial configurations, such as high/low, inside/outside or light/dark, highlight sociopolitical themes.[95] In *Submarine*, inside/outside binaries convey the fictional world into which we are entering.

Figure 9.2 The protagonist Hala walks past a real garbage dump in a dystopic sci-fi extrapolation of Lebanon's trash crisis. *Submarine* directed by Mounia Akl © Columbia University School of Arts 2016. All Rights Reserved.

Initially, the outside environment is unambiguously dystopic, signalled by abnormal piles of garbage, while the interiors, although cluttered, have a convivial ambiance and appear safe. Akl says her training in architecture before she became a filmmaker has taught her 'how to tell the story of someone through the spaces that they inhabit'.[96] Hala's living room is filled with personal possessions that reveal her past. Over the mantelpiece, a protest placard declares, in Arabic, 'The people want to topple the regime' – an 'Arab Spring' chant adopted during Lebanon's trash crisis protests. Inside/outside binaries are broken when Hala's window is shattered. Despite her attempt to seal the crack, the whole window soon collapses, bringing garbage tumbling inside. The scene vividly realizes the idea of people living in their own trash.

When Akl participated in the trash crisis protests, members of her parents' generation told her that they had lost hope. Their attitudes are shaped by the Civil War which still casts a long shadow on society, as an Amnesty Law passed by the post-war government pardoned most of the war's crimes and thus permitted perpetrators to enter politics and obtain high-ranking positions. Since some political parties today are from the same groups that carried out past crimes, it seems as if there is no escape from this cycle of history. Clinging onto hope in a seemingly hopeless situation, when all around her the country descends into despair and decay, Hala's character belongs to the younger generation, who are still trying to make change and lack the older generation's cynicism, as shown when she asks her neighbour for help fixing her window; he chides her, asking 'Why do you want to stay? Don't tell me you still have hope!' Beirut, a 'wounded city' with scars from its Civil War past, has a vibrant young generation 'trying to keep the city alive with those pubs and restaurants that are the only thing that never fails', Akl told me, before the 2020 port explosion that destroyed many bars in Gemmayzeh.[97] In the film, the Submarine Bar is based on the Torino Express bar in that area, where people united after protests. Hala enters the empty bar, where chairs are stacked away and cardboard boxes are piled on the floor in anticipation that everyone will be leaving. She turns on the lights and music and begins to dance sensuously on her own. Akl uses magic realism's porous boundaries between reality and fantasy to project her protagonist's inner world, changing the environment in a fluid shot transition. Other people enter the frame and the bar fills with the town's residents dancing (some of them still wearing their face masks) to live music. In this moment, Hala's wishful thinking about staying in Lebanon becomes a reality, although it is left open as to whether she is imagining it or it is 'really' happening.

Leaving Lebanon is a stark option facing many citizens after continual crises have convinced them that the country holds no positive future for them. Since *Submarine* was made, the port explosion and currency collapse have become further catalysts for departure. This view is shared not only by the older generation who have lived through the war. Akl reflects, 'It's sad to see that with all those increasing problems, the younger generation think a better life for them awaits outside.'[98] In the Submarine Bar, Hala's lover Elie materializes sitting alone at the counter. He tells her he has heard she is planning to stay. 'What are you trying to prove?' he asks. Tenderly they dance together to a song called 'Tango El Amal' ('Tango of Hope'). The scene poses the question of whether leaving the country is the solution, as Hala asks Elie, 'Where are you going anyway?' However, he insists that everything is over here, including the Submarine Bar itself and the politics of protest and hope it represents. Finally, he leaves, carrying his two small suitcases, packing lightly because he no longer wants to cling to things. Later, Hala goes to the beach where she encounters the townsfolk walking in the opposite direction, carrying their luggage to a ship, then she turns and follows them. She seems to change her mind, although we cannot be certain. That hopeless hope that she embodied is kept alive by this open ending.

Conclusion

We have come a long way from normative understandings of the genre but, as Sansour insists, 'The goal is not the sci-fi'; rather, science fiction is a tool to reach the goal.[99] As examples in this chapter have shown, science-fictional strategies are being used to capture surreal elements of the crises through which people in the region are living. Crossovers between fiction and reality, which point indexically to lived dystopias, are more pertinent to these strategies than hidden, allegorical meanings. Moreover, deliberately blurring fiction and reality helps to overcome political and cultural constraints. In *Atomic Heart* and *Dreamaway* this occurs through speculation provoked by the weird and eerie, while *Nation Estate* and *Submarine* use genre parameters, namely parallel world-building, to reinvigorate political and environmental debates. We have seen how, by making creative use of 'found' dystopias, filmmakers turn the limitations of their environment into assets. Moreover, genre serves as a universal language to widen their work's resonance beyond merely 'local' concerns.

Tom Moylan and Raffaella Baccolini write that dystopian texts, even as they offer us a 'pessimistic presentation of the very worst social alternatives', often 'maintain a horizon of hope'.[100] One way that they do this is 'by resisting closure: the ambiguous, open endings… maintain the utopian impulse *within* the work'.[101] Most of this chapter's films maintain 'a horizon of hope' through their open endings. In *Atomic Heart*, Arineh wins a wager with the stranger that he will be the first to jump from the roof of a building, which he claims is now their only way to the other world. A simple cut at the end leaves us with uncertainty about whether he has disappeared or not. *Dreamaway*'s ensemble cast continue to follow the Monkey, the embodiment of their hope. *Submarine*'s ending is also ambiguous, leaving a hopeful prospect. However, even if the ending remains pessimistic, as it does in *Nation Estate*, the politics of hope could be seen as intrinsic to dystopia, because its cautionary tales inspire renewed struggles and encourage us to bring about the change that will prevent current conditions from worsening. As Moylan states, 'critical dystopia' not only critiques the present order but also explores 'the oppositional spaces and possibilities from which the next round of political activism can derive imaginative sustenance and inspiration'.[102] The economic, social and political failures that drove the region's citizens to demonstrate have not gone away and new waves of protests are always being launched. Despite dismal times, their activism and these films indicate that creative resistance will always evolve and continue in response to the constraints.

Conclusion

This book has attempted to deepen and complicate the existing picture of cinematic freedom of expression in the Middle East, the world's so-called crisis hotspot. State censorship is often regarded as the main challenge for filmmakers. With a deliberate shift of focus onto constraint as a generic term for limitations upon and control of free expression, I have documented the much wider range of constraints that actually confront filmmakers and analysed nine creative strategies that they are using to tackle them. This is essential for enhancing understanding of the conditions in which independent films are made in the region and for breaking some of the stereotypes with which it is enshrouded.

The Introduction laid the groundwork for this analysis by identifying types of constraints in a twelve-part typology, which I expanded in relation to specific films within the chapters. The typology, and the book as a whole, highlights the multiple constraints that filmmakers contend with, in addition to state censorship, which is a major problem but not the only means of control; indeed, many filmmakers find that other obstacles, such as market mechanisms and lack of infrastructure, are just as restricting. Constraints also act on filmmakers differentially. Generally, filmmakers from the region face greater degrees of constrainedness depending on their status (e.g. their gender and country of residence) and the place and time in which they are working. This complex framework of constraints sets the extent of free expression under which they operate. Furthermore, as shown by the intensification of crisis as this book was being completed, new constraints, such as the COVID-19 pandemic, can arise and dramatically transform the filmmaking landscape.

My chapters have elaborated filmmakers' creative solutions for working under constraints and crisis conditions. Their resourcefulness is illustrated in the analyses of case study films which combine my perspective as a film scholar with the filmmakers' perspectives from 'behind' the works. As indicated by the chapter titles, the range of creative possibilities at filmmakers' disposal is considerable. Films often use a mixture of strategies, and this is by no means an exhaustive list as other strategies could be identified that are not discussed here.

It becomes clear that the films do not only capture the crises under which they were made in their storylines. They also capture them in their indexical relationship with their production constraints. The concept of indexicality also helps to explain why some of these films, especially *In the Last Days of the City* (Chapter 4), *Atomic Heart* and *Dreamaway* (Chapter 9), can be direct *and* elliptical: they register the circumstances in which they were made without making them explicit.

Additionally, I have discussed how filmmakers formulate practical and logistical solutions to their constraints, another way of being creative. As well as directing remotely via Skype (used to film in the Syrian war zone in *Little Gandhi*, mentioned in the Introduction), these include: location shooting, for a detailed evocation of place when limited resources are available for production design and hiring extras; non-professional actors, often playing versions of themselves; the use of small, hidden cameras for discreet or underground filmmaking; and moving vehicles as a relatively safe space for filming in conflict zones.

Creative strategies evolve as constraints alter; those creative strategies emerging from the region in the period covered in this book have become more direct than the allegorical modes that predominated in the past. Yet, allegory cannot be dispensed with altogether, as changing circumstances may demand a reversion to more guarded forms of expression; moreover, all films remain open to allegorical interpretation. At the same time, it is likely that, with ever-shifting constraints, more new creative strategies will arise in future.

Most filmmakers whom I interviewed agreed that their creativity is enhanced by constraints, whether from external pressures or self-imposed rules. However, several of them pointed cautiously to the difference between artists deciding which constraints to play with and living with imposed constraints, including state censorship. Ali Jaberansari remarks, 'In an ideal world where you create those constraints for yourself, you have the freedom to choose,' but 'in certain places you are given certain constraints which, as a survival mechanism, you have to use as a creative tool'. His film *Tehran: City of Love* (discussed in Chapters 4 and 6) is a response to those constraints without which, he believes, 'it would be a completely different film'.[1] It was instructive to hear diverging perspectives from Johanna Domke and Maraoun Omara, a German and an Egyptian filmmaker who have collaborated. Using dance as a metaphor for creativity, Domke elaborated:

It's actually quite hard to do whatever is in your head but when you're told you have to have one leg on the floor all the time, it actually gets easier because you have some sort of limitation that enables you to do other things more easily. So creativity grows when you have certain limitations because they enhance your imagination to overcome them.

'For sure, I agree', Omara responded. 'But at some moments I'm so frustrated because the limits are filling my glass... So getting around them is getting more complicated.'[2] The consensus among many filmmakers was that, while constraints stimulate creativity, they should not be glorified. Indeed, depending on their context and amount of professional experience, some of them (usually, newer filmmakers) valued constraints far less than others and wished for fewer limitations.

Interviewing filmmakers was an inspiring opportunity for me to hear them talk about their work and how they overcome their challenges. I was often struck by their fearlessness and resilience despite their numerous setbacks. In the book, I have sought to let them explain their constraints and creative solutions as voices of authority in their own right, and to emphasize their agency in the face of obstacles. Their insider knowledge of the field has offered rich and diverse insights, helping me to test my assumptions and flesh out my arguments.

The book's broad scope has made it challenging for me as a writer and has confronted me with my own constraints. However, as I stated in the Introduction, it is not a comprehensive study, but aims to create a comparative, theoretical framework for thinking about freedom of expression that may be transferable to other contexts. The book's interlocking arguments about crisis, creativity and constraints are particularly relevant to the conditions in which we now find ourselves, giving us the chance to learn from the filmmakers' innovative practices. Yet, as all filmmaking is affected by constraints, I hope the book's ramifications will be wider, illuminating the artist's role not just in sites of crisis in the Middle East but beyond.

Notes

Introduction

1. The World Free Press Index is available at https://rsf.org/en/ranking
2. The UN International Covenant on Civil and Political Rights (1966) is available at https://www.ohchr.org/en/professionalinterest/pages/ccpr.aspx
3. Marwan Kraidy, *The Naked Blogger of Cairo: Creative Insurgency in the Arab World* (Cambridge, MA: Harvard University Press, 2016), 131.
4. Joseph Fahim, 'Creators Meet Censors: The Standoff between Creators and Censors in Post-2011 Egyptian Drama', *Cairo Review* 28 (2018): 95.
5. Orwa al-Mokdad, interview by the author, 8 August 2018.
6. Nat Muller, 'Contemporary Art in the Middle East', in *Contemporary Art in the Middle East*, ed. Paul Sloman (London: Black Dog, 2009), 13.
7. Amin Saikal, 'Conclusion', in *The Arab World and Iran: A Turbulent Region in Transition*, ed. Amin Saikal (Basingstoke: Palgrave Macmillan, 2016), 183.
8. Andrew Arslan, *Lebanon: A Country in Fragments* (London: Hurst & Company, 2018), 10.
9. Timothy L. Sellnow and Matthew W. Seeger, *Theorizing Crisis Communication* (Chichester: Wiley-Blackwell, 2013), 3.
10. Craig Calhoun, 'The Idea of Emergency', in *Contemporary States of Emergency: The Politics of Humanitarian Interventions*, ed. Didier Fassin and Mariella Pandolfi (New York: Zone Books, 2010), 32.
11. Janet Roitman, *Anti-crisis* (Durham: Duke University Press, 2013), 4.
12. Marouan Omara and Johanna Domke, interview by the author, 14 October 2020.
13. Mani Haghighi, email communication with the author, 7 October 2020.
14. Beate Müller, 'Censorship and Cultural Regulation: Mapping the Territory', in *Censorship and Cultural Regulation in the Modern Age*, ed. Beate Müller (Amsterdam: Rodopi, 2004), 5.
15. See, for example, Daniel Biltereyst and Roel Vande Winkel, eds. *Silencing Cinema: Film Censorship around the World* (London: Palgrave Macmillan, 2013).
16. My account is largely based on Elster's book *Ulysses Unbound: Studies in Rationality, Precommitment and Constraints* (Cambridge: Cambridge University Press, 2000), a revision of arguments set out in his earlier essay, 'Conventions, Creativity, Originality' in *Rules and Conventions: Literature, Philosophy, Social Theory*, ed. Mette Hjort (Baltimore: Johns Hopkins University Press, 1992).

Although, for Elster, a constraint can be productive, it is different from Foucault's concept of power, which does not equate to restriction.
17 Elster, *Ulysses*, 264.
18 Khalid Abdalla, interview by the author, 8 October 2018.
19 Abdalla interview.
20 Persheng Sadegh-Vaziri, 'Iranian Documentary Filmmakers Association and the Fight for the House of Cinema', in *Iranian Cinema in a Global Context: Policy, Politics, and Form*, ed. Peter Decherney and Blake Atwood (New York: Routledge, 2015), 164.
21 Hamid Naficy, *A Social History of Iranian Cinema, Volume 4: The Globalizing Era, 1984–2010* (Durham: Duke University Press, 2012), 250.
22 Rania Stephan, interview by the author, 20 July 2018.
23 Sadegh-Vaziri, 'Iranian Documentary Filmmakers Association and the Fight for the House of Cinema', 171.
24 Ali Soozandeh, interview by the author, 23 August 2018.
25 Saeed Zeydabadi-Nejad, *The Politics of Iranian Cinema: Film and Society in the Islamic Republic* (Abingdon: Routledge, 2010), 53; Mani Haghighi, interview by the author, 13 October 2020.
26 Tamer el-Said, interview by Matt Morrison, 19 April 2018, available at https://www.filmcomment.com/blog/interview-tamer-el-said/
27 Keywan Karimi, interview by the author, 13 February 2021.
28 Tamer el-Said, The Paradox of Creative Constraints symposium, The Mosaic Rooms, London, 7 September 2019.
29 El-Said, The Paradox of Creative Constraints symposium.
30 Haghighi, email communication with the author; Gilles Deleuze, *Cinema 2: The Time-Image*, trans. Hugh Tomlinson and Robert Galeta (London: Athlone Press, 1989), 77.
31 Rana Eid, interview by the author, 7 August 2018.
32 Azadeh Farahmand, 'Perspectives on Recent (International Acclaim for) Iranian Cinema', in *The New Iranian Cinema: Politics, Representation and Identity*, ed. Richard Tapper (London: I.B. Tauris, 2002), 103.
33 Philippe Aractingi, interview by the author, 4 October 2019.
34 Shirin Barghnavard, interviewed by Christoph Dreher and Vinicius Jatobá, 'Expose yourself! Revealing the Flow of Life in Iran', 4 September 2018, available at https://schloss-post.com/expose-yourself/; Mette Hjort, 'Introduction: The Film Phenomenon and How Risk Pervades It', in *Film and Risk*, ed. Mette Hjort (Detroit: Wayne State University Press, 2012), 15.
35 Mahsa Salamati, 'Transnational Film Circulation in the Iranian Context: From Conjunctural Crisis to Discursive Heterotopia' (PhD Thesis, University of New South Wales, 2019), 50.

36 Ruth Hodgins, 'Imagination Is Power: How Bidayyat Captures Syria on Film', 11 April 2018, available at https://walkerart.org/magazine/imagination-is-power-syria-on-film-with-bidayyat
37 Al-Mokdad interview.
38 Naficy, *Social History of Iranian Cinema*, 391.
39 Mania Akbari, interview by the author, 6 September 2018.
40 Shirin Barghnavard, interview by the author, 9 September 2019.
41 Blake Atwood, *Reform Cinema in Iran: Film and Political Change in the Islamic Republic* (New York: Columbia University Press, 2016).
42 Naficy, *Social History of Iranian Cinema*, 69; Parviz Jahed, 'Underground Cinema', in *Iranian Cinema in a Global Context: Policy, Politics, and Form*, ed. Peter Decherney and Blake Atwood (New York: Routledge, 2015), 226.
43 Donatella Della Ratta, *Shooting A Revolution: Visual Media and Warfare in Syria* (London: Pluto Press, 2018), 176.
44 Kamran Rastegar, *Surviving Images: Cinema, War and Cultural Memory in the Middle East* (Oxford: Oxford University Press, 2015), 208.
45 Chibab El Khachab, 'State Control over Film Production in Egypt', *Arab Media & Society* 23 (2017), available at https://www.arabmediasociety.com/state-control-over-film-production-in-egypt
46 Kaleem Aftab, 'Why a Large Proportion of the Arab World's Best Filmmakers Are Women', *The National*, 3 December 2018, available at https://www.thenationalnews.com/arts-culture/film/why-a-large-proportion-of-the-arab-world-s-best-filmmakers-are-women-1.798541.
47 Aftab, 'Why a Large Proportion of the Arab World's Best Filmmakers Are Women'.
48 See Lila Abu-Lughod, *Do Muslim Women Need Saving?* (Cambridge, MA: Harvard University Press, 2013).
49 Mohamed Siam, interview by the author, 31 May 2018.
50 Basil Khalil, interview by the author, 17 September 2019.
51 Lisa Wedeen, *Ambiguities of Domination: Politics, Rhetoric, and Symbols in Contemporary Syria* (Chicago: University of Chicago Press, 2015), ix.
52 Sadaf Foroughi, interview by the author, 10 September 2018.
53 Hisham Fageeh, talk at NYU Abu Dhabi, organized by the author, 10 April 2017.
54 See Mette Hjort, 'Flamboyant Risk Taking: Why Some Filmmakers Embrace Avoidable and Excessive Risks', in *Film and Risk*, ed. Mette Hjort (Detroit: Wayne State University Press, 2012), 31–54, which distinguishes between 'inevitable risk' and 'excessive risks'.
55 Hodgins, 'Imagination Is Power'.
56 Sam Kadi, interview by the author, 13 March 2017.
57 Elster, 'Conventions, Creativity, Originality', 32.

58 Thomas Elsaesser, 'The Global Author: Control, Creative Constraints, and Performative Self-contradiction', in *The Global Auteur: The Politics of Authorship in 21st Century Cinema*, ed. Seung-hoon Jeong and Jeremi Szaniawski (London: Bloomsbury Academic, 2016), 25.
59 Karimi interview.
60 See, for example, Meredith Taylor, 'Tabl (2016) | Drum | Venice Settimana della Critica 2016', 5 September 2016, available at https://filmuforia.com/tabl-2016-drum-venice-settimana-della-critica-2016/
61 Virginia Woolf, *A Room of One's Own* (London: Penguin, 2020), 3.
62 Stephan interview.
63 Richard Maxwell and Toby Miller, 'Film and the Environment: Risk Off Screen', in *Film and Risk*, ed. Mette Hjort (Detroit: Wayne State University Press, 2012).
64 Omara and Domke interview.
65 Viola Shafik, *Arab Cinema: History and Cultural Identity* (Cairo: American University in Cairo Press, 2016), 26–7.
66 Elster, *Ulysses*, 190, 214.
67 Sara Afshar, interview by the author, 19 September 2018.
68 Mounia Akl, interview by the author, 12 September 2019.
69 Lara Zeidan, interview by the author, 26 August 2019.
70 Elster, *Ulysess*, 175.
71 For a detailed account of Dogme '95 as a film movement, its significance as a filmmaking strategy within Denmark and its internationalization, see Mette Hjort and Scott MacKenzie, ed. *Purity and Provocation: Dogme 95* (London: BFI, 2003).
72 Mette Hjort, *Lone Scherfig's Italian for Beginners* (Seattle: University of Washington Press, 2010), 44.
73 Aractingi interview.
74 Eid interview.
75 Raymond Williams, *Keywords: A Vocabulary of Culture and Society* (Oxford: Oxford University Press, 2015), 46.
76 Samad Seyidov, *Phenomenology of Creativity: History, Paradoxes, Personality* (Milton Keynes: AuthorHouse, 2013), 38.
77 See Henry Corbin, *Alone with the Alone: The Creative Imagination in the Sufism of Ibn 'Arabi* (Princeton, NJ: Princeton University Press, 1997).
78 Maysoon Pachachi, interview by the author, 1 May 2016.
79 Kraidy, *Naked Blogger*, 14.
80 Rob Pope, *Creativity: Theory, History, Practice* (Abingdon: Routledge, 2005).
81 Seyidov, *Phenomenology of Creativity: History, Paradoxes, Personality*, 38.
82 Andrew Sarris, 'The Auteur Theory Revisited', in *Critical Visions in Film Theory*, ed. Timothy Corrigan, Patricia White and Meta Mazaj (New York: Bedford/St Martin's, 2011), 316.

83 Mette Hjort, 'Introduction: More than Film School – Why the Full Spectrum of Practice-Based Film Education Warrants Attention', in *The Education of the Filmmaker in Africa, the Middle East, and the Americas*, ed. Mette Hjort (Basingstoke: Palgrave Macmillan, 2013), 6.
84 These terms are taken from Hjort, 'Flamboyant Risk Taking', 52.
85 Angus Fletcher, *Allegory: The Theory of a Symbolic Mode* (Ithaca, NY: Cornell University Press, 1964), 22.
86 Rasha Salti, 'Critical Nationals: The Paradoxes of Syrian Cinema', in *Insights into Syrian Cinema: Essays and Conversations with Filmmakers*, ed. Rasha Salti (New York: Rattapallax Press, 2006), 39.
87 Negar Mottahedeh, *Displaced Allegories: Post-revolutionary Iranian Cinema* (Durham: Duke University Press, 2008), 3.
88 Michelle Langford, 'The Circle', in *Directory of World Cinema: Iran 2*, ed. Parviz Jahed (Bristol: Intellect, 2017), 150.
89 Ahd Kamel, interview by the author, 10 May 2019.
90 Haghighi email.
91 Fredric Jameson, 'Third-World Literature in the Era of Multinational Capitalism', *Social Text* 15 (1986): 69.
92 See Michelle Langford, *Allegory in Iranian Cinema: The Aesthetics of Poetry and Resistance* (London: Bloomsbury, 2019).
93 Viola Shafik, 'Resisting Pleasure? Political Opposition and the Body in Arab Cinema', in *Resistance in Contemporary Middle Eastern Cultures: Literature, Cinema and Music*, ed. Karima Laachir and Saeed Talajooy (New York: Routledge, 2013), 121–37.
94 Laura Marks, *Hanan al-Cinema: Affections for the Moving Image* (Cambridge, MA: MIT Press, 2015), 73.
95 Marks, *Hanan al-Cinema*, 78.
96 Elster, *Ulysses*, 275.
97 Gilles Deleuze, *Cinema 1: The Movement-image*, trans. Hugh Tomlinson and Barbara Habberjam (London: Athlone Press, 1992), 211.
98 Michel de Certeau, *The Practice of Everyday Life*, trans. Steven F. Rendall (Berkeley: University of California, 1984), xix–xx; R.K. Khawsam, trans. *Le Livre des ruses: La stratégie politique des Arabes* (Paris: Phebus, 1976).
99 Patricia Aufderheide, 'Mainstream Documentary since 1999', in *American Film History: Selected Readings, 1960 to the Present*, ed. Cynthia Lucia, Roy Grundmann and Art Simon (Chichester: Wiley-Blackwell, 2016), 376.
100 Abdalla interview.
101 Charles Sanders Peirce, *The Essential Peirce: Selected Philosophical Writings*, vol. 1, ed. The Peirce Edition Project (Bloomington: Indiana University Press, 1998), 9.
102 Siegfried Kracauer, *Theory of Film: The Redemption of Physical Reality* (New York: Oxford University Press, 1960), ix.

103 Mary Ann Doane, *The Emergence of Cinematic Time: Modernity, Contingency, the Archive* (Cambridge, MA: Harvard University Press, 2002), 231.
104 Georgina Van Welie, interview by the author, 24 April 2018.
105 I owe this distinction between views 'in front' and 'behind' the film to conversations with Yasmin Fedda.
106 Abdalla interview.
107 Abdalla interview.

Chapter 1

1   Barbie Zelizer, 'On "Having Been There": "Eyewitnessing" as a Journalistic Key Word', *Critical Studies in Media Communication* 24.5 (2007): 410.
2   Stuart Allan, *Citizen Witnessing: Revisioning Journalism in Times of Crisis* (Cambridge: Polity Press, 2013), 2.
3   See Omar al-Ghazzi, '"Citizen Journalism" in the Syrian Uprising: Problematizing Western Narratives in a Local Context', *Communication Theory* 24.4 (2014): 435–54.
4   'Waad Al-Kateab – Activist and Filmmaker', available at https://www.actionforsama.com/waad-alkateab
5   See, for example, Shoshana Felman, 'In an Era of Testimony: Claude Lanzmann's Shoah', *Yale French Studies* 79 (1991): 39–81.
6   Zelizer, 'On "Having Been There": "Eyewitnessing" as a Journalistic Key Word', 421.
7   Hamid Naficy, *A Social History of Iranian Cinema, Volume 4: The Globalizing Era, 1984–2010* (Durham: Duke University Press, 2012), 350.
8   Similarly, in English, the word 'martyr' originates from the Greek for 'witness'.
9   Joshka Wessels, *Documenting Syria: Film-making, Video Activism and Revolution* (London: I.B. Tauris, 2019), 197. For definitions of martyrdom, see David Cook, *Martyrdom in Islam* (Cambridge: Cambridge University Press, 2007).
10 Wessels, *Documenting Syria: Film-making, Video Activism and Revolution*, 169.
11 Kari Andén-Papadopoulos, 'Journalism, Memory and the "Crowd-sourced Video Revolution"', in *Journalism and Memory*, ed. Barbie Zelizer and Keren Tenenboim-Weinblatt (Basingstoke: Palgrave Macmillan, 2014), 154.
12 Julio García Espinosa, 'For an Imperfect Cinema', trans. Julianne Burton, *Jump Cut* 20 (1979): 24–6, available at: https://www.ejumpcut.org/archive/onlinessays/JC20folder/ImperfectCinema.html
13 Naficy, *Social History of Iranian Cinema*, 356–7; Chad Elias and Zaher Omareen, 'Syria's Imperfect Cinema', in *Syria Speaks: Art and Culture from the Frontline*, ed. Malu Halasa, Zaher Omareen and Nawara Mahfoud (London: Saqi Books, 2014), 262.

14 Gala Hernández López, 'Notes on the Role of the Camera within a (Virtual) War: The Case of *Silvered Water, Syria Self-portrait*', *Digital War* 1.1 (2021): 12.
15 Naficy, *Social History of Iranian Cinema*, 356.
16 Mohammed Ali Atassi, 'The Digital Syrian Archive between Videos and Documentary Cinema', in *The Arab Archive: Mediated Memories and Digital Flows*, ed. Donatella Della Ratta, Kay Dickinson and Sune Haugbolle (Amsterdam: Institute of Network Cultures, 2020), 65.
17 William Brown, *Non-Cinema: Global Digital Filmmaking and the Multitude* (London: Bloomsbury, 2018), 4.
18 García Espinosa, 'For an Imperfect Cinema'.
19 Orwa al-Mokdad, interview by the author, 8 August 2018.
20 For further discussion of *Little Gandhi*, see Shohini Chaudhuri, 'The Alterity of the Image: The Distant Spectator and Films about the Syrian Revolution and War', *Transnational Cinemas* 9.1 (2018): 31–46.
21 Georgina Van Welie, interview by the author, 24 April 2018.
22 Naziha Arebi, interview by the author, 30 July 2019.
23 Yasmin Fedda, 'Syria on the Road: Stories of Conflict, Migration & Place', 17 November 2015, available at http://highlightarts.org/syria-on-the-road-stories-of-conflict-migration-place-by-yasmin-fedda/
24 Tamur Ashuri and Amit Pinchevski, 'Witnessing as a Field', in *Media Witnessing: Testimony in the Age of Mass Communication*, ed. Paul Frosch and Amit Pinchevski (Basingstoke: Palgrave Macmillan, 2009), 141.
25 Ashuri and Pinchevski, 'Witnessing as a Field', 144.
26 Ashuri and Pinchevski, 'Witnessing as a Field', 144.
27 Rik Smit, Ansgard Heinrich, and Marcel Broersma, 'Witnessing in the New Memory Ecology: Memory Construction of the Syrian Conflict on YouTube', *New Media & Society* 19.2 (2017): 300.
28 Sara Afshar, interview by the author, 19 September 2018.
29 Wessels, *Documenting Syria: Film-making, Video Activism and Revolution*, 205.
30 Khalid Abdalla, interview by the author, 8 October 2018.
31 Gil Z. Hochberg, *Visual Occupations: Violence and Visibility in a Conflict Zone* (Durham: Duke University Press, 2015), 19.
32 Lilie Chouliaraki, 'Digital Witnessing in Conflict Zones: The Politics of Remediation', *Information, Communication & Society* 18.11 (2015): 1372.
33 Chouliaraki, 'Digital Witnessing in Conflict Zones', 1372.
34 Donatella Della Ratta, *Shooting a Revolution: Visual Media and Warfare in Syria* (London: Pluto Press, 2018), 6.
35 Adi Kuntsman and Rebecca Stein, *Digital Militarism: Israel's Occupation in the Social Media Age* (Stanford: Stanford University Press, 2015), 58.

36 Human Rights Watch, 'Attacks on Ghouta: Analysis of Alleged Use of Chemical Weapons in Ghouta', 10 September 2013, available at https://www.hrw.org/report/2013/09/10/attacks-ghouta/analysis-alleged-use-chemical-weapons-syria#_ftn3
37 Marc Lynch, *The New Arab Wars: Uprisings and Anarchy in the Middle East* (Philadelphia: Perseus Books, 2016), xi,
38 Steve Rose, 'Lights, Camera, Revolution: The Birth of Libyan Cinema after Gaddafi's Fall', 1 October 2012, available at https://www.theguardian.com/film/2012/oct/01/libya-film-gaddafi-arab-spring
39 Leshu Torchin, *Creating the Witness: Documenting Genocide on Film, Video, and the Internet* (Minneapolis: University of Minnesota Press, 2012), 170.
40 Torchin, *Creating the Witness: Documenting Genocide on Film, Video, and the Internet*, 160.
41 See, for example, Kamran Rastegar, *Surviving Images: Cinema, War, and Cultural Memory in the Middle East* (Oxford: Oxford University Press, 2015); Miriam Cooke, *Dancing in Damascus: Creativity, Resilience, and the Syrian Revolution* (New York: Routledge 2017); Della Ratta, *Shooting a Revolution*, 159.
42 Abdalla interview. *In the Last Days of the City* is discussed as adopting another strategy, psychogeography, in Chapter 4.
43 Abdalla interview.
44 Emad Burnat, *5 Broken Cameras* Q&A, Palestine Expo, Queen Elizabeth II Conference Centre, London, 8 July 2017.
45 Emad Burnat, *5 Broken Cameras* Q&A, chaired by the author, Union Chapel, London, 5 July 2017.
46 Emad Burnat, interview by the author, 8 July 2017.
47 Burnat interview.
48 Emad Burnat and Guy Davidi, *5 Broken Cameras* Q&A, Riverside Studios, London, 21 June 2012.
49 Burnat and Davidi, *5 Broken Cameras* Q&A.
50 Burnat interview.
51 Burnat interview.
52 Yael Friedman, 'Guises of Transnationalism in Israel/ Palestine: A Few Notes on *5 Broken Cameras*', *Transnational Cinemas* 6.1 (2015): 26.
53 Burnat, *5 Broken Cameras* Q&A, chaired by the author.
54 Jonathan Robbins, 'Interview with Emad Burnat, "5 Broken Cameras"', 1 June 2012, available at https://www.filmlinc.org/daily/interview-with-emad-burnat-5-broken-cameras/
55 Torchin, *Creating the Witness: Documenting Genocide on Film, Video, and the Internet*, 8.

56 Previous Syrian films using epistolary forms include *300 Miles* (2016) (discussed in Chapter 2), *Silvered Water, Syria Self-Portrait* (2014) (in Chapter 9) and *Letters to S.* (2015) where, incidentally, S stands for Sama.
57 Donatella Della Ratta, 'Emerging from the Underground: On "For Sama" and Mainstream Filmmaking', 14 May 2020, available at https://syriauntold.com/2020/05/14/emerging-from-the-underground-on-for-sama-and-mainstream-filmmaking/
58 Waad Al-Kateab, interview with the author, 8 May 2020.
59 Al-Kateab interview.
60 Al-Kateab interview.
61 Al-Kateab interview.
62 Naficy, *Social History of Iranian Cinema*, 353.
63 Wessels, *Documenting Syria: Film-making, Video Activism and Revolution*, 188.
64 Waad Al-Kateab, *For Sama* Q&A, Curzon Soho, 14 September 2019.
65 Wessels, *Documenting Syria: Film-making, Video Activism and Revolution*, 236.
66 Al-Kateab interview.
67 Al-Kateab interview.
68 Al-Kateab interview.
69 Al-Kateab interview.
70 Al-Kateab interview.
71 Al-Kateab interview.
72 Wessels, *Documenting Syria: Film-making, Video Activism and Revolution*, 198.
73 Al-Kateab interview.
74 Al-Kateab interview.
75 Al-Kateab interview.
76 Edward Watts, interview by the author, 13 May 2020.
77 Donatella Della Ratta, 'Emerging from the Underground'.
78 Watts interview.
79 Watts interview. Watts previously made the documentary *Escape from ISIS* (2015) which departs from the sensationalism of many films made by foreigners about ISIS by focusing on survivors, Yazidi women.
80 They also had a two-week, in-person workshop together in summer 2017 while al-Kateab was still in Turkey.
81 Waad Al-Kateab, *For Sama* Q&A, Picturehouse Central, London, 13 September 2019.
82 Watts interview.
83 Watts interview.
84 Watts interview.
85 Watts interview.
86 Watts interview.

87 Ashuri and Pinchevski, 'Witnessing as a Field', 144.
88 Della Ratta, 'Emerging from the Underground'.
89 Al-Kateab, *For Sama* Q&A, Curzon Soho.
90 Wessels, *Documenting Syria: Film-making, Video Activism and Revolution*, 214.
91 Stephanie Zacharek, 'How Drones Are Revolutionizing the Way Film and Television Is Made', 31 May 2018, available at https://time.com/5295594/drones-hollywood-artists/
92 Watts interview.
93 Watts interview. Della Ratta writes, 'suddenly, we are taken to the surface, as if to be granted some precious breath'. Della Ratta, 'Emerging from the Underground'.
94 Al-Kateab interview.
95 *The Cave* (2019) is about a hospital in Ghouta built underground to avoid regime bombing.
96 Al-Kateab interview.
97 Torchin, *Creating the Witness: Documenting Genocide on Film, Video, and the Internet*, 161.
98 At the time of *For Sama*'s release in 2019, the Syrian regime had taken back control of 80 per cent of Syria.
99 Al-Kateab interview.
100 Mohamed Siam, interview by the author, 31 May 2018. There are many films about activists in the Egyptian Revolution, from Mosireen's street-based witnessing to feature documentaries such as *The Square* (2013) and *The Trials of Spring* (2015). *Amal* (2017) also focuses on activists through a teenager's perspective, as discussed in Chapter 2.
101 Scott Hibbard and Azza Salma Layton, 'The Origins and Future of Egypt's Revolt', *Journal of Islamic Law and Culture* 12.3 (2010): 204.
102 Siam interview.
103 Siam interview.
104 One Egyptian fiction film regarded as a landmark for its depiction of police brutality is *The Yacoubian Building* (2006), discussed in Walter Armbrust, 'Political Film in Egypt', in *Film in the Middle East and North Africa*, ed. Joseph Gugler (Austin: University of Texas Press, 2011), 242. Others include *Clash* (2016) and *The Nile Hilton Incident* (2017). See Joseph Fahim, 'Creators Meet Censors', *Cairo Review* 28 (2018): 92–101.
105 Siam interview.
106 Siam interview.
107 Siam interview.
108 Van Welie interview.
109 Van Welie interview.
110 Siam interview.

111 Naziha Arebi, *Freedom Fields* Q&A, Picturehouse Central, London, 21 May 2019.
112 Naziha Arebi, The Paradox of Creative Constraints symposium, The Mosaic Rooms, London, 7 September 2019.
113 Arebi, The Paradox of Creative Constraints symposium.
114 Naziha Arebi, *Freedom Fields* Q&A, Frontline Club, London, 4 June 2019.
115 Arebi, The Paradox of Creative Constraints symposium.
116 Arebi, *Freedom Fields* Q&A, Frontline Club.
117 Steve Rose, 'Lights, Camera, Revolution'.
118 Steve Rose, '"You Get Used to the Gunfire" – Filming the Libyan Women's Football Team', 31 May 2019, available at https://www.theguardian.com/film/2019/may/31/libyan-womens-football-team-freedom-fields
119 Arebi, *Freedom Fields* Q&A, Frontline Club.
120 Arebi, The Paradox of Creative Constraints symposium.
121 Arebi, The Paradox of Creative Constraints symposium.
122 Arebi, *Freedom Fields* Q&A, Frontline Club.
123 Arebi, *Freedom Fields* Q&A, Picturehouse Central.
124 Arebi, The Paradox of Creative Constraints symposium.
125 Arebi, The Paradox of Creative Constraints symposium.

Chapter 2

1   Susan Moeller, 'A Hierarchy of Innocence: The Media's use of Children in the Telling of International News', *The Harvard International Journal of Press/Politics* 7.1 (2002): 48.
2   Jamal Elias, *Alef Is for Allah: Childhood, Emotion, and Visual Culture in Islamic Societies* (Oakland: University of California Press, 2018), 2.
3   Elias, *Alef Is for Allah*, 3.
4   Omar Al-Ghazzi, 'An Archetypal Digital Witness: The Child Figure and the Media Conflict over Syria', *International Journal of Communication* 13 (2019): 3227.
5   Al-Ghazzi, 'An Archetypal Digital Witness', 3227.
6   Stephanie Hemelryk Donald, Emma Wilson, and Sarah Wright, 'Introduction', in *Childhood and Nation in Contemporary World Cinema: Borders and Encounters*, ed. Stephanie Hemelryk Donald, Emma Wilson and Sarah Wright (London: Bloomsbury, 2017), 2.
7   Hamid Naficy, *A Social History of Iranian Cinema, Volume 4: The Globalizing Era, 1984–2010* (Durham: Duke University Press, 2012), 209.
8   For critical perspectives on child performers in film history, see Michael Lawrence and Susan Smith, 'The Child Performance Dossier Introduction', *Screen* 53.4 (2012): 436–9.

9   Gilles Deleuze, *Cinema 2: The Time-Image*, trans. Hugh Tomlinson and Robert Galeta (London: Athlone Press, 1989), 2
10 Deleuze, *Cinema 2*, 3.
11 Laura E. Ruberto and Kristi M. Wilson, 'Introduction', in *Italian Neorealism and Global Cinema*, ed. Laura E. Ruberto and Kristi M. Wilson (Detroit: Wayne State University Press, 2007), 4.
12 Vadim Rizov, '"In Prison, I had Some Peace of Mind": Jafar Panahi on *Closed Curtain*', in *Jafar Panahi: Interviews*, ed. Drew Todd (Jackson: University Press of Mississippi, 2019), 139.
13 Fatima Mernissi, *Beyond the Veil: Male-female Dynamics in Modern Muslim Society* (Bloomington: Indiana University Press, 1987), 97.
14 Houshang Golmakani, 'New Times, Same Problems', *Index on Censorship* 3 (1992): 20. The post-revolutionary Iranian government did, however, periodically publish film regulations, starting with the Film, Slide and Video Monitoring, and Screening Permission Byelaw in 1982. See ASL 19, 'Censorship in Iranian Cinema', in *Iranian Cinema in a Global Context: Policy, Politics and Form*, ed. Peter Decherney and Blake Atwood (New York: Routledge, 2015), 229–42.
15 Hamid Naficy, 'Veiled Vision/Powerful Presences: Women in Post-revolutionary Iranian Cinema', in *Eye of the Storm: Women in Post-Revolutionary Iran*, ed. Mahnaz Afkhami and Erika Friedl (Syracuse: Syracuse University Press, 1994), 144. The opportunities that gender segregation affords for expressing same-sex desire are discussed in Chapter 4.
16 Hamid Reza Sadr, 'Children in Contemporary Iranian Cinema: When We Were Children', in *The New Iranian Cinema: Politics, Representation and Identity*, ed. Richard Tapper (London: I.B. Tauris, 2002), 235. Azadeh Farahmand claims that Iranian cinema became increasingly 'informed by sentimentality and an obsessive romance with children's supposed innocence, purity and beauty' in the 1990s, turning away from 'resilient' child characters in films made during the Iran-Iraq war (1980–8), such as *The Runner* and *Bashu, the Little Stranger*. See Azadeh Farahmand, 'Perspectives on Recent (International Acclaim for) Iranian Cinema', in *The New Iranian Cinema: Politics, Representation and Identity*, ed. Richard Tapper (London: I.B. Tauris, 2002), 104. Farahmand explains the shift by invoking the Islamic Republic's use of cinema, including its child protagonists, to soften Iran's image for international diplomacy. Rather than only seeing it in these terms, I would point to cinema's indexical relationship with crisis (here, the Iran-Iraq war) which produces more direct, experiential approaches to child protagonists.
17 Sadr, 'Children in Contemporary Iranian Cinema: When We Were Children', 235.
18 Sadr, 'Children in Contemporary Iranian Cinema: When We Were Children', 237.
19 Sadr, 'Children in Contemporary Iranian Cinema: When We Were Children', 236.

20 Michelle Langford, *Allegory in Iranian Cinema: The Aesthetics of Poetry and Resistance* (London: Bloomsbury, 2019), 76.
21 Karen Lury, *The Child in Film: Tears, Fears and Fairytales* (London: I.B. Tauris, 2010), 120.
22 Lury, *The Child in Film: Tears, Fears and Fairytales*, 129.
23 Sadr, 'Children in Contemporary Iranian Cinema: When We Were Children', 236.
24 Margherita Sprio, 'Performing History: Girlhood and *Sib/The Apple* (Samira Makhmalbaf, 1998)', in *International Cinema and the Girl: Local Issues, Transnational Contexts*, ed. Fiona Handyside and Kate Taylor-Jones (Basingstoke: Palgrave Macmillan, 2016), 166.
25 For further discussion of the exploitation of child labour in cinema, see Lury, *The Child in Film: Tears, Fears and Fairytales*, 145–89.
26 'Please read Amina Maher's story', Email from Mania Akbari to her mailing list, 12 September 2020.
27 Yahya al-Allaq, interview by the author, 5 May 2016. This interview was previously published in Shohini Chaudhuri, 'Hidden Outside, but Not Hidden Inside', 18 May 2016, available at https://mosaicrooms.org/blog/page/4/
28 Al-Allaq interview.
29 For discussion of an earlier landmark featuring street children from the region, the Moroccan film *Ali Zaoua, Prince of the Streets* (2000) directed by Nabil Ayouch, see Josef Gugler, 'Ali Zaoua: The Harsh Life of Street Children and the Poetics of Childhood', *The Journal of North African Studies* 12.3 (2007): 369–79.
30 *Capernaum* official website, available at https://sonyclassics.com/capernaum/
31 Pamela Hutchinson, 'City of Lost Children', *Sight & Sound* 29.3 (2019): 34.
32 Relations between the Lebanese and Syrians are further burdened by the history of Syrian occupation in Lebanon (1976–2005).
33 I discuss sensitivities around this detention centre (which was situated underneath al-Tahwita Bridge in Beirut) in relation to the censored documentary *Panoptic* (2017) in Chapter 4.
34 In the story, Sahar's parents marry her off to an older man, pointing to the practice of child marriage which is common among Syrian refugees in Beirut's Shatila camp.
35 Al-Ghazzi, 'An Archetypal Digital Witness', 3226.
36 Orwa al-Mokdad, interview by the author, 8 August 2018.
37 Al-Mokdad interview. When I interviewed al-Mokdad, Nour had not yet seen *300 Miles*, indicating that he still wanted to 'protect' her and that, although it was made *with* her, he deemed its content and approach unsuitable *for* her.
38 Eyas al-Mokdad, interview by the author, 24 April 2018. Eyas al-Mokdad is one of al-Mokdad's four brothers and is a filmmaker himself.
39 Orwa al-Mokdad interview.
40 Orwa al-Mokdad interview.

41 Orwa al-Mokdad interview.
42 Orwa al-Mokdad interview.
43 Moeller, 'Hierarchy of Innocence', 49.
44 Moeller, 'Hierarchy of Innocence', 44.
45 Anna Backman-Rogers, *American Independent Cinema: Rites of Passage and the Crisis Image* (Edinburgh: Edinburgh University Press, 2015), 16.
46 Lyn Mikel Brown, *Raising Their Voices: The Politics of Girls' Anger* (Cambridge, MA: Harvard University Press, 1998), 15–16.
47 Sarah Projansky, *Spectacular Girls: Media Fascination and Celebrity Culture* (New York: New York University Press, 2014), 6.
48 Mania Akbari, interview by the author, 6 September 2018.
49 Akbari interview.
50 Nawal Al-Saadawi, *The Hidden Face of Eve: Women in the Arab World*, trans. and ed. Sherif Hetata (London: Zed Books, 1991), 26.
51 Elizabeth Warnock Fernea, 'Childhood in the Muslim Middle East', in *Children in the Muslim Middle East*, ed. Elizabeth Warnock Fernea (Austin: University of Texas Press, 1995), 10.
52 Eric Egan, 'Regime Critics Confront Censorship in Iranian Cinema', in *Film in the Middle East and North Africa: Creative Dissidence*, ed. Josef Gugler (Austin: University of Texas Press, 2011), 55.
53 Akbari's *20 Fingers* is discussed in Chapter 5.
54 Naficy, *A Social History of Iranian Cinema, vol. 4*, 128.
55 Naficy, *A Social History of Iranian Cinema, vol. 4*, 128.
56 Naficy, *A Social History of Iranian Cinema, vol. 4*, 146.
57 Projansky defines 'tween' age as between eight and twelve. Projansky, 18.
58 Ahd Kamel, interview by the author, 10 May 2019.
59 *Wadjda* evokes the Orientalist dimensions of this in its trailer which quotes from *The Hollywood Reporter* review – 'A real discovery that throws open a previously closed world'.
60 Kamel interview.
61 Mernissi, *Beyond the Veil: Male-female Dynamics in Modern Muslim Society*, 19.
62 Mernissi, *Beyond the Veil: Male-female Dynamics in Modern Muslim Society*, 31.
63 Maria Garcia, 'A Woman's Voice Is Her Nakedness: An Interview with Haifa Al Mansour', *Cineaste* 38.4 (2013): 34.
64 Melanie Goodfellow, 'Haifaa Al Mansour on Returning Home to Saudi Arabia to Shoot TIFF Title "A Perfect Candidate"', 13 September 2019, available at https://www.screendaily.com/features/haifaa-al-mansour-on-returning-home-to-saudi-arabia-to-shoot-tiff-title-a-perfect-candidate/5142835.article
65 For a detailed discussion of the bicycle motif, including in another forerunner, *The Day I Became a Woman* (2000), see Anne Ciecko, 'Bicycle Borrowers after

Neorealism: Global Nou-Velo Cinema', in *Culture on Two Wheels: The Bicycle in Literature and Film*, ed. Jeremy Withers and Daniel P. Shea (Lincoln: University of Nebraska Press, 2016), 244–62.

66 Sadaf Foroughi, interview by the author, 10 September 2018.
67 T'cha Dunlevy, 'TIFF 2017: Iranian Montrealer Sadaf Foroughi Makes Waves with First Feature Ava', *Montreal Gazette*, 12 September 2017, available at: https://montrealgazette.com/entertainment/local-arts/tiff-2017-iranian-montrealer-sadaf-foroughi-makes-waves-with-first-feature-ava
68 Sadaf Foroughi, Screen Talk, Human Rights Watch Film Festival, London, 15 March 2018. To date, however, *Ava* has not been officially screened in Iran.
69 Sarah Hentges, *Pictures of Girlhood: Modern Female Adolescence on Film* (Jefferson, NC: McFarland, 2006), 60.
70 Peter Bradshaw, 'Ava Review – Smart Teenage Thriller Amps Up the Micro-tyrannies', *The Guardian*, 19 August 2020, available at https://www.theguardian.com/film/2020/aug/19/ava-review-smart-teenage-thriller-amps-up-the-micro-tyrannies
71 In this respect, *Ava* is similar to *Dressage* (2018), another Iranian fiction film where the teenage girl protagonist rebels against social expectations.
72 Richard Marcus, 'Ava, My Adolescent Self', 9 July 2018, available at: https://en.qantara.de/content/interview-with-award-winning-iranian-film-director-sadaf-foroughi-ava-my-adolescent-self. This closing image forms a dialogue with New Iranian Cinema's 'open images'. See Shohini Chaudhuri and Howard Finn, 'The Open Image: Poetic Realism and the New Iranian Cinema', *Screen* 44.1 (2003): 38–57.
73 See Damon Wise, 'IDFA: "Amal" Director Mohamed Siam on Documenting Disillusioned Arab Youth: "They had to swallow their dreams"', 16 November 2017, available at: https://variety.com/2017/film/festivals/idfa-amal-mohamed-siam-documenting-disillusioned-arab-youth-1202616288/
74 Erick Neher, 'Richard Linklater's Sculpture in Time', *Hudson Review* 67.3 (2014): 473.
75 'M. Siam le réalisateur, entretien "Je voulais comprendre l'Égypt à travers leurs yeux"', *Amal* dossier presse (Juste distribution: Paris, 2017).
76 'Myriam Sassine la productrice, entretien', *Amal* dossier presse (my translation).
77 Moeller, 'Hierarchy of Innocence', 44.
78 Maha El Said, Lena Meari and Nicola Pratt, 'Introduction', in *Rethinking Gender in Revolutions and Resistance in the Arab World: Lessons from the Arab World*, ed. Maha El Said, Lena Meari and Nicola Pratt (London: Zed Books, 2015), 16. See also Gini Reticker's *Trials of Spring* (2015) which documents women's participation in the Egyptian revolution (and on which Siam worked as a cinematographer).
79 Hentges, *Pictures of Girlhood: Modern Female Adolescence on Film*, 68.
80 Mohamed Siam, interview by the author, 31 May 2018.

Chapter 3

1. See Ali Jaafar, '"Persepolis" Banned in Lebanon', *Variety*, 10 March 2008, available at https://variety.com/2008/digital/markets-festivals/persepolis-banned-in-lebanon-1117982145/ In addition, the book was briefly censored in the USA; see Marie Ostby, 'Graphics and Global Dissent: Marjane Satrapi's *Persepolis*, Persian Miniatures, and the Multifaceted Power of Comic Protest', *PMLA* 132.3 (2017): 575.
2. Nea Ehrlich and Jonathan Murray, 'Introduction', in *Drawn from Life: Issues and Themes in Animated Documentary Cinema*, ed. Nea Ehrlich and Jonathan Murray (Edinburgh: Edinburgh University Press, 2019), 4.
3. See Annabelle Honess Roe, *Animated Documentary* (Basingstoke: Palgrave Macmillan, 2013), 11.
4. Cited in Janet Hetherington, '"Persepolis" in Motion', *Animation World Network*, 21 December 2007, available at https://www.awn.com/animationworld/persepolis-motion (accessed 19 January 2020).
5. Laura U. Marks, 'Calligraphic Animation: Documenting the Invisible', *Animation: An Interdisciplinary Journal* 6.4 (2011): 312.
6. Marks, 'Calligraphic Animation', 312.
7. See Giannalberto Bendazzi, *Animation: A World History* (Boca Raton, FL: CRC Press, 2016), 7.
8. Paul Wells, *Animation: Genre and Authorship* (London: Wallflower, 2002), 49.
9. Sergei Eisenstein, *On Disney*, ed. Jay Leyda, trans. Alan Upchurch (Calcutta: Seagull Books, 2017), 32.
10. Nea Ehrlich, 'Animated Documentaries: Aesthetics, Politics and Viewer Engagement', in *Pervasive Animation*, ed. Suzanne Buchan (New York: Routledge, 2013), 253.
11. Ali Soozandeh, interview by the author, 23 August 2018.
12. Wells acknowledges this as a qualification of his arguments. See Wells, *Animation: Genre and Authorship*, 16.
13. Soozandeh interview.
14. Hetherington, '"Persepolis" in Motion'.
15. Marks, 'Calligraphic Animation', 309.
16. Nargess Shahmanesh-Banks, 'Animation: Hand Over Art', *Design Week* 23.16 (2008): n.p.
17. Honess Roe, *Animated Documentary*, 3.
18. Maureen Furniss, *Art in Motion: Animation Aesthetics* (Sydney: John Libbey and Co, 1998), 170.
19. Paul Wells, *Understanding Animation: A Guide to Everything from Flipbooks to Flash* (London: Routledge, 1998), 6.
20. Wells, *Understanding Animation*, 86.

21 Furniss, *Art in Motion: Animation Aesthetics*, 163.
22 Furniss, *Art in Motion: Animation Aesthetics*, 163.
23 Fatemeh Hosseini-Shakib, 'Iranian Animation', in *Directory of World Cinema: Iran 2*, ed. Parviz Jahed (Bristol: Intellect, 2017), 230.
24 Hosseini-Shakib, 'Iranian Animation', 234.
25 Hosseini-Shakib, 'Iranian Animation', 240.
26 Tariq al-Rimawi, 'Issues of Representation in Arab Animation Cinema: Practice, History and Theory' (PhD Thesis, Loughborough University, 2014), 19.
27 *The Thousand and One Nights* is a collection of folktales that belongs to both Arabic and Persian traditions, as discussed in Chapter 7.
28 Ehrlich, 'Animated Documentaries: Aesthetics, Politics and Viewer Engagement', 251.
29 For further discussion of *The General's Boot* and its influence on other animators since the 'Arab Spring', see Stefanie Van de Peer, 'From Animated Cartoons to Suspended Animation: The History of Syrian Animation', in *Animation in the Middle East: Practice and Aesthetics from Baghdad to Casablanca*, ed. Stefanie Van de Peer (London: I.B. Tauris, 2017), 107–28.
30 Al-Rimawi, 'Issues of Representation in Arab Animation Cinema: Practice, History and Theory', 5.
31 See Stefanie Van de Peer, 'Introduction: Modelling Local Content for Animation in the Middle East', in *Animation in the Middle East: Practice and Aesthetics from Baghdad to Casablanca*, ed. Stefanie Van de Peer (London: I.B. Tauris, 2017), 11.
32 Paul Wells, 'Animation in the Gallery and the Gestalt: György Kovásznai and William Kentridge', in *Global Animation Theory: International Perspectives at Animafest Zagreb*, ed. Franziska Bruckner, Nikica Gilić, Holger Lang, Daniel Šuljić and Hrvoje Turković (London: Bloomsbury Academic, 2019), 15.
33 See Christa Blackmon, 'Animating Torture: A New Horizon in Human Rights Reporting', 17 August 2018, available at https://observatoryihr.org/priority_posts/animating-torture-a-new-horizon-in-human-rights-reporting/
34 Soozandeh interview.
35 Furniss, *Art in Motion: Animation Aesthetics*, 135–6.
36 Wells, *Understanding Animation*, 11.
37 Soozandeh interview.
38 Soozandeh interview.
39 Soozandeh interview.
40 Soozandeh interview.
41 For example, British-Iranian producer and programmer Elhum Shakerifar effectively called for *Tehran Taboo* to be censored in angry tweets to the British Board of Film Classification (BBFC), which approved the film for UK distribution under a 12A certificate. She protested against what she saw as

stereotypical representations and coarse language: 'Tehran Taboo is not a film about taboos in Iran, it's a film about all the things the Western world thinks it knows about a country that is constantly misunderstood, misrepresented and vilified'. Shakerifar, Tweet, 2 October 2018. Many diasporic Iranians are sensitive to the fact that Iran is shrouded in stereotypes and misconceptions in the West, which also affects their response to Iranian films they consider 'damaging' to Iran's image. For further discussion of Iran diasporic audiences' negative reactions to Iranian films screened in the West, see Shahab Esfandiary, *Iranian Cinema and Globalization: National, Transnational and Islamic Dimensions* (Bristol: Intellect, 2012), 74.

42 Soozandeh interview.
43 Furniss, *Art in Motion: Animation Aesthetics*, 77.
44 Honess Roe, *Animated Documentary*, 82.
45 Soozandeh interview.
46 Soozandeh interview.
47 Soozandeh interview.
48 Stanley Cavell, *The World Viewed: Reflections on the Ontology of Film* (Cambridge, MA: Harvard University Press, 1979), 170.
49 Nadia Yaqub, *Palestinian Cinema in the Days of Revolution* (Austin: University of Texas Press, 2018), 6.
50 Cited in Carol Hills, 'Why Israel Declared 18 Dairy Cows a National Security Risk', *The World*, 18 June 2015, available at https://www.pri.org/stories/2015-06-18/wanted-18-dairy-cows-considered-security-risk
51 Cited in Hills.
52 Another example is *Naila and the Uprising* (2017), set in Gaza during the First Intifada.
53 For an overview of links between animation and humour, see Wells, *Understanding Animation*, 127–86.
54 Cited in Dalia Hatuqa, 'Q&A: Middle East's Most Powerful Army Chasing 18 Cows', 21 March 2016, available at: https://www.aljazeera.com/features/2016/3/21/qa-middle-easts-most-powerful-army-chasing-18-cows
55 Cited in Hills.
56 Honess Roe, *Animated Documentary*, 79.
57 The films in *The Trilogy of Voice* (2014) are *What do you call it?* (in which Syrian women talk about the names they give to their vaginas), *Suleima* and *When I Heard My Voice for the First Time*. The first two are animated, while the third uses archival footage as visuals. See Estayqazat's YouTube channel, available at https://www.youtube.com/channel/UCx1yTQXkkeSHjl_v7Z66GVw
58 Van de Peer, 'From Animated Cartoons to Suspended Animation', 107.
59 Interview with Jalal Maghout, 5 May 2016.

60 Miriam Cooke, *Dancing in Damascus: Creativity, Resilience, and the Syrian Revolution* (New York: Routledge 2017), 101–2.
61 Maghout interview.
62 For a general elucidation of this strategy, see Honess Roe, *Animated Documentary*, 78.
63 Maghout interview.
64 Honess Roe, *Animated Documentary*, 88.
65 This is a common sentiment among Syrian revolutionaries, which I heard from several filmmakers. We also hear it in *For Sama* (2019), where Waad al-Kateab states, 'If I could rewind the days I would do exactly the same even if I never recover from the trauma'.
66 Maghout interview.
67 Ehrlich, 'Animated Documentaries: Aesthetics, Politics and Viewer Engagement', 255–6.
68 Maghout interview.

Chapter 4

1 Fuad Abdulaziz, *Sana'a: A Symphony* talk, University of Essex, 26 November 2020; Michel de Certeau, *The Practice of Everyday Life*, trans. Steven F. Rendall (Berkeley: University of California, 1984).
2 Guy Debord, 'Introduction to a Critique of Urban Geography', in *Situationist International Anthology*, ed. and trans. Ken Knabb (Berkeley: Bureau of Public Secrets, 1995), 8.
3 Guy Debord, 'Theory of the Dérive', in *Situationist International Anthology*, ed. and trans. Ken Knabb (Berkeley: Bureau of Public Secrets, 1995), 62.
4 Merlin Coverley, *Psychogeography* (Harpenden: Pocket Essentials, 2010), 12.
5 Giuliana Bruno, *Atlas of Emotion: Journeys in Art, Architecture and Film* (New York: Verso, 2002), 15.
6 Thomas Deane Tucker, *The Peripatetic Frame: Images of Walking in Cinema* (Edinburgh: Edinburgh University Press, 2020), 11.
7 Siegfried Kracauer, *Theory of Film: The Redemption of Physical Reality* (New York: Oxford University Press, 1960), 254.
8 Gilles Deleuze, *Cinema 1: The Movement-image*, trans. Hugh Tomlinson and Barbara Habberjam (London: Athlone Press, 1992), 212.
9 Viola Shafik, *Arab Cinema: History and Cultural Identity* (Cairo: American University in Cairo Press, 2016), 136.
10 Khalid Abdalla, interview by the author, 8 October 2018.

11 Blake Atwood, *Reform Cinema in Iran: Film and Political Change in the Islamic Republic* (New York: Columbia University Press, 2016), 82.
12 For details of Lefebvre's relationship with Situationist International, see Kristin Ross, 'Lefebvre on the Situationists: An Interview', *October* 79 (1997): 69–83.
13 Henri Lefebvre, *Writings on Cities*, trans. and ed. Eleonore Kaufman and Elizabeth Lebas (Oxford: Blackwell, 1996).
14 Keywan Karimi, interview by the author, 13 February 2021.
15 Karimi interview.
16 Karimi interview.
17 Karimi interview.
18 My translation. Cited in Hadrien Salducci, 'KEYWAN KARIMI, rencontre avec un cinéaste censuré', 13 June 2018, available at https://www.leblogducinema.com/portrait/keywan-karimi-interview-867162/
19 The female narrator is Farahnaz Sharifi, herself a documentary filmmaker whose co-authored work *Profession: Documentarist* (2014) is discussed in Chapter 7. With its dialectic of male and female voice-overs, *Writing on the City* is also reminiscent of Forugh Farrokhzad's *The House is Black* (1963).
20 Karimi interview.
21 Raoul Vaneigem, 'The Wall Is a Mirror', available at https://www.puntodevistafestival.com/en/noticias.asp?IdNoticia=399
22 The term 'habitus' originates from the work of sociologist Pierre Bourdieu; see Pierre Bourdieu, *Outline of a Theory of Practice*, trans. Richard Nice (Cambridge: Cambridge University Press, 1979), 72. *Tehran: City of Love* also uses deadpan humour to explore its themes, as discussed in Chapter 6.
23 An earlier film that features a *zūrkhāneh* is *Qaysar* (1969).
24 Ali Jaberansari, The Paradox of Creative Constraints symposium, The Mosaic Rooms, London, 7 September 2019.
25 Ali Jaberansari, interview by the author, 30 October 2018.
26 In earlier chapters, this is discussed as the practice of *taqieh*.
27 Jaberansari interview.
28 Henri Lefebvre, *The Production of Space*, trans. Donald Nicholson-Smith (Oxford: Blackwell, 1991), 57.
29 Ali Jaberansari, *Tehran: City of Love* Q&A, Poetry in Motion, Barbican, London, 13 April 2019.
30 Jaberansari, *Tehran: City of Love* Q&A, Poetry in Motion.
31 Jaberansari interview.
32 Pedram Partovi, *Popular Iranian Cinema before the Revolution: Family and Nation in FilmFarsi* (Abingdon: Routledge, 2017), 110. *Fīlmfārsī* is the name given to the mainstream cinema that predominated in Iran before the Islamic Republic.
33 Jaberansari, *Tehran: City of Love* Q&A, Poetry in Motion.

34 Jaberansari, The Paradox of Creative Constraints symposium.
35 Jaberansari, The Paradox of Creative Constraints symposium.
36 Lina Khatib, *Lebanese Cinema: Imagining the Civil War and beyond* (London: I.B. Tauris, 2008), 57–8.
37 T.J. Demos, *The Migrant Image: The Art and Politics of Documentary during Global Crisis* (Durham: Duke University Press, 2013), 187.
38 Rana Eid, interview by the author, 7 August 2018.
39 Nadine Labaki later filmed the same detention centre in *Capernaum* (2018), as discussed in Chapter 2. The facility has since been dismantled.
40 Eid interview.
41 Rania Stephan, interview by the author, 20 July 2018.
42 Henri Lefebvre, *Rhythmanalysis: Space, Time and Everyday Life*, trans. Stuart Elden and Gerald Moore (London: Bloomsbury, 2013), 30.
43 Eid interview.
44 Michel Foucault, *The Birth of the Clinic* (Abingdon: Routledge, 2003), 45.
45 Lefebvre, *Production of Space*, 98.
46 Eid interview.
47 Stephan interview. Stephan's own film, *The Three Disappearances of Soad Hosni* (2011), is discussed in Chapter 8.
48 Eid interview.
49 Eid interview.
50 Eid interview.
51 Eid interview. She was referring to the Civil War and, before that, several earthquakes.
52 Eid interview.
53 Stephan interview.
54 Eid interview.
55 Eid interview.
56 Geraldine Pratt and Rose Marie San Juan, *Film and Urban Space: Critical Possibilities* (Edinburgh: Edinburgh University Press, 2014), 105.
57 Pratt and San Juan, *Film and Urban Space*, 105.
58 Abdalla interview.
59 Khalid Abdalla, *In the Last Days of the City* Q&A, The Mosaic Rooms, London, 6 September 2018.
60 Abdalla interview.
61 Abdalla interview.
62 Abdalla interview.
63 Gilles Deleuze, *Cinema 2: The Time-Image*, trans. Hugh Tomlinson and Robert Galeta (London: Athlone Press, 1989), 78.
64 Abdalla interview.

65 I borrow the term *déjà disparu* from Ackbar Abbas's writing on Hong Kong cinema in the shadow of the city's 1997 handover to China. See Abbas, *Hong Kong: Culture and the Politics of Disappearance* (Minneapolis, MN: University of Minnesota Press, 1997), 25.
66 Abdalla interview.
67 Abdalla, *In the Last Days of the City* Q&A, Mosaic Rooms.
68 Abdalla, *In the Last Days of the City* Q&A, Mosaic Rooms.
69 Walter Benjamin, *Illuminations*, trans. Harry Zohn (London: Fontana Press, 1992), 230.
70 For the symbolism of the Rabea hand, see Marwan Kraidy, *The Naked Blogger of Cairo: Creative Insurgency in the Arab World* (Cambridge, MA: Harvard University Press, 2016), 104.
71 Abdalla interview.
72 Abdalla interview.
73 Abdalla interview.
74 Giuliana Bruno, 'Bodily Architectures', *Assemblage* 19 (1992): 108.
75 Debord, 'Theory of the Dérive', 62.
76 See Lina Khatib, *Image Politics in the Middle East: The Role of the Visual in Political Struggle* (London: I.B. Tauris, 2012).
77 Debord, 'Theory of the Dérive', 62.
78 Coverley, *Psychogeography*, 97.

Chapter 5

1 Kay Dickinson, 'The Palestinian Road (Block) Movie Everyday Geographies of Second Intifada Cinema', in *Cinema at the Periphery*, ed. Dina Iordanova, David Martin-Jones and Belén Vidal (Detroit: Wayne State University Press, 2010), 143.
2 Laura Marks, *Hanan al-Cinema: Affections for the Moving Image* (Cambridge, MA: MIT Press, 2015), 159.
3 Gilles Deleuze, *Cinema 1: The Movement-image*, trans. Hugh Tomlinson and Barbara Habberjam (London: Athlone Press, 1992), 208.
4 Nadia Yaqub, 'Utopia and Dystopia in Palestinian Circular Journeys from Ghassān Kanafānī to Contemporary Film', *Middle Eastern Literatures* 15.3 (2012): 306.
5 Rebecca Stein, *Itineraries in Conflict: Israelis, Palestinians, and the Political Lives of Tourism* (Durham: Duke University Press, 2008), 14.
6 Laura Berger, 'Oscars 2018: Foreign Lang Contenders: Annemarie Jacir "Wajib"', 27 November 2017, available at https://womenandhollywood.com/oscars-2018-foreign-language-contenders-annemarie-jacir-wajib-809a634d10f2/

7   However, even foreign passport holders take risks (for example, of having footage or equipment taken from them at Israeli border control) every time they enter or leave the country.
8   Annemarie Jacir, '"For Cultural Purposes Only": Curating a Palestinian Film Festival', in *Dreams of a Nation: On Palestinian Cinema*, ed. Hamid Dabashi (London: Verso, 2006), 27.
9   Jafar Panahi, interview by Tobias Grey, 'Iranian Director Flouts Ban on Filmmaking', in *Jafar Panahi: Interviews*, ed. Drew Todd (Jackson: University Press of Mississippi, 2019), 134.
10 Jafar Panahi, 'Dissident Cinema: A Conversation between Jafar Panahi and Jamsheed Akrami', *World Policy Journal* 35.1 (2018): 62.
11 Annemarie Jacir, tweet, 10 September 2018.
12 Annemarie Jacir, interview by Rolex Mentor, 'Film *Wajib* Wins Prizes and Praise', March 2018, available at https://www.rolexmentorprotege.com/journal/article/annemarie-jacir-wajib (accessed 19 September 2018).
13 Naziha Arebi, interview by the author, 30 July 2019.
14 Larissa Sansour, interview by the author, 7 August 2017. Her films are discussed in Chapter 9.
15 Marks, *Hanan al-Cinema*, 168.
16 Harriet Sherwood, 'Speed Sisters on Track for Race Equality', *The Guardian*, 18 June 2010, available at https://www.theguardian.com/world/2010/jun/18/palestine-speed-sisters-race
17 Amber Fares, interview by the author, 15 May 2020.
18 Fares interview.
19 Israeli and Palestinian territory number plates are differentiated by colour: the former are yellow, while the latter are white.
20 Fares interview.
21 Fares interview.
22 Fares interview.
23 Fares interview. Fares directed a behind-the-scenes documentary for *The Idol* (2015) in Gaza.
24 Fares interview.
25 Fares interview.
26 Fares interview.
27 Fares interview.
28 Fares interview.
29 Fares interview.
30 Fares interview.
31 A.L. Rees, 'Moving Spaces', in *Autopia: Cars and Culture*, ed. Peter Wollen and Joe Kerr (London: Reaktion Books, 2002), 93.

32 Steve Cohan and Ina Rae Hark, 'Introduction', in *The Road Movie Book*, ed. Steve Cohan and Ina Rae Hark (London: Routledge, 2002), 8.
33 For detailed discussion of Kiarostami's use of the car, see Devin Orgeron, *Road Movies: From Muybridge and Méliès to Lynch and Kiarostami* (Basingstoke: Palgrave Macmillan, 2008).
34 Geoff Andrew, *10* (London: British Film Institute, 2005), 38.
35 Mania Akbari, interview by the author, 6 September 2018.
36 Akbari interview.
37 Panahi interview by Grey, 133.
38 Panahi interview by Grey, 134.
39 Mahsa Salamati, 'Transnational Film Circulation in the Iranian Context: From Conjunctural Crisis to Discursive Heterotopia' (PhD Thesis, University of New South Wales, 2019), 193–4.
40 Panahi interview by Grey, 132.
41 Panahi, 'Dissident Cinema', 69.
42 Panahi, interview by Vadim Rizov, '"In Prison, I had Some Peace of Mind": Jafar Panahi on *Closed Curtain*', in *Jafar Panahi: Interviews*, ed. Drew Todd (Jackson: University Press of Mississippi, 2019), 138.
43 Salamati, 'Transnational Film Circulation in the Iranian Context', 224.
44 Trevor Johnston, 'Taxi Tehran', *Sight & Sound* 25.11 (2015): 68–9.
45 In Iran, movie smugglers also provide pirated movies for download from their websites or Telegram accounts.
46 Panahi, 'Dissident Cinema', 64–5.
47 The Farsi term is *qābl-e pakhsh*, literally 'worthy of distribution'.
48 Salamati, 'Transnational Film Circulation in the Iranian Context', 202.
49 Lara Zeidan, interview by the author, 26 August 2019.
50 Zeidan interview.
51 Zeidan interview.
52 Zeidan interview.
53 Lara Zeidan, interview by Jennifer Merin, 'Whistler Film Festival 2018: Lara Zeidan, director of Three Centimetres', 29 November 2018, available at https://awfj.org/female-gaze/2018/11/29/whistler-film-festival-2018-lara-zeidan-director-of-three-centimetres/?doing_wp_cron=1618823363.8232939243316650390625
54 Philippe Aractingi, interview by the author, 4 October 2019.
55 Aractingi interview.
56 Aractingi interview.
57 Ali Mostafa, *The Worthy* Q&A chaired by the author, NYU Arts Center, Abu Dhabi, 3 April 2017. Popular genres are no guarantee of commercial success, given that Mostafa's independent debut feature, *City of Life* (2009), performed better at the

box office than his subsequent Image Nation-supported popular genre films *From A to B* and *The Worthy* (2016).
58 Susan Hayward, *Cinema Studies: The Key Concepts* (London: Routledge, 2000), 313.
59 Cohan and Hark, 'Introduction', 9.
60 Roy Dib, interview by the author, 19 June 2020.
61 Dib interview.
62 Dib interview.
63 Dib interview.
64 Dib interview.
65 Dib interview.
66 Dib interview.
67 Dib interview.
68 Teresa de Lauretis, 'Film and the Visible', in *How Do I Look: Queer Film and Video*, ed. Bad Object-Choices (Seattle: Bay Press, 1991), 255.

Chapter 6

1 Larissa Sansour, interview by the author, 7 August 2017.
2 Roy Dib, interview by the author, 19 June 2020.
3 This includes scholarship on humour in the Middle East, as well as general works on the philosophy of humour. See Gayatri Devi and Najat Rahman, ed. *Humor in Middle Eastern Cinema* (Detroit: Wayne State University Press, 2014); Chrisoula Lionis, *Laughter in Occupied Palestine: Comedy and Identity in Art and Film* (London: I.B. Tauris, 2016); Simon Critchley, *On Humour* (London: Routledge, 2002); John Morreall, *Comic Relief: A Comprehensive Philosophy of Humor* (Malden: Wiley-Blackwell, 2009). There are other works that emphasize the motivation and purpose of humour, which are practitioner or activist-led, although none of these focus on cinema. See, for example, Janjira Sombatpoonsiri, *Humor and Nonviolent Struggle in Serbia* (New York: Syracuse University Press, 2015), Mahmud Farjami, *Iranian Political Satirists: Experience and Motivation in the Contemporary Era* (Amsterdam: John Benjamins Publishing Company, 2017); Amber Day, ed. *Satire and Dissent* (Bloomington: Indiana University Press, 2011).
4 I borrow the idea of comic modes from Geoff King, *Film Comedy* (New York: Columbia University Press, 2002), 2.
5 King, *Film Comedy*, 2.
6 For further discussion of safety valve theory and 'permitted criticism', see Lisa Wedeen, *Ambiguities of Domination: Politics, Rhetoric, and Symbols in Contemporary Syria* (Chicago: University of Chicago Press, 2015), 88.

7   See Lisa Wedeen, *Authoritarian Apprehensions: Ideology, Judgment, and Mourning in Syria* (Chicago: University of Chicago Press, 2019), 51.
8   Henri Bergson, *Laughter: An Essay on the Meaning of the Comic*, trans. Cloudesley Brereton and Fred Rothwell (Salt Lake City, UT: Project Gutenberg, 2009), 15.
9   Naziha Arebi, The Paradox of Creative Constraints symposium, The Mosaic Rooms, London, 7 September 2019.
10 Nacim Pak-Shiraz, 'Iranian Comedies', in *Directory of World Cinema: Iran 2*, ed. Parviz Jahed (Bristol: Intellect, 2017), 266.
11 See Sean Foley, *Changing Saudi Arabia: Art, Culture and Society in the Kingdom* (Boulder, CO: Lynne Rienner Publishers, 2019), 77–9.
12 Foley, *Changing Saudi Arabia*, 75.
13 Hisham Fageeh, talk at NYU Abu Dhabi, organized by the author, 10 April 2017.
14 Fageeh NYU Abu Dhabi talk.
15 Fageeh NYU Abu Dhabi talk.
16 Fageeh NYU Abu Dhabi talk.
17 Basil Khalil, interview by the author, 17 September 2019.
18 Khalil interview.
19 Hamid Naficy, *A Social History of Iranian Cinema, Volume 4: The Globalizing Era, 1984–2010* (Durham: Duke University Press, 2012), 190.
20 Mohamed M. Helmy and Sabine Frerichs, 'Stripping the Boss: The Powerful Role of Humor in the Egyptian Revolution 2011', *Integrative Psychological and Behavioral Science* 47 (2013): 452.
21 The collective's name, Masasit Mati, refers to the straw with which Syrians (or, more specifically, Alawites, the sect to which the al-Assad family belongs) drink Mati tea. They have since created another series, *Top Goon Reloaded*, which satirizes the international community's response to the Syrian crisis and dictators from other countries.
22 Masasit Mati, 'Who Wants to Kill a Million?' in *Syria Speaks: Art and Culture from the Frontline*, ed. Malu Halasa, Zaher Omareen and Nawara Mahfoud (London: Saqi Books, 2014), 269.
23 Jamil al-Abyad, interviewed by Annasofie Flamand and Hugh Macleod, 'Little Dictator', *Witness*, Aljazeera, 21 August 2012, available at https://www.aljazeera.com/program/episode/2012/8/21/little-dictator/
24 Wedeen, *Authoritarian Apprehensions*, 74.
25 Cited in Hugh Macleod and Annasofie Flamand, 'Top Goon: Puppet Drama Lampoons Syria's Bashar al-Assad', *Global Post*, 12 December 2011, available at https://www.pri.org/stories/2011-12-12/top-goon-puppet-drama-lampoons-syrias-bashar-al-assad
26 Amber Day, 'Introduction: Poking Holes in the Spectacle', in *Satire and Dissent*, ed. Amber Day (Bloomington: Indiana University Press, 2011), 21.

27 Cited in Macleod and Flamand, 'Top Goon: Puppet Drama Lampoons Serious Bashar al-Assad'.
28 Leila Sansour, interview by the author, 9 November 2015.
29 Leila Sansour interview.
30 Annemarie Jacir, interview by Melanie Goodfellow, 'Annemarie Jacir on the Tensions of Shooting "Wajib" in Nazareth', 15 December 2017, available at https://www.screendaily.com/features/annemarie-jacir-on-the-tensions-of-shooting-wajib-in-nazareth/5125051.article
31 Lionis, *Laughter in Occupied Palestine*, 129.
32 Leila Sansour interview.
33 André Breton claims that the term 'black humour' didn't exist as a dictionary term before *An Anthology of Black Humour*, a collection of texts that he edited in 1940 to represent surrealist notions of humour. See Breton, 'Foreword to 1966 French Edition', in *Anthology of Black Humour*, ed. André Breton, trans. Mark Polizzoti (London: Telegram, 2009), 11.
34 Chapter 9 is dedicated to science fiction and dystopia, including Larissa Sansour's works.
35 Larissa Sansour interview.
36 Larissa Sansour interview.
37 Mounia Akl, 'Tales of the Silk Road – Lebanon Chapter' Q&A, Rich Mix, London, 25 February 2019.
38 Edward Watts, interview by the author, 13 May 2020.
39 Sigmund Freud, 'On Humour', in *The Standard Edition of the Complete Psychological Works of Sigmund Freud*, vol. 21, trans. James Strachey (London: Hogarth Press, 1961), 161.
40 Jacir, interview by Leigh Singer, '"Laughing is a Way to Resist": Annemarie Jacir on Her Father-son Wedding Drama Wajib', 7 January 2019, available at https://www2.bfi.org.uk/news-opinion/sight-sound-magazine/interviews/wajib-annemarie-jacir-palestinian-father-son-wedding-drama
41 Dib interview.
42 Leila Sansour interview.
43 Larissa Sansour interview.
44 Haim Bresheeth, 'A Symphony of Absence: Borders and Liminality in Elia Suleiman's "Chronicle of a Disappearance"', *Framework: The Journal of Cinema and Media* 43.2 (2002): 73.
45 Elia Suleiman, *It Must Be Heaven* Q&A, BFI London Film Festival, 9 October 2019.
46 Elia Suleiman, interview by Linda Butler, 'The Occupation (and Life) through an Absurdist Lens', *Journal of Palestine Studies* 32.2 (2003): 72.
47 King, *Film Comedy*, 22–3.
48 Suleiman, *It Must Be Heaven* Q&A.

49 Suleiman, *It Must Be Heaven* Q&A.
50 Suleiman, *It Must Be Heaven* Q&A.
51 Basil Khalil, The Paradox of Creative Constraints symposium, The Mosaic Rooms, London, 7 September 2019.
52 Khalil interview.
53 Khalil interview.
54 Khalil interview. Khalil's comments recall Henri Bergson's view of the comic as 'something mechanical encrusted on the living'. See Bergson, *Laughter*, 49.
55 Khalil interview.
56 Khalil interview.
57 Khalil interview.
58 Mary Douglas, 'The Social Control of Cognition: Some Factors in Joke Perception', *Man* 3.3 (1968): 369.
59 Greg Philo, Alison Gilmour, Maureen Gilmour, Susanna Rust, Etta Gaskell and Lucy West, 'The Israeli-Palestinian Conflict: TV News and Public Understanding', in *War and the Media: Reporting Conflict 24/7*, ed. Daya Kishan Thussu and Des Freedman (London: Sage, 2003), 139.
60 Khalil interview.
61 Khalil interview.
62 Khalil, The Paradox of Creative Constraints symposium.
63 Liz Ferguson, 'FNC 2018: Review of Iranian Comedy Pig (Khook)', 9 October 2018, available at https://mostlymovies.ca/2018/10/09/fnc-2018-review-of-iranian-comedy-pig-khook/
64 Anne Démy-Geroe, *Iranian National Cinema: The Interaction of Policy, Genre, Funding and Reception* (Abingdon: Routledge, 2020), 47.
65 Mani Haghighi, interview by the author, 13 October 2020.
66 See Richard Brody, '"Pig," Reviewed: An Iranian Comedy about Film Makers Who Become the Targets of Murder', 7 January 2019, available at https://www.newyorker.com/culture/the-front-row/pig-reviewed-an-iranian-comedy-about-filmmakers-who-become-the-targets-of-murder
67 Haghighi interview.
68 Haghighi interview. The phrase has been attributed to Voltaire but was written by S.G. Tallentyre (pseudonym of Evelyn Beatrice Hall) in *Friends of Voltaire* (1906) in order to encapsulate Voltaire's attitude and has become the motto of some free speech advocates.
69 Haghighi interview.
70 Haghighi, email communication with the author, 7 October 2020.
71 Haghighi interview.
72 Haghighi, email communication with the author.
73 Critchley, *On Humour*, 33.

74 Haghighi interview.
75 Mani Haghighi, interview by Sanam Shantyaei, 'A Killer Comedy: France 24 Meets the Iranian Director behind "Pig"', 5 December 2018, available at https://www.youtube.com/watch?v=MTWTGc4i0MM
76 Linda Hutcheon, 'The Complex Functions of Irony', *Revista Canadiense de Estudios Hispánicos* 16.2 (1992): 220.
77 Ali Jaberansari, Paradox of Creative Constraints symposium, 7 September 2019.
78 Ali Jaberansari, interview by the author, 30 October 2018.
79 Ali Jaberansari, *Tehran: City of Love* Q&A, BFI London Film Festival, 14 October 2018.
80 James MacDowell, 'Notes on Quirky', *Movie: A Journal of Film Criticism* 1.1 (2010): 3.
81 James MacDowell, *Irony in Film* (London: Palgrave Macmillan, 2016), 145–6.
82 Cited in Thomas Austin, 'Introduction', in *The Films of Aki Kaurismäki: Ludic Engagements*, ed. Thomas Austin (New York: Bloomsbury Academic, 2018), 3.
83 Michael Lawrence, 'Deadpan Dogs: Aki Kaurismäki's Canine Comedies', in *The Films of Aki Kaurismäki: Ludic Engagements*, ed. Thomas Austin (New York: Bloomsbury Academic, 2018), 200.
84 Jaakko Seppälä, 'The Camera's Ironic Point of View: Notes on Strange and Comic Elements in the Films of Aki Kaurismäki', in *The Films of Aki Kaurismäki: Ludic Engagements*, ed. Thomas Austin (New York: Bloomsbury Academic, 2018), 83–4.
85 The term 'discrepant awareness' derives from Bertrand Evans, *Shakespeare's Comedies* (Oxford: Clarendon Press, 1960), 14. MacDowell deploys it extensively in his book *Irony in Film*.
86 I am adapting MacDowell's characterization of 'quirky'. See MacDowell, 'Notes on Quirky', 3.
87 Jonathan Romney, 'Last Exit to Helsinki: The Bleak Comedic Genius of Aki Kaurismäki, Finland's Finest', *Film Comment* 39.2 (2003): 47.
88 MacDowell, 'Notes on Quirky', 11.
89 This is how Clare Colebrook defines 'romantic irony'. See Colebrook, *Irony* (London: Routledge, 2004), 57.
90 Mahmoud Sabbagh, *Barakah Meets Barakah* Q&A, BFI London Film Festival, 8 October 2016.
91 Sabbagh, *Barakah Meets Barakah* Q&A, BFI London Film Festival.
92 Fageeh NYU Abu Dhabi talk.
93 Fageeh, *Barakah Meets Barakah* Q&A, BFI London Film Festival, 8 October 2016.
94 By the time *Barakah Meets Barakah* was released in 2016, the powers of the religious police (Committee for the Promotion of Virtue and Prevention of Vice, or *mutawwa*) had been reduced by the Council of Ministers. See Valerie Anishchenkova, *Modern Saudi Arabia* (ABC-CLIO, 2020), 95.

95   Claire Mortimer, *Romantic Comedy* (Abingdon: Routledge, 2010), 4.
96   Fageeh NYU Abu Dhabi talk.
97   Fatima al-Banawi, *Barakah Meets Barakah* Q&A, BFI London Film Festival, 8 October 2016.
98   Fageeh NYU Abu Dhabi talk. Since Fageeh made this comment in 2017, many more Saudi movies have been produced.
99   King, *Film Comedy*, 62.
100 Foley, *Changing Saudi Arabia*, 173.
101 Foley, *Changing Saudi Arabia*, 174.
102 Foley, *Changing Saudi Arabia*, 4.
103 Jane Kinninmont, 'Saudi Arabia: Why Is Going to the Cinema Suddenly OK?' 17 April 2018, available at https://www.bbc.co.uk/news/world-middle-east-43738718
104 Ahd Kamel, interview by the author, 10 May 2019.
105 Kamel interview. Furthermore, Saudi women's activism against the driving ban goes all the way back to the 1980s.
106 Day, 'Introduction', 9.
107 Fageeh NYU Abu Dhabi talk.
108 King, *Film Comedy*, 133.

Chapter 7

1   Viola Shafik, *Arab Cinema: History and Cultural Identity* (Cairo: The American University in Cairo Press, 2016), 92. This narrative structure is not unique to the region, however. It is said to have originated in Indian folktales such as *Kathasaritsagara*. See K. Ayyappa Panikkar, *Indian Narratology* (New Delhi: Indira Gandhi National Centre for the Arts, 2003).
2   Orkideh Behrouzan, 'Introduction', in *The Book of Tehran: A City in Short Fiction* (Manchester: Comma Press, 2019), xi–xii.
3   The frame story and some tales of *The Thousand and One Nights* have been traced to a Persian work, *Hazar Afsanah* ('A thousand legends'). The work was translated into Arabic in the ninth century, when its title became *Alf Layla* ('A Thousand Nights') and later *Alf Layla wa Layla* ('A Thousand and One Nights'). Indian and Arabic folktales were added by multiple scribes and editors. The arrangement of stories kept changing until a more fixed written form was adopted in the eighteenth century. It was first introduced to the West by Antoine Gallard's French translation, *Les mille et une nuits* (1704). See David Pinault, *Storytelling Techniques in the Arabian Nights* (Leiden: E.J. Brill, 1992), 6.

4   David Bordwell, *Poetics of Cinema* (New York: Routledge, 2008), 105.
5   Walter Ong, *Orality and Literacy: The Technologizing of the Word* (Abingdon: Routledge, 2006), 143.
6   María Del Mar Azcona, *The Multi-protagonist Film* (Malden, MA: Wiley-Blackwell, 2010), 33.
7   The expression 'life as lived' derives from the anthropologist Paul Riesman, *Freedom in Fulani Social Life: An Introspective Ethnography*, trans. Martha Fuller (Chicago: Chicago University Press, 1977), 1.
8   See, for example, Jack Shaheen, *Real Bad Arabs: How Hollywood Vilifies a People* (New York: Olive Branch Press, 2001), 8.
9   Michel Foucault, *Aesthetics, Method, and Epistemology: Essential Works of Foucault, 1954–1984*, ed. James D. Faubion (New York: The New Press, 1998), 139.
10 Lucien Dällenbach, '*Mise-en-abyme* and Mirror Effects in Claude Simon', in *Claude Simon*, ed. Celia Britton (New York: Longman, 1993), 141. Dällenbach treats the topic of mise en abyme more extensively in his book *The Mirror in the Text* (Chicago: University of Chicago Press, 1989).
11 Dällenbach, '*Mise-en-abyme* and Mirror Effects in Claude Simon', 142.
12 Gilles Deleuze, *Cinema 2: The Time-Image*, trans. Hugh Tomlinson and Robert Galeta (London: Athlone Press, 1989), 76.
13 Deleuze, *Cinema 2*, 76.
14 Shafik, *Arab Cinema*, 36.
15 Nacim Pak-Shiraz, 'Truth, Lies and Justice: The Fragmented Picture in Asghar Farhadi's Films', in *Muslims in the Movies*, ed. Kristian Peterson (Harvard: Harvard University Press, 2021), 156.
16 Pak-Shiraz, 'Truth, Lies and Justice', 156.
17 Cited in Lloyd Ridgeon, *Makhmalbaf's Broken Mirror: The Socio-political Significance of Modern Iranian Cinema* (Durham: University of Durham, 2000), 12.
18 Anne Démy-Geroe, *Iranian National Cinema: The Interaction of Policy, Genre, Funding and Reception* (Abingdon: Routledge, 2020), 177.
19 Mohammad Rasoulof, interview by Ali Moosavi, 'A Stranger in His Homeland', *Film International* 84 (2018): 109–10.
20 Rasoulof, interview by Moosavi, 110.
21 Rasoulof, interview by Moosavi, 110.
22 Shirin Barghnavard, The Paradox of Creative Constraints symposium, The Mosaic Rooms, London, 7 September 2019.
23 Deutsche Welle, 'Why Mohammad Rasoulof Still Makes Films Despite Iran's Threats', available at https://www.dw.com/en/why-mohammad-rasoulof-still-makes-films-despite-irans-threats/a-52575195
24 For an auteurist reading that unpacks these references to Banietemad's earlier works, see Michelle Langford, '*Tales* and the Cinematic *Divan* of Rakshan

Banietemad', in *Refocus: The Films of Rakshan Banietemad*, ed. Maryam Ghorbankarimi (Edinburgh: Edinburgh University Press, 2021).

25 Zahra Khosroshahi, 'The Films of Rakhshan Banietemad: A Gateway into the Representation of Women in Iranian Cinema' (PhD Thesis, University of East Anglia, 2019), 207.

26 Margrit Tröhler, 'Les Films à protagonistes multiples et la logique des possibles', *Iris* 29 (2000): 85–102.

27 Bordwell, *Poetics of Cinema*, 191.

28 Azcona, *The Multi-protagonist Film*, 2.

29 Shafik, *Arab Cinema*, 226.

30 Banietemad, interview by Shiva Rahbaran, 'Rakshan Bani-Etemad: Cinema as a Mirror of the Urban Image', in *Iranian Cinema Uncensored: Contemporary Film-Makers since the Islamic Revolution* (London: I.B. Tauris, 2016), 133–4.

31 Banietemad, interview by Maryam Ghorbankarimi, 'A Conversation with the Director', in *Refocus: The Films of Rakshan Banietemad*, ed. Maryam Ghorbankarimi (Edinburgh: Edinburgh University Press, 2021), 19.

32 Kay Armatage and Zahra Khosroshahi, 'An Interview with Rakhshan Banietemad', *Feminist Media Histories* 3.1 (2017): 152.

33 See Azcona, *The Multi-protagonist Film*, 39.

34 Zahra Khosroshahi, 'The Artistic and Political Implications of the Meta-cinematic in Rakshan Banietemad's Films' and Maryam Ghorbankarimi, 'Rakshan Banietemad's Art of Social Realism: Bridging Realism and Fiction', in *Refocus: The Films of Rakshan Banietemad*, ed. Maryam Ghorbankarimi (Edinburgh: Edinburgh University Press, 2021), 85, 198.

35 Banietemad, interview by Ghorbankarimi, 14.

36 Khosroshahi similarly argues that 'Banietemad uses the meta-cinematic [including the film within a film] as an artistic tool to comment on social and political issues in Iran' throughout her work. Khosroshahi, 'Implications of the Metacinematic', 93.

37 Banietemad, interview by Armatage and Khosroshahi, 153.

38 Barghnavard, The Paradox of Creative Constraints symposium.

39 For an account of problems faced by Iranian documentary filmmakers who have worked with BBC Persian, see Persheng Sadegh-Vaziri, 'The Fight for the House of Cinema', in *Iranian Cinema in a Global Context: Policy, Politics, and Form*, ed. Peter Decherney and Blake Atwood (New York: Routledge, 2015), 170–1.

40 Shirin Barghnavard, interview by the author, 9 September 2019.

41 Helen De Michiel and Patricia R. Zimmerman, *Open Space New Media Documentary: A Toolkit for Theory and Practice* (New York: Routledge, 2018), xii.

42 Barghnavard interview.

43 Barghnavard interview.

44 Barghnavard interview.
45 Sarita Malik, 'Diversity, Representation and Community Filmmaking', in *Community Filmmaking: Diversity, Practices and Places*, ed. Sarita Malik, Caroline Chapain, Roberta Comunian (New York: Routledge, 2017), 24.
46 Barghnavard interview.
47 Barghnavard, The Paradox of Creative Constraints symposium.
48 Hamid Naficy, *A Social History of Iranian Cinema, Volume 4: The Globalizing Era, 1984–2010* (Durham: Duke University Press, 2012), 344.
49 In this analysis, I use 'Shirin' to refer to the voiceover and persona constructed within the film, and 'Barghnavard' to refer to the filmmaker outside the film.
50 Barghnavard, The Paradox of Creative Constraints symposium.
51 Barghnavard interview.
52 Barghnavard interview.
53 Barghnavard interview.
54 See, for example, Ellen McLaughlin's 1995 adaptation of the play in response to the Bosnian War. Ellen McLaughlin, *The Trojan Women* (New York: Playscripts, Inc., 2011). Euripides himself used the myth of Troy to evoke the Peloponnesian War during his own time.
55 Charlotte Eager, interview by Heather McRobie, 'Trojan Women in the Twenty First Century: Women in War from Euripides to Syria', 19 June 2014, available at https://www.opendemocracy.net/en/5050/trojan-women-in-twenty-first-century-women-in-wa/
56 Nico Carpentier, 'The BBC's Video Nation as a Participatory Media Practice: Signifying Everyday Life, Cultural Diversity and Participation in an Online Community', *International Journal of Cultural Studies* 6.4 (2003): 426.
57 Yasmin Fedda, interview by the author, 4 October 2016.
58 Fedda interview.
59 Fedda interview.
60 In this respect, the women's response to the play is similar to the Bedouin women reciting a popular form of poetry known as *ghinnāwa* analysed by Lila Abu-Lughod. See Lila Abu-Lughod, *Veiled Sentiments: Honor and Poetry in a Bedouin Society* (Berkeley: University of California Press, 1999).
61 Abu-Lughod, *Veiled Sentiments*, 181.
62 Fedda interview.
63 See Margaret Litvin, 'When the Villain Steals the Show: The Character of Claudius in post-1975 Arab(ic) *Hamlet* Adaptations', *Journal of Arabic Literature* 38.2 (2007): 196–219.
64 Fedda interview.
65 Fedda interview.
66 Fedda interview.

67 Fedda interview.
68 Chapter 3 explored animation as a creative solution for precisely these sorts of constraints.
69 Fedda interview.
70 Fedda interview.
71 Fedda interview.
72 Fedda interview.
73 Fedda interview.
74 Fedda interview.
75 Fedda interview.
76 Fedda interview.

Chapter 8

1 Rania Stephan, interview by Elisabeth Stoney, 'Life on Screen: Rania Stephan', *Art Asia Pacific* 79, available at http://www.artasiapacific.com/Magazine/79/LifeOnScreenRaniaStephan
2 Jim Quilty, 'The Collection Is Safe, the Foundation's Ruined', *The Daily Star*, 25 August 2020, available at https://www.dailystar.com.lb/Arts-and-Ent/Culture/2020/Aug-25/510765-the-collection-is-safe-the-foundations-ruined.ashx (accessed 11 September 2020).
3 Mariam Ghani, 'The Artist and the Archive', in *Dissonant Archives: Contemporary Visual Culture and Contested Narratives of the Middle East*, ed. Anthony Downey (London: I.B. Tauris, 2015), 62.
4 Jaimie Baron, *The Archive Effect: Found Footage and the Audiovisual Experience of History* (Abingdon: Routledge, 2014), 7.
5 Jacques Derrida, 'Archive Fever: A Freudian Impression', trans. Eric Prenowitz, *Diacritics* 25.2 (1995): 17.
6 Derrida, 'Archive Fever: A Freudian Impression', 14.
7 The term 'microhistories' comes from the critical theory of New Historicism, influenced by the writings of Michel Foucault, Jacques Derrida and Hayden White.
8 Pad.ma, 'Theses on the Archive', in *Dissonant Archives: Contemporary Visual Culture and Contested Narratives of the Middle East*, ed. Anthony Downey (London: I.B. Tauris, 2015), 356.
9 Mary Ann Doane, *The Emergence of Cinematic Time: Modernity, Contingency, the Archive* (Cambridge, MA: Harvard University Press, 2002), 222.
10 Baron, *The Archive Effect: Found Footage and the Audiovisual Experience of History*, 17.

11 Adrian Danks, 'The Global Art of Found Footage Cinema', in *Traditions in World Cinema*, ed. Linda Badley, R. Barton Palmer and Steven Jay Schneider (Edinburgh: Edinburgh University Press, 2006), 246.
12 Paul Arthur, 'The Status of Found Footage', *Spectator* 20.1 (1999–2000): 60.
13 Baron, *The Archive Effect: Found Footage and the Audiovisual Experience of History*, 25.
14 Rik Smit, Ansgard Heinrich and Marcel Broersma, 'Witnessing in the New Memory Ecology: Memory Construction of the Syrian Conflict on YouTube', *New Media & Society* 19.2 (2017): 294.
15 Nicolas Bourriaud, *Postproduction – Culture as Screenplay: How Art Reprograms the World*, trans. Jeanine Herman (New York: Lukas & Sternberg, 2002), 24.
16 Bourriaud, *Postproduction – Culture as Screenplay: How Art Reprograms the World*, 7.
17 Guy Debord and Gil J. Wolman, 'A User's Guide to *Détournement*', in *Situationist International Anthology*, ed. and trans. Ken Knabb (Berkeley: Bureau of Public Secrets, 1995), 19.
18 Bourriaud, *Postproduction – Culture as Screenplay: How Art Reprograms the World*, 13.
19 Billy Perrigo, 'These Tech Companies Managed to Eradicate ISIS Content. But They're Also Erasing Crucial Evidence of War Crimes', *Time*, 11 April 2020, available at https://time.com/5798001/facebook-youtube-algorithms-extremism/
20 Joshka Wessels, *Documenting Syria: Film-making, Video Activism and Revolution* (London: I.B.Tauris, 2019), 178.
21 Derrida, 'Archive Fever: A Freudian Impression', 14.
22 Zaheer Omareen, interview by the author, 13 June 2016.
23 Smit et al, 'Witnessing in the New Memory Ecology: Memory Construction of the Syrian Conflict on YouTube', 293.
24 Baron, *The Archive Effect: Found Footage and the Audiovisual Experience of History*, 153.
25 Perrigo, 'These Tech Companies Managed to Eradicate ISIS Content. But They're Also Erasing Crucial Evidence of War Crimes'.
26 Hadi al-Khatib, 'Corporations Erasing History: The Case of the Syrian Archive', in *The Arab Archive: Mediated Memories and Digital Flows*, ed. Donatella Della Ratta, Kay Dickinson and Sune Haugbolle (Amsterdam: Institute of Network Cultures, 2020), 95.
27 Donatella Della Ratta, 'Why the Syrian Archive Is No Longer (only) about Syria', in *The Arab Archive: Mediated Memories and Digital Flows*, ed. Donatella Della Ratta, Kay Dickinson and Sune Haugbolle (Amsterdam: Institute of Network Cultures, 2020), 104.

28 See Wessels, *Documenting Syria: Film-making, Video activism and Revolution*, 238–40.
29 See Tiziana Terranova, 'Free Labour: Producing Culture for the Digital Economy', *Social Text* 18.2 (2000): 33–58.
30 Jon Dovey, 'Documentary Ecosystems: Collaboration and Exploitation', in *New Documentary Ecologies: Emerging Platforms, Practices and Discourses*, ed. Kate Nash, Craig Hight and Catherine Summerhayes (Basingstoke: Palgrave Macmillan, 2014), 21.
31 Abounaddara Collective, 'The Syrian Who Wanted the Revolution', 2 September 2016, available at https://www.documenta14.de/en/notes-and-works/1524/the-syrian-who-wanted-the-revolution
32 Dovey, 'Documentary Ecosystems: Collaboration and Exploitation', 22.
33 Pad.ma, 'Theses on the Archive', 360.
34 See Jeff Deutsch and Niko Para, 'Targeted Mass Archiving of Open Source Information: A Case Study', in *Digital Witness: Using Open Source Information for Human Rights Investigation, Documentation and Accountability*, ed. Sam Dubberley, Alexa Koening and Daragh Murray (Oxford: Oxford University Press, 2020), 165–84. Syrian Archive is available at https://syrianarchive.org
35 See Miriam Cooke, *Dancing in Damascus: Creativity, Resilience, and the Syrian Revolution* (New York: Routledge, 2017), 74–5.
36 Mosireen_Soursar, 'No Archive Is Innocent: On the Attempt of Archiving Revolt', in *The Arab Archive: Mediated Memories and Digital Flows*, ed. Donatella Della Ratta, Kay Dickinson and Sune Haugbolle (Amsterdam: Institute of Network Cultures, 2020), 38.
37 Yasmin Fedda, interview by Olivia Salazar-Winspear, 'Love and Loss in a Time of Revolution: "Ayouni" Documents the Forcibly Disappeared in Syria', 17 July 2020, available at https://www.france24.com/en/culture/20200717-encore-love-and-loss-in-a-time-of-revolution-ayouni-documents-the-forcibly-disappeared-in-syria
38 Mohammad Ali Atassi, 'The Digital Syrian Archive between Videos and Documentary Cinema', in *The Arab Archive: Mediated Memories and Digital Flows*, ed. Donatella Della Ratta, Kay Dickinson and Sune Haugbolle (Amsterdam: Institute of Network Cultures, 2020), 65–6.
39 Dovey, 'Documentary Ecosystems: Collaboration and Exploitation', 15.
40 André Bazin, 'In Defense of Mixed Cinema', in *What Is Cinema? Volume 1*, trans. Hugh Gray (Berkeley: University of California Press, 1967), 75. Philip Rosen claims that Hugh Gray's translation of '*cinéma impur*' (impure cinema) in Bazin's essay title as 'mixed cinema' has led to these anti-essentialist elements being overlooked in Anglophone reception of his work. Rosen, 'From Impurity to Historicity', in *Impure Cinema: Intermedial and Intercultural Approaches to Film*, ed. Lúcia Nagib and Anne Jerslev (London: I.B. Tauris, 2014), 6.

41 Rosen, 'From Impurity to Historicity', 17; Jørgen Bruhn and Anne Gjelsvik, *Cinema between Media: An Intermediality Approach* (Edinburgh: Edinburgh University Press, 2018), 4.
42 Elisabeth Stoney, 'Life on Screen: Rania Stephan', *Art Asia Pacific* 79, available at http://www.artasiapacific.com/Magazine/79/LifeOnScreenRaniaStephan
43 Marks, *Hanan al-Cinema*, 173.
44 Stephan, interview by Stoney.
45 Rania Stephan, interview by the author, 20 July 2018.
46 Stephan interview.
47 Stephan interview.
48 Stephan interview.
49 Stephan interview.
50 Bourriaud, *Postproduction – Culture as Screenplay: How Art Reprograms the World*, 18.
51 Stephan, interview by Stoney.
52 26 January is also Hosni's birthday.
53 Bourriaud, *Postproduction – Culture as Screenplay: How Art Reprograms the World*, 45.
54 Baron, *The Archive Effect: Found Footage and the Audiovisual Experience of History*, 155.
55 Catherine Russell, *Archiveology: Walter Benjamin and Archival Film Practices* (Durham: Duke University Press, 2018), 215.
56 Stoney, 'Life on Screen: Rania Stephan'.
57 Bourriaud, *Postproduction – Culture as Screenplay: How Art Reprograms the World*, 32.
58 Ossama Mohammed, interview by the author, 12 June 2016. Parts of this interview were previously published in Shohini Chaudhuri, 'Beauty Is When Justice Is Retained Somewhere, Even if This Somewhere Is in the Future', 20 June 2016, available at https://mosaicrooms.org/blog/beauty-is-when-justice-is-retained-somewhere-even-if-this-somewhere-is-in-the-future/
59 Mohammed interview.
60 See Kay Dickinson, '"Everyone's Property": Video Copying, Poetry, and Revolution in Arab West Asia', in *Asian Video Cultures in the Penumbra of the Global*, ed. Joshua Neves and Bhaskar Sarkar (Durham: Duke University Press, 2017), 310.
61 Enrico De Angelis, 'The Controversial Archive: Negotiating Horror Images in Syria', in *The Arab Archive: Mediated Memories and Digital Flows*, ed. Donatella Della Ratta, Kay Dickinson and Sune Haugbolle (Amsterdam: Institute of Network Cultures, 2020), 78.
62 See Abounaddara Collective, 'The Syrian Who wanted the Revolution'. Without naming *Silvered Water*, Abounaddara implicates it as an instance of unethical

practice when they refer to 'a documentary film that includes a scene of a Syrian boy being raped in a regime prison' as indeed *Silvered Water* does.

63 See, for example, Atassi, 'The Digital Syrian Archive between Videos and Documentary Cinema', 65–6.
64 Gala Hernández López, 'Notes on the Role of the Camera within a (Virtual) War: The Case of Silvered Water, Syria Self-portrait', *Digital War* 1.1 (2021): 8.
65 This is the nature of the critique made by Wessels, *Documenting Syria: Film-making, Video activism and Revolution*, 53.
66 Baron, *The Archive Effect: Found Footage and the Audiovisual Experience of History*, 91.
67 Danks, 'The Global Art of Found Footage Cinema', 250.
68 Baron, *The Archive Effect: Found Footage and the Audiovisual Experience of History*, 152.
69 Mohammed interview.
70 Mohammed interview.
71 Baron, *The Archive Effect: Found Footage and the Audiovisual Experience of History*, 151.
72 Mohammed interview.
73 Mohammed interview.
74 Hernández López, 'Notes on the Role of the Camera within a (Virtual) War: The Case of Silvered Water, Syria Self-portrait', 6.
75 Viola Shafik also notes Simav's collecting tendency. Shafik, *Arab Cinema: History and Cultural Identity* (Cairo: The American University in Cairo Press, 2016), 274.
76 Baron, *The Archive Effect: Found Footage and the Audiovisual Experience of History*, 150.
77 Rosen, 'From Impurity to Historicity', 9.
78 De Angelis, 'The Controversial Archive: Negotiating Horror Images in Syria', 79.
79 Mohammed interview.
80 Yasmin Fedda, interview by the author, *Ayouni*: Director Q&A, DocHouse, 24 July 2020, available at https://dochouse.org/online/video/filmed-qna/ayouni-director-qa
81 See Shohini Chaudhuri, *Cinema of the Dark Side: Atrocity and the Ethics of Spectatorship* (Edinburgh: Edinburgh University Press, 2014), 84–114.
82 Fedda, *Ayouni* Q&A. Sara Afshar faced the same challenge in her documentary *Syria's Disappeared* (2017), discussed in Chapter 1.
83 Fedda, *Ayouni* Q&A.
84 Fedda, *Ayouni* Q&A.
85 Fedda, *Ayouni* Q&A.
86 The term 'home mode' comes from Richard Chalfen, *Snapshot Versions of Life* (Bowling Green: Bowling Green State University Popular Press, 1987), 8.
87 Fedda, *Ayouni* Q&A.

88 Baron, *The Archive Effect: Found Footage and the Audiovisual Experience of History*, 84.
89 Fedda, *Ayouni* Q&A.
90 Fedda, *Ayouni* Q&A.
91 Fedda, *Ayouni* Q&A.
92 Baron, *The Archive Effect: Found Footage and the Audiovisual Experience of History*, 89.
93 Fedda, Conversation with the author, 20 July 2020.
94 Fedda, *Ayouni* Q&A.
95 Fedda, Conversation with the author, 20 July 2020.
96 Ghani, 'The Artist and the Archive', 53.
97 David Pinault, *Storytelling Techniques in the Arabian Nights* (Leiden: E.J. Brill, 1992), 107.
98 Fedda, *Ayouni* Q&A. *For Sama* is also punctuated with elements that the filmmakers felt necessary for audience respite although, as shown in Chapter 1, they were criticized for doing so.
99 Fedda, *Ayouni* Q&A.
100 In this respect, *Ayouni* recalls *Nostalgia for the Light* (2010), a documentary about the Calama women searching for their disappeared loved ones' remains in the Atacama Desert, Chile; *Nostalgia for the Light* uses metaphors of sand and skies.
101 Fedda, Conversation with the author, 20 July 2020.
102 Fedda, Conversation with the author, 20 July 2020.
103 *Ayouni* Q&A.
104 Fedda, *Ayouni* Q&A.
105 Fedda, *Ayouni* Q&A.
106 Yasmin Fedda, 'The Search for Syria's 100,000 Detained', Syria Campaign Webinar, 27 July 2020.
107 Derrida, 'Archive Fever: A Freudian Impression', 27.
108 Baron, *The Archive Effect: Found Footage and the Audiovisual Experience of History*, 110.

Chapter 9

1 Tom Moylan and Raffaella Baccolini, *Dark Horizons: Science Fiction and the Dystopian Imagination* (New York: Routledge, 2003), 1–2.
2 Darko Suvin, *Metamorphoses of Science Fiction: On the Poetics and History of a Literary Genre* (Yale: Yale University Press, 1979), 7.

3   Michael D. Gordin, Helen Tilley and Gyan Prakash, 'Introduction', in *Utopia/Dystopia: Conditions of Possibility*, ed. Michael D. Gordin, Helen Tilley, and Gyan Prakash (Princeton, NJ: Princeton University Press, 2010), 4.
4   Gregory Claeys, *Dystopia: A Natural History* (Oxford: Oxford University Press, 2020), 4.
5   May Telmissany, 'The Utopian and Dystopian Functions of Tahrir Square', *Postcolonial Studies* 17.1 (2014): 37.
6   Suvin, *Metamorphoses of Science Fiction*, 4, 8, 10.
7   Suvin, *Metamorphoses of Science Fiction*, 10.
8   Ian Campbell, *Arabic Science Fiction* (Basingstoke: Palgrave Macmillan, 2018), 7.
9   See, for example, Lejla Kucukalic, 'Arabian Wonder: Contemporary Science Fiction Transforming the Gulf', *The International Review of Science Fiction* 44.121 (2015): 8–17; Iman Haman, *Science Fiction in Arab Comics and Film* (forthcoming, Palgrave Macmillan). Furthermore, several PhD theses are being written on the subject, including by Nat Muller (Birmingham City University) and Ouissal Harize (Durham University). Muller has also interviewed Joana Hadjithomas and Khalil Joreige on their science-fictional documentary *The Lebanese Rocket Society* (2012) in 'On Being Contemporary – re-activating the Present: Joana Hadjithomas and Khalil Joreige in Conversation with Nat Muller', *Art Papers* 37.1 (2013): 33–6.
10 *The Thousand and One Nights*, with its extraordinary voyages, has been considered a forerunner of science fiction in general, serving as an early thought experiment about 'other' places. See Salvatore Proietti, 'A Groundbreaking Guide to Arab-Language SF', *Science Fiction Studies* 43 (2016): 377.
11 Campbell, *Arabic Science Fiction*, 48.
12 Laura Marks, 'Real Images Flow: Mullā Sadrā Meets Film-Philosophy', *Film-Philosophy* 20 (2016): 30.
13 One exception is the notion of 'social dreaming' that has developed out of Jungian psychoanalysis. See John Clare and Ali Zarbafi, *Social Dreaming in the 21st Century* (London: Karnac, 2009).
14 C.S. Peirce, *The Essential Peirce: Selected Philosophical Writings*, vol. 1, ed. Nathan Houser and Christian Kloesel (Bloomington: Indiana University Press, 1992), 226.
15 See Khalid Baheyeldin, 'Arabic and Islamic Themes in Frank Herbert's "Dune"', 22 January 2004, available at https://baheyeldin.com/literature/arabic-and-islamic-themes-in-frank-herberts-dune.html
16 John Rieder, *Colonialism and the Emergence of Science Fiction* (Middletown, CT: Wesleyan University Press, 2008), 31.
17 Farshid Kazemi, 'The Interpreter of Desires Iranian Cinema and Psychoanalysis' (PhD Thesis, University of Edinburgh, 2019). Kazemi develops this analysis in his book on *A Girl Walks Home Alone at Night* (Liverpool: Liverpool University Press,

2021), where he relates Fisher's 'weird and eerie' to their Persian and Arabic literary counterparts, *ajīb wa gharīb*.
18 Mark Fisher, *The Weird and the Eerie* (London: Repeater Books, 2016), 8.
19 Fisher, *The Weird and the Eerie*, 10.
20 Fisher, *The Weird and the Eerie*, 61.
21 Ahmadinejad's Subsidy Reform Plan was an attempt to remedy Iran's ailing economy by distributing cash payments to citizens.
22 Ali Ahmadzadeh, *Atomic Heart Mother* Q&A, Berlin Film Festival 2015, available at https://www.youtube.com/watch?v=cxA3wLhVs3E
23 Kazemi, 'The Interpreter of Desires Iranian Cinema and Psychoanalysis', 146–7.
24 Ali Ahmadzadeh, interview by the author, 22 October 2020. It should be noted that there *are* plenty of international influences in the film, including its title inspired by Pink Floyd's album *Atom Heart Mother* (1970).
25 Iran is not technically a dictatorship. For example, although presidential candidates are 'approved' by the Guardian Council (consisting of clerics and lawyers), presidents are elected and serve a maximum of two terms. However, Iran has been *experienced* as a dictatorship by some of its citizens and this is the perception fostered by *Atomic Heart*'s second part.
26 Ahmadzadeh interview.
27 Ahmadzadeh interview.
28 Ahmadzadeh interview.
29 Ahmadzadeh interview.
30 Fisher, *The Weird and the Eerie*, 20.
31 C-27 alludes to the film's first part, where Kami explains 'Club 27' is a group of celebrities who died at the age of twenty-seven such as Jim Morrison, Kurt Cobain, Jimi Hendrix and Amy Winehouse. Ahmadzadeh was also twenty-seven when he made *Atomic Heart*.
32 Fisher, *The Weird and the Eerie*, 19.
33 Gilles Deleuze and Félix Guattari, *What Is Philosophy?* trans. Graham Burchell and Hugh Tomlinson (London: Verso, 1994), 100.
34 Ahmadzadeh interview.
35 Ahmadzadeh interview.
36 Cited in Houshang Golmakani, 'New Times, Same Problems', *Index on Censorship* 3 (1992): 21.
37 Ahmadzadeh interview.
38 For example, J.G. Ballard, *Cocaine Nights* (London: HarperCollins, 1997). Parallels also exist between *Dreamaway* and Towfik's novel *Utopia* (2008) where, as Ian Campbell describes, 'The Egyptian masses can no longer produce anything worth buying: their only options are to work as servants for the Utopians.' Ian Campbell,

'Prefiguring Egypt's Arab Spring: Allegory and Allusion in Ahmad Tawfiq's *Utopia*', *Science-Fiction Studies* 42.3 (2015): 544.
39 Marouan Omara and Johanna Domke, interview by the author, 14 October 2020.
40 Omara and Domke interview.
41 Omara and Domke interview.
42 Omara and Domke interview. For an account of the bureaucratic permits system in Egypt, see Chibab El Khachab, 'State Control over Film Production in Egypt', *Arab Media & Society* 23 (2017), available at https://www.arabmediasociety.com/state-control-over-film-production-in-egypt
43 Omara and Domke interview.
44 Omara and Domke interview.
45 Omara and Domke interview.
46 Omara and Domke interview.
47 Omara and Domke interview.
48 Omara and Domke interview.
49 Omara and Domke interview.
50 Omara and Domke interview.
51 Omara and Domke interview.
52 Omara and Domke interview.
53 Omara and Domke interview.
54 Omara and Domke interview.
55 Omara and Domke interview.
56 Fisher, *The Weird and the Eerie,* 62.
57 Fisher, *The Weird and the Eerie,* 64.
58 Omara and Domke interview.
59 Omara and Domke interview. Due to bureaucratic processes for acquiring permits, many larger film productions in Egypt employ a worker specializing in this role. See El Khachab, 'State Control Over Film Production in Egypt'.
60 Larissa Sansour, interview by the author, 7 August 2017.
61 Sansour interview.
62 Sansour interview.
63 Sansour Interview.
64 Sansour interview.
65 Paolo Soleri, *Arcology: The City in the Image of Man* (Cambridge, MA: MIT Press, 1971).
66 Sansour interview.
67 Carol Que, 'Mechanisms of a Settler Colonial Architecture in Larissa Sansour's *Nation Estate* (2012)', *Jerusalem Quarterly* 73 (2018): 130.
68 Sansour interview.

69 Helga Tawil-Souri, 'Surveillance Sublime: The Security State in Jerusalem', *Jerusalem Quarterly* 68 (2016): 56.
70 Tawil-Souri, 'Surveillance Sublime', 58.
71 Despite indications to the contrary, several commentators assume that the window view is supposed to be real – see for example, Gil Hochberg, '"Jerusalem, We Have a Problem": Larissa Sansour's Sci-Fi Trilogy and The Impetus of Dystopic Imagination', *Arab Studies Journal* 26.1 (2018): 34–57. One exception, however, is Jussi Parikka, 'Middle East and Other Futurisms: Imaginary Temporalities in Contemporary Art and Visual Culture', *Culture, Theory and Critique* 59.1 (2018): 51.
72 Larissa Sansour, Shubbak: Imagined Futures Shorts Programme Q&A, Barbican, London, 4 July 2017. Sansour's description of the Israeli settlements encroaching upon Bethlehem 'like an army' echoes her sister Leila Sansour's documentary *Open Bethlehem* (2014).
73 Tawil-Souri, 'Surveillance Sublime', 59.
74 Eyal Weizman, *Hollow Land: Israel's Architecture of Occupation* (London: Verso, 2007), 161.
75 Sansour interview.
76 Sansour interview.
77 Sansour interview.
78 Sansour interview. The first of these exhibitions was *In the Future They Ate from the Finest Porcelain* at The Mosaic Rooms, London, June–August 2016.
79 Sansour interview.
80 Early ecological dystopias include *ZPG* (1971) and *Soylent Green* (1973) which both tackle overpopulation and air pollution.
81 Mounia Akl, Tales of the Silk Road – Lebanon Chapter Q&A, Rich Mix, London, 25 February 2019.
82 Christine Mady, 'The Imaginaries of Beirut's "Invisible" Solid Waste: Exploring Walls as Temporary Temporal Pauses amidst the Beirut Garbage Prices', in *The Temporalities of Waste: Out of Sight, Out of Time*, ed. Fiona Allon, Ruth Barcan and Karma Eddison-Cogan (Abingdon: Routledge, 2021), 100.
83 Marwan Kraidy, 'Trashing the Sectarian System? Lebanon's "You Stink" Movement and the Making of Affective Publics', *Communication and the Public* 1.1 (2016): 20.
84 Mady, 'The Imaginaries of Beirut's "Invisible" Solid Waste', 87.
85 Mounia Akl, interview by the author, 12 September 2019.
86 Akl interview.
87 Akl interview.
88 Mounia Akl, The Paradox of Creative Constraints symposium, The Mosaic Rooms, London, 7 September 2019.
89 Akl, Paradox of Creative Constraints symposium.

90 Akl interview.
91 Nadia Bozak, *The Cinematic Footprint: Lights, Camera, Natural Resources* (Rutgers: Rutgers University Press, 2011), 6.
92 Akl, The Paradox of Creative Constraints symposium.
93 Akl interview.
94 Wendy B. Faris, 'Scheherazade's Children: Magical Realism and Postmodern Fiction', in *Magic Realism: Theory, History, Community*, ed. Zamora Lois Parkinson and Wendy B. Faris (Durham: Duke University Press, 1995), 169.
95 David Desser, 'Race, Space and Class: The Politics of Cityscapes in Science Fiction Films', in *Alien Zone 2: The Spaces of Science Fiction*, ed. Annette Kuhn (London: Verso, 1999), 84.
96 Akl interview.
97 Akl interview.
98 Akl interview.
99 Sansour interview.
100 Moylan and Baccolini, *Dark Horizons*, 6.
101 Moylan and Baccolini, *Dark Horizons*, 7.
102 Tom Moylan, *Scraps of the Untainted Sky: Science Fiction, Utopia, Dystopia* (New York: Routledge, 2018), xv.

Conclusion

1 Ali Jaberansari, The Paradox of Creative Constraints symposium, The Mosaic Rooms, London, 7 September 2019.
2 Marouan Omara and Johanna Domke, interview by the author, 14 October 2020.

Bibliography

Abbas, Ackbar. *Hong Kong: Culture and the Politics of Disappearance*. Minneapolis, MN: University of Minnesota Press, 1997.

Abdalla, Khalid. *In the Last Days of the City* Q&A. The Mosaic Rooms. London, 6 September 2018.

Abdalla, Khalid. Interview by the author, 8 October 2018.

Abdulaziz, Fuad. *Sana'a: A Symphony* talk. University of Essex, 26 November 2020.

Abounaddara Collective. 'The Syrian Who Wanted the Revolution', 2 September 2016. Available at https://www.documenta14.de/en/notes-and-works/1524/the-syrian-who-wanted-the-revolution

Abu-Lughod, Lila. *Veiled Sentiments: Honor and Poetry in a Bedouin Society*. Berkeley: University of California Press, 1999.

Abu-Lughod, Lila. *Do Muslim Women Need Saving?* Cambridge, MA: Harvard University Press, 2013.

Al-Abyad, Jamil. Interview by Annasofie Flamand and Hugh Macleod. 'Little Dictator'. *Witness*. Aljazeera, 21 August 2012. Available at https://www.aljazeera.com/program/episode/2012/8/21/little-dictator/

Afshar, Sara. Interview with the author, 19 September 2018.

Aftab, Kaleem. 'Why a Large Proportion of the Arab World's Best Filmmakers Are Women'. *The National*, 3 December 2018. Available at https://www.thenationalnews.com/arts-culture/film/why-a-large-proportion-of-the-arab-world-s-best-filmmakers-are-women-1.798541.

Ahmadzadeh, Ali. *Atomic Heart Mother* Q&A, Berlin Film Festival 2015. Available at https://www.youtube.com/watch?v=cxA3wLhVs3E

Ahmadzadeh, Ali. Interview by the author, 22 October 2020.

Akbari, Mania. Interview by the author, 6 September 2018.

Akl, Mounia. 'Tales of the Silk Road – Lebanon Chapter' Q&A. Rich Mix. London, 25 February 2019.

Akl, Mounia. The Paradox of Creative Constraints symposium. The Mosaic Rooms, London, 7 September 2019.

Akl, Mounia. Interview by the author, 12 September 2019.

Allan, Stuart. *Citizen Witnessing: Revisioning Journalism in Times of Crisis*. Cambridge: Polity Press, 2013.

Al-Allaq, Yahya. Interview by the author, 5 May 2016.

Andén-Papadopoulos, Kari. 'Journalism, Memory and the "Crowd-sourced Video Revolution"'. In *Journalism and Memory*, edited by Barbie Zelizer and Keren Tenenboim-Weinblatt, 148–63. Basingstoke: Palgrave Macmillan, 2014.

Andrew, Geoff. *10*. London: British Film Institute, 2005.
Anishchenkova, Valerie. *Modern Saudi Arabia*. Santa Barbara, CA: ABC-CLIO, 2020.
Aractingi, Philippe. Interview by the author, 4 October 2019.
Arebi, Naziha. *Freedom Fields* Q&A. Picturehouse Central, London, 21 May 2019.
Arebi, Naziha. *Freedom Fields* Q&A. Frontline Club, London, 4 June 2019.
Arebi, Naziha. Interview by the author, 30 July 2019.
Arebi, Naziha. The Paradox of Creative Constraints symposium. The Mosaic Rooms, London, 7 September 2019.
Armatage, Kay and Zahra Khosroshahi. 'An Interview with Rakhshan Banietemad'. *Feminist Media Histories* 3.1 (2017): 140–55.
Armbrust, Walter. 'Political Film in Egypt'. In *Film in the Middle East and North Africa*, edited by Joseph Gugler, 228–51. Austin: University of Texas Press, 2011.
Arslan, Andrew. *Lebanon: A Country in Fragments*. London: Hurst & Company, 2018.
Arthur, Paul. 'The Status of Found Footage'. *Spectator* 20.1 (1999–2000): 57–69.
ASL 19. 'Censorship in Iranian Cinema'. In *Iranian Cinema in a Global Context: Policy, Politics and Form*, edited by Peter Decherney and Blake Atwood, 229–42. New York: Routledge, 2015.
Atwood, Blake. *Reform Cinema in Iran: Film and Political Change in the Islamic Republic*. New York: Columbia University Press, 2016.
Ashuri, Tamur and Amit Pinchevski. 'Witnessing as a Field'. In *Media Witnessing: Testimony in the Age of Mass Communication*, edited by Paul Frosch and Amit Pinchevski, 133–57. Basingstoke: Palgrave Macmillan, 2009.
Atassi, Mohammed Ali. 'The Digital Syrian Archive between Videos and Documentary Cinema'. In *The Arab Archive: Mediated Memories and Digital Flows*, edited by Donatella Della Ratta, Kay Dickinson and Sune Haugbolle, 60–8. Amsterdam: Institute of Network Cultures, 2020.
Aufderheide, Patricia. 'Mainstream Documentary since 1999'. In *American Film History: Selected Readings, 1960 to the Present*, edited by Cynthia Lucia, Roy Grundmann and Art Simon, 376–92. Chichester: Wiley-Blackwell, 2016.
Austin, Thomas. 'Introduction'. In *The Films of Aki Kaurismäki: Ludic Engagements*, edited by Thomas Austin, 1–16. New York: Bloomsbury Academic, 2018.
Azcona, María Del Mar. *The Multi-protagonist Film*. Malden, MA: Wiley-Blackwell, 2010.
Backman-Rogers, Anna. *American Independent Cinema: Rites of Passage and the Crisis Image*. Edinburgh: Edinburgh University Press, 2015.
Baheyeldin, Khalid. 'Arabic and Islamic Themes in Frank Herbert's "Dune"', 22 January 2004. Available at https://baheyeldin.com/literature/arabic-and-islamic-themes-in-frank-herberts-dune.html
Ballard, J.G. *Cocaine Nights*. London: HarperCollins, 1997.
Al-Banawi, Fatima. *Barakah Meets Barakah* Q&A. BFI London Film Festival, 8 October 2016.

Banietemad, Rakhshan. Interview by Shiva Rahbaran. 'Rakshan Bani-Etemad: Cinema as a Mirror of the Urban Image'. In *Iranian Cinema Uncensored: Contemporary Filmmakers since the Islamic Revolution*, edited by Shiva Rahbaran, 127–45. London: I.B. Tauris, 2016.

Banietemad, Rakhshan. Interview by Maryam Ghorbankarimi. 'A Conversation with the Director'. In *Refocus: The Films of Rakshan Banietemad*, edited by Maryam Ghorbankarimi, 12–24. Edinburgh: Edinburgh University Press, 2021.

Baron, Jaimie. *The Archive Effect: Found Footage and the Audiovisual Experience of History*. Abingdon: Routledge, 2014.

Barghnavard, Shirin. Interview by Christoph Dreher and Vinicius Jatobá. 'Expose Yourself! Revealing the Flow of Life in Iran', 4 September 2018, available at https://schloss-post.com/expose-yourself/

Barghnavard, Shirin. The Paradox of Creative Constraints symposium. The Mosaic Rooms, London, 7 September 2019.

Barghnavard, Shirin. Interview by the author, 9 September 2019.

Bazin, André. 'In Defense of Mixed Cinema'. In *What Is Cinema? Volume 1*, translated by Hugh Gray, 53–75. Berkeley: University of California Press, 1967.

Behrouzan, Orkideh. 'Introduction'. In *The Book of Tehran: A City in Short Fiction*, edited by Fereshteh Ahmadi, vii–xxii. Manchester: Comma Press, 2019.

Bendazzi, Giannalberto. *Animation: A World History*. Boca Raton, FL: CRC Press, 2016.

Benjamin, Walter. *Illuminations*, translated by Harry Zohn. London: Fontana Press, 1992.

Berger, Laura. 'Oscars 2018: Foreign Lang Contenders: Annemarie Jacir "Wajib"', 27 November 2017. Available at https://womenandhollywood.com/oscars-2018-foreign-language-contenders-annemarie-jacir-wajib-809a634d10f2/

Bergson, Henri. *Laughter: An Essay on the Meaning of the Comic*, translated by Cloudesley Brereton and Fred Rothwell. Salt Lake City, UT: Project Gutenberg, 2009.

Biltereyst, Daniel and Roel Vande Winkel. Eds. *Silencing Cinema: Film Censorship around the World*. London: Palgrave Macmillan, 2013.

Blackmon, Christa. 'Animating Torture: A New Horizon in Human Rights Reporting', 17 August 2018. Available at https://observatoryihr.org/priority_posts/animating-torture-a-new-horizon-in-human-rights-reporting/

Bourdieu, Pierre. *Outline of a Theory of Practice*, translated by Richard Nice. Cambridge: Cambridge University Press, 1979.

Bozak, Nadia. *The Cinematic Footprint: Lights, Camera, Natural Resources*. Rutgers: Rutgers University Press, 2011.

Bradshaw, Peter. 'Ava Review – Smart Teenage Thriller Amps up the Micro-tyrannies'. *The Guardian*, 19 August 2020. Available at https://www.theguardian.com/film/2020/aug/19/ava-review-smart-teenage-thriller-amps-up-the-micro-tyrannies

Bresheeth, Haim. 'A Symphony of Absence: Borders and Liminality in Elia Suleiman's "Chronicle of a Disappearance"'. *Framework: The Journal of Cinema and Media* 43.2. (2002): 71–84.

Breton, André. 'Foreword to 1966 French Edition'. In *Anthology of Black Humour*, edited by André Breton, translated by Mark Polizzoti, 11. London: Telegram, 2009.

Bordwell, David. *Poetics of Cinema*. New York: Routledge, 2008.

Bourriaud, Nicolas. *Postproduction – Culture as Screenplay: How Art Reprograms the World*, translated by Jeanine Herman. New York: Lukas & Sternberg, 2002.

Brody, Richard. '"Pig," Reviewed: An Iranian Comedy about Film Makers Who Become the Targets of Murder', 7 January 2019. Available at https://www.newyorker.com/culture/the-front-row/pig-reviewed-an-iranian-comedy-about-filmmakers-who-become-the-targets-of-murder

Brown, Lyn Mikel. *Raising Their Voices: The Politics of Girls' Anger*. Cambridge, MA: Harvard University Press, 1998.

Brown, William. *Non-Cinema: Global Digital Filmmaking and the Multitude*. London: Bloomsbury, 2018.

Bruhn, Jørgen and Anne Gjelsvik. *Cinema between Media: An Intermediality Approach*. Edinburgh: Edinburgh University Press, 2018.

Bruno, Giuliana. 'Bodily Architectures'. *Assemblage* 19 (1992): 106–11.

Bruno, Giuliana. *Atlas of Emotion: Journeys in Art, Architecture and Film*. New York: Verso, 2002.

Burnat, Emad. *5 Broken Cameras* Q&A, chaired by the author. Union Chapel, London, 5 July 2017.

Burnat, Emad. *5 Broken Cameras* Q&A, Palestine Expo. Queen Elizabeth II Conference Centre, London, 8 July 2017.

Burnat, Emad. Interview by the author, 8 July 2017.

Burnat, Emad and Guy Davidi, *5 Broken Cameras* Q&A. Riverside Studios, London, 21 June 2012.

Calhoun, Craig. 'The Idea of Emergency'. In *Contemporary States of Emergency: The Politics of Humanitarian Interventions*, edited by Didier Fassin and Mariella Pandolfi, 29–58. New York: Zone Books, 2010.

Campbell, Ian. 'Prefiguring Egypt's Arab Spring: Allegory and Allusion in Ahmad Tawfiq's *Utopia*'. *Science-Fiction Studies* 42.3 (2015): 541–56.

Campbell, Ian. *Arabic Science Fiction*. Basingstoke: Palgrave Macmillan, 2018.

Carpentier, Nico. 'The BBC's Video Nation as a Participatory Media Practice: Signifying Everyday Life, Cultural Diversity and Participation in an Online Community'. *International Journal of Cultural Studies* 6.4 (2003): 425–47.

Cavell, Stanley. *The World Viewed: Reflections on the Ontology of Film*. Cambridge, MA: Harvard University Press, 1979.

Chalfen, Richard. *Snapshot Versions of Life*. Bowling Green: Bowling Green State University Popular Press, 1987.

Chaudhuri, Shohini. *Cinema of the Dark Side: Atrocity and the Ethics of Spectatorship*. Edinburgh: Edinburgh University Press, 2014.

Chaudhuri, Shohini. 'The Alterity of the Image: The Distant Spectator and Films about the Syrian Revolution and War'. *Transnational Cinemas* 9.1 (2018): 31–46.

Chaudhuri, Shohini and Howard Finn. 'The Open Image: Poetic Realism and the New Iranian Cinema'. *Screen* 44.1 (2003): 38–57.

Clare, John and Ali Zarbafi. *Social Dreaming in the 21st Century*. London: Karnac, 2009.

Chouliaraki, Lilie. 'Digital Witnessing in Conflict Zones: The Politics of Remediation'. *Information, Communication & Society* 18.11 (2015): 1362–77.

Ciecko, Anne. 'Bicycle Borrowers after Neorealism: Global Nou-Velo Cinema'. In *Culture on Two Wheels: The Bicycle in Literature and Film*, edited by Jeremy Withers and Daniel P. Shea, 244–62. Lincoln: University of Nebraska Press, 2016.

Claeys, Gregory. *Dystopia: A Natural History*. Oxford: Oxford University Press, 2020.

Cohan, Steve and Ina Rae Hark. 'Introduction'. In *The Road Movie Book*, edited by Steve Cohan and Ina Rae Hark, 1–14. London: Routledge, 2002.

Colebrook, Claire. *Irony*. London: Routledge, 2004.

Cook, David. *Martyrdom in Islam*. Cambridge: Cambridge University Press, 2007.

Cooke, Miriam. *Dancing in Damascus: Creativity, Resilience, and the Syrian Revolution*. New York: Routledge 2017.

Corbin, Henry. *Alone with the Alone: The Creative Imagination in the Sufism of Ibn 'Arabi*. Princeton, NJ: Princeton University Press, 1997.

Coverley, Merlin. *Psychogeography*. Harpenden: Pocket Essentials, 2010.

Critchley, Simon. *On Humour*. London: Routledge, 2002.

Dällenbach, Lucien. *The Mirror in the Text*. Chicago: University of Chicago Press, 1989.

Dällenbach, Lucien. 'Mise-en-abyme and Mirror Effects in Claude Simon'. In *Claude Simon*, edited by Celia Britton, 140–58. New York: Longman, 1993.

Danks, Adrian. 'The Global Art of Found Footage Cinema'. In *Traditions in World Cinema*, edited by Linda Badley, R. Barton Palmer and Steven Jay Schneider, 241–53. Edinburgh: Edinburgh University Press, 2006.

Day, Amber. Ed. *Satire and Dissent*. Bloomington: Indiana University Press, 2011.

Day, Amber. 'Introduction: Poking Holes in the Spectacle'. In *Satire and Dissent*, edited by Amber Day, 1–23. Bloomington: Indiana University Press, 2011.

De Angelis, Enrico. 'The Controversial Archive: Negotiating Horror Images in Syria'. In *The Arab Archive: Mediated Memories and Digital Flows*, edited by Donatella Della Ratta, Kay Dickinson and Sune Haugbolle, 71–90. Amsterdam: Institute of Network Cultures, 2020.

De Certeau, Michel. *The Practice of Everyday Life*, translated by Steven F. Rendall. Berkeley: University of California, 1984.

De Lauretis, Teresa. 'Film and the Visible'. In *How Do I Look: Queer Film and Video*, edited by Bad Object-Choices, 223–64. Seattle: Bay Press, 1991.

De Michiel, Helen and Patricia R. Zimmerman. *Open Space New Media Documentary: A Toolkit for Theory and Practice*. New York: Routledge, 2018.

Debord, Guy. 'Introduction to a Critique of Urban Geography'. In *Situationist International Anthology*, edited and translated by Ken Knabb, 8–12. Berkeley: Bureau of Public Secrets, 1995.

Debord, Guy. 'Theory of the Dérive'. In *Situationist International Anthology*, edited and translated by Ken Knabb, 62–6. Berkeley: Bureau of Public Secrets, 1995.

Debord, Guy and Gil J. Wolman. 'A User's Guide to *Détournement*'. In *Situationist International Anthology*, edited and translated by Ken Knabb, 14–21. Berkeley: Bureau of Public Secrets, 1995.

Deleuze, Gilles. *Cinema 1: The Movement-image*, translated by Hugh Tomlinson and Barbara Habberjam. London: Athlone Press, 1992.

Deleuze, Gilles. *Cinema 2: The Time-Image*, translated by Hugh Tomlinson and Robert Galeta. London: Athlone Press, 1989.

Deleuze, Gilles and Félix Guattari. *What Is Philosophy?* translated by Graham Burchell and Hugh Tomlinson. London: Verso 1994.

Della Ratta, Donatella. *Shooting A Revolution: Visual Media and Warfare in Syria*. London: Pluto Press, 2018.

Della Ratta, Donatella. 'Emerging from the Underground: On "For Sama" and Mainstream Filmmaking', 14 May 2020. Available at https://syriauntold.com/2020/05/14/emerging-from-the-underground-on-for-sama-and-mainstream-filmmaking/

Della Ratta, Donatella. 'Why the Syrian Archive Is No Longer (only) about Syria'. In *The Arab Archive: Mediated Memories and Digital Flows*, edited by Donatella Della Ratta, Kay Dickinson and Sune Haugbolle, 101–16. Amsterdam: Institute of Network Cultures, 2020.

Demos, T.J. *The Migrant Image: The Art and Politics of Documentary during Global Crisis*. Durham: Duke University Press, 2013.

Démy-Geroe, Anne. *Iranian National Cinema: The Interaction of Policy, Genre, Funding and Reception*. Abingdon: Routledge, 2020.

Derrida, Jacques. 'Archive Fever: A Freudian Impression'. Translated by Eric Prenowitz. *Diacritics* 25.2 (1995): 9–63.

Desser, David. 'Race, Space and Class: The Politics of Cityscapes in Science Fiction Films'. In *Alien Zone 2: the Spaces of Science Fiction*, edited by Annette Kuhn, 80–96. London: Verso, 1999.

Deutsch, Jeff and Niko Para. 'Targeted Mass Archiving of Open Source Information: A Case Study'. In *Digital Witness: Using Open Source Information for Human Rights Investigation, Documentation and Accountability*, edited by Sam Dubberley, Alexa Koening and Daragh Murray, 165–84. Oxford: Oxford University Press, 2020.

Deutsche Welle. 'Why Mohammad Rasoulof Still Makes Films despite Iran's Threats'. Available at https://www.dw.com/en/why-mohammad-rasoulof-still-makes-films-despite-irans-threats/a-52575195

Devi, Gayatri and Najat Rahman. Eds. *Humor in Middle Eastern Cinema*. Detroit: Wayne State University Press, 2014/

Dib, Roy. Interview by the author, 19 June 2020.

Dickinson, Kay. 'The Palestinian Road (Block) Movie Everyday Geographies of Second Intifada Cinema'. In *Cinema at the Periphery*, edited by Dina Iordanova, David Martin-Jones and Belén Vidal. Detroit: Wayne State University Press, 2010.

Dickinson, Kay. '"Everyone's Property": Video Copying, Poetry, and Revolution in Arab West Asia'. In *Asian Video Cultures in the Penumbra of the Global*, edited by Joshua Neves and Bhaskar Sarkar, 307–26. Durham: Duke University Press, 2017.

Doane, Mary Ann. *The Emergence of Cinematic Time: Modernity, Contingency, the Archive*. Cambridge, MA: Harvard University Press, 2002.

Donald, Stephanie Hemelryk, Emma Wilson, Sarah Wright. 'Introduction'. In *Childhood and Nation in Contemporary World Cinema: Borders and Encounters*, edited by Stephanie Hemelryk Donald, Emma Wilson and Sarah Wright, 1–11. London: Bloomsbury, 2017.

Douglas, Mary. 'The Social Control of Cognition: Some Factors in Joke Perception'. *Man* 3.3 (1968): 361–76.

Dovey, Jon. 'Documentary Ecosystems: Collaboration and Exploitation'. In *New Documentary Ecologies: Emerging Platforms, Practices and Discourses*, edited by Kate Nash, Craig Hight and Catherine Summerhayes, 11–32. Basingstoke: Palgrave Macmillan, 2014.

Dunlevy, T'cha. 'TIFF 2017: Iranian Montrealer Sadaf Foroughi Makes Waves with First Feature Ava'. *Montreal Gazette*, 12 September 2017. Available at: https://montrealgazette.com/entertainment/local-arts/tiff-2017-iranian-montrealer-sadaf-foroughi-makes-waves-with-first-feature-ava

Eager, Charlotte. Interview by Heather McRobie. 'Trojan Women in the Twenty First Century: Women in War from Euripides to Syria', 19 June 2014. Available at https://www.opendemocracy.net/en/5050/trojan-women-in-twenty-first-century-women-in-wa/

Egan, Eric. 'Regime Critics Confront Censorship in Iranian Cinema'. In *Film in the Middle East and North Africa: Creative Dissidence*, edited by Josef Gugler, 37–62. Austin: University of Texas Press, 2011.

Ehrlich, Nea. 'Animated Documentaries: Aesthetics, Politics and Viewer Engagement'. In *Pervasive Animation*, edited by Suzanne Buchan, 248–71. New York: Routledge, 2013.

Ehrlich, Nea and Jonathan Murray. 'Introduction'. In *Drawn from Life: Issues and Themes in Animated Documentary Cinema*, 1–11. Edinburgh: Edinburgh University Press, 2019.

Eid, Rana. Interview with the author, 8 August 2018.

Eisenstein, Sergei. *On Disney*, edited by Jay Leyda, translated by Alan Upchurch. Calcutta: Seagull Books, 2017.

Elias, Chad and Zaher Omareen. 'Syria's Imperfect Cinema'. In *Syria Speaks: Art and Culture from the Frontline*, edited by Malu Halasa, Zaher Omareen and Nawara Mahfoud, 257–68. London: Saqi Books, 2014.

Elias, Jamal. *Alef Is for Allah: Childhood, Emotion, and Visual Culture in Islamic Societies*. Oakland: University of California Press, 2018.

Elsaesser, Thomas. 'The Global Author: Control, Creative Constraints, and Performative Self-contradiction'. In *The Global Auteur: The Politics of Authorship in*

21st Century Cinema, edited by Seung-hoon Jeong and Jeremi Szaniawski. London: Bloomsbury Academic, 2016.

Elster, Jon. 'Conventions, Creativity, Originality'. In *Rules and Conventions: Literature, Philosophy, Social Theory*, edited by Mette Hjort, 32–44. Baltimore: Johns Hopkins University Press, 1992.

Elster, Jon. *Ulysses Unbound: Studies in Rationality, Precommitment and Constraints*. Cambridge: Cambridge University Press, 2000.

Esfandiary, Shahab. *Iranian Cinema and Globalization: National, Transnational and Islamic Dimensions*. Bristol: Intellect, 2012.

Evans, Bertrand. *Shakespeare's Comedies*. Oxford: Clarendon Press, 1960.

Fageeh, Hisham. *Barakah Meets Barakah* Q&A. BFI London Film Festival, 8 October 2016.

Fageeh, Hisham. Talk at NYU Abu Dhabi. Organized by the author, 10 April 2017.

Fahim, Joseph. 'Creators Meet Censors: The Standoff between Creators and Censors in Post-2011 Egyptian Drama'. *Cairo Review* 28 (2018): 92–101.

Farahmand, Azadeh. 'Perspectives on Recent (International Acclaim for) Iranian Cinema'. In *The New Iranian Cinema: Politics, Representation and Identity*, edited by Richard Tapper, 86–108. London: I.B. Tauris, 2002.

Fares, Amber. Interview by the author, 15 May 2020.

Faris, Wendy B. 'Scheherazade's Children: Magical Realism and Postmodern Fiction'. In *Magic Realism: Theory, History, Community*, edited by Zamora Lois Parkinson and Wendy B. Faris, 163–90. Durham: Duke University Press, 1995.

Farjami, Mahmud. *Iranian Political Satirists: Experience and Motivation in the Contemporary Era*. Amsterdam: John Benjamins Publishing Company, 2017.

Fedda, Yasmin. 'Syria on the Road: Stories of Conflict, Migration & Place', 17 November 2015. Available at http://highlightarts.org/syria-on-the-road-stories-of-conflict-migration-place-by-yasmin-fedda/

Fedda, Yasmin. Interview by the author, 4 October 2016.

Fedda, Yasmin. Interview by Olivia Salazar-Winspear. 'Love and Loss in a Time of Revolution: "Ayouni" Documents the Forcibly Disappeared in Syria', 17 July 2020. Available at https://www.france24.com/en/culture/20200717-encore-love-and-loss-in-a-time-of-revolution-ayouni-documents-the-forcibly-disappeared-in-syria

Fedda, Yasmin. Interview by the author. *Ayouni*: Director Q&A. DocHouse, 24 July 2020. Available at https://dochouse.org/online/video/filmed-qna/ayouni-director-qa

Fedda, Yasmin. 'The Search for Syria's 100,000 Detained'. Syria Campaign Webinar, 27 July 2020.

Felman, Shoshana. 'In an Era of Testimony: Claude Lanzmann's *Shoah*'. *Yale French Studies* 79 (1991): 39–81.

Ferguson, Liz. 'FNC 2018: Review of Iranian Comedy Pig (Khook)', 9 October 2018. Available at https://mostlymovies.ca/2018/10/09/fnc-2018-review-of-iranian-comedy-pig-khook/

Fernea, Elizabeth Warnock. 'Childhood in the Muslim Middle East'. In *Children in the Muslim Middle East*, edited by Elizabeth Warnock Fernea, 3–16. Austin: University of Texas Press, 1995.

Fisher, Mark. *The Weird and the Eerie*. London: Repeater Books, 2016.

Fletcher, Angus. *Allegory: The Theory of a Symbolic Mode*. Ithaca, NY: Cornell University Press, 1964.

Foley, Sean. *Changing Saudi Arabia: Art, Culture and Society in the Kingdom*. Boulder, CO: Lynne Rienner Publishers, 2019.

Friedman, Yael. 'Guises of Transnationalism in Israel/Palestine: A Few Notes on *5 Broken Cameras*'. *Transnational Cinemas* 6.1 (2015): 17–32.

Foroughi, Sadaf. Screen Talk. Human Rights Watch Film Festival. London, 15 March 2018.

Foroughi, Sadaf. Interview by the author, 10 September 2018.

Foucault, Michel. *Aesthetics, Method, and Epistemology: Essential Works of Foucault, 1954–1984*, edited by James D. Faubion. New York: The New Press, 1998.

Foucault, Michel. *The Birth of the Clinic*. Abingdon: Routledge, 2003.

Freud, Sigmund. 'On Humour'. In *The Standard Edition of the Complete Psychological Works of Sigmund Freud*, vol. 21, translated by James Strachey, 159–66. London: Hogarth Press, 1961.

Furniss, Maureen. *Art in Motion: Animation Aesthetics*. Sydney: John Libbey and Co, 1998.

García Espinosa, Julio. 'For an Imperfect Cinema', translated by Julianne Burton. *Jump Cut* 20 (1979): 24–6. Available at: https://www.ejumpcut.org/archive/onlinessays/JC20folder/ImperfectCinema.html

Garcia, Maria. 'A Woman's Voice Is Her Nakedness: An Interview with Haifa Al Mansour'. *Cineaste* 38.4 (2013): 34–7.

Ghani, Mariam. 'The Artist and the Archive'. In *Dissonant Archives: Contemporary Visual Culture and Contested Narratives of the Middle East*, edited by Anthony Downey, 43–63. London: I.B. Tauris, 2015.

Al-Ghazzi, Omar. '"Citizen Journalism" in the Syrian Uprising: Problematizing Western Narratives in a Local Context'. *Communication Theory* 24.4 (2014): 435–54.

Al-Ghazzi, Omar. 'An Archetypal Digital Witness: The Child Figure and the Media Conflict over Syria'. *International Journal of Communication* 13 (2019): 3225–43.

Ghorbankarimi, Maryam. 'Rakshan Banietemad's Art of Social Realism: Bridging Realism and Fiction'. In *Refocus: The Films of Rakshan Banietemad*, edited by Maryam Ghorbankarimi, 189–205. Edinburgh: Edinburgh University Press, 2021.

Golmakani, Houshang. 'New Times, Same Problems'. *Index on Censorship* 3 (1992): 19–22.

Goodfellow, Melanie. 'Haifaa Al Mansour on Returning Home to Saudi Arabia to Shoot TIFF Title "A Perfect Candidate"', 13 September 2019. Available at https://www.screendaily.com/features/haifaa-al-mansour-on-returning-home-to-saudi-arabia-to-shoot-tiff-title-a-perfect-candidate/5142835.article

Gordin, Michael D., Helen Tilley and Gyan Prakash. 'Introduction'. In *Utopia/Dystopia: Conditions of Possibility*, edited by Michael D. Gordin, Helen Tilley, and Gyan Prakash, 1–18. Princeton, NJ: Princeton University Press, 2010.

Gugler, Josef. 'Ali Zaoua: The Harsh Life of Street Children and the Poetics of Childhood'. *The Journal of North African Studies* 12.3 (2007): 369–79.

Haghighi, Mani. Interview by Sanam Shantyaei. 'A Killer Comedy: France 24 Meets the Iranian Director behind "Pig"', 5 December 2018. Available at https://www.youtube.com/watch?v=MTWTGc4i0MM

Haghighi, Mani. Email communication with the author, 7 October 2020.

Haghighi, Mani. Interview by the author, 13 October 2020.

Hatuqa, Dalia. 'Q&A: Middle East's Most Powerful Army Chasing 18 Cows', 21 March 2016. Available at: https://www.aljazeera.com/features/2016/3/21/qa-middle-easts-most-powerful-army-chasing-18-cows

Hayward, Susan. *Cinema Studies: The Key Concepts*. London: Routledge, 2000.

Helmy, Mohamed M. and Sabine Frerichs. 'Stripping the Boss: The Powerful Role of Humor in the Egyptian Revolution 2011'. *Integrative Psychological and Behavioral Science* 47 (2013): 450–81.

Hentges, Sarah. *Pictures of Girlhood: Modern Female Adolescence on Film*. Jefferson, NC: McFarland, 2006.

Hernández López, Gala. 'Notes on the Role of the Camera within a (Virtual) War: The Case of *Silvered Water, Syria Self-portrait*'. *Digital War* 1.1 (2021): 1–15.

Hetherington, Janet. '"Persepolis" in Motion'. *Animation World Network*, 21 December 2007. Available at https://www.awn.com/animationworld/persepolis-motion (accessed 19 January 2020).

Hibbard, Scott and Azza Salma Layton, 'The Origins and Future of Egypt's Revolt'. *Journal of Islamic Law and Culture* 12.3 (2010): 197–214.

Hills, Carol. 'Why Israel Declared 18 Dairy Cows a National Security Risk'. *The World*, 18 June 2015. Available at https://www.pri.org/stories/2015-06-18/wanted-18-dairy-cows-considered-security-risk

Hjort, Mette and Scott MacKenzie. Eds. *Purity and Provocation: Dogme 95*. London: BFI, 2003.

Hjort, Mette. *Lone Scherfig's Italian for Beginners*. Seattle: University of Washington Press, 2010.

Hjort, Mette. 'Flamboyant Risk Taking: Why Some Filmmakers Embrace Avoidable and Excessive Risks'. In *Film and Risk*, edited by Mette Hjort, 31–54. Detroit, MI: Wayne State University Press, 2012.

Hjort, Mette. 'Introduction: The Film Phenomenon and How Risk Pervades It'. In *Film and Risk*, edited by Mette Hjort, 1–30. Detroit, MI: Wayne State University Press, 2012.

Hjort, Mette. 'Introduction: More than Film School – Why the Full Spectrum of Practice-Based Film Education Warrants Attention'. In *The Education of the Filmmaker in Africa, the Middle East, and the Americas*, edited by Mette Hjort, 1–22. Basingstoke: Palgrave Macmillan, 2013.

Hochberg, Gil Z. *Visual Occupations: Violence and Visibility in a Conflict Zone*. Durham: Duke University Press, 2015.

Hochberg, Gil Z. '"Jerusalem, We Have a Problem": Larissa Sansour's Sci-Fi Trilogy and The Impetus of Dystopic Imagination'. *Arab Studies Journal* 26.1 (2018): 34–57.

Hodgins, Ruth. 'Imagination Is Power: How Bidayyat Captures Syria on Film', 11 April 2018. Available at https://walkerart.org/magazine/imagination-is-power-syria-on-film-with-bidayyat

Honess Roe, Annabelle. *Animated Documentary*. Basingstoke: Palgrave Macmillan, 2013.

Hosseini-Shakib, Fatemeh. 'Iranian Animation'. In *Directory of World Cinema: Iran 2*, edited by Parviz Jahed, 228–47. Bristol: Intellect, 2017.

Human Rights Watch. 'Attacks on Ghouta: Analysis of Alleged Use of Chemical Weapons in Ghouta', 10 September 2013. Available at https://www.hrw.org/report/2013/09/10/attacks-ghouta/analysis-alleged-use-chemical-weapons-syria#_ftn3

Hutcheon, Linda. 'The Complex Functions of Irony'. *Revista Canadiense de Estudios Hispánicos* 16. 2 (1992): 219–34.

Hutchinson, Pamela. 'City of Lost Children'. *Sight & Sound* 29.3 (2019): 32–4.

Jaafar, Ali. '"Persepolis" banned in Lebanon'. *Variety*, 10 March 2008. Available at https://variety.com/2008/digital/markets-festivals/persepolis-banned-in-lebanon-1117982145/

Jaberansari, Ali. *Tehran: City of Love* Q&A. BFI London Film Festival, 14 October 2018.

Jaberansari, Ali. Interview by the author, 30 October 2018.

Jaberansari, Ali. *Tehran: City of Love* Q&A. Poetry in Motion. Barbican, London, 13 April 2019.

Jaberansari, Ali. The Paradox of Creative Constraints symposium, The Mosaic Rooms, London, 7 September 2019.

Jacir, Annemarie. '"For Cultural Purposes Only": Curating a Palestinian Film Festival'. In *Dreams of a Nation: On Palestinian Cinema*, edited by Hamid Dabashi, 23–31. London: Verso, 2006.

Jacir, Annemarie. Interview by Melanie Goodfellow. 'Annemarie Jacir on the Tensions of Shooting "Wajib" in Nazareth', 15 December 2017. Available at https://www.screendaily.com/features/annemarie-jacir-on-the-tensions-of-shooting-wajib-in-nazareth/5125051.article

Jacir, Annemarie. Interview by Rolex Mentor, 'Film *Wajib* Wins Prizes and Praise', March 2018. Available at https://www.rolexmentorprotege.com/journal/article/annemarie-jacir-wajib (accessed 19 September 2018).

Jacir, Annemarie. Interview by Leigh Singer, '"Laughing Is a Way to Resist": Annemarie Jacir on Her Father-son Wedding Drama Wajib', 7 January 2019. Available at https://www2.bfi.org.uk/news-opinion/sight-sound-magazine/interviews/wajib-annemarie-jacir-palestinian-father-son-wedding-drama

Jameson, Fredric. 'Third-World Literature in the Era of Multinational Capitalism'. *Social Text* 15 (1986): 65–88.
Johnston, Trevor. 'Taxi Tehran'. *Sight & Sound* 25.11 (2015): 68–9.
Kadi, Sam. Interview by the author, 13 March 2017.
Kamel, Ahd. Interview by the author, 10 May 2019.
Karimi, Keywan. Interview by the author, 13 February 2021.
Al-Kateab, Waad. *For Sama* Q&A. Picturehouse Central, London, 13 September 2019.
Al-Kateab, Waad. *For Sama* Q&A. Curzon Soho, 14 September 2019.
Al-Kateab, Waad. Interview with the author, 8 May 2020.
Kazemi, Farshid. 'The Interpreter of Desires Iranian Cinema and Psychoanalysis'. PhD Thesis, University of Edinburgh, 2019.
Kazemi, Farshid. *A Girl Walks Home Alone at Night*. Liverpool: Liverpool University Press, 2021.
El Khachab, Chibab. 'State Control over Film Production in Egypt'. *Arab Media & Society* 23 (2017). Available at https://www.arabmediasociety.com/state-control-over-film-production-in-egypt
Khalil, Basil. The Paradox of Creative Constraints symposium. The Mosaic Rooms, London, 7 September 2019.
Khalil, Basil. Interview by the author, 17 September 2019.
Al-Khatib, Hadi. 'Corporations Erasing History: The Case of the Syrian Archive'. In *The Arab Archive: Mediated Memories and Digital Flows*, edited by Donatella Della Ratta, Kay Dickinson and Sune Haugbolle, 91–100. Amsterdam: Institute of Network Cultures, 2020.
Khatib, Lina. *Lebanese Cinema: Imagining the Civil War and beyond*. London: I.B. Tauris, 2008.
Khatib, Lina. *Image Politics in the Middle East: The Role of the Visual in Political Struggle*. London: I.B. Tauris, 2012.
Khosroshahi, Zahra. 'The Films of Rakhshan Banietemad: A Gateway into the Representation of Women in Iranian Cinema'. PhD Thesis, University of East Anglia, 2019.
Khosroshahi, Zahra. 'The Artistic and Political Implications of the Meta-cinematic in Rakshan Banietemad's Films'. In *Refocus: The Films of Rakshan Banietemad*, edited by Maryam Ghorbankarimi, 79–93. Edinburgh: Edinburgh University Press, 2021.
King, Geoff. *Film Comedy*. New York: Columbia University Press, 2002.
Kinninmont, Jane. 'Saudi Arabia: Why Is Going to the Cinema Suddenly OK?' 17 April 2018. Available at https://www.bbc.co.uk/news/world-middle-east-43738718
Kracauer, Siegfried. *Theory of Film: The Redemption of Physical* Reality. New York: Oxford University Press, 1960.
Kraidy, Marwan. *The Naked Blogger of Cairo: Creative Insurgency in the Arab World*. Cambridge, MA: Harvard University Press, 2016.
Kraidy, Marwan. 'Trashing the Sectarian System? Lebanon's "You Stink" Movement and the Making of Affective Publics'. *Communication and the Public* 1.1 (2016): 19–26.

Kucukalic, Lejla. 'Arabian Wonder: Contemporary Science Fiction Transforming the Gulf'. *The International Review of Science Fiction* 44. 121 (2015): 8–17.

Kuntsman, Adi and Rebecca Stein. *Digital Militarism: Israel's Occupation in the Social Media Age*. Stanford: Stanford University Press, 2015.

Langford, Michelle. 'The Circle'. In *Directory of World Cinema: Iran 2*, edited by Parviz Jahed, 148–50. Bristol: Intellect, 2017.

Langford, Michelle. *Allegory in Iranian Cinema: The Aesthetics of Poetry and Resistance*. London: Bloomsbury, 2019.

Langford, Michelle. '*Tales* and the Cinematic *Divan* of Rakshan Banietemad'. In *Refocus: The Films of Rakshan Banietemad*, edited by Maryam Ghorbankarimi, 57–78. Edinburgh: Edinburgh University Press, 2021.

Lawrence, Michael. 'Deadpan Dogs: Aki Kaurismäki's Canine Comedies'. In *The Films of Aki Kaurismäki: Ludic Engagements*, edited by Thomas Austin, 187–204. New York: Bloomsbury Academic, 2018.

Lawrence, Michael and Susan Smith. Eds. 'The Child Performance Dossier'. *Screen* 53.4 (Winter 2012): 436–76.

Lefebvre, Henri. *The Production of Space*, translated by Donald Nicholson-Smith. Oxford: Blackwell, 1991.

Lefebvre, Henri. *Writings on Cities*, translated and edited by Eleonore Kaufman and Elizabeth Lebas. Oxford: Blackwell, 1996.

Lefebvre, Henri. *Rhythmanalysis: Space, Time and Everyday Life*, translated by Stuart Elden and Gerald Moore. London: Bloomsbury, 2013.

Lionis, Chrisoula. *Laughter in Occupied Palestine: Comedy and Identity in Art and Film*. London: I.B. Tauris, 2016.

Litvin, Margaret. 'When the Villain Steals the Show: The Character of Claudius in Post-1975 Arab(ic) *Hamlet* Adaptations'. *Journal of Arabic Literature* 38.2 (2007): 196–219.

Lury, Karen. *The Child in Film: Tears, Fears and Fairytales*. London: I.B. Tauris, 2010.

Lynch, Marc. *The New Arab Wars: Uprisings and Anarchy in the Middle East*. Philadelphia: Perseus Books, 2016.

MacDowell, James. 'Notes on Quirky'. *Movie: A Journal of Film Criticism* 1.1 (2010): 1–16.

MacDowell, James. *Irony in Film*. London: Palgrave Macmillan, 2016.

Macleod, Hugh and Annasofie Flamand. 'Top Goon: Puppet Drama Lampoons Syria's Bashar al-Assad'. *Global Post*. 12 December 2011. Available at https://www.pri.org/stories/2011-12-12/top-goon-puppet-drama-lampoons-syrias-bashar-al-assad

Mady, Christine. 'The Imaginaries of Beirut's "Invisible" Solid Waste: Exploring Walls as Temporary Temporal Pauses amidst the Beirut Garbage Prices'. In *The Temporalities of Waste: Out of Sight, Out of Time*, edited by Fiona Allon, Ruth Barcan and Karma Eddison-Cogan, 87–104. Abingdon: Routledge, 2021.

Maghout, Jalal. Interview with the author, 4 May 2016.

Malik, Sarita. 'Diversity, Representation and Community Filmmaking'. In *Community Filmmaking: Diversity, Practices and Places*, edited by Sarita Malik, Caroline Chapain and Roberta Comunian, 21–5. New York: Routledge, 2017.

Marcus, Richard. 'Ava, My Adolescent Self', 9 July 2018. Available at: https://en.qantara.de/content/interview-with-award-winning-iranian-film-director-sadaf-foroughi-ava-my-adolescent-self.

Marks, Laura U. 'Calligraphic Animation: Documenting the Invisible', *Animation: An Interdisciplinary Journal* 6.4 (2011): 307–23.

Marks, Laura U. *Hanan al-Cinema: Affections for the Moving Image*. Cambridge, MA: MIT, 2015.

Marks, Laura U. 'Real Images Flow: Mullā Sadrā Meets Film-Philosophy'. *Film-Philosophy* 20 (2016): 24–46.

Masasit Mati. 'Who Wants to Kill a Million?' In *Syria Speaks: Art and Culture from the Frontline*, edited by Malu Halasa, Zaher Omareen and Nawara Mahfoud, 269–75. London: Saqi Books, 2014.

Maxwell, Richard and Toby Miller. 'Film and the Environment: Risk Off Screen'. In *Film and Risk*, edited by Mette Hjort, 271–89. Detroit: Wayne State University Press, 2012.

McLaughlin, Ellen. *The Trojan Women*. New York: Playscripts, Inc., 2011.

Mernissi, Fatima. *Beyond the Veil: Male-female Dynamics in Modern Muslim Society*. Bloomington: Indiana University Press, 1987.

Meures, Susanne Regina. Interview by the author, 25 September 2018.

Moeller, Susan. 'A Hierarchy of Innocence: The Media's Use of Children in the Telling of International News'. *The Harvard International Journal of Press/Politics* 7.1 (2002): 36–56.

Mohammed, Ossama. Interview by the author, 12 June 2016.

Al-Mokdad, Eyas. Interview by the author, 24 April 2018.

Al-Mokdad, Orwa. Interview by the author, 8 August 2018.

Morreall, John. *Comic Relief: A Comprehensive Philosophy of Humor*. Malden: Wiley-Blackwell, 2009.

Mortimer, Claire. *Romantic Comedy*. Abingdon: Routledge, 2010.

Mosireen_Soursar. 'No Archive Is Innocent: On the Attempt of Archiving Revolt'. In *The Arab Archive: Mediated Memories and Digital Flows*, edited by Donatella Della Ratta, Kay Dickinson and Sune Haugbolle, 35–40. Amsterdam: Institute of Network Cultures, 2020.

Mostafa, Ali. *The Worthy* Q&A chaired by the author. NYU Arts Center, Abu Dhabi, 3 April 2017.

Mottahedeh, Negar. *Displaced Allegories: Post-revolutionary Iranian Cinema*. Durham: Duke University Press, 2008.

Moylan, Tom. *Scraps of the Untainted Sky: Science Fiction, Utopia, Dystopia*. New York: Routledge, 2018.

Moylan, Tom and Raffaella Baccolini. *Dark Horizons: Science Fiction and the Dystopian Imagination*. New York: Routledge, 2003.

'M. Siam le réalisateur, entretien "Je voulais comprendre l'Égypt à travers leurs yeux"'. *Amal* dossier presse. Juste distribution: Paris, 2017.

Müller, Beate. 'Censorship and Cultural Regulation: Mapping the Territory'. In *Censorship and Cultural Regulation in the Modern Age*, edited by Beate Müller, 1–31. Amsterdam: Rodopi, 2004.

Muller, Nat. 'Contemporary Art in the Middle East'. In *Contemporary Art in the Middle East*, edited by Paul Sloman, 12–25. London: Black Dog, 2009.

Muller, Nat. 'On Being Contemporary – re-activating the Present: Joana Hadjithomas and Khalil Joreige in Conversation with Nat Muller'. *Art Papers* 37.1 (2013): 33–6.

'Myriam Sassine la productrice, entretien'. *Amal* dossier presse. Juste distribution: Paris, 2017.

Naficy, Hamid. 'Veiled Vision/Powerful Presences: Women in Post-revolutionary Iranian Cinema'. In *Eye of the Storm: Women in Post-Revolutionary Iran*, edited by Mahnaz Afkhami and Erika Friedl, 131–50. Syracuse: Syracuse University Press, 1994.

Naficy, Hamid. *A Social History of Iranian Cinema, Volume 4: The Globalizing Era, 1984–2010*. Durham: Duke University Press, 2012.

Neher, Erick. 'Richard Linklater's Sculpture in Time'. *Hudson Review* 67.3 (2014): 470–6.

Omara, Marouan and Johanna Domke. Interview by the author, 14 October 2020.

Omareen, Zaheer. Interview by the author, 13 June 2016

Ong, Walter. *Orality and Literacy: The Technologizing of the Word*. Abingdon: Routledge, 2006.

Orgeron, Devin. *Road Movies: From Muybridge and Méliès to Lynch and Kiarostami*. Basingstoke: Palgrave Macmillan, 2008.

Ostby, Marie. 'Graphics and Global Dissent: Marjane Satrapi's *Persepolis*, Persian Miniatures, and the Multifaceted Power of Comic Protest'. *PMLA* 132.3 (2017): 558–79.

Pachachi, Maysoon. Interview by the author, 1 May 2016.

Pad.ma. 'Theses on the Archive'. In *Dissonant Archives: Contemporary Visual Culture and Contested Narratives of the Middle East*, edited by Anthony Downey, 352–63. London: I.B. Tauris, 2015.

Pak-Shiraz, Nacim. 'Iranian Comedies'. In *Directory of World Cinema: Iran 2*, edited by Parviz Jahed, 262–70. Bristol: Intellect, 2017.

Pak-Shiraz, Nacim. 'Truth, Lies and Justice: The Fragmented Picture in Asghar Farhadi's Films'. In *Muslims in the Movies*, edited by Kristian Peterson, 143–61. Harvard: Harvard University Press, 2021.

Panahi, Jafar. 'Dissident Cinema: A Conversation between Jafar Panahi and Jamsheed Akrami'. *World Policy Journal* 35.1 (2018): 56–69.

Panahi, Jafar. Interview by Tobias Grey, 'Iranian Director Flouts Ban on Filmmaking'. In *Jafar Panahi: Interviews*, edited by Drew Todd, 130–5. Jackson: University Press of Mississippi, 2019.

Panahi, Jafar. Interview by Vadim Rizov, '"In Prison, I had Some Peace of Mind": Jafar Panahi on *Closed Curtain*'. In *Jafar Panahi: Interviews*, edited by Drew Todd, 136–9. Jackson: University Press of Mississippi, 2019.

Parikka, Jussi. 'Middle East and Other Futurisms: Imaginary Temporalities in Contemporary Art and Visual Culture'. *Culture, Theory and Critique* 59.1 (2018): 40–58.

Partovi, Pedram. *Popular Iranian Cinema before the Revolution: Family and Nation in FilmFarsi*. Abingdon: Routledge, 2017.

Peirce, Charles Sanders. *The Essential Peirce: Selected Philosophical Writings*, vol. 1, edited by The Peirce Edition Project. Bloomington: Indiana University Press, 1998.

Perrigo, Billy. 'These Tech Companies Managed to Eradicate ISIS Content. But They're Also Erasing Crucial Evidence of War Crimes'. *Time*, 11 April 2020. Available at https://time.com/5798001/facebook-youtube-algorithms-extremism/

Philo, Greg, Alison Gilmour, Maureen Gilmour, Susanna Rust, Etta Gaskell and Lucy West. 'The Israeli-Palestinian Conflict: TV News and Public Understanding'. In *War and the Media: Reporting Conflict 24/7*, edited by Daya Kishan Thussu and Des Freedman, 133–48. London: Sage, 2003.

Pinault, David. *Storytelling Techniques in the Arabian Nights*. Leiden: E.J. Brill, 1992.

Pope, Rob. *Creativity: Theory, History, Practice*. Abingdon: Routledge, 2005.

Pratt, Geraldine and Rose Marie San Juan. *Film and Urban Space: Critical Possibilities*. Edinburgh: Edinburgh University Press, 2014.

Proietti, Salvatore. 'A Groundbreaking Guide to Arab-Language SF'. *Science Fiction Studies* 43 (2016): 376–9.

Projansky, Sarah. *Spectacular Girls: Media Fascination and Celebrity Culture*. New York: New York University Press, 2014.

Que, Carol. 'Mechanisms of a Settler Colonial Architecture in Larissa Sansour's *Nation Estate* (2012)'. *Jerusalem Quarterly* 73 (2018): 124–39.

Quilty, Jim. 'The Collection Is Safe, the Foundation's Ruined'. *The Daily Star*, 25 August 2020. Available at https://www.dailystar.com.lb/Arts-and-Ent/Culture/2020/Aug-25/510765-the-collection-is-safe-the-foundations-ruined.ashx (accessed 11 September 2020).

Rastegar, Kamran. *Surviving Images: Cinema, War and Cultural Memory in the Middle East*. Oxford: Oxford University Press, 2015.

Rees, A.L. 'Moving Spaces'. In *Autopia: Cars and Culture*, edited by Peter Wollen and Joe Kerr, 83–94. London: Reaktion Books, 2002.

Ridgeon, Lloyd. *Makhmalbaf's Broken Mirror: The Socio-political Significance of Modern Iranian Cinema*. Durham: University of Durham, 2000.

Rieder, John. *Colonialism and the Emergence of Science Fiction*. Middletown, CT: Wesleyan University Press, 2008.

Riesman, Paul. *Freedom in Fulani Social Life: An Introspective Ethnography*, translated by Martha Fuller. Chicago: Chicago University Press, 1977.

Al-Rimawi, Tariq. 'Issues of Representation in Arab Animation Cinema: Practice, History and Theory'. PhD Thesis, Loughborough University, 2014.

Robbins, Jonathan. 'Interview with Emad Burnat, "5 Broken Cameras"', 1 June 2012. Available at https://www.filmlinc.org/daily/interview-with-emad-burnat-5-broken-cameras/

Roitman, Janet. *Anti-crisis*. Durham: Duke University Press, 2013.

Rose, Steve. 'Lights, Camera, Revolution: The Birth of Libyan Cinema after Gaddafi's Fall', 1 October 2012. Available at https://www.theguardian.com/film/2012/oct/01/libya-film-gaddafi-arab-spring

Rose, Steve. 'You Get Used to the Gunfire' – Filming the Libyan Women's Football Team', 31 May 2019, available at https://www.theguardian.com/film/2019/may/31/libyan-womens-football-team-freedom-fields

Rosen, Philip. 'From Impurity to Historicity'. In *Impure Cinema: Intermedial and Intercultural Approaches to Film*, edited by Lúcia Nagib and Anne Jerslev, 3–20. London: I.B. Tauris, 2014.

Ross, Kristin. 'Lefebvre on the Situationists: An Interview'. *October* 79 (1997): 69–83.

Rasoulof, Mohammad. Interview by Ali Moosavi, 'A Stranger in His Homeland'. *Film International* 84 (2018): 109–13.

Ruberto, Laura E. and Kristi M. Wilson, 'Introduction'. In *Italian Neorealism and Global Cinema*, edited by Laura E. Ruberto and Kristi M. Wilson, 1–15. Detroit: Wayne State University Press, 2007.

Russell, Catherine. *Archiveology: Walter Benjamin and Archival Film Practices*. Durham: Duke University Press, 2018.

Al-Saadawi, Nawal. *The Hidden Face of Eve: Women in the Arab World*, translated and edited by Sherif Hetata. London: Zed Books, 1991.

Sabbagh, Mahmoud. *Barakah Meets Barakah* Q&A. BFI London Film Festival, 8 October 2016.

Sadegh-Vaziri, Persheng. 'Iranian Documentary Filmmakers Association and the Fight for the House of Cinema'. In *Iranian Cinema in a Global Context: Policy, Politics, and Form*, edited by Peter Decherney and Blake Atwood, 164–82. New York: Routledge, 2015.

Sadr, Hamid Reza. 'Children in Contemporary Iranian Cinema: When We Were Children'. In *The New Iranian Cinema: Politics, Representation and Identity*, edited by Richard Tapper, 227–37. London: I.B. Tauris, 2002.

Salducci, Hadrien. 'KEYWAN KARIMI, rencontre avec un cinéaste censuré', 13 June 2018. Available at https://www.leblogducinema.com/portrait/keywan-karimi-interview-867162/

El Said, Maha, Lena Meari and Nicola Pratt. 'Introduction'. In *Rethinking Gender in Revolutions and Resistance in the Arab World: Lessons from the Arab World*, 1–32. London: Zed Books, 2015.

El-Said, Tamer. Interview by Matt Morrison, 19 April 2018, available at https://www.filmcomment.com/blog/interview-tamer-el-said/

El-Said, Tamer. The Paradox of Creative Constraints symposium, The Mosaic Rooms, London, 7 September 2019.

Saikal, Amin. 'Conclusion'. In *The Arab World and Iran: A Turbulent Region in Transition*, edited by Amin Saikal, 181–6. Basingstoke: Palgrave Macmillan, 2016.

Salamati, Mahsa. 'Transnational Film Circulation in the Iranian Context: From Conjunctural Crisis to Discursive Heterotopia'. PhD Thesis, University of New South Wales, 2019.

Salti, Rasha. 'Critical Nationals: The Paradoxes of Syrian Cinema'. In *Insights into Syrian Cinema: Essays and Conversations with Filmmakers*, edited by Rasha Salti, 21–44. New York: Rattapallax Press, 2006.

Sansour, Larissa. Shubbak: Imagined Futures Shorts Programme Q&A. Barbican, London, 4 July 2017.

Sansour, Larissa. Interview by the author, 7 August 2017.

Sansour, Leila. Interview by the author, 9 November 2015.

Sarris, Andrew. 'The Auteur Theory Revisited'. In *Critical Visions in Film Theory*, edited by Timothy Corrigan, Patricia White and Meta Mazaj, 354–61. New York: Bedford/St Martin's, 2011.

Sellnow, Timothy L. and Matthew W. Seeger. *Theorizing Crisis Communication*. Chichester: Wiley-Blackwell, 2013.

Seppälä, Jaakko. 'The Camera's Ironic Point of View: Notes on Strange and Comic Elements in the Films of Aki Kaurismäki'. In *The Films of Aki Kaurismäki: Ludic Engagements*, edited by Thomas Austin, 83–101. New York: Bloomsbury Academic, 2018.

Seyidov, Samad. *Phenomenology of Creativity: History, Paradoxes, Personality*. Milton Keynes: AuthorHouse, 2013.

Shafik, Viola, 'Resisting Pleasure? Political Opposition and the Body in Arab Cinema'. In *Resistance in Contemporary Middle Eastern Cultures: Literature, Cinema and Music*, edited by Karima Laachir and Saeed Talajooy. New York: Routledge, 2013.

Shafik, Viola. *Arab Cinema: History and Cultural Identity*. Cairo: American University in Cairo Press, 2016.

Shaheen, Jack. *Real Bad Arabs: How Hollywood Vilifies a People*. New York: Olive Branch Press, 2001.

Shahmanesh-Banks, Nargess. 'Animation: Hand Over Art'. *Design Week* 23.16 (2008): n.p.

Sherwood, Harriet. 'Speed Sisters on Track for Race Equality'. *The Guardian*, 18 June 2010. Available at https://www.theguardian.com/world/2010/jun/18/palestine-speed-sisters-race

Siam, Mohamed. Interview by the author, 31 May 2018.

Smit, Rik Ansgard Heinrich, and Marcel Broersma. 'Witnessing in the New Memory Ecology: Memory Construction of the Syrian Conflict on YouTube'. *New Media & Society* 19.2 (2017): 289–307.

Soleri, Paolo. *Arcology: The City in the Image of Man*. Cambridge, MA: MIT Press, 1971.

Sombatpoonsiri, Janjira. *Humor and Nonviolent Struggle in Serbia*. New York: Syracuse University Press, 2015.

Soozandeh, Ali. Interview by the author, 23 August 2018.

Sprio, Margherita. 'Performing History: Girlhood and *Sib/The Apple* (Samira Makhmalbaf, 1998)'. In *International Cinema and the Girl: Local Issues, Transnational Contexts*, edited by Fiona Handyside and Kate Taylor-Jones, 165–177. Basingstoke: Palgrave Macmillan, 2016.

Stein, Rebecca. *Itineraries in Conflict: Israelis, Palestinians, and the Political Lives of Tourism*. Durham: Duke University Press, 2008.

Stephan, Rania. Interview by Elisabeth Stoney. 'Life on Screen: Rania Stephan'. *Art Asia Pacific* 79. Available at http://www.artasiapacific.com/Magazine/79/LifeOnScreenRaniaStephan

Stephan, Rania. Interview by the author, 20 July 2018.

Stoney, Elisabeth. 'Life on Screen: Rania Stephan'. *Art Asia Pacific* 79. Available at http://www.artasiapacific.com/Magazine/79/LifeOnScreenRaniaStephan

Suleiman, Elia. Interview by Linda Butler. 'The Occupation (and Life) through an Absurdist Lens'. *Journal of Palestine Studies* 32.2 (2003): 63–73.

Suleiman, Elia. *It Must Be Heaven* Q&A. BFI London Film Festival, 9 October 2019.

Suvin, Darko. *Metamorphoses of Science Fiction: On the Poetics and History of a Literary Genre*. Yale: Yale University Press, 1979.

Tawil-Souri, Helga. 'Surveillance Sublime: The Security State in Jerusalem'. *Jerusalem Quarterly* 68 (2016): 56–65.

Taylor, Meredith. 'Tabl (2016) | Drum | Venice Settimana della Critica 2016', 5 September 2016. Available at https://filmuforia.com/tabl-2016-drum-venice-settimana-della-critica-2016/

Telmissany, May. 'The Utopian and Dystopian Functions of Tahrir Square'. *Postcolonial Studies* 17:1 (2014): 36–46.

Terranova, Tiziana. 'Free Labour: Producing Culture for the Digital Economy'. *Social Text* 18.2 (2000): 33–58.

Torchin, Leshu. *Creating the Witness: Documenting Genocide on Film, Video, and the Internet*. Minneapolis: University of Minnesota Press, 2012.

Tröhler, Margrit. 'Les Films à protagonistes multiples et la logique des possibles'. *Iris* 29 (2000): 85–102.

Tucker, Thomas Deane. *The Peripatetic Frame: Images of Walking in Cinema*. Edinburgh: Edinburgh University Press, 2020.

Van de Peer, Stefanie. 'From Animated Cartoons to Suspended Animation: The History of Syrian Animation'. In *Animation in the Middle East: Practice and Aesthetics from Baghdad to Casablanca*, edited by Stefanie Van de Peer. London: I.B. Tauris, 2017.

Vaneigem, Raoul. 'The Wall Is a Mirror'. Available at https://www.puntodevistafestival.com/en/noticias.asp?IdNoticia=399

Van Welie, Georgina. Interview by the author, 24 April 2018.

Watts, Edward. Interview by the author, 13 May 2020.

Wedeen, Lisa. *Ambiguities of Domination: Politics, Rhetoric, and Symbols in Contemporary Syria*. Chicago: University of Chicago Press, 2015.

Wedeen, Lisa. *Authoritarian Apprehensions: Ideology, Judgment, and Mourning in Syria*. Chicago: University of Chicago Press, 2019.

Weizman, Eyal. *Hollow Land: Israel's Architecture of Occupation*. London: Verso, 2007.

Wells, Paul. *Understanding Animation: A Guide to Everything from Flipbooks to Flash*. London: Routledge, 1998.

Wells, Paul. *Animation: Genre and Authorship*. London: Wallflower, 2002.

Wells, Paul. 'Animation in the Gallery and the Gestalt: György Kovásznai and William Kentridge'. In *Global Animation Theory: International Perspectives at Animafest Zagreb*, edited by Franziska Bruckner, Nikica Gilić, Holger Lang, Daniel Šuljić and Hrvoje Turković, 11–27. London: Bloomsbury Academic, 2019.

Wessels, Joshka. *Documenting Syria: Film-making, Video Activism and Revolution*. London: I.B. Tauris, 2019.

Williams, Raymond. *Keywords: A Vocabulary of Culture and Society*. Oxford: Oxford University Press, 2015.

Wise, Damon. 'IDFA: "Amal" Director Mohamed Siam on Documenting Disillusioned Arab Youth: "They had to swallow their dreams"', 16 November 2017, available at: https://variety.com/2017/film/festivals/idfa-amal-mohamed-siam-documenting-disillusioned-arab-youth-1202616288/

Woolf, Virginia. *A Room of One's Own*. London: Penguin, 2020.

Yaqub, Nadia. 'Utopia and Dystopia in Palestinian Circular Journeys from Ghassān Kanafānī to Contemporary Film'. *Middle Eastern Literatures* 15.3 (2012): 305–18.

Yaqub, Nadia. *Palestinian Cinema in the Days of Revolution*. Austin: University of Texas Press, 2018.

Zeidan, Lara. Interview by Jennifer Merin, 'Whistler Film Festival 2018: Lara Zeidan, Director of Three Centimetres', 29 November 2018. Available at https://awfj.org/female-gaze/2018/11/29/whistler-film-festival-2018-lara-zeidan-director-of-three-centimetres/?doing_wp_cron=1618823363.8232939243316650390625

Zeidan, Lara. Interview by the author, 26 August 2019.

Zelizer, Barbie. 'On "Having Been There": "Eyewitnessing" as a Journalistic Key Word'. *Critical Studies in Media Communication* 24.5 (2007): 408–28.

Zacharek, Stephanie. 'How Drones Are Revolutionizing the Way Film and Television Is Made', 31 May 2018. Available at https://time.com/5295594/drones-hollywood-artists/

Zeydabadi-Nejad, Saeed. *The Politics of Iranian Cinema: Film and Society in the Islamic Republic*. Abingdon: Routledge, 2010.

Index

5 Broken Cameras (Burnat and Davidi) 20, 25, 28, 31, 36–9, 45, 56, 193
20 Fingers (Akbari) 69, 134, 139
300 Miles (Al-Mokdad) 10, 25, 33, 58, 65–7, 246 n. 56, 250 n. 37
858: An Archive of Resistance (Mosireen) 196

Abbas, Ackbar 259 n. 65
Abdalla, Ahmad 176
Abdalla, Khalid 6, 22, 35, 36, 104, 116–17, 119–20
Abdulaziz, Fuad 101
Abounaddara collective 196, 201
absurdity 26, 94, 96, 148, 153–61, 223
Abtahi, Sepideh 183
Abu Dhabi 141
Abu-Lughod, Lila 12, 270 n. 60
activism 19, 28, 234, 267 n. 105
activists
    as an audience 132
    constraints on free expression 43, 50
    role in witnessing and filmmaking 13, 28, 29, 31, 34, 36, 38, 65, 86, 194–5, 196
    targeted for forcible disappearance 29, 206
Adventure of a Married Couple (Karimi) 105, 28
Afshar, Sara 28, 33
agency 19, 31, 37, 45, 57, 59, 61, 64, 67, 70, 78, 79, 148, 172, 196, 211, 216, 225, 237
Agha, Akram 86
Agha-Soltan, Neda 28
Ahadi, Ali Samedi 87, 197
Ahmadinejad, Mahmoud 69, 87, 89, 106, 175, 176, 177, 178, 217, 219, 278 n. 21
Ahmadzadeh, Ali 214, 216–20, 278 n. 31
Akbari, Mania 10, 68, 69, 125, 133, 134, 137
Akl, Mounia 16, 154, 214, 229–33

al-Abed, Bana 64, 153
al-Abyad, Jamil 151
al-Allaq, Yahya 62, 63
al-Assad, Bashar 67, 121, 122, 148, 151, 152, 186
al-Assad, Hafiz 12
Alawiye, Malak 28
Aleppo 28, 40, 41–5, 47, 57, 64, 65, 66, 154
Algeria 102, 129
Ali Zaoua (Ayouch) 250 n. 29
allegory 19–21, 23, 25, 61, 101, 185, 216, 219, 236
Amal (Siam) 25, 49, 58, 75–9, 247 n. 100
And Life Goes On (Kiarostami) 173
animation 25, 81–100, 181, 197, 271 n. 68
anonymity, need for 13, 25, 30, 81, 87, 96–9, 120, 187
appropriation, practices of 192, 196, 198, 229
Apu Trilogy (Ray) 59
Arabic language 6, 16, 29, 40, 78, 119, 127, 148, 149–50, 166, 204, 209, 214, 232
Arab Image Foundation (AIF) 191
Arab Spring
    breaking the 'wall of fear' 2, 21, 30, 86, 150–1
    contrast with public space before uprisings 121
    cross-influences between different uprisings 35
    dystopian transformation of 213, 219
    effect on filmmaking 29–30, 50, 76, 117, 201, 207
    Iranian Green Movement as a forerunner of 3, 27
    relationship with anti-occupation protests in Palestine 39
    relationship with Lebanese trash crisis 232
    role of women in 43, 96, 187
    state crackdowns on 3

use of archives as a resource for future uprisings 196
  (*see also* post-Arab Spring protests)
Arab uprisings (*see* Arab Spring)
Aractingi, Philippe 9, 18, 140
archival footage, use of 26, 76, 93, 94, 107, 189, 191–211, 255 n. 57
archives
  traditional archives 93, 105, 191–2
  digital archives 26, 190, 193–6, 197, 201, 204, 206–8
Argo (Affleck) 218
Arthur, Paul 193
artisanal production 10, 198
Arebi, Naziha 28, 32, 51–5, 127, 149
Ashuri, Tamur 25, 32, 46
Assad, Maisoun 201
Atassi, Mohammed Ali 31, 197
Atomic Heart Mother (Ahmadzadeh) 26, 214, 216–20, 234, 236, 278 n. 24, 278 n. 25, 278 n. 31
auteur theory 19
authorship 19, 171, 186, 190, 196, 200
Ava (Foroughi) 25, 58, 73–5, 108
Ave Maria (Khalil) 26, 150, 157–9, 163
Ayouni (Fedda) 26, 29, 129, 197, 205–10

Babel (Iñárritu) 176
Baghdad 62–3, 117
Ballard, J.G. 221, 278 n. 38
ban
  on filmmaking 135, 159, 174, 176
  on films 81, 86, 115, 120, 137, 159, 183
  on travel 14, 52, 128, 137
al-Banawi, Fatima 165, 167, 168
Banietemad, Rakshan 104, 160, 167–79, 268 n. 24, 269 n. 36
Barakah Meets Barakah (Sabbagh) 26, 148, 149, 164–8
Barghnavard, Shirin 10, 14, 175, 179–83
Baron, Jaimie 193, 195, 200, 204
Bashu, The Little Stranger (Beyzai) 60, 249 n. 16
Bazin, André 23, 197, 205, 273 n. 40
BBC Arabic 188
BBC Persian 107, 179, 269 n. 39
Bedirxan, Wiam Simav 192, 200, 204
Beheshti, Mohammad 220
Behrouzan, Orkideh 171

Beirut 14, 63, 64, 93, 101, 110–15, 117, 138–40, 141, 142–3, 191–2, 230–2, 250 n. 33 (*see also* Lebanon)
Beit Sahour 93, 95
Bergson, Henri 148, 265 n. 54
Berlin, Symphony of a City (Ruttman) 103
Al-Bernameg (Youssef) 119, 141, 151
Bethlehem 131, 153, 154, 226, 228, 280 n. 72
Beyzai, Bahram 59
bicycle motif 58, 70, 72, 73, 251 n. 65
Bicycle Thieves (de Sica) 58, 59
Bidayyat 10
Bil'in 28, 36–9
Bin Salman, Mohammed 167
Black Audio Film Collective 179
black market 134, 137, 159
Blue-Veiled, The (Banietemad) 176
Bourriaud, Nicolas 194, 200
Boyhood (Linklater) 76
Bringing Up Baby (Hawks) 166
Bruno, Giuliana 102, 121
Burnat, Emad 28, 36–9, 45
al-Butairi, Fahad 141, 149

Cairo 15, 49, 78, 101, 115–20, 199, 225
Campbell, Ian 214, 215, 278 n. 38
Capernaum (Labaki) 25, 58, 63–4, 258 n. 39
censorship 5, 30, 37, 60, 68, 86, 138, 148, 164, 191, 200, 220, 230
  circumventing state censorship 7, 25, 26, 29, 69, 81, 84–5, 90, 99, 102, 106, 110, 189, 115, 133, 173, 174, 176, 183, 189, 222
  self-censorship 12–13, 21, 55, 187
  state censorship as one of many challenges 8–9, 104, 160–1, 168, 215, 235–6
  tendency to focus on state censorship 1, 2, 4–5, 19–20
checkpoints 66, 125, 126, 127, 130, 131, 151, 226
Cherri, Ali 201
children
  as assumed audience 83–6
  as protagonists 22, 25, 41, 46, 57–79, 93, 163, 249 n. 16
Chouliaraki, Lilie 33, 34

Chronicle of a Disappearance (Suleiman) 156
Circle, The (Panahi) 69, 70
citizen journalism 25, 27, 28, 36, 56, 182
city, representation of 25, 46–7, 62–4, 89, 92, 101–23, 136–7, 142, 144, 176, 181–2, 217–18, 221–2, 226
Closed Curtain (Panahi) 135, 136
cognitive estrangement 213–16
collective filmmaking 8, 28, 35, 96, 116, 151, 171, 179–83, 196, 200
comedy 26, 141, 147, 148–50, 153, 154, 157–9, 161–8
coming-of-age films 67–79
conflict (*see also* country-specific entries)
   association with the Middle East 1, 3
   constructing a memory of 195, 197
   effect on freedom of movement 53, 127
   effect on freedom of expression 8, 15
   filming in conflict zones 13, 25, 28, 29, 31, 32, 145, 236
   on the ground perspectives 36, 39, 40, 52, 65, 181, 203
   'view from above' media reporting 4, 33, 101, 123, 172, 201
consent 44, 62, 195
conservative values 43, 55, 70, 73, 75, 138, 148, 167, 186
constraints
   creativity within constraints 22, 54, 59, 62, 64, 74, 81, 99, 142, 148, 161, 175, 176, 192, 206, 210
   Elster's theory of constraints 5, 21
   indexical relationship with film production 20, 23, 25, 29, 32, 56, 84, 100, 120, 134, 135, 187, 236
   as a stimulus to creativity 2, 10, 18, 20, 24, 128, 215, 236–7
   typology of constraints 6–18, 235
   (*see also* different types of constraints)
copyright (*see* intellectual property)
Costa Brava Lebanon (Akl) 17
countries in transition 28, 48–56
Coup 53 (Amirani) 192
COVID-19 pandemic 4, 235
Creative Memory of the Syrian Revolution 196
creativity
   concept of 5, 18–19
   creative resistance 38
   relationship with constraints 1–2, 31 (*see also* creativity within constraints *under* constraints)
crisis 3–4
   and animation 81, 87, 100
   and archival strategies 194
   and child protagonists 58–9, 62–4
   and humour 154
   and psychogeography 25, 103
   and road movie 17, 125–6, 140
   and science fiction 17, 213
   and story within a story 26, 171–2, 173, 177
   and teen protagonists 68–70, 79
   and witnessing 27, 29, 30, 32, 33, 34, 39, 52
crisis image 21–2
Crop (Omara and Domke) 221
curfews 125, 127, 130

Dällenbach, Lucien 173, 268 n. 10
Dall'Oglio, Father Paolo 205, 206, 208, 210
Damascus 33, 97, 102, 120–3
al-Daradji, Mohamed 62–3, 173
Day, Amber 168
Day and a Button, A (Hamwi) 102, 120–3
Day I Became a Woman, The (Meshkini) 251 n. 65
De Angelis, Enrico 205
de Certeau, Michel 22, 101, 102, 105
De Michiel, Helen 179
De Sica, Vittorio 58
Death of a Salesman (Miller) 174
Debord, Guy 102, 104, 121, 122
déjà disparu 118, 259 n. 65
Del Mar Azcona, María 172
Deleuze, Gilles 8, 19, 21, 24, 220
   crisis of the action image 58, 60, 103
   crystal image 117, 173
   time image 22, 59, 68, 126
Della Ratta, Donatella 40, 45, 47
Dera'a 65, 141
dérive 102, 120, 121, 123 (*see also* psychogeography)
Derrida, Jacques 191–2, 194, 205, 211
détournement 194
desert landscape, use of 126, 142 215, 221, 229
Desser, David 231
dialects 16, 150

diaspora 90, 227
Dib, Roy 126, 142–4, 147, 155
Dickinson, Kay 125
dictatorship
    experience of living under dictatorship 21, 42, 43, 98, 186–7, 199, 217, 219, 278 n. 25
    resurgent dictatorships 3, 50, 213
digital video
    advent of digital cameras 10, 207
    distribution 127, 198
    relationship with cinema 29, 30, 197
    suspicion of 34
    (*see also* digital archives *under* archives)
dignity 87, 96, 196, 201, 204, 211
disappearance
    of cities 101, 116
    of history 191, 200, 211
    of people 27, 205–10
direct strategies
    dependent on filmmaker's situation 150, 174
    relationship with indexicality 23, 56, 120, 215
    shift towards 21, 22, 25, 26, 29, 35, 58, 79, 101, 104, 150, 168, 236
discrepant mobility 126, 144
dissent 19, 20, 21, 49, 86, 151, 167
dissimulation 12, 13, 21, 73, 150, 151, 218
Divine Intervention (Suleiman) 156, 157
documentary
    animated documentary 84, 87–9, 93–4, 96, 98
    cinéma vérité 30
    relationship with journalism 39
    rise of 22
    perceived as 'politically problematic' 179, 183, 222
documentary-fiction hybrid 22, 35–6, 58, 103, 116, 117, 220, 222
Dogme '95 17, 30, 32, 140, 241 n. 71
Domke, Johanna 214, 220–5, 237–8
Douglas, Mary 158
Dreamaway (Omara and Domke) 26, 214, 216, 220–5, 234, 236, 278 n. 3
Dreams (al-Daradji) 178
dreams, use of 18, 99, 106, 199, 214, 216, 220, 221, 223
Dressage (Badkoobeh) 252 n. 71

Drifting Clouds (Kaurismäki) 162
Drum (Karimi) 14–15
Duchamp, Michel 194
Duped, The (Saleh) 126
dystopia 26, 213–34
    critical dystopia 234
    'found' dystopia 215, 230, 234
    (*see also* utopia)

Eager, Charlotte 184
Eastern Europe 84, 85
Easy Rider (Hopper) 125
eco-disaster film 229, 231
economic constraints 5, 8–10, 18, 29, 31, 37, 59, 130
Egypt
    25 January 2011 'Day of Rage' 200
    2011 revolution 35, 48, 49, 75, 76, 77, 116, 119, 120, 150, 151, 196, 247 n. 100
    constraints of production and distribution 6, 8, 15, 51, 104, 120, 222
    counterrevolution 3, 48, 50, 78
    economic situation 221, 225
    Maspero Massacre 28
    Rabea Massacre 119
Eid, Rana 18, 111–15
Eisenstein, Sergei 82
Elster, Jon 5–6, 16, 17, 21, 238–9 n. 16
émigré filmmakers 19, 31, 81, 101
empathy 82, 95, 96, 98, 99, 155, 163
environmental constraints 15
environmental crisis 216, 229, 230, 231, 234
epistolary form 40, 246 n. 56
Alesa, Majed 169
Escape from ISIS (Watts) 246 n. 79
Estayqazat 96, 255 n. 59
ethics 13–14, 36, 44, 62, 65, 87, 97, 133, 158, 189, 191, 192, 195, 196, 201, 205, 208, 211, 223, 274
Euripides 183, 185, 270 n. 54
exile 2, 10, 15, 19, 50, 88, 96, 119, 134, 151, 184, 201
experimental filmmaking 16, 18, 74, 85, 142, 147, 198, 199, 201, 228
exploitation
    of child actors 62, 250 n. 25
    of digital labour 195, 201

Fageeh, Hisham 13, 149–50, 165, 167, 168
Fall of the Romanov Dynasty, The (Shub) 193
Farabi Cinema Foundation 176, 220
Farahmand, Azadeh 249 n. 16
Fares, Amber 125, 128–32
Farhadi, Asghar 108, 159, 174
Farrokhzad, Forugh 257 n. 19
Farsi (*see* Persian language)
Fedda, Yasmin 14, 32, 184–9, 192, 197, 205–10, 243 n. 105
female filmmakers (*see under* women)
film festivals 4, 7, 8–9, 10, 14, 16, 32, 35, 70, 85, 86, 127, 129, 138, 140, 144, 157, 159, 168, 183, 225
film funding 7, 8–10, 16, 17, 21, 37, 39, 51, 52, 54, 71, 83, 140, 141, 157, 158, 159, 168, 180, 185, 228
filmfārsī 109, 257 n. 32
film within a film 173, 177, 178, 179, 181, 200 (*see also* story within a story *under* storytelling)
Fisher, Mark 215–16, 219, 225
foreground/background dynamics 52, 126, 140–4, 145
Forgotten Village, A (Hajju) 148
formal constraints 16–17
Foroughi, Sadaf 13, 73–5, 108
For Sama (Al-Kateab and Watts) 25, 28, 31, 34, 36, 39–48, 56, 57, 65, 120, 154, 193, 256 n. 65, 276 n. 98
Foucault, Michel 5, 112, 135, 239 n. 16, 271 n. 7
found footage 26, 181, 192, 193, 203
frame story 171, 177, 267 n. 3
Free Syrian Army (FSA) 42–3, 66, 120
freedom
  of expression 1–2, 5, 6, 11, 15, 17, 21, 24, 26, 42, 50, 69, 82, 86, 96, 120, 133, 137, 148, 151, 160, 167, 168, 172, 175, 177, 185, 188, 214, 217, 223, 235–7
  of movement 3, 26, 53, 64, 125, 126, 127, 130, 131, 135, 144
Freedom Fields (Arebi) 25, 28, 32, 48, 51–6, 127, 149
Freud, Sigmund 154–5, 214
friendship, theme of 109, 117, 180, 188
In the Future They Ate from the Finest Porcelain (Sansour) 229
From A to B (Mostafa) 26, 126, 141–2, 149

al-Gaddafi, Muammar 51, 52, 152
García Espinosa, Julio 30, 31
Gaza 3, 127, 131, 228, 255, 260 n. 23
Gaza Weekend, A (Khalil) 159
gender
  constraints 12, 55, 73, 121, 168, 235
  role reversal 106, 166
  segregation 59–60, 70, 79, 148
General's Boot, The (Agha) 86
General Security, Lebanon 115, 230–1
genre
  as a formal constraint 5, 17
  transformation of existing genres 17, 26, 125, 143, 165, 214, 225, 233
  as a 'universal' language 78, 226, 234
  use of popular genres 140–1, 149, 261 n. 57
  (*see also under* individual genres)
Germany Year Zero (Rossellini) 58
Ghani, Mariam 191, 208
Ghazi Safadi, Noura 205–9
al-Ghazzi, Omar 57, 64
Ghouta 33, 34, 96, 247 n. 95
Gilaneh (Banietemad) 176
Girl in the Sneakers, The (Sadrameli) 69–70
Girl Walks Home Alone at Night, A (Amirpour) 277 n. 17
Glasgow University Media Group 158
Godard, Jean-Luc 142–3
graffiti 29, 32, 37, 98, 104–7, 122, 202
Grapes of Wrath, The (Ford) 126
Great Depression, USA 126, 179
Green Wave, The (Ahadi) 25, 81, 87–9, 90, 94, 99, 197, 198
Guattari, Félix 220
Gulf states 3, 141, 165

Hadjithomas, Joana 110, 227 n. 9
Haghighi, Mani 4, 7, 8, 148, 159–61
Hamlet (Shakespeare) 166, 173, 175
Hamwi, Azza 120–3
Hand, The (Trnka) 84–5
Hatamikia, Ebrahim 160
Hawages (Alesa) 168–9
Hebrew language 38, 150
hejāb (principle of modesty) 11, 59–60, 76, 133, 181, 217
Heliopolis (Abdalla) 176
Hezbollah 140, 219
Hjort, Mette 19

Hollywood 104, 125, 133, 218
  classical narrative 16, 142, 156
  Production Code 5, 133
Holocaust 28, 33
home mode documents 207, 275 n. 86
homosexuality 7, 107, 109, 134, 138–9, 141, 142 (*see also* same-sex desire)
homosociality 109
Homs 200, 204
Honess Roe, Annabelle 84, 97, 256 n. 62
honour 11, 68, 75, 77, 90, 96 (*see also* virginity)
hope, theme of 57, 78, 223, 232–3, 234
Hosni, Soad 198–9
House is Black, The (Farrokhzad) 257 n. 19
House of Cinema 183
human-animal transformation 94, 161
human rights 2, 50, 72, 87, 88, 136, 158, 195, 226
humanitarian gaze 93, 155
humour 71, 94, 130, 136, 147–69, 225, 225 n 53, 262 n. 3
  black humour 147, 148, 160, 264 n 33
  deadpan humour 26, 148, 154, 161–4, 257 n. 22
  surrealist humour 26, 153–61
  translatability of 149–50
  (*see also* irony, jokes, laughter *and* satire)
Hussein, Saddam 219
Hutcheon, Linda 161

Idol, The (Abu-Assad) 260 n. 23
Image Nation, Abu Dhabi 141, 261 n. 57
Immortal Sergeant, The (Kalthoum) 173
independent cinema 1, 4, 8, 10, 12, 14, 21, 54, 104, 126, 167, 177, 235
indexicality 22–3, 25, 29, 56, 58, 83–4, 148, 181, 192, 215, 234, 236
indirect strategies 5, 13, 21, 26, 30, 90, 91, 148, 150, 161, 168, 174, 185, 209
individuals at risk 13–14, 19, 29, 30, 37, 50, 62, 87
infrastructural constraints 7–8, 10, 25, 79, 103–4, 120, 123
Inside Aleppo (Channel 4, UK) 41–2, 44, 45
Institute for the Intellectual Development of Children and Young Adults 59, 85
intellectual property 195, 196
intentional disparity 193, 202
intermediality 197

Internet
  as an archive 194, 196
  censorship of 11, 127, 195, 197
  as a distribution platform 1, 10, 11, 34, 35, 150, 151
  slow speed of 15, 197
  (*see also* social media, YouTube *and* web 2.0)
interview methodology 23–4
intimacy, depiction of 12, 54, 107, 108, 109, 133, 142, 207
Invisible (Barghnavard) 14
Iran
  1978–9 revolution 8, 59, 104, 105, 179, 183
  Chain Murders 160, 175
  Green Movement 3, 30, 27, 29, 87, 88, 104, 106–7, 175, 178, 182, 194, 213, 218
  Iran-Iraq war 60, 81, 106, 181–2, 249 n. 16
  Islamic Republic of 11–12, 20, 60, 62, 75, 85, 106, 216–19, 249 n. 16
  Koker earthquake 173
  nuclear anxiety 3, 216, 218
Iraq
  Iraq war 34, 62
  US-led invasion and occupation 3, 116, 173, 182
Iron Island (Rasoulof) 174
irony 147, 148, 161–8
Islam 12, 68, 72, 73, 161
  attitudes to image-making 82
  Shi'a 12, 73, 174
  Sunni 70
  Wahhabi 70
Islamic philosophy 21, 214
Islamic State of Iraq and Syria (ISIS) 3, 13, 33, 187, 195, 205, 221
Israel-Hezbollah War (*see* July 2006 War *under* Lebanon)
It Happened One Night (Capra) 133
It Must Be Heaven (Suleiman) 26, 156, 157
Izzam, Itab 184

Jaberansari, Ali 107–10, 148, 161–3, 176, 236
Jacir, Annemarie 12, 126, 127, 154, 155
Jaffa 130
Jahanpanah, Mohammad Reza 163, 180

Jeddah 150, 165
Jenin 128, 131
Jericho 131
Jerusalem 3, 128, 130, 228
jokes 149, 150, 154, 158, 159 (*see also* humour)
Jordan 141, 142, 183, 186, 226
Joreige, Khalil 110, 277 n. 9

Kabyle 102
Kadi, Sam 13, 31
Kalthoum, Ziad 173
Kamel, Ahd 20, 71, 72, 168
Kami's Party (Ahmadzadeh) 217
Kanun (*see* Institute for the Intellectual Development of Children and Young Adults)
Karimi, Keywan 7, 14, 104–7
al-Karnak (Badrakhan) 200
al-Kateab, Waad 28, 39–48, 154, 256 n. 65
Kaurismäki, Aki 162, 164
Kazemi, Farshid 215, 216, 277 n. 17
Keaton, Buster 162
Keshavarz, Mina 183
Khalatbari, Mitra 89
Khalil, Basil 12, 148, 150, 157–9
Khameni, Ayatollah 89
Khatami, Mohammad 68–9, 90, 104, 106
Khosroshahi, Zahra 176, 178
Khosrovani, Firouzeh 182
Kiarostami, Abbas 18, 59, 62, 125, 133, 139, 159, 173, 261 n. 33
King, Geoff 148, 262 n. 4
Kracauer, Siegfried 23, 103
Kraidy, Marwan 2, 19, 259 n. 70
Kuntsman, Adi 34

Labaki, Nadine 63, 64, 258 n. 39
Ladder to Damascus (Malas) 173
Land Confiscation Order (Sansour) 226
Langford, Michelle 21, 61, 268 n. 24
In the Last Days of the City (el-Said) 8, 25, 35, 101, 115–20, 236
laughter 94, 99, 148, 150, 155 (*see also* humour)
Lawrence, Michael 162, 248 n. 8
Lebanese Rocket Society, The (Hadjithomas and Joreige) 277 n. 9
Lebanon
 Amnesty law 110, 232

 Beirut Port explosion 111, 114, 191, 192, 233
 civil war 3, 18, 110–15, 230, 232–3
 economic crisis 3, 111, 233
 immigration detention 111, 115, 258 n. 39
 July 2006 War 110, 116, 140, 141
 relationship with Israel 128
 Syrian occupation 111, 113, 114, 250 n. 32
 Syrian refugees in 3, 14, 63
 trash crisis 230–2
Lefebvre, Henri 105, 108, 112, 257 n. 12
Letters to S. (Abyad) 246 n. 56
'life as lived' 172, 268 n. 7
limitation (*see* constraints)
Libya
 2011 revolution 51
 civil war 3, 34, 51–6, 127
limits of representation (*see* representational limits)
linguistic constraints 15–16, 38
Lionis, Chrisoula 154
Little Gandhi (Kadi) 13, 31, 192, 236, 244 n. 20
live action 81, 82, 83, 84, 91, 92, 96, 99
Lizard, The (Tabrizi) 149
location shooting 90, 103, 104, 112, 116, 123, 229, 231, 236
Lost Highway (Lynch) 216
Lynch, David 216–17, 219
Lynch, Marc 34

Mad, Mad, Mad World (Zarrinkelk) 85
Mady, Christine 230
Maghout, Jalal 96–9
magic realism 214, 231, 233
Mainline (Banietemad) 176
Maklouf, Mohammed 35
Malas, Mohamed 173
male guardianship 53, 169
Man with a Movie Camera (Vertov) 103
Man without a Past (Kaurismäki) 164
Al-Mansour, Haifaa 12, 70–3
Manuscripts Don't Burn (Rasoulof) 174–5
Marks, Laura 21, 82, 83, 125, 128, 198, 214
Masasit Mati 151, 263 n. 21
Master and Margarita, The (Bulgakov) 175, 216
May Lady (Banietemad) 178

Mernissi, Fatima 72
microhistories 26, 192, 271 n. 7
Middle East
    as a crisis hotspot 1–4, 101, 235
    as a problematic term 3–4
Mikhail, Dunya 209
Milani, Tahmineh 108
Ministry of Culture and Islamic Guidance (MCIG) 73, 138, 161, 176, 181
Mirtahmasb, Mojtiba 135
Mirror (Tarkovsky) 61
Mirror, The (Panahi) 59, 78
mise-en-abyme structure 117, 173–6, 181, 268 n. 10
mobility restrictions 14, 73, 125, 126, 127, 131, 135 (*see also* freedom of movement *and* travel restrictions)
Mohammed, Ossama 20, 192, 200–5
Al-Mokdad, Orwa 2, 10, 14, 31, 33, 65–7
Mondial 2010 (Dib) 26, 126, 142–4, 147
Morsi, Mohamed 3, 50, 78, 119, 151
Mosireen 8, 28, 35, 116, 117, 196, 247 n. 100
Mossadegh, Mohammad 193
Mostafa, Ali 126, 141–2, 176, 261 n. 57
Mottahedeh, Negar 20
Motorcycle Diaries (Salles) 140, 141
Mousavi, Mir-Hussein 87, 89
Mubarak, Hosni 3, 49, 78, 116, 120, 152, 199
Mulholland Drive (Lynch) 216
multi-protagonist film 172, 176
multi-strand narrative 171, 172, 176, 177, 180, 202
Muslim ban, USA 127

Naficy, Hamid 30, 31, 57, 70
Naila and the Uprising (Bacha) 255 n. 52
Nargess (Banietemad) 176
Nation Estate (Sansour) 26, 214, 216, 225–9, 234
National Film Organisation (NFO), Syria
Nematollah, Hamid 160
neorealism 58–62, 63, 64, 79, 103, 126
news reporting 4, 33, 67, 155, 203
No Woman No Drive (Fageeh and al-Butairi) 149, 169
non-professional actors 58–62, 63–4, 76, 133, 140, 236
Nostalgia for the Light (Guzmán) 276 n. 100
Notre musique (Godard) 142, 143

obstacles (*see* constraints)
Off-Limits (Banietemad) 176
Offside (Panahi) 159
Through the Olive Trees (Kiarostami) 173
Omara, Marouan 4, 15, 214, 221–5, 236–7
Omareen, Zaher 30, 194
Omari, Mansour 27, 29
Open Bethlehem (Sansour) 153, 280
Oppenheim, Meret 154
Orientalism 3, 9, 16, 45, 70, 86, 172, 189, 201, 251
Oulipo 5, 18

Pachachi, Maysoon 18
Pak-Shiraz, Nacim 174
Palestine
    First Intifada 93, 94, 225 n. 52
    Nakba 126, 143, 227
    occupation and colonization of 3, 14, 131, 155, 156, 213, 228–9
    relationship with Israel 158
    Second Intifada 125
    Separation Wall 28, 36, 38, 130, 228
Panahi, Jafar 9, 14, 59, 69, 76, 125, 127, 128, 134–8, 159, 161, 174
Panoptic (Eid) 18, 25, 103, 111–15, 120, 199, 250 n. 33
parallel world-building 225–33, 234
Partovi, Kambuzia 135
patriarchy 70, 75, 165
Peirce, C.S. 22, 215
Perfect Candidate, The (al-Mansour) 73
permits
    for filmmaking and screening 6, 10, 53, 73, 76, 110, 115, 120, 135, 144, 164, 174, 175, 177, 178, 179, 183, 198, 217, 220, 221, 222, 225, 229, 249 n. 14, 279 n. 42
    for travel 126, 127, 130
permitted criticism 148, 262 n. 6
Persepolis (Satrapi) 81, 82, 83, 85, 86, 87, 88, 98, 99
Persian language 16, 29, 68, 75, 109, 162, 277 n. 17
Pig (Haghighi) 26, 148, 159–61
Pinchevski, Amit 25, 32, 46
piracy 137–8
Pixelated Revolution, The (Mroué) 30
poetry
    citation of poetry 209, 270 n. 60

poetic language in cinema 21, 103, 105, 201, 202, 204, 252 n. 72
police brutality 49, 89, 200, 247 n. 104
political constraints 2, 6–7, 10, 12, 15, 25, 32, 56, 76, 120, 187, 221–2, 234
political filmmaking 21–3, 30
political prisoners 105, 137, 209
post-Arab Spring protests 3, 11, 28, 234
postproduction, practices of 192, 194, 198
practitioner's agency 19
prison experience, depiction of 18, 27, 29, 87, 99, 111, 112, 202, 209, 275 n. 62
private space 59, 123, 125, 130, 133–6, 139, 144, 150, 172, 181, 207, 217
Profession: Documentarist (Barghnavard et al) 26, 171, 172, 175, 179–83, 257 n. 19
psychogeography 25, 101–23
public space 12, 29, 54, 59, 60, 72, 73, 106, 121, 123, 125, 133–6, 139, 144, 148, 150, 165, 207, 217
puppets, use of 84–5, 96, 148, 151–3

Queens of Syria (Fedda) 14, 26, 171, 172, 183–9, 208
queer cinema 140, 144
Quran 72, 171, 132
Qashami, Walid 203

Raheb, Eliane 13
Ramallah 142, 143
Raqqa 205
Rasoulof, Mohammed 174–6
Ray, Satyajit 59
Rees, A.L. 133
representational limits 20, 28
Rezaei, Nahid 180, 183
al-Rimawi, Tariq 86
refugees 3, 14, 53, 63, 93, 94, 126, 128, 183, 184, 250 n. 34
restriction (*see* constraints)
Report, The (Lahham) 173
Reporters without Borders 1
Rieder, John 215
Risk of Acid Rain (Sanaeeha) 163
road movie 14, 17, 26, 123, 125–45, 217
romantic comedy 26, 147, 147, 164–7
Rossellini, Roberto 58
Rouhani, Hasan 177, 178, 183, 217, 220

Runner, The (Naderi) 249 n. 16
Rumi, Jalal al-Din Muhammad 174
Russell, Catherine 200

Sabbagh, Mahmoud 148, 164–8
Sadegh-Vaziri, Persheng 269 n. 39
Sadeghi, Ali Akbar 85
Sadr, Hamid Reza 60, 61
Sadrameli, Rasoul 69
Safadi, Bassel 29, 205–10
safety valve theory 148, 262 n. 6
El-Said, Tamer 7, 8, 115–20
Salahshoor, Sahar 183
Salamati, Mahsa 135
Salesman, The (Farhadi) 174
Salt of this Sea (Jacir) 12
same-sex desire (*see also* homosexuality) 108, 109, 110, 134, 138, 164
Sanaʻa 101
Sanaʻa: A Symphony (Abdulaziz) 101, 103, 127
Sansour, Larissa 17, 128, 147, 154, 214, 225–9, 233
Sansour, Leila 153, 155
Sassine, Myriam 76
satire 26, 85, 147, 148, 150–3, 160, 168, 178
Satrapi, Marjane 81, 82, 83, 84, 85, 86
Saudi Arabia
    ban on cinema exhibition 70, 73, 167, 168
    ban on women driving 72–3, 149, 166, 167, 168, 267 n. 105
    religious police 165, 266 n. 94
Scheherazade/Shahrazad 171, 172, 190, 204 (see also *The Thousand and One Nights*)
science fiction 17, 154, 213–34
Second World War 22, 28, 58, 59
security risks 2, 9, 11, 13–14, 19, 21, 29, 30, 33, 37, 44, 50, 96, 107, 120, 121, 135, 151, 172, 173, 179, 186–7, 189, 194, 197, 239, 230, 260 n. 7
self-imposed constraints 5, 17–18, 24, 63, 85, 108, 133, 134, 139, 141, 236
self-reflexivity 35, 78, 135, 136, 173, 178
Senna (Kapadia) 129
Separation, The (Farhadi) 174
Shafik, Viola 21, 104

Sharifi, Farahnaz 181, 257 n. 19
Sharm el-Sheik 221–4
Shomali, Amer 93–6
Short Cuts (Altman) 176
short films 1, 16–17, 28, 175, 176, 177, 179, 226
siāh-namāyi (showing the negative aspects) 7, 137, 138, 218
Siam, Mohamed 12, 28, 48–51, 55, 75–9
Silvered Water, Syria Self-Portrait (Mohammad and Bedirxan) 26, 189, 192, 193, 198, 200–5, 207, 274 n. 62
Sinking of the Lusitania, The (McCay) 84
el-Sisi, Abdel Fattah 3, 120, 151
Situationist International 102, 105, 107, 120, 194, 257 n. 12
Under the Skin of the City (Banietemad) 104, 176, 178
smuggling of films 9, 13, 127, 137–8, 261 n. 45
Soleri, Paolo 226
Soozandeh, Ali 7, 83, 88, 90–3
Sotoudeh, Nasrin 135
Space Exodus, A 226
Speed Sisters (Fares) 26, 125, 128–33
Spotlight (Hajju) 148
Square, The (Noujaim) 247 n. 100
social media 3, 34, 150, 159, 160, 165, 189, 194, 195, 197
social and religious constraints 5, 11–13, 21, 55, 70, 73, 148, 149, 168, 187, 234
songs, use of 63, 79, 122, 129, 149, 150, 199, 233
sound design 18, 99, 103, 111–15, 74, 118, 129, 142, 156, 180, 199, 202, 219, 204, 223
Soviet Union 193
Star Wars: A New Hope (Lucas) 215
Stars in Broad Daylight (Mohammed) 20
Steamboat Bill, Jr (Keaton) 162
Stein, Rebecca 34, 126
Stephan, Rania 15, 113, 191, 192, 198–200
storytelling 16, 26, 40, 45, 87, 108, 154, 171–2
  oral storytelling 171, 180, 209
  sharing stories 186, 189
  story within a story 171–90
  women's stories 172, 176–89
strategy, as a concept 22, 24–5, 59 (*see also* tactic)
Submarine (Akl) 17, 26, 214, 216, 229–33, 234
subtitles, use of 16, 149–50, 153, 192, 197, 210
Sufism 18, 19, 24, 174
Suleima (Maghout) 25, 81, 91, 96–9
Suleiman, Elia 148, 156–7, 161
Sur 231
surrealism 102, 153–61, 194, 199, 214, 231
surveillance 21, 74, 98, 112, 113, 122, 214, 227, 228
Suvin, Darko 213, 214
Syria
  Ghouta chemical attack 34
  Hama massacre 98, 152
  Syrian opposition 42, 64–6, 96, 122, 202
  Syrian uprising 2, 10, 30, 33, 41, 44, 47, 98, 120, 152–3, 173, 187, 196, 200, 201, 203, 206
  Syrian War 8, 13, 27, 31, 42–3, 64, 66, 96, 120, 154, 183, 200, 236
Syrian Archive 196
Syria's Disappeared (Afshar) 27, 28, 33

tactic, as a concept 22, 23, 125
Take Care of Your Scarf, Tatiana (Kaurismäki) 162
Tales (Banietemad) 26, 172, 176–9, 183
taqiya 12, 73 (*see also* dissimulation)
Tash ma Tash (al-Hamoud and al-Ghanim) 149
Tawil-Souri, Helga 227
Taxi Tehran (Panahi) 26, 125, 134–8
technological constraints 5, 10–11, 31, 83
teenagers 58, 67–79, 247 n. 100
Tehran 10, 14, 92, 101, 104–10, 134, 136, 163, 175, 181–2, 216–18
Tehran: City of Love (Jaberansari) 25, 26, 101, 107–10, 148, 161–4, 236
Tehran Taboo (Soozandeh) 7, 25, 81, 83, 90–3, 94, 99, 254 n. 41
Telfaz 11 149
temporal constraints 14–15, 29, 76, 8 , 100, 235

Ten on 10 (Kiarostami) 133
testimony 27, 35, 36, 37, 46, 49, 84, 87, 89, 96, 99, 210
theatre production 151, 166, 184
Thelma and Louise (Scott) 125
Third Cinema 23, 30, 179
This is Not a Film (Panahi) 9, 135
Thousand and One Nights, The 86, 171, 172, 181, 189, 190, 200, 201, 202, 214, 254 n. 27, 267 n. 3, 277 n. 10
Three Centimetres (Zeidan) 17, 26, 126, 138–40
Three Disappearances of Soad Hosni, The (Stephan) 26, 192, 198–200, 258 n. 47
Time for Drunken Horses, A (Ghobadi) 60
Time That Remains, The (Suleiman) 156
Top Goon: Diaries of a Little Dictator 26, 148, 151–3
Torchin, Leshu 35, 48
Towfik, Ahmed 214, 278 n. 38
trauma 43, 53, 65, 114, 134, 172, 173, 188, 256 n. 65
travel restrictions 14, 125–8 (*see also* mobility restrictions *and* discrepant mobility)
Trials of Spring, The (Reticker) 247 n. 100, 252 n. 78
Trilogy of Voice (Estayqazat) 96, 255 n. 57
Trojan Women, The (Euripides)
Trump, Donald 127, 181, 214
Tunisia 21, 81, 86, 215
Turkey 13, 42, 45
Turtles Can Fly (Ghobadi) 60
Tyre (*see* Sur)

Under the Bombs (Aractingi) 140
Under the Skin of the City (Banietemad) 104, 176, 178
underground films 10–11, 29, 69, 102, 134, 175, 236
United Arab Emirates (UAE) 141, 176
utopia 213, 218, 220, 226–7, 234
Utopia (Towfik) 214, 278 n. 38

Van Welie, Georgina 32, 51
veiling as a creative strategy 96, 148, 150
verification of digital artefacts 34, 196

Vie de Bohème, La (Kaurismäki) 162
view from 'behind' the film 23, 243 n. 105
violence
  depiction of 75, 81, 87, 92, 93, 182, 187, 200, 201
  experience of 29, 37, 66, 67, 110, 111, 154, 189
virginity 68, 69, 72, 74, 75, 77, 90, 138–9 (*see also* honour)
visa restrictions 14, 127, 128
voice
  double-voicing 185
  politics of 24, 41, 68, 72, 75, 106, 143, 172, 184, 205
voice-over, construction of 42, 46, 51, 77, 96–7, 105, 142, 180–1, 202, 204, 220
Voyage to Italy (Rossellini) 126
vulnerable groups / individuals (*see* individuals at risk)

Wadjda (al-Mansour) 12, 26, 58, 70–3, 74, 251 n. 59
Wajib (Jacir) 127
Wanted 18, The (Shomali and Cowan) 25, 81, 93–6, 99, 161
Waltz with Bashir (Folman) 81, 83
war (*see under* conflict *and* country-specific entries)
War Canister (Al-Allaq) 25, 58, 62–3
War, Love, God & Madness (al-Daradji) 173
Watts, Edward 28, 45–8, 154, 245 n. 79
web 2.0 27, 189 (*see also* Internet *and* social media *and* YouTube)
weird and eerie, concept of 215, 216, 277 n. 17
Wells, Paul 82, 84, 255 n. 53
Wessels, Joshka 30, 195
West Bank, Palestine 3, 28, 36, 93, 126–7, 130, 131, 156, 157, 226, 228
Where is the Friend's House (Kiarostami) 173
White Balloon, The (Panahi) 59, 60, 62
White Meadows, The (Rasoulof) 174
To Whom Do You Show these Films? (Banietemad) 178

Whose Country? (Siam) 28, 32, 48–51, 52, 75, 76
witnessing 25, 26, 27–56, 65, 67, 87, 101, 117, 144, 192, 197, 210
women
   as filmmakers 11, 12, 54, 70, 73, 168, 172, 179, 180
   representation of 9, 53, 58, 60, 69–70, 96, 132, 133, 172, 181, 184, 187, 189, 217
   (*see also* Arab Spring, role of women in)
World Free Press Index 1
Writing on the City (Karimi) 25, 101, 104–7

Yacoubian Building, The (Hamed) 247 n. 104
Yaqub, Nadia 126
Yemen
   civil war 3, 101, 119, 127
Youssef, Bassem 119, 151
YouTube, use of 14, 28, 41, 47, 86, 88, 96, 105, 148, 149, 150, 151, 190, 194, 195, 200–4, 206–7

Zarrinkelk, Nourredin 85
Zeidan, Lara 17, 126, 138–40
Zelizer, Barbie 27
Zimmerman, Patricia 179

www.ingramcontent.com/pod-product-compliance
Lightning Source LLC
Chambersburg PA
CBHW052148300426
44115CB00011B/1576